PLATO
SELECTIONS

PLATO
SELECTIONS

EDITED BY
RAPHAEL DEMOS

CHARLES SCRIBNER'S SONS
NEW YORK

INTRODUCTION

PLATO has exerted a greater influence over human thought than any other individual with the possible exception of Aristotle; this is due both to the intrinsic vitality of his ideas and to the fact that he appears at a comparatively early stage in Western culture. His ideas affect the intellectual climate of our day in two important ways: first, by entering into our Christian theology and contributing especially to its doctrine of the opposition between the spirit and the flesh; secondly, by entering into our scientific mentality. The fundamental assumption of modern science is the importance of the mathematical method in the understanding of things, and this was Plato's cherished doctrine. Moreover, from amongst the works of the ancient Greek writers, those of Plato alone have survived in their totality. Undoubtedly, the leading factor in the remarkable preservation of the Platonic writings was the existence of the Platonic Academy, founded in 387 B. C. and enjoying a life of about eight centuries up to 529 A. D., when its funds were embezzled by Justinian.

A philosopher in our day is considered a specialist in a field of knowledge distinct from that of science. Plato was a philosopher in a totally different sense. For him, philosophy was insight into the whole of truth, the study of reality in all its aspects; he was unaware of any barriers between this or that field of inquiry such as we erect today. Common sense ran into physics, physics into mathematics, mathematics into metaphysics; metaphysics, in its turn, led into ethics, politics, and religion. In reading the dialogues of Plato, we find abstruse discussions of ultimate principles joined to

v

detailed descriptions of the parts of the human body, and investigations into the properties of geometrical figures along with inquiries as to the nature of the good life. Nor was philosophy confined to science; it included art. Plato is equally at home in the highly technical treatment of negation in the *Sophist* and in the poetical rhapsodies of the *Symposium;* his work is great both as thought and as literature, and is indeed great in the one category through its greatness in the other. Plato is a mystic and a mathematician together, and to enter into his meaning one must read him with one's emotions as well as with one's intellect. Finally, philosophy, for Plato, is a form of life, in fact, the distinctive form of life; far from being the indulgence of a mere instinct of curiosity, the toying of a dilettante with this or that amusing idea, it is a serious, a passionate business; it is the way to salvation, the endeavor to live one's life in the setting of the universe. Philosophy requires not only keenness of intellect but courage to face the truth, moral integrity, and a magnificence of soul; it calls on the resources of the entire personality. And Plato found in the person of Socrates a perfect embodiment of his ideal of the philosopher. Is philosophy, then, coextensive with the whole range of human activity? Rather, it is its central core; in knowledge, it is the perception of the ultimate truths which lie at the root of our thinking; in life, it supplies the fundamental criteria by which we may evaluate action. Therefore only a philosopher can be a statesman. One might say that two unshakeable convictions determine Plato's thinking; one, that the philosopher seeks and finds what is absolute and permanent behind appearances, the other, that the philosopher, just because he grasps the absolute, should be at the head of affairs in the community.

It would not be an exaggeration to say that Plato's thought constitutes the most complete realization of the Greek genius. In his conviction that logical analysis and clear thinking are the gateways to wisdom, in his relentless tracking of a doctrine to its ultimate presuppositions, in his conception of reality as a stately edifice of timeless essences, in his moral seriousness and yet also in his delightful playfulness and irony, in the splendor and restraint of his style, in the soaring quality of his speculative imagination, finally in his opposition to whatever is fragmentary and provincial in thought and in his insistence that life should form a unified whole, Plato resumes more adequately than any other Greek, and perfects the classical point of view.

Plato hardly claims the power to grasp absolute truth for himself. Very often, when approaching the territory of final metaphysical ideas, he abandons the style of logical exposition for that of myth or poetry. There is something characteristically unfinished about his thought; he eschews neat systems and his intuitions often jostle one another. By contrast, the works of any commonplace thinker leave an impression of extreme artificiality in their orderly array of premises leading inevitably to the one possible conclusion. That is not— one reflects—how the thinker actually arrived at the solution; those neat proofs do not represent the complex processes of his mind in its fumbling quest. Only after he had worked out his thought to its conclusion, did he conceive of the systematic pattern which he sets down in his book. Nor is he really as pleased with the solution as he claims to be; in his mind, the conclusion is rather a tentative answer standing uncertainly against a background of aggressive alternatives impatient to replace it. Now, in Plato's works, we have not the manufactured article, but the real thing; we have the

picture of a mind caught in the toils of thinking, we
get the concrete process by which he struggled to a conclusion, the hesitation amongst the thousand different
standpoints, the doubts and the certainties together.
The dialogues are, each one, a drama of ideas; in their
totality, they depict the voyage of a mind in which any
number of ports are visited before the anchor is finally
cast. And at the end, it is as though the ship of
thought were unable to stay in the harbor but had to cast
anchor outside; for according to Plato the mind must
be satisfied with a distant vision of the truth, though it
may grasp reality intimately at fleeting intervals.

To understand the place of Plato in Greek civilization, one must have a picture of Athens in his time and
before. Greek culture originated in the Greek colonies,
in the islands of the Ægean, in Sicily, in the cities
along the Ionian coast and the shores of the Black Sea.
Before Athens had produced any great figure in the
world of thought, the colonies had their full quota of
poets, philosophers, and mathematicians. Sappho and
Alcæus, Thales the Milesian, Anaxagoras of Clazo-
menæ, Heraclitus of Ephesus, Pythagoras of Samos,
Empedocles of Sicily,—these are only a few of the illus-
trious names that may be cited. When the Persians and
Lydians began their advance westward, the Ionian colonists were compelled to retire and many of them to return to the mainland. In Athens, their thinkers were
at first suspected as radicals, atheists, bearers of strange
doctrines, but Pericles was possessed of enough vision
to perceive their value for the city; he gave them protection and liberty of expression. The truth is that the
colonists were in continuous touch with the mother country. The colonies may be regarded as links between
Athens and the world at large and Athens itself must
have been like New York of today, a world's fair,

where all sorts of sects and religions and philosophies were displayed and brought together. The Sophists came from distant parts, foreigners within the city's gates, offering their doctrine of the relativity of truth; the Ionians introduced the Asiatic view of the perishableness of all tangible things, while from Elea came the conception of the permanence of being. The Pythagorean philosophy of number and the transmigration of the soul met the kindred mystical teaching of the Orphic cults from the north. The significance of Plato lies in the fact that he converted this cultural Babel into a city; what was a heterogeneous mixture became welded into a system. In his philosophy, the miscellaneous cults and doctrines from all over the world are fused into a whole and through this fusion are made to yield a new and a significant conception of the universe. In Plato, Greece, and through Greece, the world of the day, first achieves intellectual unity, and the Greek view of life comes into self-consciousness as an explicit and coördinated attitude.

Plato forms the middle link in the great triad of Greek philosophers, of whom Socrates and Aristotle are the other two members. Socrates was Plato's teacher, the man who probably turned him in the direction of philosophy. Socrates was the prophet, Plato the metaphysician; Socrates wrote nothing, Plato was a prolific writer; Socrates was a moralist, intent on conduct, averse to speculations about nature, Plato was interested in the general view of the universe which would make a scaffolding for our concrete ethical insights. At least such was the accepted opinion among scholars, until very recently when an entirely different view as to the relation of Socrates with Plato was put forward and defended with great vigor by two distinguished British students of Greek philosophy, A. E. Taylor and

John Burnet.   In their view, Socrates was an exponent
of the Pythagorean doctrine that numbers are the essences of things and is to be held responsible for what
has been regarded as the keystone of the Platonic system, namely the theory of ideas, while Plato's contribution is confined to the more technical discussions of
the later dialogues.   Among many arguments, the most
important brought forward is that a cleavage exists between the doctrines of the earlier and those of the later
dialogues.   To debate the merits of this view with any
thoroughness would be out of question in this essay.
But this at least may be argued: an apparent difference
of doctrine in works purporting to come from one and
the same man is no evidence of multiple authorship.
A philosopher is a multiple personality in himself;
moreover, his works represent his thought as it developed through a long interval, in fact, through a lifetime.
Plato's writings occupy about forty years of his life.
It should occasion no surprise that Plato in his later
dialogues altered the distribution of emphasis.   In his
earlier philosophical period—and let us say while under
the influence of the Pythagoreans or of Socrates—Plato
took the rather extreme attitude of separating the world
of ideas from the world of particulars, whereas in his
maturer and more emancipated period, he insisted upon
the connectedness of the two worlds.   Such a change
of emphasis is no more radical than we might expect
from any growing and active mind.   Another point to
be noted is that the integrity of an author is in no way
affected by the fact that his thought reveals the influence of other minds.   Every thinker grows out of the
tradition of his epoch; every idea has its parents, like
all living things.   The achievement of the great thinker
is that he produces a creative fusion of pre-existing material; a new idea is a new way of taking account of

the data, a new pattern into which the elements of the
past are fitted. Thus, the fact that Pythagorean elements (whether as introduced by Socrates or not) are
to be traced in Plato's thought means simply that
Plato's philosophy emerged from a fusion which included the Pythagorean tradition among its components.
But he made this tradition his own, by interpreting it
in terms of his own insight. In his system, it is an
aspect of Platonism, part of his mind; not an alien doctrine added on to his own.

Plato was born in Athens in 427 and died in 346 B. C.
He was of aristocratic descent. In his early youth he
showed leanings to poetry, but on meeting Socrates decided to devote his life to philosophy; though he did
become a philosopher, he remained a poet writing prose.
Plato studied with Socrates during the period between
his twentieth and twenty-eighth years; after the death
of his master, he retired from Athens and traveled. It
is difficult to distinguish legend from history at this
point; the story goes that Plato visited Cyrene, where
he came in touch with the mathematical school, Egypt
where he heard the wisdom of the priests, Italy where
he met the Pythagoreans, and Sicily where he was invited into the court of Dionysius I, the ruler of Syracuse. He was not as successful at court as with the
wise men. According to the legend, he soon made himself obnoxious to the court circle by his outspokenness,
was kidnapped, put to sale in the slave-market, and
was saved in the nick of time by a friend who ran-
somed him and sent him to Athens. There he inaugu-
rated the Academy at the age of forty and devoted his
time to teaching and writing. Twenty years later, he
returned, on invitation, to Syracuse, to help reorganize
the government; his reception was at first very cordial
but soon violent opposition developed to his drastic

measures and Plato, realizing that his schemes could not succeed, withdrew to Athens. Plato had the opportunity to embody in his own person his ideal of the philosopher-king, and he seems to have failed—such has been the comment of cynics. But there is no reason to believe that Plato's failure was any more remarkable than that of any reformer who is ahead of his public. He died at the age of eighty-one.

His works fall into three groups. These are (a) the early writings known as the Socratic dialogues—short, dealing with ethical problems, charming in style; the *Apology, Crito, Charmides, Laches, Euthyphro, Euthydemus, Cratylus, Protagoras,* and *Gorgias* belong to this group. (b) Then there are the dialogues of the middle period, in which the interest is more clearly metaphysical and the theory of ideas receives explicit formulation. These include the *Meno, Symposium, Phædo, Republic, Phædrus.* (c) Finally, we have the later dialogues, more dialetical and technical in character, in which the world of nature comes for its share of attention; their tone is growingly religious. These dialogues comprise the *Theætetus, Parmenides, Sophist, Statesman, Philebus, Timæus,* and the *Laws.*

Despite its extreme complexity, Plato's thought easily divides itself into two large sections: his theory of reality and his theory of life; his metaphysics and his ethics. His metaphysics includes his physics and his theory of knowledge; its basic doctrine is the theory of ideas. His ethics is really his politics; it is his doctrine of the state as inclusive of the individual. We will begin with his metaphysics.

In the philosophy of Plato, the theory of ideas is the focal point toward which all problems converge and from which all solutions take their rise. To understand what Plato meant by ideas (we will speak of 'essences' or 'universals,' since the term 'ideas' has a subjectivistic connotation which is misleading) we must go back to two of his predecessors, Heraclitus and Parmenides. Heraclitus, whom Plato later called the river-philosopher, had taught that all things are in flux and that reality is like a river in which one cannot step twice; to be is to change. Parmenides maintained the opposite doctrine that to be is to be permanent and change is an illusion; reality is one, indivisible, and timeless. Plato's own doctrine may be regarded as issuing from a desire to reconcile these conflicting insights. There are, he said, two worlds, that of flux, which is the world of opinion, and that of permanence, which is the world of true knowledge.[1] The world of opinion comprises particular objects, the world of true knowledge comprises universals. We have, for instance, this or that individual being, Socrates or Alcibiades, Smith or Jones, and we have, over and above these, man as such; there are just acts and there is the principle of justice; there are beautiful landscapes and there is the sheer essence of beauty. The primary beings are the universals while particulars are real only in so far as they participate in the universals; in their mere particularity they have no being at all.

Now this way of describing things seems to be on first thought one which puts the cart before the horse. The instinctive feeling of the man in the street is that Plato has taken facts and explained them by fictions, that man and justice and beauty in the abstract are but names for the groups of instances which they designate. Let us see. Take the field of science. What is

---

[1] Both Heraclitus and Parmenides had tried to supplement their views, the one by asserting that there is a permanent law of change, the other by making room for change in what he called the 'way of opinion.'

it that an entomologist, for example, is interested in while exploring his world? He takes up this bee or moth, scrutinizes its wings, counts its legs; so far his interest seems to be in particular things. As a matter of fact, the scientist, while observing the individual moth or bee, is trying to find what is true of moths and bees *in general;* he is studying this insect only in order to elicit from it hints about the *nature* of insects as such; he does not trouble to investigate the casual peculiarities of the insect, its special biography, in other words, its unique individuality. His mind is wrapped up in what is universal in the individual insect, and when he has seized and recorded that, he tosses his moth or bee away. The primary being, then, for the entomologist is the essence of bees or moths as such; the individual case suggests the general essence, and the general essence explains the particular case. Take laws as against particular events. The scientist is not concerned about the event; that he leaves to the historian or rather to the chronicler, while he seeks the law. Plato's universals are precisely the laws of the scientist.

The mathematician deals with extensionless points, lines without thickness, perfect circles, and abstract numbers, none of which are given in concrete experience. Are they to be regarded as figments of the imagination? If so, our algebras and our geometries are fairy-tales and it is puzzling that serious people should have dwelt so intently upon them. According to Plato, the mathematician is confronted with a world ruled by necessity no less than is the world of the astronomer. If I construct a mermaid in my imagination, I can endow her with long or short hair, with blue or green eyes, but the mathematician cannot give his triangle any property he pleases; given any triangle, the sum of its angles must be equal to two right angles. Here then is an abstract world which is just as real and, for Plato, more genuinely real than the world of experience. Perfection is of its essence; a circle is perfectly round, a line perfectly straight. Concrete objects are only approximations of their abstract counterparts; there is no ring which is completely round, no ruler which is completely straight. In short, to be rationally minded, whether in science or in mathematics, is to move away from particulars to essences, from the concrete to the abstract, from the imperfect to the perfect. The Platonic universal is neither mental nor physical; it is not the latter because it is changeless and abstract; it is not the former because its being does not depend on its being thought. A universal is not an 'idea' and it is not a 'thing'; it belongs to a new category of reality.

Proceed to the field of art. The painter seems to be drawing the model; actually, the model serves merely as a point of departure. Mona Lisa is not the picture of this or that individual woman, it is the portrait of the eternal elusive feminine. The essence of painting as an art, as distinguished from photography, lies in this: the photographer reproduces the particular object while the painter reproduces the type embodied in the particular. Hamlet may have never lived in the time and space of history, but Hamlet is nonetheless real, more real than any individual, because he embodies an eternal human type. All great art goes beyond the particular and yet great art is not mere fancy; it is the representation of the type which is obscurely disclosed in the particular.[1]

---

[1] Plato would not have admitted the above application of his theory of ideas; he regarded art rather as the representation of particulars. It remained for Aristotle to do justice to art in terms of Plato's conceptions.

Action and life reveal similar characteristics. We have the statesman, the seer, the uncompromising prophet, as contrasted with the politician, the sophist, the man of expediency. The latter look to immediate, the former to remote results; the latter to consequences, the former to principles, the latter to the actual, the former to the ideal. Moral insight is the vision of ideals which are never attained in life, but to which life constantly tends; the prophet proclaims standards by which actual achievements are tested and criticized. Ethics deals not with what is but with what should be; it is an account not of this actual man, with his virtues and vices, but of the ideal man, and of the supreme good. The Sophists had preached that moral ideals are conventions, private desires projected into society and raised to the dignity of principles, that standards represent the interest of the stronger enforced against the weaker. Socrates and Plato are as vehement as they possibly can be in their denunciation of the sophistical doctrine; what they have most at heart is the view that moral standards are moral truths, absolute principles, and that no amount of might can convert a private interest into a right.

So the standpoint of commonsense, which would regard universals as fanciful fictions, is completely reversed. The scientist, the mathematician, the artist, the moralist, and the statesman join in vouching for their reality. To sum up, we have two worlds, that of universals—timeless, unchanging, general, abstract, perfect—and that of particulars—temporal, perishable, individual, concrete, imperfect. The perfect world is also the more real; don't we speak of a 'real' battle, a 'real' man, meaning what is perfect in its kind? Particulars participate in universals in varying degrees. The ideal is very faintly realized in the objects of nature; more vividly in the lives of individuals, and still more in institutions. And the soul may gradually ascend to the level of the eternal by an intelligent apprehension of particulars. Plato is not consistent on this point; there are passages both in the *Phædo* and in the *Republic* in which he depicts the world of opinion not as a step to but as a step away from the world of knowledge. Life gives a distorted view of universals just as water gives a distorted appearance of a stick. In a famous allegory in the sixth book of the *Republic,* Plato compares empirically minded people to prisoners chained in a cave, watching the play of shadows on a fire-lit wall. When reason awakes, the prisoner breaks his chains, goes out into the sun, and sees the objects themselves. He returns to the cave but is received with jeers as soon as he proclaims that what they have all along been looking at are shadows, not realities. The state of being in a cave describes the condition of the majority of men, for the true philosophers are very few; and the chains which confine men to the cave are not only those of sense-experience but of private desire, of passion, of habit and convention. To become free is to reflect for oneself instead of imitating, to resign passion for contemplation, to fix one's eyes on the principle and not on the fugitive events.

The doctrine of ideas has been justly characterized as one of the enduring possessions of humanity. One may or may not believe that universals subsist independently of particulars; and indeed, it would be rash to claim that Plato himself subscribed to such a view. The essential achievement of Plato lies in another direction. Our horizon in life is bounded by what we can see and touch and handle; Plato enlarges this horizon indefinitely by adding a totally different type of being, the type of timeless, abstract reality. We are apt to regard

the concrete world as absolute and self-sustaining;
Plato suggests that the temporal is the image of the
eternal. The truth of Platonism is the truth of mysticism. Yet this mysticism is not vague and incoherent
like that of the Orient. It is tempered by the fact of
its being a Western growth; it is a rational mysticism.
For Plato the timeless universe is definite, articulated,
and orderly. And this brings us to the question of the
relationship of essences.

The universals constitute a system; the particular
laws are subsumed under one ultimate law, the virtues
are aspects of one general principle, the mathematical
theorems all issue from one fundamental truth. The
primary categories under which the universals are
brought together are those of beauty, truth, goodness,
and the greatest of these is goodness. Correspondingly,
there are three avenues to the universals: love, thought,
and moral insight. Just as the particulars are instances
of universals, so are the universals instances of the
good. Plato compares the good to the sun. The sun
is both the source of things and, through its light, the
revealer of things; so the good is both the source of all
being and the means by which all being is understood.
What does this mean? Everything, whether natural or
artificial, has a purpose, is 'good for' something; its
existence follows from the fact that it fulfils an end.
Likewise, to know a thing is to understand its purpose,
what it is 'good for'; one does not define a table by saying that it is a plank of wood on four legs, because the
plank may not be wooden and the legs may be only)
three; the essence of the table is its function—its good;
a table is something to write on, just as a chair is something to sit on. The meaning of Plato goes still deeper.
The pervading nature of essences is their eternity, their
universality, their ideality, in other words, their per-

fection; in a similar way, the essential nature of particulars is their participation in essence and hence in perfection. Perfection is the principle of being. Evil is nothing positive; it is absence of being, a lesser degree of good. A criminal—shall we say—is a very low-grade saint. We are now better prepared to understand Plato's statement that perfection is the principle of existence and of knowledge. To understand this or that object is to find the ideal type to which it belongs, the eternal laws of which it is a passing instance, the context of relations into which it fits. To study the earth is to perceive its place in the solar system and as a stage in the evolution of the heavenly bodies; to see its motion as taking place in accordance with the law of gravity. Thus, to know what the earth is, is to see the earth as part of a systematic order, and so, of perfection.

How is knowledge possible? Not through experience but through reason; the senses, at best, wake up the reason to a consciousness of what it already possesses; and at worst, they mislead it. The universals are innate, not learned. Experience could never be made to yield knowledge of principles, for principles are universal and necessary whereas experience reveals what is particular and casual. Counting may teach me that two pairs of apples are four apples, but no amount of countings will give me the truth that two and two are four; the instances of counting will always be so many and not more, while the arithmetical proposition extends to all possible as well as actual cases. Again, empirical objects are crude and imperfect, whereas conceptions deal with pure types. The circles—the wheels and the rings—that I observe in experience are never quite round. The whiteness of the paper on which I am writing is not pure whiteness, it is a blackish or brownish

whiteness, yet I do have the conception of a pure un-
adulterated whiteness. Have I obtained it perchance
by arranging the empirical whitenesses in an ascending
order of purity and conceiving pure whiteness as the
limit of the series? But in order to arrange them in
that order I must already have the conception of pure
whiteness. Experience presupposes the universals;
there must be something already in the mind by which
one may interpret one's impressions. Plato maintains
that knowledge is inborn; in a well-known passage in
the *Meno,* he depicts a scene in which an uneducated
slave-boy, faced by questions from philosophers and
mathematicians is able, with a little prodding, to dis-
play a knowledge of arithmetic and geometry. Plato's
point is that teaching only evokes what is already latent,
that the teacher with his geometrical figures and concrete examples never proves his theorem but only illus-
trates it.

A theory of knowledge such as the above, whatever
its philosophical merits, provides an exceptionally fruit-
ful conception of education. Socrates says that as a
teacher he is only a midwife to his pupils' thoughts.
Now, a midwife is old and barren; similarly, a teacher
does not furnish ideas but helps the student bring forth
his own, and if the intellectual infant is a monster, he
puts it to death. The teacher is no more than a stimu-
lus and a critic.

If we have knowledge at birth, how did we get it in
the first place? Through a previous state of existence.
There was a time when the soul, unencumbered by the
body, freely roamed among the ideal essences and came
to know the good by immediate inspection. Experience serves to recall what we discovered in a previous
life; the process of learning now, is that of recovering
deep distant memories lying buried in the tomb of the

body. There is a story that Shelley, while a youth at Oxford and fresh from studies in Plato, encountered a beggar woman with her baby while crossing one of the bridges on the Thames. Impatient to test Plato's theory of reminiscence, he seized the baby and called upon it to reveal its innate knowledge. "My lord, the baby is only three months old; it cannot speak," protested the mother. "So much the better," answered Shelley, "it has had no chance to forget." But the baby only cried. Yet, as we know from the poetry he wrote later, Shelley did not lose his Platonism.

To some, the conception of a previous life with its opportunity for a glimpse of the eternal essences may appear fantastic. Yet to any one who believes that the soul survives the body the view that the soul antecedes the body should not seem unreasonable. In any case, the transcendental theory is only an interpretation of the immediate fact that experience fails to account for all of knowledge. The doctrine of the limitation of empiricism remains, whatever one's view about the origin of abstract ideas may be. We cannot derive our categories—thinghood, quality, relation, causality,—from experience, because we use them in understanding experience; we cannot derive our laws of thought—such as the law of contradiction—from experience, because they are presupposed in any actual process of thinking; we cannot derive universal principles from experience, because experience is limited to particular cases; finally, we cannot derive any concepts (such as white, square) from experience, because they constitute standards by which the data of experience are measured. The kernel of the Platonic theory is rationalism, namely that there is a non-empirical element in knowledge.

Plato resorts to the figure of a divided line in which the lower section corresponds to experience and the higher to reason. Each side is subdivided in its turn; within experience, there is first 'guessing'—the state of dream and illusion, and there is, further, 'belief' which is normal sense-perception. In the lower half of reason, there is understanding which includes science and mathematics. These latter do not represent the highest stage of knowledge; to be sure, they deal with essence but they make use of concrete examples and unproved assumptions. Finally, we have the stage of dialectic, in which the mind grasps essences independently of symbols. This is philosophy; it is the business of the mind at this stage to analyze the undefined notions of science and mathematics, and test their unproved assumptions. Philosophy both criticizes science and mathematics and develops their implications. It is all one continuous process of knowledge with different stages. The meaning of the figure of the divided line is that the various types of knowledge are different not in kind but in degree, that together they form the ladder of the soul to truth. And as the process is continuous we cannot stop short of the final stage; apart from philosophy, science is not knowledge at all; it starts with assumptions, and unless these are proved, the conclusions based on them, in short, the whole structure of science falls to pieces.

The ladder to the supreme good reappears in Plato's discussion of desire. Parallel to contemplation there is action. The motive force of life has been variously described by modern philosophers; Schopenhauer speaks of a primary will-to-live; Bergson of an *élan vital,* while Freud makes sex the primary motive. Plato regards life as the expression of an impetus which he calls *'eros'* or love; this impetus is not purposeless, as with Bergson; it is directed toward an end and is therefore an aspiration; and it is not physical as with Freud—

it is an aspiration for the ideal. Love is the desire of the soul for the good apprehended as beauty, just as contemplation is union of the soul with the good in its aspect of truth. Love is not of the flesh primarily, nor of individual persons; it is an attraction to essence. For Christianity the highest love is of a person—namely God; for Plato, the object of desire, though ideal, is impersonal. Love is creative, leading as it does to re-production; sex is desire for more and more life. Back of the effort to multiply life, there is the desire for im-mortality, the endeavor to achieve eternity through an endless series of temporal lives; love is the impulse to realize the eternal in time. There is not only physical but intellectual creation as well, creation of opinions. The steps of the ladder are as follows. There is first the love of bodies, then of persons, then of theories, then of institutions and communities, finally of beauty itself, each step leading to the next. And at every step, the earlier as well as the later ones, love is really di-rected to the ideal; sex-attraction and affection are love of the beauty and the excellence which the person em-bodies; only derivatively can there be love of a con-crete object at all.

The contrast with Freud is obvious; both Plato and Freud (and Christianity, for that matter) agree that love is the root impulse of life; but whereas Freud would represent all idealistic impulses—such as those of religion, affection, poetry—as 'sublimations' of phys-ical desire, Plato would represent physical desire as a distorted manifestation of a spiritual impulse. If it is legitimate for Freud to go behind the apparent content of an impulse, so it is for Plato; and the question whether the 'lower' or the 'higher' impulses should be taken as fundamental cannot be settled except by ref-erence to a general metaphysical standpoint. For Plato, perfection is the principle of reality, and therefore to desire an object is to desire the good.]

One would naturally expect art to play a central rôle in the passion for beauty; in fact, for Plato, it plays no rôle at all, or rather it plays the rôle of a villain. The paradox of Plato is that he, one of the supreme artists of the world, should exclude artists from his republic. When the poets come to our gates, he says in so many words, we should be very courteous to them and give them wreaths, but we shall keep them out of the state. Like Tolstoy, Plato decries art as immoral. Is it the master despising his craft? Is it a puritan fearful of the frivolities of art? Or is it a genius indulging in an eccentricity? In reflecting upon this difficult problem, it is well to remember that Plato was an Athenian commenting upon the contemporary scene. Plato's criticism of art in general must be viewed as a criticism of the art of his day, especially of the drama, which tended to abandon all serious purpose and take the aspect of a trivial entertainment; even tragedy was losing its dignity and lapsing into melodrama. But his attitude meant much more; it reflected a general metaphysical theory. According to Plato, art contemplates the particular. In art, the soul turns away from essence to the concrete; it goes down the ladder instead of going up. At the top, there is the universal—let us say the essence of a bed; lower down, there is the particular bed made by the carpenter according to the ideal pattern; lowest down, there is the picture of a bed, made by the painter after the pattern of the particular bed. Thus, art is the imitation of an imitation; worse, it is the distortion of a distortion; the particular distorts the universal and the picture distorts the particular in the sense that the painter views the object from a special angle and not as one sees it in normal

life. Beauty lies beyond all art and all symbolism; it
is an ineffable essence, grasped only in the moment of
ecstasy.

Our problem is still unsolved; it is Plato's own view
that essences may be approached via the route of the
particulars in which they are embodied; why then does
he not define art as an ascent rather than as a descent
—as the attempt of the soul to seize the universal
through a particular embodiment? Perhaps it is because art is unique among all the mental attitudes; unlike them, it brings the concrete to the foreground, by
regarding the universal as *constituted in the particular.*
The analogy between science and art is really very limited. Sooner or later, science abandons the particular
in its quest for the universal; art, however, sees the universal as inextricably bound up with the particular.
Consider, for instance, the treatment of the theme of
jealousy by a psychologist and by a dramatist. The
psychologist will define jealousy as a complex of universals; his account will consist of general concepts
alone. The dramatist, on the other hand, will represent jealousy through a concrete image, say Othello.
The distinctive significance of art is its affirmation of
the metaphysical value of the individual. To the extent then that he denies the ultimate reality of the particular, Plato is consistent in his attack on art. One
may go so far as to say that art supplies the touchstone by which Platonism may be judged and its possible weakness displayed. However, Plato has a way of
confuting his critics by meeting their objections in advance, even at the cost of apparent inconsistency on his
part. Thus, he says that beauty makes the ideas visible to sense; and on a number of occasions he intimates
that universals may not be separated from particulars.

The place of God in the Platonic system has been

the subject of long controversy among scholars. Too
often the tendency has been to regard the idea of God
as an undigested concept in Plato's mind, an after-
thought, or, at best, a symbolic expression for the idea
of the good. Yet, a study of the later dialogues, notably
the Philebus, shows that God plays a necessary role in
the Platonic metaphysics, and one distinct from that of
the ideas. In the earlier dialogues God is mentioned
rather incidentally; and a student who takes up the
later dialogues after he has formed his views upon the
basis of the earlier ones, is liable to interpret all references to God as implied references to the ideas. But it
is not a question of how far one can go in interpreting
one conception in terms of another, but of what Plato
himself believed; and an unprejudiced reading of the
later dialogues suggests that God, in Plato's mind,
stands only for Himself, and is not a name for anything
else. A question of this sort cannot be settled by a
mechanical comparison of words and passages; Plato
is at no point explicit on the connection of God with the
good; one has to steep oneself in Plato and get, if possible, the pattern, the 'feel' of his mind. Clearly, to
Plato religion is a genuine personal experience; in his
references to God there is a suggestion at once of reverence and of intimacy; God seems to have been for
him not an abstract conception but an immediate in-
tuition. To reduce God to the ideas is to fail to do
justice to the religious nature of Plato as distinct from
his detached contemplative attitude. We will say then
that for Plato God is coördinate with the Ideas, and
even distinct from them, in so far as ultimates may be
said to be distinct from one another. God is the energy
of creation; the ideas, the pattern of creation; matter,
the stuff of creation. God finds a chaos and transforms
it into a cosmos.

Why did God make the world? "Let me tell you, then, why the creator of the world generated and created this universe. He was good, and no goodness can ever have any jealousy of anything. And being free from jealousy, he desired that all things should be as like himself as possible. This is the true beginning of creation and of the world, which we shall do well in receiving from the testimony of wise men: God desired that all things should be good and nothing bad as far as this could be accomplished." The Christian God creates the world out of nothing, but Plato's God is less of a creator and more of an architect, fashioning a universe out of existing material. He is finite, in the sense that his action is limited by the possibilities of his material. Good in the world is not an actuality but an achievement. God finds the world bad, or rather indifferent, and introduces good into it. God is in the world fighting for the victory of good and against evil. "For as we acknowledge the heaven to be full of many goods and also of evils, and of more evils than goods, there is, as we affirm, an immortal conflict going on among us, which requires marvelous watchfulness; and in that conflict the gods and demigods are our allies, and we are their property.' [1] Plato's God bears a remarkable similarity to modern conceptions of God, especially that of James; according to James, too, God is finite and wages a battle against the forces of evil in the world.

God cares for the least as well as for the greatest of creatures; he not only makes the world but watches over it; he is a Providence. Aristotle's God is aloof, subsisting in Olympian detachment and contemplating

[1] It is not easy to reconcile this phrase with those passages in the *Republic* in which he speaks of the good as the principle of being.

only himself; love is *of* the world *to* God. But Plato's
God is in the world and with man; he seeks out his
creatures; love flows *from* him *to* the world. Whether
it be true that Aristotle is less of a dualist than Plato
so far as philosophy of nature is concerned, there can
be no doubt that in the sphere of philosophy of religion Plato is much less a dualistic than Aristotle. Aristotle emphasizes the detachment of God from the world,
Plato the presence of God in the world. But whereas
pantheism interprets the divine presence as an identity
of God with the whole, and is therefore led to regard
evil as illusory, Plato regards God as present *with* the
world, and evil as a reality to be combated. In sum,
the metaphysical situation is analyzable into three ultimate factors: God, the principle of the finite (or the
ideas, or the good), and the principle of the infinite (or
matter, or the indeterminate). The actual order is explained by reference to these three factors. An actual
entity is a mixture of the finite with the infinite, brought
about by God—an infusion of form into the indeterminate, an organization of material according to the pattern of the ideas. The created world comprises both
physical objects and souls. The former are temporal
and perishable; souls too are temporal, since they are
'mixtures', i. e., created objects. But they are so created as to endure forever.

Plato's social philosophy is refreshingly modern;
eugenics, rights of women, socialism, and projects whose
application still lies in the future crowd his pages. The
notorious doctrine that might is right is stated and attacked; the issue of democracy *versus* aristocracy is
debated with great vigor. In treating of social conditions, Plato is at once a detached onlooker and an intimate participator in the contemporary scene; he is in
turn suave, ironical, enthusiastic, pessimistic. His work

surpasses the limits of a theoretical analysis; he is a historian and a prophet. The reader gets the impression of a mind of tremendous vitality, of a titanic force from which ideas leap in profusion as though from an inexhaustible source. One wonders whether Plato's hesitations about the relation of particulars to universals may not be a reflection of his varying feeling to his social environment; when democracy has committed some especially heinous crime (such as the condemnation of Socrates to death) he is disgusted with life; then he leans to the view that the physical is only a prison house for the spiritual, the philosopher must flee the world, the eternal is beyond the temporal. But when the heat of his indignation has subsided, then his natural sympathy for life comes to the foreground; he is no longer averse to the temporal; the body is the servant of the soul, the universal finds its realization in the particular.

Plato's genius is exhibited in the fact that he succeeded in eliciting from his observations of the Athenian state reflections on society and government that are true everywhere. Of course the city of Athens was an exceptionally favorable field for a student seeking generalizations concerning social life. The history of Athens has all the sweep of a classical tragedy; it mirrors the rise and fall of a far-flung empire, a great sea-power, an extremely prosperous commercial state, a thorough-going democracy, a community in which material prosperity went together with a magnificent culture, a culture in which art went together with science and both were overtopped by philosophy.

Plato's republic is one of the notable utopias in the history of thought. In giving a picture of the state he is depicting a universal essence, in other words he is drawing an ideal. When a friend objected that his con-

ception of the state was unrealizable on earth, he replied that he is only offering an ideal to man. No ideal
is ever realized, and yet no ideal need on that account
be useless; it is the function of an ideal to be beyond
realization and by this fact to inspire and guide human
effort. The reader must guard against using the term
'utopia' too loosely. Plato is not concerned with giving
a beautiful picture of a fantastic state; in depicting an
ideal he is describing what is for him the only genuine
reality. A physiologist is not primarily concerned with
cripples and invalids; he gives an account of the normal
body and the laws of its functioning. So Plato is painting the image of society in its normal condition and of
the moral principles which govern its operation.

Plato comes in sharpest opposition with modern ten-
dencies in his treatment of democracy. He favors aristocracy as against democracy. This is putting it too
mildly: Plato detests democracy. He lived his youth
in the aftermath of the Sicilian expedition when the
deficiencies of democracy were exposed in their naked-
ness; besides, the condemnation of Socrates to death by
the jury of the Athenian public could not fail to impress
him profoundly. Yet once more, his intuitive judgment stands against a background of a general theory.
Democracy is a denial of the principle of qualification;
it holds that every citizen has a right to participate in
government; but a right must correspond to capacity,
and Plato believes that the average person has neither
the knowledge nor the native intelligence requisite for
government. Politics is an art and it is a science; we
demand that a doctor should be trained in medicine and
a pilot in navigation, yet we permit any one to govern
irrespective of his equipment. Government is a complicated function, the highest function of man, and one
which must be mastered in order that it may be exer-

cised responsibly. Democracy affirms that all men are equal; in fact, all are not equal; the majority are incapable of ruling, and of those that are, some are more capable than others. Instead of government by all, good as well as bad, stupid as well as intelligent, Plato advocates aristocracy which is government by the best, the reign of the philosophers. For Plato, aristocracy is the rule of reason. We must not misunderstand Plato's meaning; aristocracy is not exploitation; it is not a condition in which the interests of the many are sacrificed to the interests of the few; in aristocracy, the interests of the group are paramount, and the rulers will be the servants of the community; they will indeed not be rulers but leaders; aristocracy is a polity in which the interests of all are safeguarded by the exceptional intelligence of the few. Such a state will be like a family in which the head works for the good of its weaker members.

The word democracy designates not only a form of government but a form of life, individual and social. Democracy in the individual is equality of all desires, failure to discriminate between the better and the worse, giving the lower an equal voice with the higher; it is the absence of standards. The democratic régime in the soul is one of genial license. The democratic man is not bad, he is both bad and good, or rather he is neither; he has no character, but only impulse. Every impulse, whether good or bad, has its day, but its day is very short. So the life of the democratic individual is protean, lacking all stability. He "lives through the day, indulging the appetite of the hour; and sometimes he is lapped in drink and strains of the flute; then he is for total abstinence, and tries to get thin; then, again, he is at gymnastics; sometimes idling and neglecting everything, then once more living the life of a philosopher;

often he is at politics, and starts to his feet and says and
does anything that may turn up; and if he is emulous
of anyone who is a warrior, off he is in that direction,
or of men of business, once more in that. His life has
neither order nor law". Plato's account applies to conditions in our day. We have a gospel of individualism
according to which an artist may utilize any feeling or
impression; a work of art is approved if sincere, if expressing a feeling which is there, no matter if the feeling be itself profound or not; we have the democracy of
impulse in art. In conduct, the same gospel leads to
the denial of self-discipline in favor of a uniform gratification of all desires; with the aid of catch-words from
modern psychology we are now formulating a code of
equal rights for all impulses, according to which sup-
pression, and even control, are condemned as unhealthy.

In social life, democracy means that anyone is as good
as anyone else in any respect; it is the denial of the
expert, or rather the setting up of everyone as his own
expert. Take our own times. If it is a problem affecting organic evolution, the man in the street or on
the farm regards his opinion as of equal importance
with that of the biologist. "Asses and horses march
along with all the dignities and rights of freemen." This
is individualism gone mad. Nowadays, the intellectual
atmosphere is filled with the vapor of uncriticized, in-
expert opinions; this makes for picturesqueness and variety "and just as women and children think variety
charming, so there are many men who will deem this the
fairest of states." But on the other hand, it makes for
the cult of the average, the gradual destruction of excellence. Leadership is coming to be a lost function;
in our reaction against servile obedience to authority,
we have become needlessly suspicious of all forms of
guidance. And the disappearance of leaders is a much

greater social revolution than the overthrow of mon-
archs; the untitled prophets whose authority reposed on
the respect in which they were held by the public exercised a much greater power than kings ever did.

The present fear of leaders is unjustified; leaders are
not rulers but guides; they play the function in democracy of upholding standards and formulating for the
public its dumb and instinctive aspirations. No democracy is healthy unless it provides a mechanism for continuous self-criticism, in the shape either of a stable,
though growing, tradition or of a forceful personality.
In the absence of such an agency, standards tend to
weaken and institutions to pander to the public instead
of leading it; our press, our literature, our drama, sometimes our educational establishments give the public
what it wants, instead of raising the public from the
level of its wants to the level of its ideals. "Little
things of this sort happen: the master fears and imitates
his scholars, and the scholars despise their masters and
tutors; and in general, young and old are alike, and the
young man is on a level with the old, and is ready to
compete with him in word or deed; and old men conde-
scend to the young . . . and they imitate the young."

Plato divides the social organism into three classes
the philosophers, the warriors, and the artisans. It is a
division of society upon the basis of function; the first
class rules, the second protects the state, the third provides for its physical needs. Two features stand out in
Plato's conception. First, that leadership is in the
hands of the intelligent group, the producing class being
allowed the least power of any. Modern society often
tends to reverse this order and to establish the business
group as dominant, as the one which sets the tone and
pulls the strings in politics and in the other spheres of
life. Second, there are class-distinctions in Plato's re-

public, based—be it noted—on the principle of function and not on any hereditary principle. We have to-day the viewpoint that any man may begin in a log-cabin and end in the White House; and this is a conception which we must cherish. Nevertheless, Plato's social philosophy supplies a useful check to whatever temptation there may be to carry our contemporary viewpoint to an extreme. For Plato, every individual has a natural orbit which prescribes the boundaries of his career; to-day many an individual is rendered unhappy by continually trying to rise to a more commanding position than the one in which he finds himself and so to rise into a sphere beyond his abilities. An apprentice must become a shop keeper, the shop keeper must become a professional man, the professional man must become a manufacturer or a political chief. In this there lurks a false standard of values. According to Plato, a man can realize his function as a human being and become happy no matter what the rank of his position, provided it be socially useful. The ideal of boundless ambition means that man moves continually from function to function and from position to position without catching root at any point and without ever enjoying the fruits of his labor; the business man must keep on making more money and the official must keep on being promoted to a 'higher' rank. But this fitful restless change makes for shallowness; only in repose may depth of experience be achieved. Culture develops through concentration, and in that atmosphere of leisure which enables the mind to dwell upon and explore all the possibilities of its environment and of itself.

Plato's social philosophy revolves around two foci; first, the doctrine that society is an organic whole; second, that society is a hierarchical whole, with higher and lower levels. We have discussed the second and

we shall now proceed to the first. The individual has
no being apart from the community; there is no such
thing as the good of the individual in distinction from
that of the group. The unit *is* the group; and ethics
is part of politics. Every action of any importance
is a public function and a public trust. Plato must
not be taken as standing for a social good over and
above the good of the individual; the state is a community of persons and its good is their good. A social
good by itself is as much of an abstraction as a merely
individual good. Society and individual exist in re-
ciprocal dependence. The doctrine of the social organism leads Plato to some drastic conceptions regarding
property and the family. There must be no private property for the guardians of the state; they constitute a
unity and private property is a denial of this unity.
There should be no 'mine' and 'thine' in the common
family which is the group. Possession of wealth must
be divorced from possession of political power. We have
in Plato's republic what is perhaps the first formulation
of the ideal of communism, and a defence of it not on
economic but on moral grounds. It is more like the
communism of the monastic orders among the early
Christians, for Plato is opposed not only to the privacy
of property but to its material quality.

The state will be in charge of production in the
sphere both of physical goods and of life. It will regulate marriages and the breeding of children. Here we
have a remarkable foreshadowing of modern theories
of eugenics; there will be selective breeding as with animals, and bad specimens of humanity will be ruthlessly
destroyed at birth. There will be no individual families
because there is only the one family of the state. The
latter will control mating among the sexes, and when
children are born, they will be brought up by the state.

Thus, both the breeding and the rearing of children will be in the hands of the community. There will not be that atmosphere of seclusion in the relations of parents with one another and with their children which constitutes the institution of the family. The child will know neither its father nor its mother; it will recognize the state alone at its parent. The implications of the principle that the social group is an organism are carried out by Plato in the most rigid and uncompromising fashion. And doubtless, his disgust with the instability of political forms in Athens converted Plato into a fervent advocate of the Spartan system. Women are part of the community no less than men. There will be no disqualification on the basis of sex; women will participate in public affairs and in war on an equal footing with men, that is to say, without prejudice on account of their sex. They will be treated as persons; they will have the rights and duties of citizens because they form an integral part of the social organism. The fact that it took the world more than two thousand years to grasp and apply Plato's ideal of feminism should give courage to despondent reformers. While insisting that there is no difference in kind between the sexes, Plato maintains that there is a difference in degree; women are in all respects weaker than men.

The above is all too brief a survey of the thought of one of the greatest of philosophers; and, in fact, no attempt has been made to cover the ground. Plato's thought has an intimate personal quality which it is impossible to convey in a general exposition; it must be obtained from his own words. And in reading him, one comes face to face not only with an exceptional individual but with an exceptional civilization—Hellenism. The problem as to whether the great man is merely a symptom of his age or a creator of it is significantly illustrated in the case of Plato: Plato gathers together all the threads of the Greek genius, but in so doing he creates a new pattern which is a genuine contribution to Hellenism. He combines a singular freshness of insight with great subtlety of analysis; and he combines subtlety with honesty of thought. Plato never forces the solution; if he has none, he does not invent one; so he is often baffling and even provoking in his inconclusiveness. While his problems are transcendent and universal, his style is concrete and his starting point is in the immediate situation. If the function of philosophy is to enable the man whose outlook is bounded by his private and practical interests to become a "spectator of all time and all existence," then Plato has succeeded. It has often been urged against philosophers that, in contrast to scientists, they fail to reach unanimity of opinion. But though scientists agree on a theory (more or less) at any one time, they change their views, from epoch to epoch. All scientific theories of the past have undergone modification, and no scientist expects the present theories to remain unaltered in the future; scientific hypotheses are always subject to correction. On the other hand, though at no one time is there unanimity among philosophers on any theory, there are several doctrines which are bound to have a good number of devoted followers at all times. The history of philosophy is the continuous recurrence and resuscitation of certain well-defined points of view, such as empiricism, rationalism, mysticism, realism, idealism, etc.; in these the mind seems to have achieved a final insight into the nature of things, in the sense that they represent permanent possibilities of explaining the universe. In short, scientists are unanimous at a given time; philosophers throughout time. And among the philosophical doctrines which seem destined thus to remain forever part of the intellectual heritage of the human race, Platonism is sure to occupy a commanding position.[1]

[1] There are no selections in this volume from Plato's *Republic,* as the *Republic* had been issued entire in a separate volume of this series. An attempt has been made to include selections both from the literary and the technical dialogues, but on account of the limitation of space, it has been found necessary to omit important passages. Thus, this volume includes nothing from the *Sophist* and all too little from the *Philebus.* It has been difficult to decide among alternative sets of selections; but something had to be excluded, and where the arguments on either side seemed equally strong, the choice had to be made arbitrarily.

RAPHAEL DEMOS.

CONTENTS

PLATO
SELECTIONS

APOLOGY

How you, O Athenians, have been affected by my accusers, I cannot tell; but I know that they almost made me forget who I was—so persuasively did they speak; and yet they have hardly uttered a word of truth. But of the many falsehoods told by them, there was one which quite amazed me;—I mean when they said that you should be upon your guard and not allow yourselves to be deceived by the force of my eloquence. To say this, when they were certain to be detected as soon as I opened my lips and proved myself to be anything but a great speaker, did indeed appear to me most shameless —unless by the force of eloquence they mean the force of truth; for if such is their meaning, I admit that I am eloquent. But in how different a way from theirs! Well, as I was saying, they have scarcely spoken the truth at all; but from me you shall hear the whole truth: not, however, delivered after their manner in a set oration duly ornamented with words and phrases. No, by heaven! but I shall use the words and arguments which occur to me at the moment; for I am confident in the justice of my cause: at my time of life I ought not to be appearing before you, O men of Athens, in the character of a juvenile orator—let no one expect it of me. And I must beg of you to grant me a favour:—If I defend myself in my accustomed manner, and you hear me using the words which I have been in the habit of using in the agora, at the tables of the money-changers, or anywhere else, I would ask you not to be surprised, and not to interrupt me on this account. For I am more

than seventy years of age, and appearing now for the
first time in a court of law, I am quite a stranger to the
language of the place; and therefore I would have you
regard me as if I were really a stranger, whom you
would excuse if he spoke in his native tongue, and after
the fashion of his country:—Am I making an unfair
request. of you? Never mind the manner, which may
or may not be good; but think only of the truth of my
words, and give heed to that: let the speaker speak
truly and the judge decide justly.

And first, I have to reply to the older charges and
to my first accusers, and then I will go on to the later
ones. For of old I have had many accusers, who have
accused me falsely to you during many years; and I am
more afraid of them than of Anytus and his associates,
who are dangerous, too, in their own way. But far more
dangerous are the others, who began when you were
children, and took possession of your minds with their
falsehoods, telling of one Socrates, a wise man, who
speculated about the heaven above, and searched into the
earth beneath, and made the worse appear the better
cause. The disseminators of this tale are the accusers
whom I dread; for their hearers are apt to fancy that
such enquirers do not believe in the existence of the
gods. And they are many, and their charges against
me are of ancient date, and they were made by them
in the days when you were more impressible than you
are now—in childhood, or it may have been in youth—
and the cause when heard went by default, for there
was none to answer. And hardest of all, I do not know
and cannot tell the names of my accusers; unless in the
chance case of a Comic poet. All who from envy
and malice have persuaded you—some of them having
first convinced themselves—all this class of men are
most difficult to deal with; for I cannot have them up

here, and cross-examine them, and therefore I must
simply fight with shadows in my own defence, and argue
when there is no one who answers. I will ask you
then to assume with me, as I was saying, that my op-
ponents are of two kinds; one recent, the other ancient;
and I hope that you will see the propriety of my answering the latter first, for these accusations you heard
long before the others, and much oftener.

Well, then, I must make my defence, and endeavour
to clear away in a short time, a slander which has lasted
a long time. May I succeed, if to succeed be for my
good and yours, or likely to avail me in my cause! The
task is not an easy one; I quite understand the nature
of it. And so leaving the event with God, in obedience
to the law I will now make my defence.

I will begin at the beginning, and ask what is the accusation which has given rise to the slander of me, and
in fact has encouraged Meletus to prefer this charge
against me. Well, what do the slanderers say? They
shall be my prosecutors, and I will sum up their words
in an affidavit: 'Socrates is an evil-doer, and a curious
person, who searches into things under the earth and in
heaven, and he makes the worse appear the better cause;
and he teaches the aforesaid doctrines to others.' Such
is the nature of the accusation: it is just what you have
yourselves seen in the comedy of Aristophanes,[1] who
has introduced a man whom he calls Socrates, going
about and saying that he walks in air, and talking a
deal of nonsense concerning matters of which I do not
pretend to know either much or little—not that I mean
to speak disparagingly of any one who is a student of
natural philosophy. I should be very sorry if Meletus
could bring so grave a charge against me. But the simple truth is, O Athenians, that I have nothing to do

[1] Aristoph., *Clouds*, 225 ff.

with physical speculations. Very many of those here
present are witnesses to the truth of this, and to them
I appeal. Speak then, you who have heard me, and tell
your neighbours whether any of you have ever known
me hold forth in few words or in many upon such matters. . . . You hear their answer. And from what they
say of this part of the charge you will be able to judge
of the truth of the rest.

As little foundation is there for the report that I am
a teacher, and take money; this accusation has no more
truth in it than the other. Although, if a man were
really able to instruct mankind, to receive money for
giving instruction would, in my opinion, be an honour
to him. There is Gorgias of Leontium, and Prodicus
of Ceos, and Hippias of Elis, who go the round of the
cities, and are able to persuade the young men to leave
their own citizens by whom they might be taught for
nothing, and come to them whom they not only pay, but
are thankful if they may be allowed to pay them. There
is at this time a Parian philosopher residing in Athens,
of whom I have heard; and I came to hear of him in
this way:—I came across a man who has spent a world
of money on the Sophists, Callias, the son of Hipponicus, and knowing that he had sons, I asked him: 'Callias,' I said, 'if your two sons were foals or calves,
there would be no difficulty in finding some one to put
over them; we should hire a trainer of horses, or a
farmer probably, who would improve and perfect them
in their own proper virtue and excellence; but as they
are human beings, whom are you thinking of placing
over them? Is there any one who understands human
and political virtue? You must have thought about the
matter, for you have sons; is there any one?' 'There
is,' he said. 'Who is he?' said I; 'and of what country? and what does he charge?' 'Evenus the Parian,'

he replied; 'he is the man, and his charge is five minae.'
Happy is Evenus, I said to myself, if he really has this
wisdom, and teaches at such a moderate charge. Had
I the same, I should have been very proud and con-
ceited; but the truth is that I have no knowledge of the
kind.

I dare say, Athenians, that some one among you will
reply, 'Yes, Socrates, but what is the origin of these
accusations which are brought against you; there must
have been something strange which you have been doing? All these rumours and this talk about you would
never have arisen if you had been like other men: tell
us, then, what is the cause of them, for we should be
sorry to judge hastily of you.' Now I regard this as a
fair challenge, and I will endeavour to explain to you
the reason why I am called wise and have such an evil
fame. Please to attend then. And although some of
you may think that I am joking, I declare that I will
tell you the entire truth. Men of Athens, this reputation of mine has come of a certain sort of wisdom which
I possess. If you ask me what kind of wisdom, I reply,
wisdom such as may perhaps be attained by man, for to
that extent I am inclined to believe that I am wise;
whereas the persons of whom I was speaking have a
superhuman wisdom, which I may fail to describe, because I have it not myself; and he who says that I have,
speaks falsely, and is taking away my character. And
here, O men of Athens, I must beg you not to interrupt
me, even if I seem to say something extravagant. For
the word which I will speak is not mine. I will refer
you to a witness who is worthy of credit; that witness
shall be the God of Delphi—he will tell you about my
wisdom, if I have any, and of what sort it is. You must
have known Chaerephon; he was early a friend of mine,
and also a friend of yours, for he shared in the recent

exile of the people, and returned with you. Well, Chaerephon, as you know, was very impetuous in all his doings, and he went to Delphi and boldly asked the oracle to tell him whether—as I was saying, I must beg you not to interrupt—he asked the oracle to tell him whether any one was wiser than I was, and the Pythian prophetess answered, that there was no man wiser. Chaerephon is dead himself; but his brother, who is in court, will confirm the truth of what I am saying.

Why do I mention this? Because I am going to explain to you why I have such an evil name. When I heard the answer, I said to myself, What can the god mean? and what is the interpretation of his riddle? for I know that I have no wisdom, small or great. What then can he mean when he says that I am the wisest of men? And yet he is a god, and cannot lie; that would be against his nature. After long consideration, I thought of a method of trying the question. I reflected that if I could only find a man wiser than myself, then I might go to the god with a refutation in my hand. I should say to him, 'Here is a man who is wiser than I am; but you said that I was the wisest.' Accordingly I went to one who had the reputation of wisdom, and observed him—his name I need not mention; he was a politician whom I selected for examination—and the result was as follows: When I began to talk with him, I could not help thinking that he was not really wise, although he was thought wise by many, and still wiser by himself; and thereupon I tried to explain to him that he thought himself wise, but was not really wise; and the consequence was that he hated me, and his enmity was shared by several who were present and heard me. So I left him, saying to myself, as I went away: Well, although I do not suppose that either of us knows anything really beautiful and good, I am better off than he is,—for he knows nothing, and thinks that he knows; I neither know nor think that I know. In this latter particular, then, I seem to have slightly the advantage of him. Then I went to another who had still higher pretensions to wisdom, and my conclusion was exactly the same. Whereupon I made another enemy of him, and of many others besides him.⟩

Then I went to one man after another, being not unconscious of the enmity which I provoked, and I lamented and feared this: but necessity was laid upon me,—the word of God, I thought, ought to be considered first. And I said to myself, Go I must to all who appear to know, and find out the meaning of the oracle. And I swear to you, Athenians, by the dog I swear!—for I must tell you the truth—the result of my mission was just this: I found that the men most in repute were all but the most foolish; and that others less esteemed were really wiser and better.⟩ I will tell you the tale of my wanderings and of the 'Herculean' labours, as I may call them, which I endured only to find at last the oracle irrefutable. After the politicians, I went to the poets; tragic, dithyrambic, and all sorts. And there, I said to myself, you will be instantly detected; now you will find out that you are more ignorant than they are. Accordingly, I took them some of the most elaborate passages in their own writings, and asked what was the meaning of them—thinking that they would teach me something. Will you believe me? I am almost ashamed to confess the truth, but I must say that there is hardly a person present who would not have talked better about their poetry than they did themselves. Then I knew that not by wisdom do poets write poetry, but by a sort of genius and inspiration; they are like diviners or soothsayers who also say many fine things, but do not understand the meaning of them. The poets appeared to me to be much in the same case; and I further observed that upon the strength of their poetry they believed themselves to be the wisest of men in other things in which they were not wise. So I departed, conceiving myself to be superior to them for the same reason that I was superior to the politicians.

At last I went to the artisans. I was conscious that I knew nothing at all, as I may say, and I was sure that they knew many fine things; and here I was not mistaken, for they did know many things of which I was ignorant, and in this they certainly were wiser than I was. But I observed that even the good artisans fell into the same error as the poets;—because they were good workmen they thought that they also knew all sorts of high matters, and this defect in them overshadowed their wisdom; and therefore I asked myself on behalf of the oracle, whether I would like to be as I was, neither having their knowledge nor their ignorance, or like them in both; and I made answer to myself and to the oracle that I was better off as I was.

This inquisition has led to my having many enemies of the worst and most dangerous kind, and has given occasion also to many calumnies. And I am called wise, for my hearers always imagine that I myself possess the wisdom which I find wanting in others: but the truth is, O men of Athens, that God only is wise; and by his answer he intends to show that the wisdom of men is worth little or nothing; he is not speaking of Socrates, he is only using my name by way of illustration, as if he said, He, O men, is the wisest, who, like Socrates, knows that his wisdom is in truth worth nothing. And so I go about the world, obedient to the god, and search and make enquiry into the wisdom of any one, whether citizen or stranger, who appears to be wise; and if he is not wise, then in vindication of the oracle I show him that he is

not wise; and my occupation quite absorbs me, and I
have no time to give either to any public matter of interest or to any concern of my own, but I am in utter poverty by reason of my devotion to the god.

There is another thing:—young men of the richer
classes, who have not much to do, come about me of their
own accord; they like to hear the pretenders examined,
and they often imitate me, and proceed to examine others; there are plenty of persons, as they quickly discover, who think that they know something, but really
know little or nothing; and then those who are examined
by them instead of being angry with themselves are
angry with me: This confounded Socrates, they say; this
villainous misleader of youth!—and then if somebody
asks them, Why, what evil does he practise or teach?
they do not know, and cannot tell; but in order that they
may not appear to be at a loss, they repeat the ready-
made charges which are used against all philosophers
about teaching things up in the clouds and under the
earth, and having no gods, and making the worse appear
the better cause; for they do not like to confess that
their pretence of knowledge has been detected—which
is the truth; and as they are numerous and ambitious
and energetic, and are drawn up in battle array and have
persuasive tongues, they have filled your ears with their
loud and inveterate calumnies. And this is the reason
why my three accusers, Meletus and Anytus and Lycon,
have set upon me; Meletus, who has a quarrel with me
on behalf of the poets; Anytus, on behalf of the crafts-
men and politicians; Lycon, on behalf of the rhetoricians: and as I said at the beginning, I cannot expect
to get rid of such a mass of calumny all in a moment.
And this, O men of Athens, is the truth and the whole
truth; I have concealed nothing, I have dissembled nothing. And yet, I know that my plainness of speech

makes them hate me, and what is their hatred but a proof that I am speaking the truth?—Hence has arisen the prejudice against me; and this is the reason of it, as you will find out either in this or in any future enquiry. ——I have said enough in my defence against the first class of my accusers; I turn to the second class. They are headed by Meletus, that good man and true lover of his country, as he calls himself. Against these, too, I must try to make a defence:—Let their affidavit be read: it contains something of this kind: It says that Socrates is a doer of evil, who corrupts the youth; and who does not believe in the gods of the state, but has other new divinities of his own. Such is the charge; and now let us examine the particular counts. He says that I am a doer of evil, and corrupt the youth; but I say, O men of Athens, that Meletus is a doer of evil, in that he pretends to be in earnest when he is only in jest, and is so eager to bring men to trial from a pretended zeal and interest about matters in which he really never had the smallest interest. And the truth of this I will endeavour to prove to you.

Come hither, Meletus, and let me ask a question of you. You think a great deal about the improvement of youth?

Yes, I do.

Tell the judges, then, who is their improver; for you must know, as you have taken the pains to discover their corrupter, and are citing and accusing me before them. Speak, then, and tell the judges who their improver is. —Observe, Meletus, that you are silent, and have nothing to say. But is not this rather disgraceful, and a very considerable proof of what I was saying, that you have no interest in the matter? Speak up, friend, and tell us who their improver is.

The laws.

But that, my good sir, is not my meaning. I want to know who the person is, who, in the first place, knows the laws.

The judges, Socrates, who are present in court.

What, do you mean to say, Meletus, that they are able to instruct and improve youth?

Certainly they are.

What, all of them, or some only and not others?

All of them.

By the goddess Herè, that is good news! There are plenty of improvers, then. And what do you say of the audience,—do they improve them?

Yes, they do.

And the senators?

Yes, the senators improve them.

But perhaps the members of the assembly corrupt them?—or do they too improve them?

They improve them.

Then every Athenian improves and elevates them; all with the exception of myself; and I alone am their corrupter? Is that what you affirm?

That is what I stoutly affirm.

I am very unfortunate if you are right. But suppose I ask you a question: How about horses? Does one man do them harm and all the world good? Is not the exact opposite the truth? One man is able to do them good, or at least not many;—the trainer of horses, that is to say, does them good, and others who have to do with them rather injure them? Is not that true, Meletus, of horses, or of any other animals? Most assuredly it is; whether you and Anytus say yes or no. Happy indeed would be the condition of youth if they had one corrupter only, and all the rest of the world were their improvers. But you, Meletus, have sufficiently shown that you never had a thought about the young: your carelessness is seen in your not caring about the very things which you bring against me.

And now, Meletus, I will ask you another question— by Zeus I will: Which is better, to live among bad citizens, or among good ones? Answer, friend, I say; the question is one which may be easily answered. Do not the good do their neighbours good, and the bad do them evil?

Certainly.

And is there any one who would rather be injured than benefited by those who live with him? Answer, my good friend, the law requires you to answer—does any one like to be injured?

Certainly not.

And when you accuse me of corrupting and deteriorating the youth, do you allege that I corrupt them intentionally or unintentionally?

Intentionally, I say.

But you have just admitted that the good do their neighbours good, and the evil do them evil. Now, is that a truth which your superior wisdom has recognized thus early in life, and am I, at my age, in such darkness and ignorance as not to know that if a man with whom I have to live is corrupted by me, I am very likely to be harmed by him; and yet I corrupt him, and intentionally, too—so you say, although neither I nor any other human being is ever likely to be convinced by you. But either I do not corrupt them, or I corrupt them unintentionally; and on either view of the case you lie. If my offence is unintentional, the law has no cognizance of unintentional offences: you ought to have taken me privately, and warned and admonished me; for if I had been better advised, I should have left off doing what I only did unintentionally—no doubt I should; but you would have nothing to say to me and refused to teach me. And now you bring me up in this court, which is a place not of instruction, but of punishment.

It will be very clear to you, Athenians, as I was saying, that Meletus has no care at all, great or small, about the matter. But still I should like to know, Meletus, in what I am affirmed to corrupt the young. I suppose you mean, as I infer from your indictment, that I teach them not to acknowledge the gods which the state acknowledges, but some other new divinities or spiritual agencies in their stead. These are the lessons by which I corrupt the youth, as you say.

Yes, that I say emphatically.

Then, by the gods, Meletus, of whom we are speaking, tell me and the court, in somewhat plainer terms, what you mean! for I do not as yet understand whether you affirm that I teach other men to acknowledge some gods, and therefore that I do believe in gods, and am not an entire atheist—this you do not lay to my charge, —but only you say that they are not the same gods which the city recognizes—the charge is that they are different gods. Or, do you mean that I am an atheist simply, and a teacher of atheism?

I mean the latter—that you are a complete atheist.

What an extraordinary statement! Why do you think so, Meletus? Do you mean that I do not believe in the godhead of the sun or moon, like other men?

I assure you, judges, that he does not: for he says that the sun is stone, and the moon earth.

Friend Meletus, you think that you are accusing Anaxagoras: and you have but a bad opinion of the judges, if you fancy them illiterate to such a degree as not to know that these doctrines are found in the books of Anaxagoras the Clazomenian, which are full of them. And so, forsooth, the youth are said to be taught them by Socrates, when there are not unfrequently exhibitions of them at the theatre [1] (price of admission one drachma at the most); and they might pay their money, and laugh at Socrates if he pretends to father these extraordinary views. And so, Meletus, you really think that I do not believe in any god?

I swear by Zeus that you believe absolutely in none at all.

Nobody will believe you, Meletus, and I am pretty sure that you do not believe yourself. I cannot help thinking, men of Athens, that Meletus is reckless and impudent, and that he has written this indictment in a spirit of mere wantonness and youthful bravado. Has he not compounded a riddle, thinking to try me? He said to himself:—I shall see whether the wise Socrates will discover my facetious contradiction, or whether I shall be able to deceive him and the rest of them. For he certainly does appear to me to contradict himself in the indictment as much as if he said that Socrates is guilty of not believing in the gods, and yet of believing in them—but this is not like a person who is in earnest.

I should like you, O men of Athens, to join me in examining what I conceive to be his inconsistency; and do you, Meletus, answer. And I must remind the audience of my request that they would not make a disturbance if I speak in my accustomed manner:

Did ever man, Meletus, believe in the existence of human things, and not of human beings? . . . I wish, men of Athens, that he would answer, and not be always trying to get up an interruption. Did ever any man believe in horsemanship, and not in horses? or in flute-playing, and not in flute-players? No, my friend; I will answer to you and to the court, as you refuse to answer for yourself. There is no man who ever did.

[1] Probably in allusion to Aristophanes who caricatured, and to Euripides who borrowed the notions of Anaxagoras, as well as to other dramatic poets.

WHO KNOWS

But now please to answer the next question: Can a man believe in spiritual and divine agencies, and not in spirits or demigods?

He cannot.

How lucky I am to have extracted that answer, by the assistance of the court! But then you swear in the indictment that I teach and believe in divine or spiritual agencies (new or old, no matter for that); at any rate, I believe in spiritual agencies,—so you say and swear in the affidavit; and yet if I believe in divine beings, how can I help believing in spirits or demigods;—must I not? To be sure I must; and therefore I may assume that your silence gives consent. Now what are spirits or demigods? are they not either gods or the sons of gods?

Certainly they are.

But this is what I call the facetious riddle invented by you: the demigods or spirits are gods, and you say first that I do not believe in gods, and then again that I do believe in gods; that is, if I believe in demigods. For if the demigods are the illegitimate sons of gods, whether by the nymphs or by any other mothers, of whom they are said to be the sons—what human being will ever believe that there are no gods if they are the sons of gods? You might as well affirm the existence of mules, and deny that of horses and asses. Such nonsense, Meletus, could only have been intended by you to make trial of me. You have put this into the indictment because you had nothing real of which to accuse me. But no one who has a particle of understanding will ever be convinced by you that the same men can believe in divine and superhuman things, and yet not believe that there are gods and demigods and heroes.

I have said enough in answer to the charge of Meletus: any elaborate defence is unnecessary; but I know

only too well how many are the enmities which I have
incurred, and this is what will be my destruction if I
am destroyed;—not Meletus, nor yet Anytus, but the
envy and detraction of the world, which has been the
death of many good men, and will probably be the death
of many more; there is no danger of my being the last
of them.

Some one will say: And are you not ashamed, Socrates, of a course of life which is likely to bring you
to an untimely end? To him I may fairly answer: There
you are mistaken: a man who is good for anything
ought not to calculate the chance of living or dying; he
ought only to consider whether in doing anything he is
doing right or wrong—acting the part of a good man or
of a bad. Whereas, upon your view, the heroes who fell
at Troy were not good for much, and the son of Thetis
above all, who altogether despised danger in comparison with disgrace; and when he was so eager to slay
Hector, his goddess mother said to him, that if he
avenged his companion Patroclus, and slew Hector, he
would die himself—'Fate,' she said, in these or the like
words, 'waits for you next after Hector;' he, receiving
this warning, utterly despised danger and death, and
instead of fearing them, feared rather to live in dishonour, and not to avenge his friend. 'Let me die forth-
with,' he replies, 'and be avenged of my enemy, rather
than abide here by the beaked ships, a laughing-stock
and a burden of the earth.' Had Achilles any thought
of death and danger? For wherever a man's place is,
whether the place which he has chosen or that in which
he has been placed by a commander, there he ought to
remain in the hour of danger; he should not think of
death or of anything but of disgrace. And this, O men
of Athens, is a true saying.

Strange, indeed, would be my conduct, O men of

Athens, if I who, when I was ordered by the generals whom you chose to command me at Potidaea and Amphipolis and Delium, remained where they placed me, like any other man, facing death—if now, when, as I conceive and imagine, God orders me to fulfil the philosopher's mission of searching into myself and other men, I were to desert my post through fear of death, or any other fear; that would indeed be strange, and I might justly be arraigned in court for denying the existence of the gods, if I disobeyed the oracle because I was afraid of death, fancying that I was wise when I was not wise. For the fear of death is indeed the pretence of wisdom, and not real wisdom, being a pretence of knowing the unknown; and no one knows whether death, which men in their fear apprehend to be the greatest evil, may not be the greatest good. Is not this ignorance of a disgraceful sort, the ignorance which is the conceit that a man knows what he does not know? And in this respect only I believe myself to differ from men in general, and may perhaps claim to be wiser than they are:—that whereas I know but little of the world below, I do not suppose that I know: but I do know that injustice and disobedience to a better, whether God or man, is evil and dishonourable, and I will never fear or avoid a possible good rather than a certain evil. And therefore if you let me go now, and are not convinced by Anytus, who said that since I had been prosecuted I must be put to death; (or if not that I ought never to have been prosecuted at all); and that if I escape now, your sons will all be utterly ruined by listening to my words—if you say to me, Socrates, this time we will not mind Anytus, and you shall be let off, but upon one condition, that you are not to enquire and speculate in this way any more, and that if you are caught doing so again you shall die;—if this was the condition on which you

let me go, I should reply: Men of Athens, I honour and
love you; but I shall obey God rather than you, and
while I have life and strength I shall never cease from
the practice and teaching of philosophy, exhorting any
one whom I meet and saying to him after my manner:
You, my friend,—a citizen of the great and mighty and
wise city of Athens,—are you not ashamed of heaping
up the greatest amount of money and honour and reputation, and caring so little about wisdom and truth and
the greatest improvement of the soul, which you never
regard or heed at all? And if the person with whom I
am arguing, says: Yes, but I do care; then I do not leave
him or let him go at once; but I proceed to interrogate
and examine and cross-examine him, and if I think that
he has no virtue in him, but only says that he has, I reproach him with undervaluing the greater, and over-
valuing the less. And I shall repeat the same words to
every one whom I meet, young and old, citizen and
alien, but especially to the citizens, inasmuch as they
are my brethren. For know that this is the command
of God; and I believe that no greater good has ever happened in the state than my service to the God. For I
do nothing but go about persuading you all, old and
young alike, not to take thought for your persons or
your properties, but first and chiefly to care about the
greatest improvement of the soul. I tell you that virtue
is not given by money, but that from virtue comes money
and every other good of man, public as well as private.
This is my teaching, and if this is the doctrine which
corrupts the youth, I am a mischievous person. But if
any one says that this is not my teaching, he is speaking
an untruth. Wherefore, O men of Athens, I say to you,
do as Anytus bids or not as Anytus bids, and either acquit me or not; but whichever you do, understand that

I shall never alter my ways, not even if I have to die many times.

Men of Athens, do not interrupt, but hear me; there was an understanding between us that you should hear me to the end: I have something more to say, at which you may be inclined to cry out; but I believe that to hear me will be good for you, and therefore I beg that you will not cry out. I would have you know, that if you kill such an one as I am, you will injure yourselves more than you will injure me. Nothing will injure me, not Meletus nor yet Anytus—they cannot, for a bad man is not permitted to injure a better than himself. I do not deny that Anytus may, perhaps, kill him, or drive him into exile, or deprive him of civil rights; and he may imagine, and others may imagine, that he is inflicting a great injury upon him: but there I do not agree. For the evil of doing as he is doing—the evil of unjustly taking away the life of another—is greater far.

And now, Athenians, I am not going to argue for my own sake, as you may think, but for yours, that you may not sin against the God by condemning me, who am his gift to you. For if you kill me you will not easily find a successor to me, who, if I may use such a ludicrous figure of speech, am a sort of gadfly, given to the state by God; and the state is a great and noble steed who is tardy in his motions owing to his very size, and requires to be stirred into life. I am that gadfly which God has attached to the state, and all day long and in all places am always fastening upon you, arousing and persuading and reproaching you. You will not easily find another like me, and therefore I would advise you to spare me. I dare say that you may feel out of temper (like a person who is suddenly awakened from sleep), and you think that you might easily strike me dead as Anytus advises, and then you would sleep on for the remainder of your lives, unless God in his care of you sent you another gadfly. When I say that I am given to you by God, the proof of my mission is this:— if I had been like other men, I should have not neglected all my own concerns or patiently seen the neglect of them during all these years, and have been doing yours, coming to you individually like a father or elder brother, exhorting you to regard virtue; such conduct, I say, would be unlike human nature. If I had gained anything, or if my exhortations had been paid, there would have been some sense in my doing so; but now, as you will perceive, not even the impudence of my accusers dares to say that I have ever exacted or sought pay of any one; of that they have no witness. And I have a sufficient witness to the truth of what I say—my poverty.

Some one may wonder why I go about in private giving advice and busying myself with the concerns of others, but do not venture to come forward in public and advise the state. I will tell you why. You have heard me speak at sundry times and in divers places of an oracle or sign which comes to me, and is the divinity which Meletus ridicules in the indictment. This sign, which is a kind of voice, first began to come to me when I was a child; it always forbids but never commands me to do anything which I am going to do. This is what deters me from being a politician. And rightly, as I think. For I am certain, O men of Athens, that if I had engaged in politics, I should have perished long ago, and done no good either to you or to myself. And do not be offended at my telling you the truth: for the truth is, that no man who goes to war with you or any other multitude, honestly striving against the many lawless and unrighteous deeds which are done in a state, will save his life; he who will fight for the right, if he

would live even for a brief space, must have a private
station and not a public one.

I can give you convincing evidence of what I say, not
words only, but what you value far more—actions. Let
me relate to you a passage of my own life which will
prove to you that I should never have yielded to injustice from any fear of death, and that 'as I should have
refused to yield' I must have died at once. I will tell
you a tale of the courts, not very interesting perhaps,
but nevertheless true. The only office of state which I
ever held, O men of Athens, was that of senator: the
tribe Antiochis, which is my tribe, had the presidency
at the trial of the generals who had not taken up the
bodies of the slain after the battle of Arginusae; and
you proposed to try them in a body, contrary to law, as
you all thought afterwards; but at the time I was the
only one of the Prytanes who was opposed to the illegal-
ity, and I gave my vote against you; and when the orators threatened to impeach and arrest me, and you called
and shouted, I made up my mind that I would run the
risk, having law and justice with me, rather than take
part in your injustice because I feared imprisonment
and death. This happened in the days of the democracy. But when the oligarchy of the Thirty was in
power, they sent for me and four others into the rotunda, and bade us bring Leon the Salaminian from
Salamis, as they wanted to put him to death. This was
a specimen of the sort of commands which they were always giving with the view of implicating as many as
possible in their crimes; and then I showed, not in word
only but in deed, that, if I may be allowed to use such
an expression, I cared not a straw for death, and that
my great and only care was lest I should do an unrighteous or unholy thing. For the strong arm of that
oppressive power did not frighten me into doing wrong;

and when we came out of the rotunda the other four went to Salamis and fetched Leon, but I went quietly home. For which I might have lost my life, had not the power of the Thirty shortly afterwards come to an end. And many will witness to my words.

Now do you really imagine that I could have survived all these years, if I had led a public life, supposing that like a good man I had always maintained the right and had made justice, as I ought, the first thing? No indeed, men of Athens, neither I nor any other man. But I have been always the same in all my actions, public as well as private, and never have I yielded any base compliance to those who are slanderously termed my disciples, or to any other. Not that I have any regular disciples. But if any one likes to come and hear me while I am pursuing my mission, whether he be young or old, he is not excluded. Nor do I converse only with those who pay; but any one, whether he be rich or poor, may ask and answer me and listen to my words; and whether he turns out to be a bad man or a good one, neither result can be justly imputed to me; for I never taught or professed to teach him anything. And if any one says that he has ever learned or heard anything from me in private which all the world has not heard, let me tell you that he is lying.

But I shall be asked, Why do people delight in continually conversing with you? I have told you already, Athenians, the whole truth about this matter: they like to hear the cross-examination of the pretenders to wisdom; there is amusement in it. Now this duty of cross-examining other men has been imposed upon me by God; and has been signified to me by oracles, visions, and in every way in which the will of divine power was ever intimated to any one. This is true, O Athenians; or, if not true, would be soon refuted. If I am or have been corrupting the youth, those of them who are now grown up and have become sensible that I gave them bad advice in the days of their youth should come forward as accusers, and take their revenge; or if they do not like to come themselves, some of their relatives, fathers, brothers, or other kinsmen, should say what evil their families have suffered at my hands. Now is their time. Many of them I see in the court. There is Crito, who is of the same age and of the same deme with myself, and there is Critobulus his son, whom I also see. Then again there is Lysanias of Sphettus, who is the father of Aeschines—he is present; and also there is Antiphon of Cephisus, who is the father of Epigenes; and there are the brothers of several who have associated with me. There is Nicostratus the son of Theosdotides, and the brother of Theodotus (now Theodotus himself is dead, and therefore he, at any rate, will not seek to stop him); and there is Paralus the son of Demodocus, who had a brother Theages; and Adeimantus the son of Ariston, whose brother Plato is present; and Aeantodorus, who is the brother of Apollodorus, whom I also see. I might mention a great many others, some of whom Meletus should have produced as witnesses in the course of his speech; and let him still produce them, if he has forgotten—I will make way for him. And let him say, if he has any testimony of the sort which he can produce. Nay, Athenians, the very opposite is the truth. For all these are ready to witness on behalf of the corrupter, of the injurer of their kindred, as Meletus and Anytus call me; not the corrupted youth only—there might have been a motive for that—but their uncorrupted elder relatives. Why should they too support me with their testimony? Why, indeed, except for the sake of truth and justice, and because they know that I am speaking the truth, and that Meletus is a liar.

Well, Athenians, this and the like of this is all the defence which I have to offer. Yet a word more. Perhaps there may be some one who is offended at me, when he calls to mind how he himself on a similar, or even a less serious occasion, prayed and entreated the judges with many tears, and how he produced his children in court, which was a moving spectacle, together with a host of relations and friends; whereas I, who am probably in danger of my life, will do none of these things. The contrast may occur to his mind, and he may be set against me, and vote in anger because he is displeased at me on this account. Now if there be such a person among you,—mind, I do not say that there is,—to him I may fairly reply: My friend, I am a man, and like other men, a creature of flesh and blood, and not 'of wood or stone,' as Homer says; and I have a family, yes, and sons, O Athenians, three in number, one almost a man, and two others who are still young; and yet I will not bring any of them hither in order to petition you for an acquittal. And why not? Not from any self-assertion or want of respect for you. Whether I am or am not afraid of death is another question, of which I will not now speak. But, having regard to public opinion, I feel that such conduct would be discreditable to myself, and to you, and to the whole state. One who has reached my years, and who has a name for wisdom, ought not to demean himself. Whether this opinion of me be deserved or not, at any rate the world has decided that Socrates is in some way superior to other men. And if those among you who are said to be superior in wisdom and courage, and any other virtue, demean themselves in this way, how shameful is their conduct! I have seen men of reputation, when they have been condemned, behaving in the strangest manner: they seemed to fancy that they were going to suffer something dreadful if they died, and that they could be immortal if you only allowed them to live; and I think that such are a dishonour to the state, and that any stranger coming in would have said of them that the most eminent men of Athens, to whom the Athenians themselves give honour and command, are no better than women. And I say that these things ought not to be done by those of us who have a reputation; and if they are done, you ought not to permit them; you ought rather to show that you are far more disposed to condemn the man who gets up a doleful scene and makes the city ridiculous, than him who holds his peace.

But, setting aside the question of public opinion, there seems to be something wrong in asking a favour of a judge, and thus procuring an acquittal, instead of informing and convincing him. For his duty is, not to make a present of justice, but to give judgment; and he has sworn that he will judge according to the laws, and not according to his own good pleasure; and we ought not to encourage you, nor should you allow yourselves to be encouraged, in this habit of perjury—there can be no piety in that. Do not then require me to do what I consider dishonourable and impious and wrong, especially now, when I am being tried for impiety on the indictment of Meletus. For if, O men of Athens, by force of persuasion and entreaty I could overpower your oaths, then I should be teaching you to believe that there are no gods, and in defending should simply convict myself of the charge of not believing in them. But that is not so—far otherwise. For I do believe that there are gods, and in a sense higher than that in which any of my accusers believe in them. And to you and to God I commit my cause, to be determined by you as is best for you and me.

There are many reasons why I am not grieved, O men of Athens, at the vote of condemnation. I expected it, and am only surprised that the votes are so nearly equal; for I had thought that the majority against me would have been far larger; but now, had thirty votes gone over to the other side, I should have been acquitted. And I may say, I think, that I have escaped Meletus. I may say more; for without the assistance of Anytus and Lycon, any one may see that he would not have had a fifth part of the votes, as the law requires, in which case he would have incurred a fine of a thousand drachmae.

And so he proposes death as the penalty. And what shall I propose on my part, ● men of Athens? Clearly that which is my due. And what is my due? What return shall be made to the man who has never had the wit to be idle during his whole life; but has been careless of what the many care for—wealth, and family interests, and military offices, and speaking in the assembly, and magistracies, and plots, and parties. Reflecting that I was really too honest a man to be a politician and live, I did not go where I could do no good to you or to myself; but where I could do the greatest good privately to every one of you, thither I went, and sought to persuade every man among you that he must look to himself, and seek virtue and wisdom before he looks to his private interests, and look to the state before he looks to the interests of the state; and that this should be the order which he observes in all his actions. What shall be done to such an one? Doubtless some good thing, O men of Athens, if he has his reward; and the good should be of a kind suitable to him. What would be a reward suitable to a poor man who is your benefactor, and who desires leisure that he may instruct you? There can be no reward so fitting as maintenance in the Prytaneum, O men of Athens, a reward which he deserves far more than the citizen who has won the prize at Olympia in the horse or chariot race, whether the chariots were drawn by two horses or by many. For I am in want, and he has enough; and he only gives you the appearance of happiness, and I give you the reality. And if I am to estimate the penalty fairly, I should say that maintenance in the Prytaneum is the just return.

Perhaps you think that I am braving you in what I am saying now, as in what I said before about the tears and prayers. But this is not so. I speak rather because I am convinced that I never intentionally wronged any one, although I cannot convince you—the time has been too short; if there were a law at Athens, as there is in other cities, that a capital cause should not be decided in one day, then I believe that I should have convinced you. But I cannot in a moment refute great slanders; and, as I am convinced that I never wronged another, I will assuredly not wrong myself. I will not say of myself that I deserve any evil, or propose any penalty. Why should I? Because I am afraid of the penalty of death which Meletus proposes? When I do not know whether death is a good or an evil, why should I propose a penalty which would certainly be an evil? Shall I say imprisonment? And why should I live in prison, and be the slave of the magistrates of the year —of the Eleven? Or shall the penalty be a fine, and imprisonment until the fine is paid? There is the same objection. I should have to lie in prison, for money I have none, and cannot pay. And if I say exile (and this may possibly be the penalty which you will affix), I must indeed be blinded by the love of life, if I am so irrational as to expect that when you, who are my own citizens, cannot endure my discourses and words, and have found them so grievous and odious that you will have no more of them, others are likely to endure me. No indeed, men of Athens, that is not very likely. And what a life should I lead, at my age, wandering from city to city, ever changing my place of exile, and always being driven out! For I am quite sure that wherever I go, there, as here, the young men will flock to me; and if I drive them away, their elders will drive me out at their request; and if I let them come, their fathers and friends will drive me out for their sakes.

Some one will say: Yes, Socrates, but cannot you hold your tongue, and then you may go into a foreign city, and no one will interfere with you? Now I have great difficulty in making you understand my answer to this. For if I tell you that to do as you say would be a disobedience to the God, and therefore that I cannot hold my tongue, you will not believe that I am serious; and if I say again that daily to discourse about virtue, and of those other things about which you hear me examining myself and others, is the greatest good of man, and that the unexamined life is not worth living, you are still less likely to believe me. Yet I say what is true, although a thing of which it is hard for me to persuade you. Also, I have never been accustomed to think that I deserve to suffer any harm. Had I money I might have estimated the offence at what I was able to pay, and not have been much the worse. But I have none, and therefore I must ask you to proportion the fine to my means. Well, perhaps I could afford a mina, and therefore I propose that penalty: Plato, Crito, Critobulus, and Apollodorus, my friends here, bid me say thirty minae, and they will be the sureties. Let thirty minae be the penalty; for which sum they will be ample security to you.

———

Not much time will be gained, O Athenians, in return for the evil name which you will get from the detractors of the city, who will say that you killed Socrates, a wise man; for they will call me wise, even although I am not wise, when they want to reproach you. If you had waited a little while, your desire would have been fulfilled in the course of nature. For I am far advanced in years, as you may perceive, and not far from death. I am speaking now not to all of you, but only to those who have condemned me to death. And I have another thing to say to them: You think that I was convicted because I had no words of the sort which would have procured my acquittal—I mean, if I had thought fit to leave nothing undone or unsaid. Not so; the deficiency which led to my conviction was not of words—certainly not. But I had not the boldness or impudence or inclination to address you as you would have liked me to do, weeping and wailing and lamenting, and saying and doing many things which you have been accustomed to hear from others, and which, as I maintain, are unworthy of me. I thought at the time that I ought not to do anything common or mean when in danger: nor do I now repent of the style of my defence; I would rather die having spoken after my manner, than speak in your manner and live. For neither in war nor yet at law ought I or any man to use every way of escaping death. Often in battle there can be no doubt that if a man will throw away his arms, and fall on his knees before his pursuers, he may escape

death; and in other dangers there are other ways of
escaping death, if a man is willing to say and do anything. The difficulty, my friends, is not to avoid death,
but to avoid unrighteousness; for that runs faster than
death. I am old and move slowly, and the slower runner has overtaken me, and my accusers are keen and
quick, and the faster runner, who is unrighteousness,
has overtaken them. And now I depart hence condemned by you to suffer the penalty of death,—they too
go their ways condemned by the truth to suffer the penalty of villainy and wrong; and I must abide by my
award—let them abide by theirs. I suppose that these
things may be regarded as fated,—and I think that they
are well.

And now, O men who have condemned me, I would
fain prophesy to you; for I am about to die, and in the
hour of death men are gifted with prophetic power. And
I prophesy to you who are my murderers, that immediately after my departure punishment far heavier than
you have inflicted on me will surely await you. Me you
have killed because you wanted to escape the accuser,
and not to give an account of your lives. But that will
not be as you suppose: far otherwise. For I say that
there will be more accusers of you than there are now;
accusers whom hitherto I have restrained: and as they
are younger they will be more inconsiderate with you,
and you will be more offended at them. If you think
that by killing men you can prevent some one from cen-
suring your evil lives, you are mistaken; that is not a
way of escape which is either possible or honourable;
the easiest and the noblest way is not to be disabling
others, but to be improving yourselves. This is the
prophecy which I utter before my departure to the
judges who have condemned me.

Friends, who would have acquitted me, I would like

also to talk with you about the thing which has come
to pass, while the magistrates are busy, and before I go
to the place at which I must die. Stay then a little, for
we may as well talk with one another while there is
time. You are my friends, and I should like to show
you the meaning of this event which has happened to
me. O my judges—for you I may truly call judges—
I should like to tell you of a wonderful circumstance.
Hitherto the divine faculty of which the internal oracle
is the source has constantly been in the habit of opposing me even about trifles, if I was going to make a slip
or error in any matter; and now as you see there has
come upon me that which may be thought, and is generally believed to be, the last and worst evil. But the
oracle made no sign of opposition, either when I was
leaving my house in the morning, or when I was on my
way to the court, or while I was speaking, at anything
which I was going to say; and yet I have often been
stopped in the middle of a speech, but now in nothing I
either said or did touching the matter in hand has the
oracle opposed me. What do I take to be the explanation of this silence? I will tell you. It is an intimation
that what has happened to me is a good, and that those
of us who think that death is an evil are in error. For
the customary sign would surely have opposed me had
I been going to evil and not to good.

Let us reflect in another way, and we shall see that
there is great reason to hope that death is a good; for
one of two things—either death is a state of nothingness
and utter unconsciousness, or, as men say, there is a
change and migration of the soul from this world to another. Now if you suppose that there is no consciousness, but a sleep like the sleep of him who is undisturbed even by dreams, death will be an unspeakable
gain. For if a person were to select the night in which

his sleep was undisturbed even by dreams, and were to
compare with this the other days and nights of his life,
and then were to tell us how many days and nights he
had passed in the course of his life better and more
pleasantly than this one, I think that any man, I will
not say a private man, but even the great king will not
find many such days or nights, when compared with the
others. Now if death be of such a nature, I say that to
die is gain; for eternity is then only a single night. But
if death is the journey to another place, and there, as
men say, all the dead abide, what good, O my friends
and judges, can be greater than this? If indeed when
the pilgrim arrives in the world below, he is delivered
from the professors of justice in this world, and finds
the true judges who are said to give judgment there,
Minos and Rhadamanthus and Aeacus and Triptolemus,
and other sons of God who were righteous in their own
life, that pilgrimage will be worth making. What would
not a man give if he might converse with Orpheus and
Musaeus and Hesiod and Homer? Nay, if this be true,
let me die again and again. I myself, too, shall have
a wonderful interest in there meeting and conversing
with Palamedes, and Ajax the son of Telamon, and any
other ancient hero who has suffered death through an
unjust judgment; and there will be no small pleasure,
as I think, in comparing my own sufferings with theirs.
Above all, I shall then be able to continue my search
into true and false knowledge; as in this world, so also
in the next; and I shall find out who is wise, and who
pretends to be wise, and is not. What would not a man
give, O judges, to be able to examine the leader of the
great Trojan expedition; or Odysseus or Sisyphus, or
numberless others, men and women too! What infinite
delight would there be in conversing with them and asking them questions! In another world they do not put

a man to death for asking questions: assuredly not. For besides being happier than we are, they will be immortal, if what is said is true.

Wherefore, O judges, be of good cheer about death, and know of a certainty, that no evil can happen to a good man, either in life or after death. He and his are not neglected by the gods; nor has my own approaching end happened by mere chance. But I see clearly that the time had arrived when it was better for me to die and be released from trouble; wherefore the oracle gave no sign. For which reason, also, I am not angry with my condemners, or with my accusers; they have done me no harm, although they did not mean to do me any good; and for this I may gently blame them.

Still I have a favour to ask of them. When my sons are grown up, I would ask you, ❶ my friends, to punish them; and I would have you trouble them, as I have troubled you, if they seem to care about riches, or anything, more than about virtue; or if they pretend to be something when they are really nothing,—then reprove them, as I have reproved you, for not caring about that for which they ought to care, and thinking that they are something when they are really nothing. And if you do this, both I and my sons will have received justice at your hands.

The hour of departure has arrived, and we go our ways—I to die, and you to live. Which is better God only knows.

CRITO

PERSONS OF THE DIALOGUE

SOCRATES   CRITO

SCENE:—The Prison of Socrates

Socrates. WHY have you come at this hour, Crito? it must be quite early?

Crito. Yes, certainly.

Soc. What is the exact time?

Cr. The dawn is breaking.

Soc. I wonder that the keeper of the prison would let you in.

Cr. He knows me, because I often come, Socrates; moreover, I have done him a kindness.

Soc. And are you only just arrived?

Cr. No, I came some time ago.

Soc. Then why did you sit and say nothing, instead of at once awakening me?

Cr. I should not have liked myself, Socrates, to be in such great trouble and unrest as you are—indeed I should not: I have been watching with amazement your peaceful slumbers; and for that reason I did not awake you, because I wished to minimize the pain. I have always thought you to be of a happy disposition; but never did I see anything like the easy, tranquil manner in which you bear this calamity.

Soc. Why, Crito, when a man has reached my age he ought not to be repining at the approach of death.

Cr. And yet other old men find themselves in similar misfortunes, and age does not prevent them from repining.

Soc. That is true. But you have not told me why you come at this early hour.

Cr. I come to bring you a message which is sad and painful; not, as I believe, to yourself, but to all of us who are your friends, and saddest of all to me.

Soc. What? Has the ship come from Delos, on the arrival of which I am to die?

Cr. No, the ship has not actually arrived, but she will probably be here to-day, as persons who have come from Sunium tell me that they left her there; and therefore to-morrow, Socrates, will be the last day of your life.

Soc. Very well, Crito; if such is the will of God, I am willing; but my belief is that there will be a delay of a day.

Cr. Why do you think so?

Soc. I will tell you. I am to die on the day after the arrival of the ship.

Cr. Yes; that is what the authorities say.

Soc. But I do not think that the ship will be here until to-morrow; this I infer from a vision which I had last night, or rather only just now, when you fortunately allowed me to sleep.

Cr. And what was the nature of the vision?

Soc. There appeared to me the likeness of a woman, fair and comely, clothed in bright raiment, who called to me and said: O Socrates,

'The third day hence to fertile Phthia shalt thou go.' [1]

Cr. What a singular dream, Socrates!

Soc. There can be no doubt about the meaning, Crito, I think.

[1] Homer, *Il.* ix. 363.

Cr. Yes; the meaning is only too clear. But, oh! my beloved Socrates, let me entreat you once more to take my advice and escape. For if you die I shall not only lose a friend who can never be replaced, but there is another evil: people who do not know you and me will believe that I might have saved you if I had been willing to give money, but that I did not care. Now, can there be a worse disgrace than this—that I should be thought to value money more than the life of a friend? For the many will not be persuaded that I wanted you to escape, and that you refused.

Soc. But why, my dear Crito, should we care about the opinion of the many? Good men, and they are the only persons who are worth considering, will think of these things truly as they occurred.

Cr. But you see, Socrates, that the opinion of the many must be regarded, for what is now happening shows that they can do the greatest evil to any one who has lost their good opinion.

Soc. I only wish it were so, Crito; and that the many could do the greatest evil; for then they would also be able to do the greatest good—and what a fine thing this would be! But in reality they can do neither; for they cannot make a man either wise or foolish; and whatever they do is the result of chance.

Cr. Well, I will not dispute with you; but please to tell me, Socrates, whether you are not acting out of regard to me and your other friends: are you not afraid that if you escape from prison we may get into trouble with the informers for having stolen you away, and lose either the whole or a great part of our property; or that even a worse evil may happen to us? Now, if you fear on our account, be at ease; for in order to save you, we ought surely to run this, or even a greater risk; be persuaded, then, and do as I say.

Soc. Yes, Crito, that is one fear which you mention, but by no means the only one.

Cr. Fear not—there are persons who are willing to get you out of prison at no great cost; and as for the informers, they are far from being exorbitant in their demands—a little money will satisfy them. My means, which are certainly ample, are at your service, and if you have a scruple about spending all mine, here are strangers who will give you the use of theirs; and one of them, Simmias the Theban, has brought a large sum of money for this very purpose; and Cebes and many others are prepared to spend their money in helping you to escape. I say, therefore, do not hesitate on our account, and do not say, as you did in the court, that you will have a difficulty in knowing what to do with yourself anywhere else. For men will love you in other places to which you may go, and not in Athens only; there are friends of mine in Thessaly, if you like to go to them, who will value and protect you, and no Thessalian will give you any trouble. Nor can I think that you are at all justified, Socrates, in betraying your own life when you might be saved; in acting thus you are playing into the hands of your enemies, who are hurrying on your destruction. And further I should say that you are deserting your own children; for you might bring them up and educate them; instead of which you go away and leave them, and they will have to take their chance; and if they do not meet with the usual fate of orphans, there will be small thanks to you. No man should bring children into the world who is unwilling to persevere to the end in their nurture and education. But you appear to be choosing the easier part, not the better and manlier, which would have been more becoming in one who professes to care for virtue in all his actions, like yourself. And indeed, I am ashamed not only of you, but of us who are your friends, when I reflect that the whole business will be attributed entirely to our want of courage. The trial need never have come on, or might have been managed differently; and this last act, or crowning folly, will seem to have occurred through our negligence and cowardice, who might have saved you, if we had been good for anything; and you might have saved yourself, for there was no difficulty at all. See now, Socrates, how sad and discreditable are the consequences, both to us and you. Make up your mind then, or rather have your mind already made up, for the time of deliberation is over, and there is only one thing to be done, which must be done this very night, and if we delay at all will be no longer practicable or possible; I beseech you therefore, Socrates, be persuaded by me, and do as I say.

Soc. Dear Crito, your zeal is invaluable, if a right one; but if wrong, the greater the zeal the greater the danger; and therefore we ought to consider whether I shall or shall not do as you say. For I am and always have been one of those natures who must be guided by reason, whatever the reason may be which upon reflection appears to me to be the best; and now that this chance has befallen me, I cannot repudiate my own words: the principles which I have hitherto honoured and revered I still honour, and unless we can at once find other and better principles, I am certain not to agree with you; no, not even if the power of the multitude could inflict many more imprisonments, confiscations, deaths, frightening us like children with hobgoblin terrors. What will be the fairest way of considering the question? Shall I return to your old argument about the opinions of men?—we were saying that some of them are to be regarded, and others not. Now were we right in maintaining this before I was condemned? And has the argument which was once good now proved to be talk for the sake of talking—mere childish nonsense? That is what I want to consider with your help, Crito: —whether, under my present circumstances, the argument appears to be in any way different or not; and is to be allowed by me or disallowed. That argument, which, as I believe, is maintained by many persons of authority, was to the effect, as I was saying, that the opinions of some men are to be regarded, and of other men not to be regarded. Now you, Crito, are not going to die to-morrow—at least, there is no human probability of this—and therefore you are disinterested and not liable to be deceived by the circumstances in which you are placed. Tell me then, whether I am right in saying that some opinions, and the opinions of some men only, are to be valued, and that other opinions, and the opinions of other men, are not to be valued. I ask you whether I was right in maintaining this?

Cr. Certainly.

Soc. The good are to be regarded, and not the bad?

Cr. Yes.

Soc. And the opinions of the wise are good, and the opinions of the unwise are evil?

Cr. Certainly.

Soc. And what was said about another matter? Is the pupil who devotes himself to the practice of gymnastics supposed to attend to the praise and blame and opinion of every man, or of one man only—his physician or trainer, whoever he may be?

Cr. Of one man only.

Soc. And he ought to fear the censure and welcome the praise of that one only, and not of the many?

Cr. Clearly so.

Soc. And he ought to act and train, and eat and drink in the way which seems good to his single master who has understanding, rather than according to the opinion of all other men put together?

Cr. True.

Soc. And if he disobeys and disregards the opinion and approval of the one, and regards the opinion of the many who have no understanding, will he not suffer evil?

Cr. Certainly he will.

Soc. And what will the evil be, whither tending and what affecting, in the disobedient person?

Cr. Clearly, affecting the body; that is what is destroyed by the evil.

Soc. Very good; and is not this true, Crito, of other things which we need not separately enumerate? In questions of just and unjust, fair and foul, good and evil, which are the subjects of our present consultation, ought we to follow the opinion of the many and to fear them; or the opinion of the one man who has understanding? ought we not to fear and reverence him more than all the rest of the world: and if we desert him shall we not destroy and injure that principle in us which may be assumed to be improved by justice and deteriorated by injustice;—there is such a principle?

Cr. Certainly there is, Socrates.

Soc. Take a parallel instance:—if, acting under the advice of those who have no understanding, we destroy that which is improved by health and is deteriorated by disease, would life be worth having? And that which has been destroyed is—the body?

Cr. Yes.

Soc. Could we live, having an evil and corrupted body?

Cr. Certainly not.

Soc. And will life be worth having, if that higher part of man be destroyed, which is improved by justice and depraved by injustice? Do we suppose that principle, whatever it may be in man, which has to do with justice and injustice, to be inferior to the body?

Cr. Certainly not.

Soc. More honourable than the body?

Cr. Far more.

Soc. Then, my friend, we must not regard what the many say of us: but what he, the one man who has understanding of just and unjust, will say, and what the truth will say. And therefore you begin in error when you advise that we should regard the opinion of the many about just and unjust, good and evil, honourable and dishonourable.—'Well,' some one will say, 'but the many can kill us.'

Cr. Yes, Socrates; that will clearly be the answer.

Soc. And it is true: but still I find with surprise that the old argument is unshaken as ever. And I should like to know whether I may say the same of another proposition—that not life, but a good life, is to be chiefly valued?

Cr. Yes, that also remains unshaken.

Soc. And a good life is equivalent to a just and honourable one—that holds also?

Cr. Yes, it does.

Soc. From these premisses I proceed to argue the question whether I ought or ought not to try and escape without the consent of the Athenians: and if I am clearly right in escaping, then I will make the attempt; but if not, I will abstain. The other considerations which you mention, of money and loss of character and the duty of educating one's children, are, I fear, only the doctrines of the multitude, who would be as ready to restore people to life, if they were able, as they are to put them to death—and with as little reason. But now, since the argument has thus far prevailed, the only question which remains to be considered is, whether we shall do rightly either in escaping or in suffering others to aid in our escape and paying them in money and thanks, or whether in reality we shall not do rightly; and if the latter, then death or any other calamity which may ensue on my remaining here must not be allowed to enter into the calculation.

Cr. I think that you are right, Socrates; how then shall we proceed?

Soc. Let us consider the matter together, and do you either refute me if you can, and I will be convinced; or else cease, my dear friend, from repeating to me that I ought to escape against the wishes of the Athenians: for I highly value your attempts to persuade me to do so, but I may not be persuaded against my own better judgment. And now please to consider my first position, and try how you can best answer me.

Cr. I will.

Soc. Are we to say that we are never intentionally to do wrong, or that in one way we ought and in another way we ought not to do wrong, or is doing wrong always evil and dishonourable, as I was just now saying, and as has been already acknowledged by us? Are all our former admissions which were made within a few days to be thrown away? And have we, at our age, been earnestly discoursing with one another all our life long only to discover that we are no better than children? Or, in spite of the opinion of the many, and in spite of consequences whether better or worse, shall we insist on the truth of what was then said, that injustice is always an evil and dishonour to him who acts unjustly? Shall we say so or not?

Cr. Yes.

Soc. Then we must do no wrong?

Cr. Certainly not.

Soc. Nor when injured injure in return, as the many imagine; for we must injure no one at all?

Cr. Clearly not.

Soc. Again, Crito, may we do evil?

Cr. Surely not, Socrates.

Soc. And what of doing evil in return for evil, which is the morality of the many—is that just or not?

Cr. Not just.

Soc. For doing evil to another is the same as injuring him?

Cr. Very true.

Soc. Then we ought not to retaliate or render evil for evil to any one, whatever evil we may have suffered from him. But I would have you consider, Crito, whether you really mean what you are saying. For this opinion has never been held, and never will be held, by any considerable number of persons; and those who are agreed and those who are not agreed upon this point have no common ground, and can only despise one another when they see how widely they differ. Tell me, then, whether you agree with and assent to my first principle, that neither injury nor retaliation nor warding off evil by evil is ever right. And shall that be the premiss of our argument? Or do you decline and dissent from this? For so I have ever thought, and continue to think; but, if you are of another opinion, let me hear what you have to say. If, however, you remain of the same mind as formerly, I will proceed to the next step.

Cr. You may proceed, for I have not changed my mind.

Soc. Then I will go on to the next point, which may be put in the form of a question:—Ought a man to do

what he admits to be right, or ought he to betray the
right?

Cr. He ought to do what he thinks right.

Soc. But if this is true, what is the application? In
leaving the prison against the will of the Athenians, do
I wrong any? or rather do I not wrong those whom I
ought least to wrong? Do I not desert the principles
which were acknowledged by us to be just—what do you
say?

Cr. I cannot tell, Socrates; for I do not know.

Soc. Then consider the matter in this way:—Imagine that I am about to play truant (you may call the
proceeding by any name which you like), and the laws
and the government come and interrogate me: 'Tell us,
Socrates,' they say; 'what are you about? are you not
going by an act of yours to overturn us—the laws, and
the whole state, as far as in you lies? Do you imagine
that a state can subsist and not be overthrown, in which
the decisions of law have no power, but are set aside
and trampled upon by individuals?' What will be our
answer, Crito, to these and the like words? Any one,
and especially a rhetorician, will have a good deal to
say on behalf of the law which requires a sentence to be
carried out. He will argue that this law should not be
set aside; and shall we reply, 'Yes; but the state has
injured us and given an unjust sentence.' Suppose I
say that?

Cr. Very good, Socrates.

Soc. 'And was that our agreement with you?' the
law would answer; 'or were you to abide by the sentence of the state?' And if I were to express my astonishment at their words, the law would probably add:
'Answer, Socrates, instead of opening your eyes—you
are in the habit of asking and answering questions. Tell
us,—What complaint have you to make against us which

justifies you in attempting to destroy us and the state?
In the first place did we not bring you into existence?
Your father married your mother by our aid and begat
you.   Say whether you have any objection to urge
against those of us who regulate marriage?' None, I
should reply.   'Or against those of us who after birth
regulate the nurture and education of children, in which
you also were trained?   Were not the laws, which have
the charge of education, right in commanding your
father to train you in music and gymnastics?' Right, I
should reply.   'Well then, since you were brought into
the world and nurtured and educated by us, can you
deny in the first place that you are our child and slave,
as your fathers were before you?   And if this is true
you are not on equal terms with us; nor can you think
that you have a right to do to us what we are doing to
you.   Would you have any right to strike or revile or
do any other evil to your father or your master, if you
had one, because you have been struck or reviled by
him, or received some other evil at his hands?—you
would not say this?   And because we think right to
destroy you, do you think that you have any right
to destroy us in return, and your country as far as in
you lies?   Will you, O professor of true virtue, pretend
that you are justified in this?   Has a philosopher like
you failed to discover that our country is more to be
valued and higher and holier far than mother or father
or any ancestor, and more to be regarded in the eyes of
the gods and of men of understanding? also to be
soothed, and gently and reverently entreated when
angry, even more than a father, and either to be persuaded, or if not persuaded, to be obeyed?   And when
we are punished by her, whether with imprisonment or
stripes, the punishment is to be endured in silence; and
if she lead us to wounds or death in battle, thither we

follow as is right; neither may any one yield or retreat or leave his rank, but whether in battle or in a court of law, or in any other place, he must do what his city and his country order him; or he must change their view of what is just: and if he may do no violence to his father or mother, much less may he do violence to his country.' What answer shall we make to this, Crito? Do the laws speak truly, or do they not?

Cr. I think that they do.

Soc. Then the laws will say: 'Consider, Socrates, if we are speaking truly that in your present attempt you are going to do us an injury. For, having brought you into the world, and nurtured and educated you, and given you and every other citizen a share in every good which we had to give, we further proclaim to any Athenian by the liberty which we allow him, that if he does not like us when he has become of age and has seen the ways of the city, and made our acquaintance, he may go where he pleases and take his goods with him. None of us laws will forbid him or interfere with him. Any one who does not like us and the city, and who wants to emigrate to a colony or to any other city, may go where he likes, retaining his property. But he who has experience of the manner in which we order justice and administer the state, and still remains, has entered into an implied contract that he will do as we command him. And he who disobeys us is, as we maintain, thrice wrong; first, because in disobeying us he is disobeying his parents; secondly, because we are the authors of his education; thirdly, because he has made an agreement with us that he will duly obey our commands; and he neither obeys them nor convinces us that our commands are unjust; and we do not rudely impose them, but give him the alternative of obeying or convincing us;—that is what we offer, and he does neither.

'These are the sort of accusations to which, as we were saying, you, Socrates, will be exposed if you accomplish your intentions; you, above all other Athenians.' Suppose now I ask, why I rather than anybody else? they will justly retort upon me that I above all other men have acknowledged the agreement. 'There is clear proof,' they will say, 'Socrates, that we and the city were not displeasing to you. Of all Athenians you have been the most constant resident in the city, which, as you never leave, you may be supposed to love. For you never went out of the city either to see the games, except once when you went to the Isthmus, or to any other place unless when you were on military service; nor did you travel as other men do. Nor had you any curiosity to know other states or their laws: your affections did not go beyond us and our state; we were your special favourites, and you acquiesced in our government of you; and here in this city you begat your children, which is a proof of your satisfaction. Moreover, you might in the course of the trial, if you had liked, have fixed the penalty at banishment; the state which refuses to let you go now would have let you go then. But you pretended that you preferred death to exile, and that you were not unwilling to die. And now you have forgotten these fine sentiments, and pay no respect to us the laws, of whom you are the destroyer; and are doing what only a miserable slave would do, running away and turning your back upon the compacts and agreements which you made as a citizen. And first of all answer this very question: Are we right in saying that you agreed to be governed according to us in deed, and not in word only? Is that true or not?' How shall we answer, Crito? Must we not assent?

Cr. We cannot help it, Socrates.

Soc. Then will they not say: 'You, Socrates, are

breaking the covenants and agreements which you made with us at your leisure, not in any haste or under any compulsion or deception, but after you have had seventy years to think of them, during which time you were at liberty to leave the city, if we were not to your mind, or if our covenants appeared to you to be unfair. You had your choice, and might have gone either to Lacedaemon or Crete, both which states are often praised by you for their good government, or to some other Hellenic or foreign state. Whereas you, above all other Athenians, seemed to be so fond of the state, or, in other words, of us her laws (and who would care about a state which has no laws?), that you never stirred out of her; the halt, the blind, the maimed were not more stationary in her than you were. And now you run away and forsake your agreements. Not so, Socrates, if you will take our advice; do not make yourself ridiculous by escaping out of the city.

'For just consider, if you transgress and err in this sort of way, what good will you do either to yourself or to your friends? That your friends will be driven into exile and deprived of citizenship, or will lose their property, is tolerably certain; and you yourself, if you fly to one of the neighbouring cities, as, for example, Thebes or Megara, both of which are well governed, will come to them as an enemy, Socrates, and their government will be against you, and all patriotic citizens will cast an evil eye upon you as a subverter of the laws, and you will confirm in the minds of the judges the justice of their own condemnation of you. For he who is a corrupter of the laws is more than likely to be a corrupter of the young and foolish portion of mankind. Will you then flee from well-ordered cities and virtuous men? and is existence worth having on these terms? Or will you go to them without shame, and talk to them,

Socrates? And what will you say to them? What you
say here about virtue and justice and institutions and
laws being the best things among men? Would that be
decent of you? Surely not. But if you go away from
well-governed states to Crito's friends in Thessaly,
where there is great disorder and licence, they will be
charmed to hear the tale of your escape from prison, set
off with ludicrous particulars of the manner in which
you were wrapped in a goatskin or some other disguise,
and metamorphosed as the manner is of runaways; but
will there be no one to remind you that in your old age
you were not ashamed to violate the most sacred laws
from a miserable desire of a little more life? Perhaps
not, if you keep them in a good temper; but if they are
out of temper you will hear many degrading things;
you will live, but how?—as the flatterer of all men, and
the servant of all men; and doing what?—eating and
drinking in Thessaly, having gone abroad in order that
you may get a dinner. And where will be your fine sentiments about justice and virtue? Say that you wish
to live for the sake of your children—you want to bring
them up and educate them—will you take them into
Thessaly and deprive them of Athenian citizenship? Is
this the benefit which you will confer upon them? Or
are you under the impression that they will be better
cared for and educated here if you are still alive, although absent from them; for your friends will take
care of them? Do you fancy that if you are an inhabitant of Thessaly they will take care of them, and if you
are an inhabitant of the other world that they will not
take care of them? Nay; but if they who call themselves friends are good for anything, they will—to be
sure they will.

'Listen, then, Socrates, to us who have brought you
up. Think not of life and children first, and of justice

afterwards, but of justice first, that you may be justified before the princes of the world below. For neither will you nor any that belong to you be happier or holier or juster in this life, or happier in another, if you do as Crito bids. Now you depart in innocence, a sufferer and not a doer of evil; a victim, not of the laws but of men. But if you go forth, returning evil for evil, and injury for injury, breaking the covenants and agreements which you have made with us, and wronging those whom you ought least of all to wrong, that is to say, yourself, your friends, your country, and us, we shall be angry with you while you live, and our brethren, the laws in the world below, will receive you as an enemy; for they will know that you have done your best to destroy us. Listen, then, to us and not to Crito.'

This, dear Crito, is the voice which I seem to hear murmuring in my ears, like the sound of the flute in the ears of the mystic; that voice, I say, is humming in my ears, and prevents me from hearing any other. And I know that anything more which you may say will be vain. Yet speak, if you have anything to say.

Cr. I have nothing to say, Socrates.

Soc. Leave me then, Crito, to fulfil the will of God, and to follow whither he leads.

PROTAGORAS

PERSONS OF THE DIALOGUE

SOCRATES, *who is the narrator of the Dialogue to his Companion*
HIPPOCRATES
ALCIBIADES
CRITIAS

PROTAGORAS
HIPPIAS   } *Sophists*
PRODICUS

CALLIAS, *a wealthy Athenian*

SCENE:—The House of Callias

Companion. WHERE do you come from, Socrates? And yet I need hardly ask the question, for I know that you have been in chase of the fair Alcibiades. I saw him the day before yesterday; and he had got a beard like a man,—and he is a man, as I may tell you in your ear. But I thought he was still very charming.

Socrates. What of his beard? Are you not of Homer's opinion, who says [1]

'Youth is most charming when the beard first appears'?

And that is now the charm of Alcibiades.

Com. Well, and how do matters proceed? Have you been visiting him, and was he gracious to you?

Soc. Yes, I thought that he was very gracious; and especially to-day, for I have just come from him, and he has been helping me in an argument. But shall I tell you a strange thing? I paid no attention to him, and several times I quite forgot that he was present.

Com. What is the meaning of this? Has anything

[1] *Il.* xxiv. 348.

happened between you and him? For surely you cannot have discovered a fairer love than he is; certainly not in this city of Athens.

Soc. Yes, much fairer.

Com. What do you mean—a citizen or a foreigner?

Soc. A foreigner.

Com. Of what country?

Soc. Of Abdera.

Com. And is this stranger really in your opinion a fairer love than the son of Cleinias?

Soc. And is not the wiser always the fairer, sweet friend?

Com. But have you really met, Socrates, with some wise one?

Soc. Say rather, with the wisest of all living men, if you are willing to accord that title to Protagoras.

Com. What! Is Protagoras in Athens?

Soc. Yes; he has been here two days.

Com. And do you just come from an interview with him?

Soc. Yes; and I have heard and said many things.

Com. Then, if you have no engagement, suppose that you sit down and tell me what passed, and my attendant here shall give up his place to you.

Soc. To be sure; and I shall be grateful to you for listening.

Com. Thank you, too, for telling us.

Soc. That is thank you twice over. Listen then:—

Last night, or rather very early this morning, Hippocrates, the son of Apollodorus and the brother of Phason, gave a tremendous thump with his staff at my door; some one opened to him, and he came rushing in and bawled out: Socrates, are you awake or asleep?

I knew his voice, and said: Hippocrates, is that you? and do you bring any news?

Good news, he said; nothing but good.

Delightful, I said; but what is the news? and why have you come hither at this unearthly hour?

He drew nearer to me and said: Protagoras is come.

Yes, I replied; he came two days ago: have you only just heard of his arrival?

Yes, by the gods, he said; but not until yesterday evening.

At the same time he felt for the truckle-bed, and sat down at my feet, and then he said: Yesterday quite late in the evening, on my return from Oenoe whither I had gone in pursuit of my runaway slave Satyrus, as I meant to have told you, if some other matter had not come in the way;—on my return, when we had done supper and were about to retire to rest, my brother said to me: Protagoras is come. I was going to you at once, and then I thought that the night was far spent. But the moment sleep left me after my fatigue, I got up and came hither direct.

I, who knew the very courageous madness of the man, said: What is the matter? Has Protagoras robbed you of anything?

He replied, laughing: Yes, indeed he has, Socrates, of the wisdom which he keeps from me.

But, surely, I said, if you give him money, and make friends with him, he will make you as wise as he is himself.

Would to heaven, he replied, that this were the case! He might take all that I have, and all that my friends have, if he pleased. But that is why I have come to you now, in order that you may speak to him on my behalf; for I am young, and also I have never seen nor heard him; (when he visited Athens before I was but a child;) and all men praise him, Socrates; he is reputed to be the most accomplished of speakers. There is no reason why we should not go to him at once, and then we shall find him at home. He lodges, as I hear, with Callias the son of Hipponicus: let us start.

I replied: Not yet, my good friend; the hour is too early. But let us rise and take a turn in the court and wait about there until day-break; when the day breaks, then we will go. For Protagoras is generally at home, and we shall be sure to find him; never fear.

Upon this we got up and walked about in the court, and I thought that I would make trial of the strength of his resolution. So I examined him and put questions to him. Tell me, Hippocrates, I said, as you are going to Protagoras, and will be paying your money to him, what is he to whom you are going? and what will he make of you? If, for example, you had thought of going to Hippocrates of Cos, the Asclepiad, and were about to give him your money, and some one had said to you: You are paying money to your namesake Hippocrates, O Hippocrates; tell me, what is he that you give him money? how would you have answered?

I should say, he replied, that I gave money to him as a physician.

And what will he make of you?

A physician, he said.

And if you were resolved to go to Polycleitus the Argive, or Pheidias the Athenian, and were intending to give them money, and some one had asked you: What are Polycleitus and Pheidias? and why do you give them this money?—how would you have answered?

I should have answered, that they were statuaries.

And what will they make of you?

A statuary, of course.

Well now, I said, you and I are going to Protagoras, and we are ready to pay him money on your behalf. If our own means are sufficient, and we can gain him with these, we shall be only too glad; but if not, then we are to spend the money of your friends as well. Now suppose, that while we are thus enthusiastically pursuing our object some one were to say to us: Tell me, Socrates, and you Hippocrates, what is Protagoras, and why are you going to pay him money,—how should we answer? I know that Pheidias is a sculptor, and that Homer is a poet; but what appellation is given to Protagoras? how is he designated?

They call him a Sophist, Socrates, he replied.

Then we are going to pay our money to him in the character of a Sophist?

Certainly.

But suppose a person were to ask this further question: And how about yourself? What will Protagoras make of you, if you go to see him?

He answered, with a blush upon his face (for the day was just beginning to dawn, so that I could see him): Unless this differs in some way from the former instances, I suppose that he will make a Sophist of me.

By the gods, I said, and are you not ashamed at having to appear before the Hellenes in the character of a Sophist?

Indeed, Socrates, to confess the truth, I am.

But you should not assume, Hippocrates, that the instruction of Protagoras is of this nature: may you not learn of him in the same way that you learned the arts of the grammarian, or musician, or trainer, not with the view of making any of them a profession, but only as a part of education, and because a private gentleman and freeman ought to know them?

Just so, he said; and that, in my opinion, is a far truer account of the teaching of Protagoras.

I said: I wonder whether you know what you are doing?

And what am I doing?

You are going to commit your soul to the care of a man whom you call a Sophist. And yet I hardly think that you know what a Sophist is; and if not, then you do not even know to whom you are committing your soul and whether the thing to which you commit yourself be good or evil.

I certainly think that I do know, he replied.

Then tell me, what do you imagine that he is?

I take him to be one who knows wise things, he replied, as his name implies.

And might you not, I said, affirm this of the painter and of the carpenter also: Do not they, too, know wise things? But suppose a person were to ask us: In what are the painters wise? We should answer: In what relates to the making of likenesses, and similarly of other things. And if he were further to ask: What is the wisdom of the Sophist, and what is the manufacture over which he presides?—how should we answer him?

How should we answer him, Socrates? What other answer could there be but that he presides over the art which makes men eloquent?

Yes, I replied, that is very likely true, but not enough; for in the answer a further question is involved: Of what does the Sophist make a man talk eloquently? The player on the lyre may be supposed to make a man talk eloquently about that which he makes him understand, that is about playing the lyre. Is not that true?

Yes.

Then about what does the Sophist make him eloquent? Must not he make him eloquent in that which he understands?

Yes, that may be assumed.

And what is that which the Sophist knows and makes his disciple know?

Indeed, he said, I cannot tell.

Then I proceeded to say: Well, but are you aware of the danger which you are incurring? If you were going to commit your body to some one, who might do good or harm to it, would you not carefully consider and ask the opinion of your friends and kindred, and deliberate many days as to whether you should give him the care of your body? But when the soul is in question, which you hold to be of far more value than the body, and upon the good or evil of which depends the well-being of your all,—about this you never consulted either with your father or with your brother or with any one of us who are your companions. But no sooner does this foreigner appear, than you instantly commit your soul to his keeping. In the evening, as you say, you hear of him, and in the morning you go to him, never deliberating or taking the opinion of any one as to whether you ought to intrust yourself to him or not; —you have quite made up your mind that you will at all hazards be a pupil of Protagoras, and are prepared to expend all the property of yourself and of your friends in carrying out at any price this determination, although, as you admit, you do not know him, and have never spoken with him: and you call him a Sophist, but are manifestly ignorant of what a Sophist is; and yet you are going to commit yourself to his keeping.

When he heard me say this, he replied: No other inference, Socrates, can be drawn from your words.

I proceeded: Is not a Sophist, Hippocrates, one who deals wholesale or retail in the food of the soul? To me that appears to be his nature.

And what, Socrates, is the food of the soul?

Surely, I said, knowledge is the food of the soul; and we must take care, my friend, that the Sophist does not deceive us when he praises what he sells, like the dealers wholesale or retail who sell the food of the body; for they praise indiscriminately all their goods, without knowing what are really beneficial or hurtful: neither do their customers know, with the exception of any trainer or physician who may happen to buy of them. In like manner those who carry about the wares of knowledge, and make the round of the cities, and sell or retail them to any customer who is in want of them, praise them all alike; though I should not wonder, O my friend, if many of them were really ignorant of their effect upon the soul; and their customers equally ignorant, unless he who buys of them happens to be a physician of the soul. If, therefore, you have understanding of what is good and evil, you may safely buy knowledge of Protagoras or of any one; but if not, then, O my friend, pause, and do not hazard your dearest interests at a game of chance. For there is far greater peril in buying knowledge than in buying meat and drink: the one you purchase of the wholesale or retail dealer, and carry them away in other vessels, and before you receive them into the body as food, you may deposit them at home and call in any experienced friend who knows what is good to be eaten or drunken, and what not, and how much, and when; and then the danger of purchasing them is not so great. But you cannot buy the wares of knowledge and carry them away in another vessel; when you have paid for them you must receive them into the soul and go your way, either greatly harmed or greatly benefited; and therefore we should deliberate and take counsel with our elders; for we are still young—too young to determine such a matter. And now let us go, as we were intending, and hear Protagoras;

and when we have heard what he has to say, we may take counsel of others; for not only is Protagoras at the house of Callias, but there is Hippias of Elis, and, if I am not mistaken, Prodicus of Ceos, and several other wise men.

To this we agreed, and proceeded on our way until we reached the vestibule of the house; and there we stopped in order to conclude a discussion which had arisen between us as we were going along; and we stood talking in the vestibule until we had finished and come to an understanding. And I think that the door-keeper, who was a eunuch, and who was probably annoyed at the great inroad of the Sophists, must have heard us talking. At any rate, when we knocked at the door, and he opened and saw us, he grumbled: They are Sophists —he is not at home; and instantly gave the door a hearty bang with both his hands. Again we knocked, and he answered without opening: Did you not hear me say that he is not at home, fellows? But, my friend, I said, you need not be alarmed; for we are not Sophists, and we are not come to see Callias, but we want to see Protagoras; and I must request you to announce us. At last, after a good deal of difficulty, the man was persuaded to open the door.

When we entered, we found Protagoras taking a walk in the cloister; and next to him, on one side, were walking Callias, the son of Hipponicus, and Paralus, the son of Pericles, who, by the mother's side, is his half-brother, and Charmides, the son of Glaucon. On the other side of him were Xanthippus, the other son of Pericles, Philippides, the son of Philomelus; also Antimoerus of Mende, who of all the disciples of Protagoras is the most famous, and intends to make sophistry his profession. A train of listeners followed him; the greater part of them appeared to be foreigners, whom Protagoras had brought with him out of the various cities visited by him in his journeys, he, like Orpheus, attracting them by his voice, and they following. I should mention also that there were some Athenians in the company. Nothing delighted me more than the precision of their movements: they never got into his way at all; but when he and those who were with him turned back, then the band of listeners parted regularly on either side; he was always in front, and they wheeled round and took their places behind him in perfect order.

After him, as Homer says,[1] 'I lifted up my eyes and saw' Hippias the Elean sitting in the opposite cloister on a chair of state, and around him were seated on benches Eryximachus, the son of Acumenus, and Phaedrus the Myrrhinusian, and Andron the son of Androtion, and there were strangers whom he had brought with him from his native city of Elis, and some others: they were putting to Hippias certain physical and astronomical questions, and he, *ex cathedrâ,* was determining their several questions to them, and discoursing of them.

Also, 'my eyes beheld Tantalus;'[2] for Prodicus the Cean was at Athens: he had been lodged in a room which, in the days of Hipponicus, was a storehouse; but, as the house was full, Callias had cleared this out and made the room into a guest-chamber. Now Prodicus was still in bed, wrapped up in sheepskins and bedclothes, of which there seemed to be a great heap; and there was sitting by him on the couches near, Pausanias of the deme of Cerameis, and with Pausanias was a youth quite young, who is certainly remarkable for his good looks, and, if I am not mistaken, is also of a fair

[1] *Od.* xi. 601 foll.
[2] *Od.* xi. 582.

and gentle nature. I thought that I heard him called
Agathon, and my suspicion is that he is the beloved of
Pausanias. There was this youth, and also there were
the two Adeimantuses, one the son of Cepis, and the
other of Leucolophides, and some others. I was very
anxious to hear what Prodicus was saying, for he seems
to me to be an all-wise and inspired man; but I was not
able to get into the inner circle, and his fine deep voice
made an echo in the room which rendered his words
inaudible.

No sooner had we entered than there followed us
Alcibiades the beautiful, as you say, and I believe you;
and also Critias the son of Calleschrus.

On entering we stopped a little, in order to look about
us, and then walked up to Protagoras, and I said: Protagoras, my friend Hippocrates and I have come to see
you.

Do you wish, he said, to speak with me alone, or in
the presence of the company?

Whichever you please, I said; you shall determine
when you have heard the purpose of our visit.

And what is your purpose? he said.

I must explain, I said, that my friend Hippocrates is
a native Athenian; he is the son of Apollodorus, and of
a great and prosperous house, and he is himself in natural ability quite a match for anybody of his own age.
I believe that he aspires to political eminence; and this
he thinks that conversation with you is most likely to
procure for him. And now you can determine whether
you would wish to speak to him of your teaching alone
or in the presence of the company.

Thank you, Socrates, for your consideration of me.
For certainly a stranger finding his way into great cities,
and persuading the flower of the youth in them to leave
the company of their kinsmen or any other acquaintances,

old or young, and live with him, under the idea that they will be improved by his conversation, ought to be very cautious; great jealousies are aroused by his proceedings, and he is the subject of many enmities and conspiracies. Now the art of the Sophist is, as I believe, of great antiquity; but in ancient times those who practised it, fearing this odium, veiled and disguised themselves under various names, some under that of poets, as Homer, Hesiod, and Simonides, some, of hierophants and prophets, as Orpheus and Musaeus, and some, as I observe, even under the name of gymnastic-masters, like Iccus of Tarentum, or the more recently celebrated Herodicus, now of Selymbria and formerly of Megara, who is a first-rate Sophist. Your own Agathocles pretended to be a musician, but was really an eminent Sophist; also Pythocleides the Cean; and there were many others; and all of them, as I was saying, adopted these arts as veils or disguises because they were afraid of the odium which they would incur. But that is not my way, for I do not believe that they effected their purpose, which was to deceive the government, who were not blinded by them; and as to the people, they have no understanding, and only repeat what their rulers are pleased to tell them. Now to run away, and to be caught in running away, is the very height of folly, and also greatly increases the exasperation of mankind; for they regard him who runs away as a rogue, in addition to any other objections which they have to him; and therefore I take an entirely opposite course, and acknowledge myself to be a Sophist and instructor of mankind; such an open acknowledgment appears to me to be a better sort of caution than concealment. Nor do I neglect other precautions, and therefore I hope, as I may say, by the favour of heaven that no harm will come of the acknowledgment that I am a Sophist. And I

have been now many years in the profession—for all my
years when added up are many: there is no one here
present of whom I might not be the father. Wherefore I should much prefer conversing with you, if you
want to speak with me, in the presence of the company.

As I suspected that he would like to have a little dis-
play and glorification in the presence of Prodicus and
Hippias, and would gladly show us to them in the light
of his admirers, I said: But why should we not summon
Prodicus and Hippias, and their friends to hear us?

Very good, he said.

Suppose, said Callias, that we hold a council in which
you may sit and discuss.—This was agreed upon, and
great delight was felt at the prospect of hearing wise
men talk; we ourselves took the chairs and benches, and
arranged them by Hippias, where the other benches had
been already placed. Meanwhile Callias and Alcibiades
got Prodicus out of bed and brought in him and his
companions.

When we were all seated, Protagoras said: Now that
the company are assembled, Socrates, tell me about the
young man of whom you were just now speaking.

I replied: I will begin again at the same point, Protagoras, and tell you once more the purport of my visit:
this is my friend Hippocrates, who is desirous of making your acquaintance; he would like to know what will
happen to him if he associates with you. I have no more
to say.

Protagoras answered: Young man, if you associate
with me, on the very first day you will return home a
better man than you came, and better on the second day
than on the first, and better every day than you were on
the day before.

When I heard this, I said: Protagoras, I do not at all
wonder at hearing you say this; even at your age, and

with all your wisdom, if any one were to teach you what
you did not know before, you would become better no
doubt: but please to answer in a different way—I will
explain how by an example. Let me suppose that Hippocrates, instead of desiring your acquaintance, wished
to become acquainted with the young man Zeuxippus of
Heraclea, who has lately been in Athens, and he had
come to him as he has come to you, and had heard him
say, as he has heard you say, that every day he would
grow and become better if he associated with him: and
then suppose that he were to ask him, 'In what shall I
become better, and in what shall I grow?'—Zeuxippus
would answer, 'In painting.' And suppose that he went
to Orthagoras the Theban, and heard him say the same
thing, and asked him, 'In what shall I become better day
by day?' he would reply, 'In flute-playing.' Now I
want you to make the same sort of answer to this young
man and to me, who am asking questions on his account.
When you say that on the first day on which he associates with you he will return home a better man, and
on every day will grow in like manner,—in what, Protagoras, will he be better? and about what?

When Protagoras heard me say this, he replied: You
ask questions fairly, and I like to answer a question
which is fairly put. If Hippocrates comes to me he will
not experience the sort of drudgery with which other
Sophists are in the habit of insulting their pupils; who,
when they have just escaped from the arts, are taken
and driven back into them by these teachers, and made
to learn calculation, and astronomy, and geometry, and
music (he gave a look at Hippias as he said this); but
if he comes to me, he will learn that which he comes to
learn. And this is prudence in affairs private as well as
public; he will learn to order his own house in the best

manner, and he will be able to speak and act for the best in the affairs of the state.

Do I understand you, I said; and is your meaning that you teach the art of politics, and that you promise to make men good citizens?

That, Socrates, is exactly the profession which I make.

Then, I said, you do indeed possess a noble art, if there is no mistake about this; for I will freely confess to you, Protagoras, that I have a doubt whether this art is capable of being taught, and yet I know not how to disbelieve your assertion. And I ought to tell you why I am of opinion that this art cannot be taught or communicated by man to man. I say that the Athenians are an understanding people, and indeed they are esteemed to be such by the other Hellenes. Now I observe that when we are met together in the assembly, and the matter in hand relates to building, the builders are summoned as advisers; when the question is one of shipbuilding, then the ship-wrights; and the like of other arts which they think capable of being taught and learned. And if some person offers to give them advice who is not supposed by them to have any skill in the art, even though he be good-looking, and rich, and noble, they will not listen to him, but laugh and hoot at him, until either he is clamoured down and retires of himself; or if he persist, he is dragged away or put out by the constables at the command of the prytanes. This is their way of behaving about professors of the arts. But when the question is an affair of state, then everybody is free to have a say—carpenter, tinker, cobbler, sailor, passenger; rich and poor, high and low—any one who likes gets up, and no one reproaches him, as in the former case, with not having learned, and having no teacher, and yet giving advice; evidently because they are under the impression that this sort of knowledge cannot be taught. And not only is this true of the state, but of individuals; the best and wisest of our citizens are unable to impart their political wisdom to others: as for example, Pericles, the father of these young men, who gave them excellent instruction in all that could be learned from masters, in his own department of politics neither taught them, nor gave them teachers; but they were allowed to wander at their own free will in a sort of hope that they would light upon virtue of their own accord. Or take another example: there was Cleinias the younger brother of our friend Alcibiades, of whom this very same Pericles was the guardian; and he being in fact under the apprehension that Cleinias would be corrupted by Alcibiades, took him away, and placed him in the house of Ariphron to be educated; but before six months had elapsed, Ariphron sent him back, not knowing what to do with him. And I could mention numberless other instances of persons who were good themselves, and never yet made any one else good, whether friend or stranger. Now I, Protagoras, having these examples before me, am inclined to think that virtue cannot be taught. But then again, when I listen to your words, I waver; and am disposed to thing that there must be something in what you say, because I know that you have great experience, and learning, and invention. And I wish that you would, if possible, show me a little more clearly that virtue can be taught. Will you be so good?

That I will, Socrates, and gladly. But what would you like? Shall I, as an elder, speak to you as younger men in an apologue or myth, or shall I argue out the question?

To this several of the company answered that he should choose for himself.

Well, then, he said, I think that the myth will be more interesting.

Once upon a time there were gods only, and no mortal creatures. But when the time came that these also should be created, the gods fashioned them out of earth and fire and various mixtures of both elements in the interior of the earth; and when they were about to bring them into the light of day, they ordered Prometheus and Epimetheus to equip them, and to distribute to them severally their proper qualities. Epimetheus said to Prometheus: 'Let me distribute, and do you inspect.' This was agreed, and Epimetheus made the distribution. There were some to whom he gave strength without swiftness, while he equipped the weaker with swiftness; some he armed, and others he left unarmed; and devised for the latter some other means of preservation, making some large, and having their size as a protection, and others small, whose nature was to fly in the air or burrow in the ground; this was to be their way of escape. Thus did he compensate them with the view of preventing any race from becoming extinct. And when he had provided against their destruction by one another, he contrived also a means of protecting them against the seasons of heaven; clothing them with close hair and thick skins sufficient to defend them against the winter cold and able to resist the summer heat, so that they might have a natural bed of their own when they wanted to rest; also he furnished them with hoofs and hair and hard and callous skins under their feet. Then he gave them varieties of food,—herb of the soil to some, to others fruits of trees, and to others roots, and to some again he gave other animals as food. And

some he made to have few young ones, while those who
were their prey were very prolific; and in this manner
the race was preserved. Thus did Epimetheus, who,
not being very wise, forgot that he had distributed
among the brute animals all the qualities which he had
to give,—and when he came to man, who was still un-
provided, he was terribly perplexed. Now while he was
in this perplexity, Prometheus came to inspect the distribution, and he found that the other animals were
suitably furnished, but that man alone was naked and
shoeless, and had neither bed nor arms of defence. The
appointed hour was approaching when man in his turn
was to go forth into the light of day; and Prometheus,
not knowing how he could devise his salvation, stole the
mechanical arts of Hephaestus and Athene, and fire
with them (they could neither have been acquired nor
used without fire), and gave them to man. Thus man
had the wisdom necessary to the support of life, but political wisdom he had not; for that was in the keeping
of Zeus, and the power of Prometheus did not extend
to entering into the citadel of heaven, where Zeus dwelt,
who moreover had terrible sentinels; but he did enter
by stealth into the common workshop of Athene and
Hephaestus, in which they used to practise their favourite arts, and carried off Hephaestus' art of working by
fire, and also the art of Athene, and gave them to man.
And in this way man was supplied with the means of
life. But Prometheus is said to have been afterwards
prosecuted for theft, owing to the blunder of Epimetheus.

Now man, having a share of the divine attributes, was
at first the only one of the animals who had any gods,
because he alone was of their kindred; and he would
raise altars and images of them. He was not long in
inventing articulate speech and names; and he also con-

structed houses and clothes and shoes and beds, and drew sustenance from the earth. Thus provided, mankind at first lived dispersed, and there were no cities. But the consequence was that they were destroyed by the wild beasts, for they were utterly weak in comparison of them, and their art was only sufficient to provide them with the means of life, and did not enable them to carry on war against the animals: food they had, but not as yet the art of government, of which the art of war is a part. After a while the desire of self-preservation gathered them into cities; but when they were gathered together, having no art of government, they evil intreated one another, and were again in process of dispersion and destruction. Zeus feared that the entire race would be exterminated, and so he sent Hermes to them, bearing reverence and justice to be the ordering principles of cities and the bonds of friendship and conciliation. Hermes asked Zeus how he should impart justice and reverence among men:—Should he distribute them as the arts are distributed; that is to say, to a favoured few only, one skilled individual having enough of medicine or of any other art for many unskilled ones? 'Shall this be the manner in which I am to distribute justice and reverence among men, or shall I give them to all?' 'To all,' said Zeus; 'I should like them all to have a share; for cities cannot exist, if a few only share in the virtues, as in the arts. And further, make a law by my order, that he who has no part in reverence and justice shall be put to death, for he is a plague of the state.'

And this is the reason, Socrates, why the Athenians and mankind in general, when the question relates to carpentering or any other mechanical art, allow but a few to share in their deliberations; and when any one else interferes, then, as you say, they object, if he be not of the favoured few; which, as I reply, is very natural. But when they meet to deliberate about political virtue, which proceeds only by way of justice and wisdom, they are patient enough of any man who speaks of them, as is also natural, because they think that every man ought to share in this sort of virtue, and that states could not exist if this were otherwise. I have explained to you, Socrates, the reason of this phenomenon.

And that you may not suppose yourself to be deceived in thinking that all men regard every man as having a share of justice or honesty and of every other political virtue, let me give you a further proof, which is this. In other cases, as you are aware, if a man says that he is a good flute-player, or skilful in any other art in which he has no skill, people either laugh at him or are angry with him, and his relations think that he is mad and go and admonish him; but when honesty is in question, or some other political virtue, even if they know that he is dishonest, yet, if the man comes publicly forward and tells the truth about his dishonesty, then, what in the other case was held by them to be good sense, they now deem to be madness. They say that all men ought to profess honesty whether they are honest or not, and that a man is out of his mind who says anything else. Their notion is, that a man must have some degree of honesty; and that if he has none at all he ought not to be in the world.

I have been showing that they are right in admitting every man as a counsellor about this sort of virtue, as they are of opinion that every man is a partaker of it. And I will now endeavour to show further that they do not conceive this virtue to be given by nature, or to grow spontaneously, but to be a thing which may be taught; and which comes to a man by taking pains. No one would instruct, no one would rebuke, or be angry with those whose calamities they suppose to be due to nature or chance; they do not try to punish or to prevent them from being what they are; they do but pity them. Who is so foolish as to chastise or instruct the ugly, or the diminutive, or the feeble? And for this reason. Because he knows that good and evil of this kind is the work of nature and of chance; whereas if a man is wanting in those good qualities which are attained by study and exercise and teaching, and has only the contrary evil qualities, other men are angry with him, and punish and reprove him—of these evil qualities one is impiety, another injustice, and they may be described generally as the very opposite of political virtue. In such cases any man will be angry with another, and reprimand him,—clearly because he thinks that by study and learning, the virtue in which the other is deficient may be acquired. If you will think, Socrates, of the nature of punishment, you will see at once that in the opinion of mankind virtue may be acquired; no one punishes the evil-doer under the notion, or for the reason, that he has done wrong,—only the unreasonable fury of a beast acts in that manner. But he who desires to inflict rational punishment does not retaliate for a past wrong which cannot be undone; he has regard to the future, and is desirous that the man who is punished, and he who sees him punished, may be deterred from doing wrong again. He punishes for the sake of prevention, thereby clearly implying that virtue is capable of being taught. This is the notion of all who retaliate upon others either privately or publicly. And the Athenians, too, your own citizens, like other men, punish and take vengeance on all whom they regard as evil doers; and hence, we may infer them to be of the number of those who think that virtue may be acquired and taught. Thus far, Socrates, I have shown you clearly enough, if I am not mistaken, that your countrymen are right in admitting the tinker and the cobbler to advise about politics, and also that they deem virtue to be capable of being taught and acquired.

There yet remains one difficulty which has been raised by you about the sons of good men. What is the reason why good men teach their sons the knowledge which is gained from teachers, and make them wise in that, but do nothing towards improving them in the virtues which distinguish themselves? And here, Socrates, I will leave the apologue and resume the argument. Please to consider: Is there or is there not some one quality of which all the citizens must be partakers, if there is to be a city at all? In the answer to this question is contained the only solution of your difficulty; there is no other. For if there be any such quality, and this quality or unity is not the art of the carpenter, or the smith, or the potter, but justice and temperance and holiness and, in a word, manly virtue—if this is the quality of which all men must be partakers, and which is the very condition of their learning or doing anything else, and if he who is wanting in this, whether he be a child only or a grown-up man or woman, must be taught and punished, until by punishment he becomes better, and he who rebels against instruction and punishment is either exiled or condemned to death under the idea that he is incurable—if what I am saying be true, good men have their sons taught other things and not this, do consider how extraordinary their conduct would appear to be. For we have shown that they think virtue capable of being taught and cultivated both in private and public; and, notwithstanding, they have their sons taught lesser matters, ignorance of which does not involve the punishment of death: but greater things, of which the ignorance may cause death and exile to those who have no

training or knowledge of them—aye, and confiscation
as well as death, and, in a word, may be the ruin of
families—those things, I say, they are supposed not
to teach them,—not to take the utmost care that they
should learn. How improbable is this, Socrates!

Education and admonition commence in the first years
of childhood, and last to the very end of life. Mother
and nurse and father and tutor are vying with one another about the improvement of the child as soon as ever
he is able to understand what is being said to him: he
cannot say or do anything without their setting forth to
him that this is just and that is unjust; this is honourable, that is dishonourable; this is holy, that is unholy;
do this and abstain from that. And if he obeys, well
and good; if not, he is straightened by threats and blows,
like a piece of bent or warped wood. At a later stage
they send him to teachers, and enjoin them to see to his
manners even more than to his reading and music; and
the teachers do as they are desired. And when the boy
has learned his letters and is beginning to understand
what is written, as before he understood only what was
spoken, they put into his hands the works of great poets,
which he reads sitting on a bench at school; in these
are contained many admonitions, and many tales, and
praises, and encomia of ancient famous men, which he
is required to learn by heart, in order that he may imitate or emulate them and desire to become like them.
Then, again, the teachers of the lyre take similar care
that their young disciple is temperate and gets into no
mischief; and when they have taught him the use of the
lyre, they introduce him to the poems of other excellent
poets, who are the lyric poets; and these they set to
music, and make their harmonies and rhythms quite familiar to the children's souls, in order that they may
learn to be more gentle, and harmonious, and rhythmical,

and so more fitted for speech and action; for the life
of man in every part has need of harmony and rhythm.
Then they send them to the master of gymnastics, in
order that their bodies may better minister to the virtuous mind, and that they may not be compelled through
bodily weakness to play the coward in war or on any
other occasion. This is what is done by those who have
the means, and those who have the means are the rich;
their children begin to go to school soonest and leave off
latest. When they have done with masters, the state
again compels them to learn the laws, and live after the
pattern which they furnish, and not after their own
fancies; and just as in learning to write, the writing-
master first draws lines with a style for the use of the
young beginner, and gives him the tablet and makes him
follow the lines, so the city draws the laws, which were
the invention of good lawgivers living in the olden time;
these are given to the young man, in order to guide him
in his conduct whether he is commanding or obeying;
and he who transgresses them is to be corrected, or, in
other words, called to account, which is a term used not
only in your country, but also in many others, seeing
that justice calls men to account. Now when there is
all this care about virtue private and public, why, Socrates, do you still wonder and doubt whether virtue can
be taught? Cease to wonder, for the opposite would be
far more surprising.

But why then do the sons of good fathers often turn
out ill? There is nothing very wonderful in this; for,
as I have been saying, the existence of a state implies
that virtue is not any man's private possession. If so
—and nothing can be truer—then I will further ask
you to imagine, as an illustration, some other pursuit or
branch of knowledge which may be assumed equally to
be the condition of the existence of a state. Suppose

that there could be no state unless we were all flute-
players, as far as each had the capacity, and everybody
was freely teaching everybody the art, both in private
and public, and reproving the bad player as freely and
openly as every man now teaches justice and the laws,
not concealing them as he would conceal the other arts,
but imparting them—for all of us have a mutual interest in the justice and virtue of one another, and this is
the reason why every one is so ready to teach justice
and the laws;—suppose, I say, that there were the same
readiness and liberality among us in teaching one another flute-playing, do you imagine, Socrates, that the
sons of good flute-players would be more likely to be
good than the sons of bad ones? I think not. Would
not their sons grow up to be distinguished or undistin-
guished according to their own natural capacities as
flue-players, and the son of a good player would often
turn out to be a bad one, and the son of a bad player
to be a good one, and all flute-players would be good
enough in comparison of those who were ignorant and
unacquainted with the art of flute-playing? In like
manner I would have you consider that he who appears
to you to be the worst of those who have been brought
up in laws and humanities, would appear to be a just
man and a master of justice if he were to be compared
with men who had no education, or courts of justice, or
laws, or any restraints upon them which compelled them
to practise virtue—with the savages, for example, whom
the poet Pherecrates exhibited on the stage at the last
year's Lenaean festival. If you were living among men
such as the man-haters in his Chorus, you would be only
too glad to meet with Eurybates and Phrynondas, and
you would sorrowfully long to revisit the rascality of
this part of the world. And you, Socrates, are discontented, and why? Because all men are teachers of vir-

tue, each one according to his ability; and you say, Where are the teachers? You might as well ask, Who teaches Greek? For of that too there will not be any teachers found. Or you might ask, Who is to teach the sons of our artisans this same art which they have learned of their fathers? He and his fellow-workmen have taught them to the best of their ability,—but who will carry them further in their arts? And you would certainly have a difficulty, Socrates, in finding a teacher of them; but there would be no difficulty in finding a teacher of those who are wholly ignorant. And this is true of virtue or of anything else; if a man is better able than we are to promote virtue ever so little, we must be content with the result. A teacher of this sort I believe myself to be, and above all other men to have the knowledge which makes a man noble and good; and I give my pupils their money's-worth, and even more, as they themselves confess. And therefore I have introduced the following mode of payment:—When a man has been my pupil, if he likes he pays my price, but there is no compulsion; and if he does not like, he has only to go into a temple and take an oath of the value of the instructions, and he pays no more than he declares to be their value.

Such is my Apologue, Socrates, and such is the argument by which I endeavour to show that virtue may be taught, and that this is the opinion of the Athenians. And I have also attempted to show that you are not to wonder at good fathers having bad sons, or at good sons having bad fathers, of which the sons of Polycleitus afford an example, who are the companions of our friends here, Paralus and Xanthippus, but are nothing in comparison with their father; and this is true of the sons of many other artists. As yet I ought not to say

the same of Paralus and Xanthippus themselves, for
they are young and there is still hope of them.

Protagoras ended, and in my ear

'So charming left his voice, that I the while
Thought him still speaking; still stood fixed to hear.' [1]

At length, when the truth dawned upon me, that he had
really finished, not without difficulty I began to collect
myself, and looking at Hippocrates, I said to him: O
son of Apollodorus, how deeply grateful I am to you
for having brought me hither; I would not have missed
the speech of Protagoras for a great deal. For I used to
imagine that no human care could make men good; but
I know better now. Yet I have still one very small difficulty which I am sure that Protagoras will easily explain, as he has already explained so much. If a man
were to go and consult Pericles or any of our great
speakers about these matters, he might perhaps hear as
fine a discourse, but then when one has a question to ask
of any of them, like books, they can neither answer nor
ask; and if any one challenges the least particular of
their speech, they go ringing on in a long harangue, like
brazen pots, which when they are struck continue to
sound unless some one puts his hand upon them; whereas
our friend Protagoras can not only make a good speech,
as he has already shown, but when he is asked a question he can answer briefly; and when he asks he will
wait and hear the answer; and this is a very rare gift.
Now I, Protagoras, want to ask of you a little question,
which if you will only answer, I shall be quite satisfied. You were saying that virtue can be taught;—that
I will take upon your authority, and there is no one to

[1] Borrowed by Milton, *Paradise Lost*, viii. 2, 3.

whom I am more ready to trust. But I marvel at one thing about which I should like to have my mind set at rest. You were speaking of Zeus sending justice and reverence to men; and several times while you were speaking, justice, and temperance, and holiness, and all these qualities, were described by you as if together they made up virtue. Now I want you to tell me truly whether virtue is one whole, of which justice and temperance and holiness are parts; or whether all these are only the names of one and the same thing: that is the doubt which still lingers in my mind.

There is no difficulty, Socrates, in answering that the qualities of which you are speaking are the parts of virtue which is one.

And are they parts, I said, in the same sense in which mouth, nose, and eyes, and ears, are the parts of a face; or are they like the parts of gold, which differ from the whole and from one another only in being larger or smaller?

I should say that they differed, Socrates, in the first way; they are related to one another as the parts of a face are related to the whole face.

And do men have some one part and some another part of virtue? Or if a man has one part, must he also have all the others?

By no means, he said; for many a man is brave and not just, or just and not wise.

You would not deny, then, that courage and wisdom are also parts of virtue?

Most undoubtedly they are, he answered; and wisdom is the noblest of the parts.

And they are all different from one another? I said. Yes.

And has each of them a distinct function like the parts of the face;—the eye, for example, is not like the ear, and has not the same functions; and the other parts are none of them like one another, either in their functions, or in any other way? I want to know whether the comparison holds concerning the parts of virtue. Do they also differ from one another in themselves and in their functions? For that is clearly what the simile would imply.

Yes, Socrates, you are right in supposing that they differ.

Then, I said, no other part of virtue is like knowledge, or like justice, or like courage, or like temperance, or like holiness?

No, he answered.

Well then, I said, suppose that you and I enquire into their natures. And first, you would agree with me that justice is of the nature of a thing, would you not? That is my opinion: would it not be yours also?

Mine also, he said.

And suppose that some one were to ask us, saying, 'O Protagoras, and you, Socrates, what about this thing which you were calling justice, is it just or unjust?'— and I were to answer, just: would you vote with me or against me?

With you, he said.

Thereupon I should answer to him who asked me, that justice is of the nature of the just: would not you?

Yes, he said.

And suppose that he went on to say: 'Well, now, is there also such a thing as holiness?'—we should answer, 'Yes,' if I am not mistaken?

Yes, he said.

Which you would also acknowledge to be a thing— should we not say so?

He assented.

'And is this a sort of thing which is of the nature of

the holy, or of the nature of the unholy?' I should be angry at his putting such a question, and should say, 'Peace, man; nothing can be holy if holiness is not holy.' What would you say? Would you not answer in the same way?

Certainly, he said.

And then after this suppose that he came and asked us, 'What were you saying just now? Perhaps I may not have heard you rightly, but you seemed to me to be saying that the parts of virtue were not the same as one another.' I should reply, 'You certainly heard that said, but not, as you imagine, by me; for I only asked the question; Protagoras gave the answer.' And suppose that he turned to you and said, 'Is this true, Protagoras? and do you maintain that one part of virtue is unlike another, and is this your position?'—how would you answer him?

I could not help acknowledging the truth of what he said, Socrates.

Well then, Protagoras, we will assume this; and now supposing that he proceeded to say further, 'Then holiness is not of the nature of justice, nor justice of the nature of holiness, but of the nature of unholiness; and holiness is of the nature of the not just, and therefore of the unjust, and the unjust is the unholy:' how shall we answer him? I should certainly answer him on my own behalf that justice is holy, and that holiness is just; and I would say in like manner on your behalf also, if you would allow me, that justice is either the same with holiness, or very nearly the same; and above all I would assert that justice is like holiness and holiness is like justice; and I wish that you would tell me whether I may be permitted to give this answer on your behalf, and whether you would agree with me.

He replied, I cannot simply agree, Socrates, to the

proposition that justice is holy and that holiness is just, for there appears to me to be a difference between them. But what matter? if you please I please; and let us assume, if you will, that justice is holy, and that holiness is just.

Pardon me, I replied; I do not want this 'if you wish' or 'if you will' sort of conclusion to be proven, but I want you and me to be proven: I mean to say that the conclusion will be best proven if there be no 'if.'

Well, he said, I admit that justice bears a resemblance to holiness, for there is always some point of view in which everything is like every other thing; white is in a certain way like black, and hard is like soft, and the most extreme opposites have some qualities in common; even the parts of the face which, as we were saying before, are distinct and have different functions, are still in a certain point of view similar, and one of them is like another of them. And you may prove that they are like one another on the same principle that all things are like one another; and yet things which are alike in some particular ought not to be called alike, nor things which are unlike in some particular, however slight, unlike.

And do you think, I said in a tone of surprise, that justice and holiness have but a small degree of likeness?

Certainly not; any more than I agree with what I understand to be your view.

Well, I said, as you appear to have a difficulty about this, let us take another of the examples which you mentioned instead. Do you admit the existence of folly?

I do.

And is not wisdom the very opposite of folly?

That is true, he said.

And when men act rightly and advantageously they seem to you to be temperate?

Yes, he said.

And temperance makes them temperate?

Certainly.

And they who do not act rightly act foolishly, and in acting thus are not temperate?

I agree, he said.

Then to act foolishly is the opposite of acting temperately?

He assented.

And foolish actions are done by folly, and temperate actions by temperance?

He agreed.

And that is done strongly which is done by strength, and that which is weakly done, by weakness?

He assented.

And that which is done with swiftness is done swiftly, and that which is done with slowness, slowly?

He assented again.

And that which is done in the same manner, is done by the same; and that which is done in an opposite manner by the opposite?

He agreed.

Once more, I said, is there anything beautiful?

Yes.

To which the only opposite is the ugly?

There is no other.

And is there anything good?

There is.

To which the only opposite is the evil?

There is no other.

And there is the acute in sound?

True.

To which the only opposite is the grave?

There is no other, he said, but that.

Then every opposite has one opposite only and no more?

He assented.

Then now, I said, let us recapitulate our admissions. First of all we admitted that everything has one opposite and not more than one?

We did so.

And we admitted also that what was done in opposite ways was done by opposites?

Yes.

And that which was done foolishly, as we further admitted, was done in the opposite way to that which was done temperately?

Yes.

And that which was done temperately was done by temperance, and that which was done foolishly by folly?

He agreed.

And that which is done in opposite ways is done by opposites?

Yes.

And one thing is done by temperance, and quite another thing by folly?

Yes.

And in opposite ways?

Certainly.

And therefore by opposites:—then folly is the opposite of temperance?

Clearly.

And do you remember that folly has already been acknowledged by us to be the opposite of wisdom?

He assented.

And we said that everything has only one opposite?

Yes.

Then, Protagoras, which of the two assertions shall

we renounce? One says that everything has but one opposite; the other that wisdom is distinct from temperance, and that both of them are parts of virtue; and that they are not only distinct, but dissimilar, both in themselves and in their functions, like the parts of a face. Which of these two assertions shall we renounce? For both of them together are certainly not in harmony; they do not accord or agree: for how can they be said to agree if everything is assumed to have only one opposite and not more than one, and yet folly, which is one, has clearly the two opposites—wisdom and temperance? Is not that true, Protagoras? What else would you say?

He assented, but with great reluctance.

Then temperance and wisdom are the same, as before justice and holiness appeared to us to be nearly the same. And now, Protagoras, I said, we must finish the enquiry, and not faint. Do you think that an unjust man can be temperate in his injustice?

I should be ashamed, Socrates, he said, to acknowledge this, which nevertheless many may be found to assert.

And shall I argue with them or with you? I replied.

I would rather, he said, that you should argue with the many first, if you will.

Whichever you please, if you will only answer me and say whether you are of their opinion or not. My object is to test the validity of the argument; and yet the result may be that I who ask and you who answer may both be put on our trial.

Protagoras at first made a show of refusing, as he said that the argument was not encouraging; at length, he consented to answer.

Now then, I said, begin at the beginning and answer me. You think that some men are temperate, and yet unjust?

Yes, he said; let that be admitted.

And temperance is good sense?

Yes.

And good sense is good counsel in doing injustice?

Granted.

If they succeed, I said, or if they do not succeed?

If they succeed.

And you would admit the existence of goods?

Yes.

And is the good that which is expedient for man?

Yes, indeed, he said: and there are some things which may be inexpedient, and yet I call them good.

I thought that Protagoras was getting ruffled and excited; he seemed to be setting himself in an attitude of war. Seeing this, I minded my business, and gently said:—

When you say, Protagoras, that things inexpedient are good, do you mean inexpedient for man only, or inexpedient altogether? and do you call the latter good?

Certainly not the last, he replied; for I know of many things,—meats, drinks, medicines, and ten thousand other things, which are inexpedient for man, and some which are expedient; and some which are neither expedient nor inexpedient for man, but only for horses; and some for oxen only, and some for dogs; and some for no animals, but only for trees; and some for the roots of trees and not for their branches, as for example, manure, which is a good thing when laid about the roots of a tree, but utterly destructive if thrown upon the shoots and young branches; or I may instance olive oil, which is mischievous to all plants, and generally most injurious to the hair of every animal with the exception of man, but beneficial to human hair and to the human body generally; and even in this application (so various and changeable is the nature of the benefit), that which is the greatest good to the outward parts of a man, is a very great evil to his inward parts: and for this reason physicians always forbid their patients the use of oil in their food, except in very small quantities, just enough to extinguish the disagreeable sensation of smell in meats and sauces.

When he had given this answer, the company cheered him. And I said: Protagoras, I have a wretched memory, and when any one makes a long speech to me I never remember what he is talking about. As then, if I had been deaf, and you were going to converse with me, you would have had to raise your voice; so now, having such a bad memory, I will ask you to cut your answers shorter, if you would take me with you.

[*Here occurs a long digression on the poets after which Socrates proceeds as follows:*]

Do not imagine, Protagoras, that I have any other interest in asking questions of you but that of clearing up my own difficulties. For I think that Homer was very right in saying that

'When two go together, one sees before the other,' [1]

for all men who have a companion are readier in deed, word, or thought; but if a man

'Sees a thing when he is alone,'

he goes about straightway seeking until he finds some one to whom he may show his discoveries, and who may confirm him in them. And I would rather hold discourse with you than with any one, because I think that no man has a better understanding of most things which a good man may be expected to understand, and in par-

[1] *Il.* x. 224.

ticular of virtue. For who is there, but you?—who not
only claim to be a good man and a gentleman, for many
are this, and yet have not the power of making others
good—whereas you are not only good yourself, but also
the cause of goodness in others. Moreover such confidence have you in yourself, that although other Sophists
conceal their profession, you proclaim in the face of
Hellas that you are a Sophist or teacher of virtue and
education, and are the first who demanded pay in return. How then can I do otherwise than invite you to
the examination of these subjects, and ask questions and
consult with you? I must, indeed. And I should like
once more to have my memory refreshed by you about
the questions which I was asking you at first, and also
to have your help in considering them. If I am not mistaken the question was this: Are wisdom and temperance
and courage and justice and holiness five names of the
same thing? or has each of the names a separate under-
lying essence and corresponding thing having a peculiar
function, no one of them being like any other of them?
And you replied that the five names were not the names
of the same thing, but that each of them had a separate
object, and that all these objects were parts of virtue,
not in the same way that the parts of gold are like each
other and the whole of which they are parts, but as the
parts of the face are unlike the whole of which they are
parts and one another, and have each of them a distinct
function. I should like to know whether this is still
your opinion; or if not, I will ask you to define your
meaning, and I shall not take you to task if you now
make a different statement. For I dare say that you
may have said what you did only in order to make
trial of me.

I answer, Socrates, he said, that all these qualities
are parts of virtue, and that four out of the five are to

some extent similar, and that the fifth of them, which
is courage, is very different from the other four, as I
prove in this way: You may observe that many men are
utterly unrighteous, unholy, intemperate, ignorant, who
are nevertheless remarkable for their courage.

Stop, I said; I should like to think about that. When
you speak of brave men, do you mean the confident, or
another sort of nature?

Yes, he said; I mean the impetuous, ready to go at
that which others are afraid to approach.

In the next place, you would affirm virtue to be a good
thing, of which good thing you assert yourself to be a
teacher.

Yes, he said; I should say the best of all things, if I
am in my right mind.

And is it partly good and partly bad, I said, or wholly
good?

Wholly good, and in the highest degree.

Tell me then; who are they who have confidence when
diving into a well?

I should say, the divers.

And the reason of this is that they have knowledge?

Yes, that is the reason.

And who have confidence when fighting on horseback
—the skilled horseman or the unskilled?

The skilled.

And who when fighting with light shields—the peltasts or the nonpeltasts?

The peltasts.   And that is true of all other things, he
said, if that is your point: those who have knowledge
are more confident than those who have no knowledge,
and they are more confident after they have learned than
before.

And have you not seen persons utterly ignorant, I
said, of these things, and yet confident about them?

Yes, he said, I have seen such persons far too confident.

And are not these confident persons also courageous?

In that case, he replied, courage would be a base thing, for the men of whom we are speaking are surely madmen.

Then who are the courageous? Are they not the confident?

Yes, he said; to that statement I adhere.

And those, I said, who are thus confident without knowledge are really not courageous, but mad; and in that case the wisest are also the most confident, and being the most confident are also the bravest, and upon that view again wisdom will be courage.

Nay, Socrates, he replied, you are mistaken in your remembrance of what was said by me. When you asked me, I certainly did say that the courageous are the confident; but I was never asked whether the confident are the courageous; if you had asked me, I should have answered, 'Not all of them:' and what I did answer you have not proved to be false, although you proceeded to show that those who have knowledge are more courageous than they were before they had knowledge, and more courageous than others who have no knowledge, and were then led on to think that courage is the same as wisdom. But in this way of arguing you might come to imagine that strength is wisdom. You might begin by asking whether the strong are able, and I should say 'Yes;' and then whether those who know how to wrestle are not more able to wrestle than those who do not know how to wrestle, and more able after than before they had learned, and I should assent. And when I had admitted this, you might use my admissions in such a way as to prove that upon my view wisdom is strength; whereas in that case I should not have admitted, any more than in the other, that the able are strong, although I have admitted that the strong are able. For there is a difference between ability and strength; the former is given by knowledge as well as by madness or rage, but strength comes from nature and a healthy state of the body. And in like manner I say of confidence and courage, that they are not the same; and I argue that the courageous are confident, but not all the confident courageous. For confidence may be given to men by art, and also, like ability, by madness and rage; but courage comes to them from nature and the healthy state of the soul.

I said: You would admit, Protagoras, that some men live well and others ill?

He assented.

And do you think that a man lives well who lives in pain and grief?

He does not.

But if he lives pleasantly to the end of his life, will he not in that case have lived well?

He will.

Then to live pleasantly is a good, and to live unpleasantly an evil?

Yes, he said, if the pleasure be good and honourable.

And do you, Protagoras, like the rest of the world, call some pleasant things evil and some painful things good?—for I am rather disposed to say that things are good in as far as they are pleasant, if they have no consequences of another sort, and in as far as they are painful they are bad.

I do not know, Socrates, he said, whether I can venture to assert in that unqualified manner that the pleasant is the good and the painful the evil. Having regard not only to my present answer, but also to the whole of my life, I shall be safer, if I am not mistaken, in saying that there are some pleasant things which are not good, and that there are some painful things which are good, and some which are not good, and that there are some which are neither good nor evil.

And you would call pleasant, I said, the things which participate in pleasure or create pleasure?

Certainly, he said.

Then my meaning is, that in as far as they are pleasant they are good; and my question would imply that pleasure is a good in itself.

According to your favourite mode of speech, Socrates, 'let us reflect about this,' he said; and if the reflection is to the point, and the result proves that pleasure and good are really the same, then we will agree; but if not, then we will argue.

And would you wish to begin the enquiry? I said; or shall I begin?

You ought to take the lead, he said; for you are the author of the discussion.

May I employ an illustration? I said. Suppose some one who is enquiring into the health or some other bodily quality of another:—he looks at his face and at the tips of his fingers, and then he says, Uncover your chest and back to me that I may have a better view:—that is the sort of thing which I desire in this speculation. Having seen what your opinion is about good and pleasure, I am minded to say to you: Uncover your mind to me, Protagoras, and reveal your opinion about knowledge, that I may know whether you agree with the rest of the world. Now the rest of the world are of opinion that knowledge is a principle not of strength, or of rule, or of command: their notion is that a man may have knowledge, and yet that the knowledge which is in him may be overmastered by anger, or pleasure, or pain, or love, or perhaps by fear,—just as if knowledge were a slave, and might be dragged about anyhow. Now is that your view? or do you think that knowledge is a noble and commanding thing, which cannot be overcome, and will not allow a man, if he only knows the difference of good and evil, to do anything which is contrary to knowledge, but that wisdom will have strength to help him?

I agree with you, Socrates, said Protagoras; and not only so, but I, above all other men, am bound to say that wisdom and knowledge are the highest of human things.

Good, I said, and true. But are you aware that the majority of the world are of another mind; and that men are commonly supposed to know the things which are best, and not to do them when they might? And most persons whom I have asked the reason of this have said that when men act contrary to knowledge they are overcome by pain, or pleasure, or some of those affections which I was just now mentioning.

Yes, Socrates, he replied; and that is not the only point about which mankind are in error.

Suppose, then, that you and I endeavour to instruct and inform them what is the nature of this affection which they call 'being overcome by pleasure,' and which they affirm to be the reason why they do not always do what is best. When we say to them: Friends, you are mistaken, and are saying what is not true, they would probably reply: Socrates and Protagoras, if this affection of the soul is not to be called 'being overcome by pleasure,' pray, what is it, and by what name would you describe it?

But why, Socrates, should we trouble ourselves about the opinion of the many, who just say anything that happens to occur to them?

I believe, I said, that they may be of use in helping

us to discover how courage is related to the other parts of virtue. If you are disposed to abide by our agreement, that I should show the way in which, as I think, our recent difficulty is most likely to be cleared up, do you follow; but if not, never mind.

You are quite right, he said; and I would have you proceed as you have begun.

Well then, I said, let me suppose that they repeat their question, What account do you give of that which, in our way of speaking, is termed being overcome by pleasure? I should answer thus: Listen, and Protagoras and I will endeavour to show you. When men are overcome by eating and drinking and other sensual desires which are pleasant, and they, knowing them to be evil, nevertheless indulge in them, would you not say that they were overcome by pleasure? They will not deny this. And suppose that you and I were to go on and ask them again: 'In what way do you say that they are evil,—in that they are pleasant and give pleasure at the moment, or because they cause disease and poverty and other like evils in the future? Would they still be evil, if they had no attendant evil consequences, simply because they give the consciousness of pleasure of whatever nature?'—Would they not answer that they are not evil on account of the pleasure which is immediately given by them, but on account of the after consequences —diseases and the like?

I believe, said Protagoras, that the world in general would answer as you do.

And in causing diseases do they not cause pain? and in causing poverty do they not cause pain;—they would agree to that also, if I am not mistaken?

Protagoras assented.

Then I should say to them, in my name and yours: Do

you think them evil for any other reason, except because they end in pain and rob us of other pleasures:—there again they would agree?

We both of us thought that they would.

And then I should take the question from the opposite point of view, and say: 'Friends, when you speak of goods being painful, do you not mean remedial goods, such as gymnastic exercises, and military service, and the physician's use of burning, cutting, drugging, and starving? Are these the things which are good but painful?' —they would assent to me?

He agreed.

'And do you call them good because they occasion the greatest immediate suffering and pain; or because, afterwards, they bring health and improvement of the bodily condition and the salvation of states and power over others and wealth?'—they would agree to the latter alternative, if I am not mistaken?

He assented.

'Are these things good for any other reason except that they end in pleasure, and get rid of and avert pain? Are you looking to any other standard but pleasure and pain when you call them good?'—they would acknowledge that they were not?

I think so, said Protagoras.

'And do you not pursue after pleasure as a good, and avoid pain as an evil?'

He assented.

'Then you think that pain is an evil and pleasure is a good: and even pleasure you deem an evil, when it robs you of greater pleasures than it gives, or causes pains greater than the pleasure. If, however, you call pleasure an evil in relation to some other end or standard, you will be able to show us that standard. But you have none to show.'

I do not think that they have, said Protagoras.

'And have you not a similar way of speaking about pain? You call pain a good when it takes away greater pains than those which it has, or gives pleasures greater than the pains: then if you have some standard other than pleasure and pain to which you refer when you call actual pain a good, you can show what that is. But you cannot.'

True, said Protagoras.

Suppose again, I said, that the world says to me: 'Why do you spend many words and speak in many ways on this subject?' Excuse me, friends, I should reply; but in the first place there is a difficulty in explaining the meaning of the expression 'overcome by pleasure;' and the whole argument turns upon this. And even now, if you see any possible way in which evil can be explained as other than pain, or good as other than pleasure, you may still retract. Are you satisfied, then, at having a life of pleasure which is without pain? If you are, and if you are unable to show any good or evil which does not end in pleasure and pain, hear the consequences:—If what you say is true, then the argument is absurd which affirms that a man often does evil knowingly, when he might abstain, because he is seduced and overpowered by pleasure, or again, when you say that a man knowingly refuses to do what is good because he is overcome at the moment by pleasure. And that this is ridiculous will be evident if only we give up the use of various names, such as pleasant and painful, and good and evil. As there are two things, let us call them by two names—first, good and evil, and then pleasant and painful. Assuming this, let us go on to say that a man does evil knowing that he does evil. But some one will ask, Why? Because he is overcome, is the first answer. And by

what is he overcome? the enquirer will proceed to ask.
And we shall not be able to reply 'By pleasure,' for the
name of pleasure has been exchanged for that of good.
In our answer, then, we shall only say that he is overcome. 'By what?' he will reiterate. By the good, we
shall have to reply; indeed we shall. Nay, but our
questioner will rejoin with a laugh, if he be one of the
swaggering sort, 'That is too ridiculous, that a man
should do what he knows to be evil when he ought not,
because he is overcome by good. Is that,' he will ask,
'because the good was worthy or not worthy of con-
quering the evil?' And in answer to that we shall
clearly reply, Because it was not worthy; for if it had
been worthy, then he who, as we say, was overcome by
pleasure, would not have been wrong. 'But how,' he
will reply, 'can the good be unworthy of the evil, or the
evil of the good?' Is not the real explanation that they
are out of proportion to one another, either as greater
and smaller, or more and fewer? This we cannot deny.
And when you speak of being overcome—'what do you
mean,' he will say, 'but that you choose the greater evil
in exchange for the lesser good?' Admitted. And now
substitute the names of pleasure and pain for good and
evil, and say, not as before, that a man does what is evil
knowingly, but that he does what is painful knowingly,
and because he is overcome by pleasure, which is unworthy to overcome. What measure is there of the relations of pleasure to pain other than excess and defect,
which means that they become greater and smaller, and
more and fewer, and differ in degree? For if any one
says: 'Yes, Socrates, but immediate pleasure differs
widely from future pleasure and pain—To that I should
reply: And do they differ in anything but in pleasure
and pain? There can be no other measure of them. And
do you, like a skilful weigher, put into the balance the

pleasures and the pains, and their nearness and distance, and weigh them, and then say which outweighs the other. If you weigh pleasures against pleasures, you of course take the more and greater; or if you weigh pains against pains, you take the fewer and the less; or if pleasures against pains, then you choose that course of action in which the painful is exceeded by the pleasant, whether the distant by the near or the near by the distant; and you avoid that course of action in which the pleasant is exceeded by the painful. Would you not admit, my friends, that this is true? I am confident that they cannot deny this.

He agreed with me.

Well then, I shall say, if you agree so far, be so good as to answer me a question: Do not the same magnitudes appear larger to your sight when near, and smaller when at a distance? They will acknowledge that. And the same holds of thickness and number; also sounds, which are in themselves equal, are greater when near, and lesser when at a distance. They will grant that also. Now suppose happiness to consist in doing or choosing the greater, and in not doing or in avoiding the less, what would be the saving principle of human life? Would not the art of measuring be the saving principle; or would the power of appearance? Is not the latter that deceiving art which makes us wander up and down and take the things at one time of which we repent at another, both in our actions and in our choice of things great and small? But the art of measurement would do away with the effect of appearances, and, showing the truth, would fain teach the soul at last to find rest in the truth, and would thus save our life. Would not mankind generally acknowledge that the art which accomplishes this result is the art of measurement?

Yes, he said, the art of measurement.

Suppose, again, the salvation of human life to depend on the choice of odd and even, and on the knowledge of when a man ought to choose the greater or less, either in reference to themselves or to each other, and whether near or at a distance; what would be the saving principle of our lives? Would not knowledge?—a knowledge of measuring, when the question is one of excess and defect, and a knowledge of number, when the question is of odd and even? The world will assent, will they not?

Protagoras himself thought that they would.

Well then, my friends, I say to them; seeing that the salvation of human life has been found to consist in the right choice of pleasures and pains,—in the choice of the more and the fewer, and the greater and the less, and the nearer and remoter, must not this measuring be a consideration of their excess and defect and equality in relation to each other?

This is undeniably true.

And this, as possessing measure, must undeniably also be an art and science?

They will agree, he said.

The nature of that art or science will be a matter of future consideration; but the existence of such a science furnishes a demonstrative answer to the question which you asked of me and Protagoras. At the time when you asked the question, if you remember, both of us were agreeing that there was nothing mightier than knowledge, and that knowledge, in whatever existing, must have the advantage over pleasure and all other things; and then you said that pleasure often got the advantage even over a man who has knowledge; and we refused to allow this, and you rejoined: O Protagoras and Socrates, what is the meaning of being overcome by pleasure if not this?—tell us what you call such a state:—if we had immediately and at the time answered 'Igno-

rance,' you would have laughed at us. But now, in
laughing at us, you will be laughing at yourselves: for
you also admitted that men err in their choice of pleasures and pains; that is, in their choice of good and evil,
from defect of knowledge; and you admitted further,
that they err, not only from defect of knowledge in general, but of that particular knowledge which is called
measuring. And you are also aware that the erring
act which is done without knowledge is done in ignorance. This, therefore, is the meaning of being overcome by pleasure;—ignorance, and that the greatest.
And our friends Protagoras and Prodicus and Hippias
declare that they are the physicians of ignorance; but
you, who are under the mistaken impression that ignorance is not the cause, and that the art of which I am
speaking cannot be taught, neither go yourselves, nor
send your children, to the Sophists, who are the teachers of these things—you take care of your money and
give them none; and the result is, that you are the worse
off both in public and private life:—Let us suppose this
to be our answer to the world in general: And now I
should like to ask you, Hippias, and you, Prodicus, as
well as Protagoras (for the argument is to be yours as
well as ours), whether you think that I am speaking the
truth or not?

They all thought that what I said was entirely true.

Then you agree, I said, that the pleasant is the good,
and the painful evil. And here I would beg my friend
Prodicus not to introduce his distinction of names,
whether he is disposed to say pleasurable, delightful,
joyful. However, by whatever name he prefers to call
them, I will ask you, most excellent Prodicus, to answer
in my sense of the words.

Prodicus laughed and assented, as did the others.

Then, my friends, what do you say to this? Are not

all actions honourable and useful, of which the tendency is to make life painless and pleasant? The honourable work is also useful and good?

This was admitted.

Then, I said, if the pleasant is the good, nobody does anything under the idea or conviction that some other thing would be better and is also attainable, when he might do the better. And this inferiority of a man to himself is merely ignorance, as the superiority of a man to himself is wisdom.

They all assented.

And is not ignorance the having a false opinion and being deceived about important matters?

To this also they unanimously assented.

Then, I said, no man voluntarily pursues evil, or that which he thinks to be evil. To prefer evil to good is not in human nature; and when a man is compelled to choose one of two evils, no one will choose the greater when he may have the less.

All of us agreed to every word of this.

Well, I said, there is a certain thing called fear or terror; and here, Prodicus, I should particularly like to know whether you would agree with me in defining this fear or terror as expectation of evil.

Protagoras and Hippias agreed, but Prodicus said that this was fear and not terror.

Never mind, Prodicus, I said; but let me ask whether, if our former assertions are true, a man will pursue that which he fears when he is not compelled? Would not this be in flat contradiction to the admission which has been already made, that he thinks the things which he fears to be evil; and no one will pursue or voluntarily accept that which he thinks to be evil?

That also was universally admitted.

Then, I said, these, Hippias and Prodicus, are our

premisses; and I would beg Protagoras to explain to us how he can be right in what he said at first. I do not mean in what he said quite at first, for his first statement, as you may remember, was that whereas there were five parts of virtue none of them was like any other of them; each of them had a separate function. To this, however, I am not referring, but to the assertion which he afterwards made that of the five virtues four were nearly akin to each other, but that the fifth, which was courage, differed greatly from the others. And of this he gave me the following proof. He said: You will find, Socrates, that some of the most impious, and unrighteous, and intemperate, and ignorant of men are among the most courageous; which proves that courage is very different from the other parts of virtue. I was surprised at his saying this at the time, and I am still more surprised now that I have discussed the matter with you. So I asked him whether by the brave he meant the confident. Yes, he replied, and the impetuous or goers. (You may remember, Protagoras, that this was your answer.)

He assented.

Well then, I said, tell us against what are the courageous ready to go—against the same dangers as the cowards?

No, he answered.

Then against something different?

Yes, he said.

Then do cowards go where there is safety, and the courageous where there is danger?

Yes, Socrates, so men say.

Very true, I said. But I want to know against what do you say that the courageous are ready to go—against dangers, believing them to be dangers, or not against dangers?

No, said he; the former case has been proved by you in the previous argument to be impossible.

That, again, I replied, is quite true. And if this has been rightly proven, then no one goes to meet what he thinks to be dangers, since the want of self-control, which makes men rush into dangers, has been shown to be ignorance.

He assented.

And yet the courageous man and the coward alike go to meet that about which they are confident; so that, in this point of view, the cowardly and the courageous go to meet the same things.

And yet, Socrates, said Protagoras, that to which the coward goes is the opposite of that to which the courageous goes; the one, for example, is ready to go to battle, and the other is not ready.

And is going to battle honourable or disgraceful? I said.

Honourable, he replied.

And if honourable, then already admitted by us to be good; for all honourable actions we have admitted to be good.

That is true; and to that opinion I shall always adhere.

True, I said. But which of the two are they who, as you say, are unwilling to go to war, which is a good and honourable thing?

The cowards, he replied.

And what is good and honourable, I said, is also pleasant?

It has certainly been acknowledged to be so, he replied.

And do the cowards knowingly refuse to go to the nobler, and pleasanter, and better?

The admission of that, he replied, would belie our former admissions.

But does not the courageous man also go to meet the better, and pleasanter, and nobler?

That must be admitted.

And the courageous man has no base fear or base confidence?

True, he replied.

And if not base, then honourable?

He admitted this.

And if honourable, then good?

Yes.

But the fear and confidence of the coward or foolhardy or madman, on the contrary, are base?

He assented.

And these base fears and confidences originate in ignorance and uninstructedness?

True, he said.

Then as to the motive from which the cowards act, do you call it cowardice or courage?

I should say cowardice, he replied.

And have they not been shown to be cowards through their ignorance of dangers?

Assuredly, he said.

And because of that ignorance they are cowards?

He assented.

And the reason why they are cowards is admitted by you to be cowardice?

He again assented.

Then the ignorance of what is and is not dangerous is cowardice?

He nodded assent.

But surely courage, I said, is opposed to cowardice?

Yes.

Then the wisdom which knows what are and are not dangers is opposed to the ignorance of them?

To that again he nodded assent.

And the ignorance of them is cowardice?

To that he very reluctantly nodded assent.

And the knowledge of that which is and is not dangerous is courage, and is opposed to the ignorance of these things?

At this point he would no longer nod assent, but was silent.

And why, I said, do you neither assent nor dissent, Protagoras?

Finish the argument by yourself, he said.

I only want to ask one more question, I said. I want to know whether you still think that there are men who are most ignorant and yet most courageous?

You seem to have a great ambition to make me answer, Socrates, and therefore I will gratify you, and say, that this appears to me to be impossible consistently with the argument.

My only object, I said, in continuing the discussion, has been the desire to ascertain the nature and relations of virtue; for if this were clear, I am very sure that the other controversy which has been carried on at great length by both of us—you affirming and I denying that virtue can be taught—would also become clear. The result of our discussion appears to me to be singular. For if the argument had a human voice, that voice would be heard laughing at us and saying: 'Protagoras and Socrates, you are strange beings; there are you, Socrates, who were saying that virtue cannot be taught, contradicting yourself now by your attempt to prove that all things are knowledge, including justice, and temperance, and courage,—which tends to show that virtue can certainly be taught; for if virtue were other than knowledge, as Protagoras attempted to prove, then clearly virtue cannot be taught; but if virtue is entirely knowledge, as you are seeking to show, then I cannot but suppose that virtue is capable of being taught. Protagoras, on the other hand, who started by saying that it might be taught, is now eager to prove it to be anything rather than knowledge; and if this is true, it must be quite incapable of being taught.' Now I, Protagoras, perceiving this terrible confusion of our ideas, have a great desire that they should be cleared up. And I should like to carry on the discussion until we ascertain what virtue is, and whether capable of being taught or not, lest haply Epimetheus should trip us up and deceive us in the argument, as he forgot us in the story; I prefer your Prometheus to your Epimetheus, for of him I make use, whenever I am busy about these questions, in Promethean care of my own life. And if you have no objection, as I said at first, I should like to have your help in the enquiry.

Protagoras replied: Socrates, I am not of a base nature, and I am the last man in the world to be envious. I cannot but applaud your energy and your conduct of an argument. As I have often said, I admire you above all men whom I know, and far above all men of your age; and I believe that you will become very eminent in philosophy. Let us come back to the subject at some future time; at present we had better turn to something else.

By all means, I said, if that is your wish; for I too ought long since to have kept the engagement of which I spoke before, and only tarried because I could not refuse the request of the noble Callais. So the conversation ended, and we went our way.

GORGIAS

PERSONS OF THE DIALOGUE

CALLICLES SOCRATES CHAEREPHON
GORGIAS POLUS
SCENE:—The house of Callicles

[*The dialogue opens with a discussion of the nature
of rhetoric; then Socrates, by a bold transition, raises
the question whether the unjust man can be happy, and
answers it indirectly with the paradox that it is better
to suffer than to do injustice.*]

Socrates. Which of the two, Polus, in your opin-
ion, is the worst?—to do injustice or to suffer?
Polus. I should say that suffering was worst.
Soc. And which is the greater disgrace?—Answer.
Pol. To do.
Soc. And the greater disgrace is the greater evil?
Pol. Certainly not.
Soc. I understand you to say, if I am not mistaken,
that the honourable is not the same as the good, or the
disgraceful as the evil?
Pol. Certainly not.
Soc. Let me ask a question of you: When you speak
of beautiful things, such as bodies, colours, figures,
sounds, institutions, do you not call them beautiful in
reference to some standard: bodies, for example, are
beautiful in proportion as they are useful, or as the
sight of them gives pleasure to the spectators; can you
give any other account of personal beauty?

Pol. I cannot.

Soc. And you would say of figures or colours generally that they were beautiful, either by reason of the pleasure which they give, or of their use, or of both?

Pol. Yes, I should.

Soc. And you would call sounds and music beautiful for the same reason?

Pol. I should.

Soc. Laws and institutions also have no beauty in them except in so far as they are useful or pleasant or both?

Pol. I think not.

Soc. And may not the same be said of the beauty of knowledge?

Pol. To be sure, Socrates; and I very much approve of your measuring beauty by the standard of pleasure and utility.

Soc. And deformity or disgrace may be equally measured by the opposite standard of pain and evil?

Pol. Certainly.

Soc. Then when of two beautiful things one exceeds in beauty, the measure of the excess is to be taken in one or both of these; that is to say, in pleasure or utility or both?

Pol. Very true.

Soc. And of two deformed things, that which exceeds in deformity or disgrace, exceeds either in pain or evil—must it not be so?

Pol. Yes.

Soc. But then again, what was the observation which you just now made, about doing and suffering wrong? Did you not say, that suffering wrong was more evil, and doing wrong more disgraceful?

Pol. I did.

Soc. Then, if doing wrong is more disgraceful than

suffering, the more disgraceful must be more painful and must exceed in pain or in evil or both: does not that also follow?

Pol. Of course.

Soc. First, then, let us consider whether the doing of injustice exceeds the suffering in the consequent pain: Do the injurers suffer more than the injured?

Pol. No, Socrates; certainly not.

Soc. Then they do not exceed in pain?

Pol. No.

Soc. But if not in pain, then not in both?

Pol. Certainly not.

Soc. Then they can only exceed in the other?

Pol. Yes.

Soc. That is to say, in evil?

Pol. True.

Soc. Then doing injustice will have an excess of evil, and will therefore be a greater evil than suffering injustice?

Pol. Clearly.

Soc. But have not you and the world already agreed that to do injustice is more disgraceful than to suffer?

Pol. Yes.

Soc. And that is now discovered to be more evil?

Pol. True.

Soc. And would you prefer a greater evil or a greater dishonour to a less one? Answer, Polus, and fear not; for you will come to no harm if you nobly resign yourself into the healing hand of the argument as to a physician without shrinking, and either say 'Yes' or 'No' to me.

Pol. I should say 'No.'

Soc. Would any other man prefer a greater to a less evil?

Pol. No, not according to this way of putting the case, Socrates.

Soc. Then I said truly, Polus, that neither you, nor I, nor any man, would rather do than suffer injustice; for to do injustice is the greater evil of the two.

Pol. That is the conclusion.

Soc. You see, Polus, when you compare the two kinds of refutations, how unlike they are. All men, with the exception of myself, are of your way of thinking; but your single assent and witness are enough for me,—I have no need of any other; I take your suffrage, and am regardless of the rest. Enough of this, and now let us proceed to the next question; which is, Whether the greatest of evils to a guilty man is to suffer punishment, as you supposed, or whether to escape punishment is not a greater evil, as I supposed. Consider:— You would say that to suffer punishment is another name for being justly corrected when you do wrong?

Pol. I should.

Soc. And would you not allow that all just things are honourable in so far as they are just? Please to reflect, and tell me your opinion.

Pol. Yes, Socrates, I think that they are.

Soc. Consider again:—Where there is an agent, must there not also be a patient?

Pol. I should say so.

Soc. And will not the patient suffer that which the agent does, and will not the suffering have the quality of the action? I mean, for example, that if a man strikes, there must be something which is stricken?

Pol. Yes.

Soc. And if the striker strikes violently or quickly, that which is struck will be struck violently or quickly?

Pol. True.

Soc. And the suffering to him who is stricken is of the same nature as the act of him who strikes?

Pol. Yes.

Soc. And if a man burns, there is something which is burned?

Pol. Certainly.

Soc. And if he burns in excess or so as to cause pain, the thing burned will be burned in the same way?

Pol. Truly.

Soc. And if he cuts, the same argument holds— there will be something cut?

Pol. Yes.

Soc. And if the cutting be great or deep or such as will cause pain, the cut will be of the same nature?

Pol. That is evident.

Soc. Then you would agree generally to the universal proposition which I was just now asserting: that the affection of the patient answers to the act of the agent?

Pol. I agree.

Soc. Then, as this is admitted, let me ask whether being punished is suffering or acting?

Pol. Suffering, Socrates; there can be no doubt of that.

Soc. And suffering implies an agent?

Pol. Certainly, Socrates; and he is the punisher.

Soc. And he who punishes rightly, punishes justly?

Pol. Yes.

Soc. And therefore he acts justly?

Pol. Justly.

Soc. Then he who is punished and suffers retribution, suffers justly?

Pol. That is evident.

Soc. And that which is just has been admitted to be honourable?

Pol.   Certainly.

Soc.   Then the punisher does what is honourable, and the punished suffers what is honourable?

Pol.   True.

Soc.   And if what is honourable, then what is good, for the honourable is either pleasant or useful?

Pol.   Certainly.

Soc.   Then he who is punished suffers what is good?

Pol.   That is true.

Soc.   Then he is benefited?

Pol.   Yes.

Soc.   Do I understand you to mean what I mean by the term 'benefited'?   I mean, that if he be justly punished his soul is improved.

Pol.   Surely.

Soc.   Then he who is punished is delivered from the evil of his soul?

Pol.   Yes.

Soc.   And is he not then delivered from the greatest evil?   Look at the matter in this way:—In respect of a man's estate, do you see any greater evil than poverty?

Pol.   There is no greater evil.

Soc.   Again, in a man's bodily frame, you would say that the evil is weakness and disease and deformity?

Pol.   I should.

Soc.   And do you not imagine that the soul likewise has some evil of her own?

Pol.   Of course.

Soc.   And this you would call injustice and ignorance and cowardice, and the like?

Pol.   Certainly.

Soc.   So then, in mind, body, and estate, which are three, you have pointed out three corresponding evils—injustice, disease, poverty?

Pol.   True.

Soc. And which of the evils is the most disgraceful?
—Is not the most disgraceful of them injustice, and in general the evil of the soul?

Pol. By far the most.

Soc. And if the most disgraceful, then also the worst?

Pol. What do you mean, Socrates?

Soc. I mean to say, that what is most disgraceful has been already admitted to be most painful or hurtful, or both.

Pol. Certainly.

Soc. And now injustice and all evil in the soul has been admitted by us to be most disgraceful?

Pol. It has been admitted.

Soc. And most disgraceful either because most painful and causing excessive pain, or most hurtful, or both?

Pol. Certainly.

Soc. And therefore to be unjust and intemperate, and cowardly and ignorant, is more painful than to be poor and sick?

Pol. Nay, Socrates; the painfulness does not appear to me to follow from your premises.

Soc. Then, if, as you would argue, not more painful, the evil of the soul is of all evils the most disgraceful; and the excess of disgrace must be caused by some preternatural greatness, or extraordinary hurtfulness of the evil.

Pol. Clearly.

Soc. And that which exceeds most in hurtfulness will be the greatest of evils?

Pol. Yes.

Soc. Then injustice and intemperance, and in general the depravity of the soul, are the greatest of evils?

Pol. That is evident.

Soc. Now, what art is there which delivers us from poverty? Does not the art of making money?

Pol. Yes.

Soc. And what art frees us from disease? Does not the art of medicine?

Pol. Very true.

Soc. And what from vice and injustice? If you are not able to answer at once, ask yourself whither we go with the sick, and to whom we take them.

Pol. To the physicians, Socrates.

Soc. And to whom do we go with the unjust and intemperate?

Pol. To the judges, you mean.

Soc. —Who are to punish them?

Pol. Yes.

Soc. And do not those who rightly punish others, punish them in accordance with a certain rule of justice?

Pol. Clearly.

Soc. Then the art of money-making frees a man from poverty; medicine from disease; and justice from intemperance and injustice?

Pol. That is evident.

Soc. Which, then, is the best of these three?

Pol. Will you enumerate them?

Soc. Money-making, medicine, and justice.

Pol. Justice, Socrates, far excels the two others.

Soc. And justice, if the best, gives the greatest pleasure or advantage or both?

Pol. Yes.

Soc. But is the being healed a pleasant thing, and are those who are being healed pleased?

Pol. I think not.

Soc. A useful thing, then?

Pol. Yes.

Soc. Yes, because the patient is delivered from a great evil; and this is the advantage of enduring the pain—that you get well?

Pol. Certainly.

Soc. And would he be the happier man in his bodily condition, who is healed, or who never was out of health?

Pol. Clearly he who was never out of health.

Soc. Yes; for happiness surely does not consist in being delivered from evils, but in never having had them.

Pol. True.

Soc. And suppose the case of two persons who have some evil in their bodies, and that one of them is healed and delivered from evil, and another is not healed, but retains the evil—which of them is the most miserable?

Pol. Clearly he who is not healed.

Soc. And was not punishment said by us to be a deliverance from the greatest of evils, which is vice?

Pol. True.

Soc. And justice punishes us, and makes us more just, and is the medicine of our vice?

Pol. True.

Soc. He, then, has the first place in the scale of happiness who has never had vice in his soul; for this has been shown to be the greatest of evils.

Pol. Clearly.

Soc. And he has the second place, who is delivered from vice?

Pol. True.

Soc. That is to say, he who receives admonition and rebuke and punishment?

Pol. Yes.

Soc. Then he lives worst, who, having been unjust, has no deliverance from injustice?

Pol. Certainly.

Soc. That is, he lives worst who commits the greatest crimes, and who, being the most unjust of men, succeeds in escaping rebuke or correction or punishment; and this, as you say, has been accomplished by Archelaus and other tyrants and rhetoricians and potentates?

Pol. True.

Soc. May not their way of proceeding, my friend, be compared to the conduct of a person who is afflicted with the worst of diseases and yet contrives not to pay the penalty to the physician for his sins against his constitution, and will not be cured, because, like a child, he is afraid of the pain of being burned or cut:—Is not that a parallel case?

Pol. Yes, truly.

Soc. He would seem as if he did not know the nature of health and bodily vigour; and if we are right, Polus, in our previous conclusions, they are in a like case who strive to evade justice, which they see to be painful, but are blind to the advantage which ensues from it, not knowing how far more miserable a companion a diseased soul is than a diseased body; a soul, I say, which is corrupt and unrighteous and unholy. And hence they do all that they can to avoid punishment and to avoid being released from the greatest of evils; they provide themselves with money and friends, and cultivate to the utmost their powers of persuasion. But if we, Polus, are right, do you see what follows, or shall we draw out the consequences in form?

Pol. If you please.

Soc. Is it not a fact that injustice, and the doing of injustice, is the greatest of evils?

Pol. That is quite clear.

Soc. And further, that to suffer punishment is the way to be released from this evil?

Soc. And not to suffer, is to perpetuate the evil?

Pol. Yes.

Soc. To do wrong, then, is second only in the scale of evils; but to do wrong and not to be punished, is first and greatest of all?

Pol. That is true.

Soc. Well, and was not this the point in dispute, my friend? You deemed Archelaus happy, because he was a very great criminal and unpunished: I, on the other hand, maintained that he or any other who like him has done wrong and has not been punished, is, and ought to be, the most miserable of all men; and that the doer of injustice is more miserable than the sufferer; and he who escapes punishment, more miserable than he who suffers.—Was not that what I said?

Pol. Yes.

Soc. And it has been proved to be true?

Pol. Certainly.

Soc. Well, Polus, but if this is true, where is the great use of rhetoric? If we admit what has been just now said, every man ought in every way to guard himself against doing wrong, for he will thereby suffer great evil?

Pol. True.

Soc. And if he, or any one about whom he cares, does wrong, he ought of his own accord to go where he will be immediately punished; he will run to the judge, as he would to the physician, in order that the disease of injustice may not be rendered chronic and become the incurable cancer of the soul; must we not allow this consequence, Polus, if our former admissions are to stand:—is any other inference consistent with them?

Pol. To that, Socrates, there can be but one answer.

Soc. Then rhetoric is of no use to us, Polus, in helping a man to excuse his own injustice, or that of his parents or friends, or children or country; but may be of use to any one who holds that instead of excusing he ought to accuse—himself above all, and in the next degree his family or any of his friends who may be doing wrong; he should bring to light the iniquity and not conceal it, that so the wrong-doer may suffer and be made whole; and he should even force himself and others not to shrink, but with closed eyes like brave men to let the physician operate with knife or searing iron, not regarding the pain, in the hope of attaining the good and the honourable; let him who has done things worthy of stripes, allow himself to be scourged, if of bonds, to be bound, if of a fine, to be fined, if of exile, to be exiled, if of death, to die, himself being the first to accuse himself and his own relations, and using rhetoric to this end, that his and their unjust actions may be made manifest, and that they themselves may be delivered from injustice, which is the greatest evil. Then, Polus, rhetoric would indeed be useful. Do you say 'Yes' or 'No' to that?

Pol. To me, Socrates, what you are saying appears very strange, though probably in agreement with your premises.

Soc. Is not this the conclusion, if the premises are not disproven?

Pol. Yes; it certainly is.

Soc. And from the opposite point of view, if indeed it be our duty to harm another, whether an enemy or not—I except the case of self-defence—then I have to be upon my guard—but if my enemy injures a third person, then in every sort of way, by word as well as deed, I should try to prevent his being punished, or appearing before the judge; and if he appears, I should contrive that he should escape, and not suffer punishment: if he has stolen a sum of money, let him keep

what he has stolen and spend it on him and his, regardless of religion and justice; and if he have done things
worthy of death, let him not die, but rather be immortal
in his wickedness; or, if this is not possible, let him at
any rate be allowed to live as long as he can. For such
purposes, Polus, rhetoric may be useful, but is of small
if of any use to him who is not intending to commit injustice; at least, there was no such use discovered by us
in the previous discussion.

Cal. Tell me, Chaerephon, is Socrates in earnest, or
is he joking?

Chaer. I should say, Callicles, that he is in most
profound earnest; but you may as well ask him.

Cal. By the gods, and I will. Tell me, Socrates, are
you in earnest, or only in jest? For if you are in
earnest, and what you say is true, is not the whole of
human life turned upside down; and are we not doing,
as would appear, in everything the opposite of what we
ought to be doing?

Soc. O Callicles, if there were not some community
of feelings among mankind, however varying in different persons—I mean to say, if every man's feelings were
peculiar to himself and were not shared by the rest of
his species—I do not see how we could ever commu-
nicate our impressions to one another. I make this remark because I perceive that you and I have a common
feeling. For we are lovers both, and both of us have
two loves apiece:—I am the lover of Alcibiades, the son
of Cleinias, and of philosophy; and you of the Athenian Demus, and of Demus the son of Pyrilampes. Now,
I observe that you, with all your cleverness, do not venture to contradict your favourite in any word or opinion
of his; but as he changes you change, backwards and
forwards. When the Athenian Demus denies anything
that you are saying in the assembly, you go over to his

opinion; and you do the same with Demus, the fair
young son of Pyrilampes. For you have not the power
to resist the words and ideas of your loves; and if a
person were to express surprise at the strangeness of
what you say from time to time when under their influence, you would probably reply to him, if you were honest, that you cannot help saying what your loves say
unless they are prevented; and that you can only be
silent when they are. Now you must understand that
my words are an echo too, and therefore you need not
wonder at me; but if you want to silence me, silence
philosophy, who is my love, for she is always telling me
what I am now telling you, my friend; neither is she
capricious like my other love, for the son of Cleinias
says one thing to-day and another thing to-morrow, but
philosophy is always true. She is the teacher at whose
words you are now wondering, and you have heard her
yourself. Her you must refute, and either show, as I
was saying, that to do injustice and to escape punishment is not the worst of all evils; or, if you leave her
word unrefuted, by the dog the god of Egypt, I declare, O Callicles, that Callicles will never be at one with
himself, but that his whole life will be a discord. And
yet, my friend, I would rather that my lyre should be
inharmonious, and that there should be no music in the
chorus which I provided; aye, or that the whole world
should be at odds with me, and oppose me, rather than
that I myself should be at odds with myself, and contradict myself.

Cal. O Socrates, you are a regular declaimer, and
seem to be running riot in the argument. And now you
are declaiming in this way because Polus has fallen into
the same error himself of which he accused Gorgias:—
for he said that when Gorgias was asked by you,
whether, if some one came to him and wanted to learn

rhetoric, and did not know justice, he would teach him justice, Gorgias in his modesty replied that he would, because he thought that mankind in general would be displeased if he answered 'No'; and then in consequence of this admission, Gorgias was compelled to contradict himself, that being just the sort of thing in which you delight. Whereupon Polus laughed at you deservedly, as I think; but now he has himself fallen into the same trap. I cannot say very much for his wit when he conceded to you that to do is more dishonourable than to suffer injustice, for this was the admission which led to his being entangled by you; and because he was too modest to say what he thought, he had his mouth stopped. For the truth is, Socrates, that you, who pretend to be engaged in the pursuit of truth, are appealing now to the popular and vulgar notions of right, which are not natural, but only conventional. Convention and nature are generally at variance with one another: and hence, if a person is too modest to say what he thinks, he is compelled to contradict himself; and you, in your ingenuity perceiving the advantage to be thereby gained, slyly ask of him who is arguing conventionally a question which is to be determined by the rule of nature; and if he is talking of the rule of nature, you slip away to custom: as, for instance, you did in this very discussion about doing and suffering injustice. When Polus was speaking of the conventionally dishonourable, you assailed him from the point of view of nature; for by the rule of nature, to suffer injustice is the greater disgrace because the greater evil; but conventionally, to do evil is the more disgraceful. For the suffering of injustice is not the part of a man, but of a slave, who indeed had better die than live; since when he is wronged and trampled upon, he is unable to help himself, or any other about whom he cares. The rea-

son, as I conceive, is that the makers of laws are the
majority who are weak; and they make laws and distribute praises and censures with a view to themselves
and to their own interests; and they terrify the stronger
sort of men, and those who are able to get the better
of them, in order that they may not get the better of
them; and they say, that dishonesty is shameful and unjust; meaning, by the word injustice, the desire of a
man to have more than his neighbours; for knowing
their own inferiority, I suspect that they are too glad
of equality. And therefore the endeavour to have more
than the many, is conventionally said to be shameful
and unjust, and is called injustice, whereas nature herself intimates that it is just for the better to have more
than the worse, the more powerful than the weaker; and
in many ways she shows, among men as well as among
animals, and indeed among whole cities and races, that
justice consists in the superior ruling over and having more than the inferior. For on what principle of
justice did Xerxes invade Hellas, or his father the
Scythians? (not to speak of numberless other examples). Nay, but these are the men who act according
to nature; yes, by Heaven, and according to the law of
nature: not, perhaps, according to that artificial law,
which we invent and impose upon our fellows, of whom
we take the best and strongest from their youth upwards, and tame them like young lions,—charming them
with the sound of the voice, and saying to them, that
with equality they must be content, and that the equal
is the honourable and the just. But if there were a man
who had sufficient force, he would shake off and break
through, and escape from all this; he would trample
under foot all our formulas and spells and charms, and
all our laws which are against nature: the slave would

rise in rebellion and be lord over us, and the light of natural justice would shine forth. And this I take to be the sentiment of Pindar, when he says in his poem, that

"Law is the king of all, of mortals as well as of immortals;'

this, as he says,

'Makes might to be right, doing violence with highest hand; as I infer from the deeds of Heracles, for without buying them—'

—I do not remember the exact words, but the meaning is, that without buying them, and without their being given to him, he carried off the oxen of Geryon, according to the law of natural right, and that the oxen and other possessions of the weaker and inferior properly belong to the stronger and superior. And this is true, as you may ascertain, if you will leave philosophy and go on to higher things: for philosophy, Socrates, if pursued in moderation and at the proper age, is an elegant accomplishment, but too much philosophy is the ruin of human life. Even if a man has good parts, still, if he carries philosophy into later life, he is necessarily ignorant of all those things which a gentleman and a person of honour ought to know; he is inexperienced in the laws of the State, and in the language which ought to be used in the dealings of man with man, whether private or public, and utterly ignorant of the pleasures and desires of mankind and of human character in general. And people of this sort, when they betake themselves to politics or business, are as ridiculous as I imagine the politicians to be, when they make their appearance in the arena of philosophy. For, as Euripides says,

'Every man shines in that and pursues that, and devotes the greatest portion of the day to that in which he most excels.'

but anything in which he is inferior, he avoids and depreciates, and praises the opposite from partiality to himself, and because he thinks that he will thus praise himself. The true principle is to unite them. Philosophy, as a part of education, is an excellent thing, and there is no disgrace to a man while he is young in pursuing such a study; but when he is more advanced in years, the thing becomes ridiculous, and I feel towards philosophers as I do towards those who lisp and imitate children. For I love to see a little child, who is not of an age to speak plainly, lisping at his play; there is an appearance of grace and freedom in his utterance, which is natural to his childish years. But when I hear some small creature carefully articulating its words, I am offended; the sound is disagreeable, and has to my ears the twang of slavery. So when I hear a man lisping, or see him playing like a child, his behaviour appears to me ridiculous and unmanly and worthy of stripes. And I have the same feeling about students of philosophy; when I see a youth thus engaged,—the study appears to me to be in character, and becoming a man of a liberal education, and him who neglects philosophy I regard as an inferior man, who will never aspire to anything great or noble. But if I see him continuing the study in later life, and not leaving off, I should like to beat him, Socrates; for, as I was saying, such a one, even though he have good natural parts, becomes effeminate. He flies from the busy centre and the market-place, in which, as the poet says, men become distinguished; he creeps into a corner for the rest of his life, and talks in a whisper with three or four admiring youths, but never speaks out like a freeman in a satisfactory manner. Now I, Socrates, am very well inclined towards you, and my feeling may be compared with that of Zethus towards Amphion, in the play of Euripides, whom I was mentioning just now: for I am disposed to say to you much what Zethus said to his brother, that you, Socrates, are careless about the things of which you ought to be careful; and that you

> 'Who have a soul so noble, are remarkable for a pue-
>   rile exterior;
> Neither in a court of justice could you state a case,
>   or give any reason or proof,
> Or offer valiant counsel on another's behalf.'

And you must not be offended, my dear Socrates, for I am speaking out of good-will towards you, if I ask whether you are not ashamed of being thus defenceless; which I affirm to be the condition not of you only but of all those who will carry the study of philosophy too far. For suppose that some one were to take you, or any one of your sort, off to prison, declaring that you had done wrong when you had done no wrong, you must allow that you would not know what to do:—there you would stand giddy and gaping, and not having a word to say; and when you went up before the Court, even if the accuser were a poor creature and not good for much, you would die if he were disposed to claim the penalty of death. And yet, Socrates, what is the value of

> 'An art which converts a man of sense into a fool,'

who is helpless, and has no power to save either himself or others, when he is in the greatest danger and is going to be despoiled by his enemies of all his goods, and has to live, simply deprived of his rights of citizenship?—he being a man who, if I may use the expression, may be boxed on the ears with impunity. Then, my good friend, take my advice, and refute no more:

'Learn the philosopny of business, and acquire the
  reputation of wisdom.
But leave to others these niceties,'

whether they are to be described as follies or absurdities:

'For they will only
Give you poverty for the inmate of your dwelling.'

Cease, then, emulating these paltry splitters of words, and emulate only the man of substance and honour, who is well to do.

Soc. If my soul, Callicles, were made of gold, should I not rejoice to discover one of those stones with which they test gold, and the very best possible one to which I might bring my soul; and if the stone and I agreed in approving of her training, then I should know that I was in a satisfactory state, and that no other test was needed by me.

Cal. What is your meaning, Socrates?

Soc. I will tell you; I think that I have found in you the desired touchstone.

Cal. Why?

Soc. Because I am sure that if you agree with me in any of the opinions which my soul forms, I have at last found the truth indeed. For I consider that if a man is to make a complete trial of the good or evil of the soul, he ought to have three qualities—knowledge, good-will, outspokenness, which are all possessed by you. Many whom I meet are unable to make trial of me, because they are not wise as you are; others are wise, but they will not tell me the truth, because they have not the same interest in me which you have; and these two strangers, Gorgias and Polus, are undoubtedly wise men and my very good friends, but they are not out-spoken enough, and they are too modest. Why, their modesty is so great that they are driven to contradict themselves, first one and then the other of them, in the face of a large company, on matters of the highest mo-ment. But you have all the qualities in which these others are deficient, having received an excellent educa-tion; to this many Athenians can testify. And you are my friend. Shall I tell you why I think so? I know that you, Callicles, and Tisander of Aphidnae, and An-dron the son of Androtion, and Nausicydes of the deme of Cholarges, studied together: there were four of you, and I once heard you advising with one another as to the extent to which the pursuit of philosophy should be carried, and, as I know, you came to the conclusion that the study should not be pushed too much into de-tail. You were cautioning one another not to be over-wise; you were afraid that too much wisdom might unconsciously to yourselves be the ruin of you. And now when I hear you giving the same advice to me which you then gave to your most intimate friends, I have a sufficient evidence of your real good-will to me. And of the frankness of your nature and freedom from modesty I am assured by yourself, and the assurance is confirmed by your last speech. Well then, the infer-ence in the present case clearly is, that if you agree with me in an argument about any point, that point will have been sufficiently tested by us, and will not require to be submitted to any further test. For you could not have agreed with me, either from lack of knowledge or from superfluity of modesty, nor yet from a desire to deceive me, for you are my friend, as you tell me yourself. And therefore when you and I are agreed, the result will be the attainment of perfect truth. Now there is no nobler enquiry, Callicles, than that which you censure me for making,—What ought the character of a man to be, and what his pursuits, and how far is he to go, both in maturer years and in youth? For be assured that if I err in my own conduct I do not err intentionally, but from ignorance. Do not then desist from advising me, now that you have begun, until I have learned clearly what this is which I am to practise, and how I may acquire it. And if you find me assenting to your words, and hereafter not doing that to which I assented, call me 'dolt,' and deem me unworthy of receiving further instruction. Once more, then, tell me what you and Pindar mean by natural justice: Do you not mean that the superior should take the property of the inferior by force; that the better should rule the worse, the noble have more than the mean? Am I not right in my recollection?

Cal. Yes; that is what I was saying, and so I still aver.

Soc. And do you mean by the better the same as the superior? for I could not make out what you were saying at the time—whether you meant by the superior the stronger, and that the weaker must obey the stronger, as you seemed to imply when you said that great cities attack small ones in accordance with natural right, because they are superior and stronger, as though the superior and stronger and better were the same; or whether the better may be also the inferior and weaker, and the superior the worse, or whether better is to be defined in the same way as superior:—this is the point which I want to have cleared up. Are the superior and better and stronger the same or different?

Cal. I say unequivocally that they are the same.

Soc. Then the many are by nature superior to the one, against whom, as you were saying, they make the laws?

Cal. Certainly.

Soc. Then the laws of the many are the laws of the superior?

Cal. Very true.

Soc. Then they are the laws of the better; for the superior class are far better, as you were saying?

Cal. Yes.

Soc. And since they are superior, the laws which are made by them are by nature good?

Cal. Yes.

Soc. And are not the many of opinion, as you were lately saying, that justice is equality, and that to do is more disgraceful than to suffer injustice?—is that so or not? Answer, Callicles, and let no modesty be found to come in the way; do the many think, or do they not think thus?—I must beg of you to answer, in order that if you agree with me I may fortify myself by the assent of so competent an authority.

Cal. Yes; the opinion of the many is what you say.

Soc. Then not only custom but nature also affirms that to do is more disgraceful than to suffer injustice, and that justice is equality; so that you seem to have been wrong in your former assertion, when accusing me you said that nature and custom are opposed, and that I, knowing this, was dishonestly playing between them, appealing to custom when the argument is about nature, and to nature when the argument is about custom?

Cal. This man will never cease talking nonsense. At your age, Socrates, are you not ashamed to be catching at words and chuckling over some verbal slip? do you not see—have I not told you already, that by superior I mean better: do you imagine me to say, that if a rabble of slaves and nondescripts, who are of no use except perhaps for their physical strength, get together, their ipsissima verba are laws?

Soc. Ho! my philosopher, is that your line?

Cal. Certainly.

Soc. I was thinking, Callicles, that something of the kind must have been in your mind, and that is why I repeated the question,—What is the superior? I wanted to know clearly what you meant; for you surely do not think that two men are better than one, or that your slaves are better than you because they are stronger? Then please to begin again, and tell me who the better are, if they are not the stronger; and I will ask you, great Sir, to be a little milder in your instructions, or I shall have to run away from you.

Cal. You are ironical.

Soc. No, by the hero Zethus, Callicles, by whose aid you were just now saying (486 A) many ironical things against me, I am not;—tell me, then, whom you mean by the better?

Cal. I mean the more excellent.

Soc. Do you not see that you are yourself using words which have no meaning and that you are explaining nothing?—will you tell me whether you mean by the better and superior the wiser, or if not, whom?

Cal. Most assuredly, I do mean the wiser.

Soc. Then according to you, one wise man may often be superior to ten thousand fools, and he ought to rule them, and they ought to be his subjects, and he ought to have more than they should. This is what I believe that you mean (and you must not suppose that I am word-catching), if you allow that the one is superior to the ten thousand?

Cal. Yes; that is what I mean, and that is what I conceive to be natural justice—that the better and wiser should rule and have more than the inferior.

Soc. Stop there, and let me ask you what you would say in this case: Let us suppose that we are all together as we are now; there are several of us, and we have a large common store of meats and drinks, and there are all sorts of persons in our company having various degrees of strength and weakness, and one of us, being a physician, is wiser in the matter of food than all the rest, and he is probably stronger than some and not so strong as others of us—will he not, being wiser, be also better than we are, and our superior in this matter of food?

Cal. Certainly.

Soc. Either, then, he will have a larger share of the meats and drinks, because he is better, or he will have the distribution of all of them by reason of his authority, but he will not expend or make use of a larger share of them on his own person, or if he does, he will be punished;—his share will exceed that of some, and be less than that of others, and if he be the weakest of all, he being the best of all will have the smallest share of all, Callicles:—am I not right, my friend?

Cal. You talk about meats and drinks and physicians and other nonsense; I am not speaking of them.

Soc. Well, but do you admit that the wiser is the better? Answer 'Yes' or 'No.'

Cal. Yes.

Soc. And ought not the better to have a larger share?

Cal. Not of meats and drinks.

Soc. I understand: then, perhaps, of coats—the skilfullest weaver ought to have the largest coat, and the greatest number of them, and go about clothed in the best and finest of them?

Cal. Fudge about coats!

Soc. Then the skilfullest and best in making shoes ought to have the advantage in shoes; the shoemaker, clearly, should walk about in the largest shoes, and have the greatest number of them?

Cal. Fudge about shoes! What nonsense are you talking?

Soc. Or, if this is not your meaning, perhaps you would say that the wise and good and true husbandman should actually have a larger share of seeds, and have as much seed as possible for his own land?

Cal. How you go on, always talking in the same way, Socrates!

Soc. Yes, Callicles, and also about the same things.

Cal. Yes, by the Gods, you are literally always talking of cobblers and fullers and cooks and doctors, as if this had to do with our argument.

Soc. But why will you not tell me in what a man must be superior and wiser in order to claim a larger share; will you neither accept a suggestion, nor offer one?

Cal. I have already told you. In the first place, I mean by superiors not cobblers or cooks, but wise politicians who understand the administration of a state, and who are not only wise, but also valiant and able to carry out their designs, and not the men to faint from want of soul.

Soc. See now, most excellent Callicles, how different my charge against you is from that which you bring against me, for you reproach me with always saying the same; but I reproach you with never saying the same about the same things, for at one time you were defining the better and the superior to be the stronger, then again as the wiser, and now you bring forward a new notion; the superior and the better are now declared by you to be the more courageous: I wish, my good friend, that you would tell me, once for all, whom you affirm to be the better and superior, and in what they are better?

Cal. I have already told you that I mean those who are wise and courageous in the administration of a state —they ought to be the rulers of their states, and justice consists in their having more than their subjects.

Soc. But whether rulers or subjects will they or will they not have more than themselves, my friend?

Cal. What do you mean?

Soc. I mean that every man is his own ruler; but perhaps you think that there is no necessity for him to rule himself; he is only required to rule others?

Cal. What do you mean by his 'ruling over himself'?

Soc. A simple thing enough; just what is commonly said, that a man should be temperate and master of himself, and ruler of his own pleasures and passions.

Cal. What innocence! you mean those fools,—the temperate?

Soc. Certainly:—any one may know that to be my meaning.

Cal. Quite so, Socrates; and they are really fools, for how can a man be happy who is the servant of anything? On the contrary, I plainly assert, that he who would truly live ought to allow his desires to wax to the uttermost, and not to chastise them; but when they have grown to their greatest he should have courage and intelligence to minister to them and to satisfy all his longings. And this I affirm to be natural justice and nobility. To this however the many cannot attain; and they blame the strong man because they are ashamed of their own weakness, which they desire to conceal, and hence they say that intemperance is base. As I have remarked already, they enslave the nobler natures, and being unable to satisfy their pleasures, they praise temperance and justice out of their own cowardice. For if a man had been originally the son of a king, or had a nature capable of acquiring an empire or a tyranny or sovereignty, what could be more truly base or evil than temperance—to a man like him, I say, who might freely be enjoying every good, and has no one to stand in his way, and yet has admitted custom and reason and the opinion of other men to be lords over him?—must not he be in a miserable plight whom the reputation of justice and temperance hinders from giving more to his friends than to his enemies, even though he be a ruler in his city? Nay, Socrates, for you profess to be a votary of the truth, and the truth is this:—that luxury and intemperance and licence, if they be provided with means, are virtue and happiness—all the rest is a mere bauble, agreements contrary to nature, foolish talk of men, nothing worth.

Soc. There is a noble freedom, Callicles, in your way of approaching the argument; for what you say is what the rest of the world think, but do not like to say. And I must beg of you to persevere, that the true rule of human life may become manifest. Tell me, then:—you say, do you not, that in the rightly-developed man the passions ought not to be controlled, but that we should let them grow to the utmost and somehow or other satisfy them, and that this is virtue?

Cal. Yes; I do.

Soc. Then those who want nothing are not truly said to be happy?

Cal. No indeed, for then stones and dead men would be the happiest of all.

Soc. But surely life according to your view is an awful thing; and indeed I think that Euripides may have been right in saying,

'Who knows if life be not death and death life;'

and that we are very likely dead; I have heard a philosopher say that at this moment we are actually dead, and that the body (σῶμα) is our tomb (σῆμα), and that the part of the soul which is the seat of the desires is liable to be tossed about by words and blown up and down; and some ingenious person, probably a Sicilian or an Italian, playing with the word, invented a tale in which he called the soul—because of its believing and make-believe nature—a vessel,[1] and the ignorant he called the uninitiated or leaky, and the place in the souls of the uninitiated in which the desires are seated, being the intemperate and incontinent part, he compared to a vessel full of holes, because it can never be satisfied. He is not of your way of thinking, Callicles, for he declares, that of all the souls in Hades, meaning the invisible world (ἀειδὲς), these uninitiated or leaky persons are the most miserable, and that they pour water into a vessel which is full of holes out of a colander which is similarly perforated. The colander, as my informer assures me, is the soul, and the soul which he compares to a colander is the soul of the ignorant, which is likewise full of holes, and therefore incontinent, owing to a bad memory and want of faith. These notions are strange enough, but they show the principle which, if I can, I would fain prove to you; that you

---

[1] An untranslateable pun,—διὰ τὸ πιθανόν τε καὶ πιστικὸν ὠνόμασε πίθον.

should change your mind, and, instead of the intemperate and insatiate life, choose that which is orderly and sufficient and has a due provision for daily needs. Do I make any impression on you, and are you coming over to the opinion that the orderly are happier than the intemperate? Or do I fail to persuade you, and, however many tales I rehearse to you, do you continue of the same opinion still?

Cal. The latter, Socrates, is more like the truth.

Soc. Well, I will tell you another image, which comes out of the same school:—Let me request you to consider how far you would accept this as an account of the two lives of the temperate and intemperate in a figure:—There are two men, both of whom have a number of casks; the one man has his casks sound and full, one of wine, another of honey, and a third of milk, besides others filled with other liquids, and the streams which fill them are few and scanty, and he can only obtain them with a great deal of toil and difficulty; but when his casks are once filled he has no need to feed them any more, and has no further trouble with them or care about them. The other, in like manner, can procure streams, though not without difficulty; but his vessels are leaky and unsound, and night and day he is compelled to be filling them, and if he pauses for a moment, he is in an agony of pain. Such are their respective lives:—And now would you say that the life of the intemperate is happier than that of the temperate? Do I not convince you that the opposite is the truth?

Cal. You do not convince me, Socrates, for the one who has filled himself has no longer any pleasure left; and this, as I was just now saying, is the life of a stone: he has neither joy nor sorrow after he is once filled; but the pleasure depends on the superabundance of the influx.

Soc. But the more you pour in, the greater the waste; and the holes must be large for the liquid to escape.

Cal. Certainly.

Soc. The life which you are now depicting is not that of a dead man, or of a stone, but of a cormorant; you mean that he is to be hungering and eating?

Cal. Yes.

Soc. And he is to be thirsting and drinking?

Cal. Yes, that is what I mean; he is to have all his desires about him, and to be able to live happily in the gratification of them.

Soc. Capital, excellent; go on as you have begun, and have no shame; I, too, must disencumber myself of shame: and first, will you tell me whether you include itching and scratching, provided you have enough of them and pass your life in scratching, in your notion of happiness?

Cal. What a strange being you are, Socrates! a regular mob-orator.

Soc. That was the reason, Callicles, why I scared Polus and Gorgias, until they were too modest to say what they thought; but you will not be too modest and will not be scared, for you are a brave man. And now, answer my question.

Cal. I answer, that even the scratcher would live pleasantly.

Soc. And if pleasantly, then also happily?

Cal. To be sure.

Soc. But what if the itching is not confined to the head? Shall I pursue the question? And here, Callicles, I would have you consider how you would reply if consequences are pressed upon you, especially if in the last resort you are asked, whether the life of a catamite is not terrible, foul, miserable? Or would you venture to say, that they too are happy, if they only get enough of what they want?

Cal. Are you not ashamed, Socrates, of introducing such topics into the argument?

Soc. Well, my fine friend, but am I the introducer of these topics, or he who says without any qualification that all who feel pleasure in whatever manner are happy, and who admits of no distinction between good and bad pleasures? And I would still ask, whether you say that pleasure and good are the same, or whether there is some pleasure which is not a good?

Cal. Well, then, for the sake of consistency, I will say that they are the same.

Soc. You are breaking the original agreement, Callicles, and will no longer be a satisfactory companion in the search after truth, if you say what is contrary to your real opinion.

Cal. Why, that is what you are doing too, Socrates.

Soc. Then we are both doing wrong. Still, my dear friend, I would ask you to consider whether pleasure, from whatever source derived, is the good; for, if this be true, then the disagreeable consequences which have been darkly intimated must follow, and many others.

Cal. That, Socrates, is only your opinion.

Soc. And do you, Callicles, seriously maintain what you are saying?

Cal. Indeed I do.

Soc. Then, as you are in earnest, shall we proceed with the argument?

Cal. By all means.[1]

Soc. Well, if you are willing to proceed, determine this question for me:—There is something, I presume, which you would call knowledge?

Cal. There is.

[1] Or, 'I am in profound earnest.'

Soc. And were you not saying just now, that some courage implied knowledge?

Cal. I was.

Soc. And you were speaking of courage and knowledge as two things different from one another?

Cal. Certainly I was.

Soc. And would you say that pleasure and knowledge are the same, or not the same?

Cal. Not the same, O man of wisdom.

Soc. And would you say that courage differed from pleasure?

Cal. Certainly.

Soc. Well, then, let us remember that Callicles, the Acharnian, says that pleasure and good are the same; but that knowledge and courage are not the same, either with one another, or with the good.

Cal. And what does our friend Socrates, of Foxton, say—does he assent to this, or not?

Soc. He does not assent; neither will Callicles, when he sees himself truly. You will admit, I suppose, that good and evil fortune are opposed to each other?

Cal. Yes.

Soc. And if they are opposed to each other, then, like health and disease, they exclude one another; a man cannot have them both, or be without them both, at the same time?

Cal. What do you mean?

Soc. Take the case of any bodily affection:—a man may have the complaint in his eyes which is called ophthalmia?

Cal. To be sure.

Soc. But he surely cannot have the same eyes well and sound at the same time?

Cal. Certainly not.

Soc. And when he has got rid of his ophthalmia,

has he got rid of the health of his eyes too? Is the final result, that he gets rid of them both together?

Cal. Certainly not.

Soc. That would surely be marvellous and absurd?

Cal. Very.

Soc. I suppose that he is affected by them, and gets rid of them in turns?

Cal. Yes.

Soc. And he may have strength and weakness in the same way, by fits?

Cal. Yes.

Soc. Or swiftness and slowness?

Cal. Certainly.

Soc. And does he have and not have good and happiness, and their opposites, evil and misery, in a similar alternation?

Cal. Certainly he has.

Soc. If then there be anything which a man has and has not at the same time, clearly that cannot be good and evil—do we agree? Please not to answer without consideration.

Cal. I entirely agree.

Soc. Go back now to our former admissions. Did you say that to hunger, I mean the mere state of hunger, was pleasant or painful?

Cal. I said painful, but that to eat when you are hungry is pleasant.

Soc. I know; but still the actual hunger is painful: am I not right?

Cal. Yes.

Soc. And thirst, too, is painful?

Cal. Yes, very.

Soc. Need I adduce any more instances, or would you agree that all wants or desires are painful?

Cal.   I agree, and therefore you need not adduce any more instances.

Soc.   Very good.   And you would admit that to drink, when you are thirsty, is pleasant?

Cal.   Yes.

Soc.   And in the sentence which you have just uttered, the word 'thirsty' implies pain?

Cal.   Yes.

Soc.   And the word 'drinking' is expressive of pleasure, and of the satisfaction of the want?

Cal.   Yes.

Soc.   There is pleasure in drinking?

Cal.   Certainly.

Soc.   When you are thirsty?

Cal.   Yes.

Soc.   And in pain?

Cal.   Yes.

Soc.   Do you see the inference:——that pleasure and pain are simultaneous, when you say that being thirsty, you drink?   For are they not simultaneous, and do they not affect at the same time the same part, whether of the soul or the body?——which of them is affected cannot be supposed to be of any consequence: Is not this true?

Cal.   It is.

Soc.   You said also, that no man could have good and evil fortune at the same time?

Cal.   Yes, I did.

Soc.   But you admitted, that when in pain a man might also have pleasure?

Cal.   Clearly.

Soc.   Then pleasure is not the same as good fortune, or pain the same as evil fortune, and therefore the good is not the same as the pleasant?

Cal.   I wish I knew, Socrates, what your quibbling means.

Soc. You know, Callicles, but you affect not to know.

Cal. Well, get on, and don't keep fooling: then you will know what a wiseacre you are in your admonition of me.

Soc. Does not a man cease from his thirst and from his pleasure in drinking at the same time?

Cal. I do not understand what you are saying.

Gor. Nay, Callicles, answer, if only for our sakes; —we should like to hear the argument out.

Cal. Yes, Gorgias, but I must complain of the habitual trifling of Socrates; he is always arguing about little and unworthy questions.

Gor. What matter? Your reputation, Callicles, is not at stake. Let Socrates argue in his own fashion.

Cal. Well, then, Socrates, you shall ask these little peddling questions, since Gorgias wishes to have them.

Soc. I envy you, Callicles, for having been initiated into the great mysteries before you were initiated into the lesser. I thought that this was not allowable. But to return to our argument:—Does not a man cease from thirsting and from the pleasure of drinking at the same moment?

Cal. True.

Soc. And if he is hungry, or has any other desire, does he not cease from the desire and the pleasure at the same moment?

Cal. Very true.

Soc. Then he ceases from pain and pleasure at the same moment?

Cal. Yes.

Soc. But he does not cease from good and evil at the same moment, as you have admitted: do you still adhere to what you said?

Cal. Yes, I do; but what is the inference?

Soc. Why, my friend, the inference is that the good is not the same as the pleasant, or the evil the same as the painful; there is a cessation of pleasure and pain at the same moment; but not of good and evil, for they are different. How then can pleasure be the same as good, or pain as evil? And I would have you look at the matter in another light, which could hardly, I think, have been considered by you when you identified them: Are not the good good because they have good present with them, as the beautiful are those who have beauty present with them?

Cal. Yes.

Soc. And do you call the fools and cowards good men? For you were saying just now that the courageous and the wise are the good—would you not say so?

Cal. Certainly.

Soc. And did you never see a foolish child rejoicing?

Cal. Yes, I have.

Soc. And a foolish man too?

Cal. Yes, certainly; but what is your drift?

Soc. Nothing particular, if you will only answer.

Cal. Yes, I have.

Soc. And did you ever see a sensible man rejoicing or sorrowing?

Cal. Yes.

Soc. Which rejoice and sorrow most—the wise or the foolish?

Cal. They are much upon a par, I think, in that respect.

Soc. Enough: And did you ever see a coward in battle?

Cal. To be sure.

Soc. And which rejoiced most at the departure of the enemy, the coward or the brave?

Cal. I should say 'most' of both; or at any rate, they rejoiced about equally.

Soc. No matter; then the cowards, and not only the brave, rejoice?

Cal. Greatly.

Soc. And the foolish; so it would seem?

Cal. Yes.

Soc. And are only the cowards pained at the approach of their enemies, or are the brave also pained?

Cal. Both are pained.

Soc. And are they equally pained?

Cal. I should imagine that the cowards are more pained.

Soc. And are they not better pleased at the enemy's departure?

Cal. I dare say.

Soc. Then are the foolish and the wise and the cowards and the brave all pleased and pained, as you were saying, in nearly equal degree; but are the cowards more pleased and pained than the brave?

Cal. Yes.

Soc. But surely the wise and brave are the good, and the foolish and the cowardly are the bad?

Cal. Yes.

Soc. Then the good and the bad are pleased and pained in a nearly equal degree?

Cal. Yes.

Soc. Then are the good and bad good and bad in a nearly equal degree, or have the bad the advantage both in good and evil? [i. e. in having more pleasure and more pain.]

Cal. I really do not know what you mean.

Soc. Why, do you not remember saying that the good were good because good was present with them, and the evil because evil; and that pleasures were goods and pains evils?

Cal. Yes, I remember.

Soc. And are not these pleasures or goods present to those who rejoice—if they do rejoice?

Cal. Certainly.

Soc. Then those who rejoice are good when goods are present with them?

Cal. Yes.

Soc. And those who are in pain have evil or sorrow present with them?

Cal. Yes.

Soc. And would you still say that the evil are evil by reason of the presence of evil?

Cal. I should.

Soc. Then those who rejoice are good, and those who are in pain evil?

Cal. Yes.

Soc. The degrees of good and evil vary with the degrees of pleasure and of pain?

Cal. Yes.

Soc. Have the wise man and the fool, the brave and the coward, joy and pain in nearly equal degrees? or would you say that the coward has more?

Cal. I should say that he has.

Soc. Help me then to draw out the conclusion which follows from our admissions; for it is good to repeat and review what is good twice and thrice over, as they say. Both the wise man and the brave man we allow to be good?

Cal. Yes.

Soc. And the foolish man and the coward to be evil?

Cal. Certainly.

Soc. And he who has joy is good?

Cal. Yes.

Soc. And he who is in pain is evil?

Cal. Certainly.

Soc. The good and evil both have joy and pain, but, perhaps, the evil has more of them?

Cal. Yes.

Soc. Then must we not infer, that the bad man is as good and bad as the good, or, perhaps, even better?—is not this a further inference which follows equally with the preceding from the assertion that the good and the pleasant are the same:—can this be denied, Callicles?

Cal. I have been listening and making admissions to you, Socrates; and I remark that if a person grants you anything in play, you, like a child, want to keep hold and will not give it back. But do you really suppose that I or any other human being denies that some pleasures are good and others bad?

Soc. Alas, Callicles, how unfair you are! you certainly treat me as if I were a child, sometimes saying one thing, and then another, as if you were meaning to deceive me. And yet I thought at first that you were my friend, and would not have deceived me if you could have helped. But I see that I was mistaken; and now I suppose that I must make the best of a bad business, as they said of old, and take what I can get out of you. —Well, then, as I understand you to say, I may assume that some pleasures are good and others evil?

Cal. Yes.

Soc. The beneficial are good, and the hurtful are evil?

Cal. To be sure.

Soc. And the beneficial are those which do some good, and the hurtful are those which do some evil?

Cal. Yes.

Soc. Take, for example, the bodily pleasures of eat-

ing and drinking, which we were just now mentioning
—you mean to say that those which promote health, or
any other bodily excellence, are good, and their opposites evil?

Cal.   Certainly.

Soc.   And in the same way there are good pains and
there are evil pains?

Cal.   To be sure.

Soc.   And ought we not to choose and use the good
pleasures and pains?

Cal.   Certainly.

Soc.   But not the evil?

Cal.   Clearly.

Soc.   Because, if you remember, Polus and I have
agreed that all our actions are to be done for the sake
of the good;—and will you agree with us in saying,
that the good is the end of all our actions, and that all
our actions are to be done for the sake of the good, and
not the good for the sake of them?—will you add a third
vote to our two?

Cal.   I will.

Soc.   Then pleasure, like everything else, is to be
sought for the sake of that which is good, and not that
which is good for the sake of pleasure?

Cal.   To be sure.

[*The rest of the dialogue is omitted.*]

PHAEDO

PERSONS OF THE DIALOGUE

PHAEDO, *who is the narrator*   APOLLODORUS
of the Dialogue to   SIMMIAS
Echecrates of Phlius   CEBES
SOCRATES   CRITO
ATTENDANT OF THE PRISON

SCENE:—The Prison of Socrates

PLACE OF THE NARRATION—Phlius

Echecrates. WERE you yourself, Phaedo, in the prison with Socrates on the day when he drank the poison?

Phaedo. Yes, Echecrates, I was.

Ech. I should so like to hear about his death. What did he say in his last hours? We were informed that he died by taking poison, but no one knew anything more; for no Phliasian ever goes to Athens now, and it is a long time since any stranger from Athens has found his way hither; so that we had no clear account.

Phaed. Did you not hear of the proceedings at the trial?

Ech. Yes; some one told us about the trial, and we could not understand why, having been condemned, he should have been put to death, not at the time, but long afterwards. What was the reason of this?

Phaed. An accident, Echecrates: the stern of the ship which the Athenians send to Delos happened to have been crowned on the day before he was tried.

Ech. What is this ship?

Phaed. It is the ship in which, according to Athenian tradition, Theseus went to Crete when he took with him the fourteen youths, and was the saviour of them and of himself. And they are said to have vowed to Apollo at the time, that if they were saved they would send a yearly mission to Delos. Now this custom still continues, and the whole period of the voyage to and from Delos, beginning when the priest of Apollo crowns the stern of the ship, is a holy season, during which the city is not allowed to be polluted by public executions; and when the vessel is detained by contrary winds, the time spent in going and returning is very considerable. As I was saying, the ship was crowned on the day before the trial, and this was the reason why Socrates lay in prison and was not put to death until long after he was condemned.

Ech. What was the manner of his death, Phaedo? What was said or done? And which of his friends were with him? Or did the authorities forbid them to be present—so that he had no friends near him when he died?

Phaed. No; there were several of them with him.

Ech. If you have nothing to do, I wish that you would tell me what passed, as exactly as you can.

Phaed. I have nothing at all to do, and will try to gratify your wish. To be reminded of Socrates is always the greatest delight to me, whether I speak myself or hear another speak of him.

Ech. You will have listeners who are of the same mind with you, and I hope that you will be as exact as you can.

Phaed. I had a singular feeling at being in his company. For I could hardly believe that I was present at the death of a friend, and therefore I did not pity him, Echecrates; he died so fearlessly, and his words and bearing were so noble and gracious, that to me he appeared blessed. I thought that in going to the other world he could not be without a divine call, and that he would be happy, if any man ever was, when he arrived there; and therefore I did not pity him as might have seemed natural at such an hour. But I had not the pleasure which I usually feel in philosophical discourse (for philosophy was the theme of which we spoke). I was pleased, but in the pleasure there was also a strange admixture of pain; for I reflected that he was soon to die, and this double feeling was shared by us all; we were laughing and weeping by turns, especially the excitable Apollodorus—you know the sort of man?

Ech. Yes.

Phaed. He was quite beside himself; and I and all of us were greatly moved.

Ech. Who were present?

Phaed. Of native Athenians there were, besides Apollodorus, Critobulus and his father Crito, Hermogenes, Epigenes, Aeschines, Antisthenes; likewise Ctesippus of the deme of Paeania, Menexenus, and some others; Plato, if I am not mistaken, was ill.

Ech. Were there any strangers?

Phaed. Yes, there were; Simmias the Theban, and Cebes, and Phaedondes; Euclid and Terpsion, who came from Megara.

Ech. And was Aristippus there, and Cleombrotus?

Phaed. No, they were said to be in Aegina.

Ech. Any one else?

Phaed. I think that these were nearly all.

Ech. Well, and what did you talk about?

Phaed. I will begin at the beginning, and endeavour to repeat the entire conversation. On the previous days we had been in the habit of assembling early in the morning at the court in which the trial took place, and which is not far from the prison. There used to wait talking with one another until the opening of the doors (for they were not opened very early); then we went in and generally passed the day with Socrates. On the last morning we assembled sooner than usual, having heard on the day before when we quitted the prison in the evening that the sacred ship had come from Delos; and so we arranged to meet very early at the accustomed place. On our arrival the jailer who answered the door, instead of admitting us, came out and told us to stay until he called us. 'For the Eleven,' he said, 'are now with Socrates; they are taking off his chains, and giving orders that he is to die to-day.' He soon returned and said that we might come in. On entering we found Socrates just released from chains, and Xanthippè, whom you know, sitting by him, and holding his child in her arms. When she saw us she uttered a cry and said, as women will: "O Socrates, this is the last time that either you will converse with your friends, or they with you." Socrates turned to Crito and said: 'Crito, let some one take her home.' Some of Crito's people accordingly led her away, crying out and beating herself. And when she was gone, Socrates, sitting up on the couch, bent and rubbed his leg, saying, as he was rubbing: How singular is the thing called pleasure, and how curiously related to pain, which might be thought to be the opposite of it; for they are never present to a man at the same instant, and yet he who pursues either is generally compelled to take the other; their bodies are two, but they are joined by a single head. And I cannot help thinking that if Aesop had remembered them, he would have made a fable about God trying to reconcile their strife, and how, when he could not, he fastened their heads together; and this is the reason why when one comes the other follows: as I know by my own experience now, when after the pain in my leg which was caused by the chain pleasure appears to succeed.

Upon this Cebes said: I am glad, Socrates, that you have mentioned the name of Aesop. For it reminds me of a question which has been asked by many, and was asked of me only the day before yesterday by Evenus the poet—he will be sure to ask it again, and therefore if you would like me to have an answer ready for him, you may as well tell me what I should say to him:— he wanted to know why you, who never before wrote a line of poetry, now that you are in prison are turning Aesop's fables into verse, and also composing that hymn in honour of Apollo.

Tell him, Cebes, he replied, what is the truth—that I had no idea of rivalling him or his poems; to do so, as I knew, would be no easy task. But I wanted to see whether I could purge away a scruple which I felt about the meaning of certain dreams. In the course of my life I have often had intimations in dreams 'that I should compose music.' The same dream came to me sometimes in one form, and sometimes in another, but always saying the same or nearly the same words: 'Cultivate and make music,' said the dream. And hitherto I had imagined that this was only intended to exhort and encourage me in the study of philosophy, which has been the pursuit of my life, and is the noblest and best of music. The dream was bidding me do what I was already doing, in the same way that the competitor in a race is bidden by the spectators to run when he is already running. But I was not certain of this; for the dream might have meant music in the popular sense of the word, and being under sentence of death, and the festival giving me a respite, I thought that it would be safer for me to satisfy the scruple, and, in obedience to the dream, to compose a few verses before I departed. And first I made a hymn in honour of the god of the festival, and then considering that a poet, if he is really to be a poet, should not only put together words, but should invent stories, and that I have no invention, I took some fables of Aesop, which I had ready at hand and which I knew—they were the first I came upon— and turned them into verse. Tell this to Evenus, Cebes, and bid him be of good cheer; say that I would have him come after me if he be a wise man, and not tarry; and that to-day I am likely to be going, for the Athenians say that I must.

Simmias said: What a message for such a man! having been a frequent companion of his I should say that, as far as I know him, he will never take your advice unless he is obliged.

Why, said Socrates,—is not Evenus a philosopher?

I think that he is, said Simmias.

Then he, or any man who has the spirit of philosophy, will be willing to die; but he will not take his own life, for that is held to be unlawful.

Here he changed his position, and put his legs off the couch on to the ground, and during the rest of the conversation he remained sitting.

Why do you say, enquired Cebes, that a man ought not to take his own life, but that the philosopher will be ready to follow the dying?

Socrates replied: And have you, Cebes and Simmias, who are the disciples of Philolaus, never heard him speak of this?

Yes, but his language was obscure, Socrates.

My words, too, are only an echo; but there is no reason why I should not repeat what I have heard: and indeed, as I am going to another place, it is very meet for me to be thinking and talking of the nature of the pilgrimage which I am about to make. What can I do better in the interval between this and the setting of the sun?

Then tell me, Socrates, why is suicide held to be unlawful? as I have certainly heard Philolaus, about whom you were just now asking, affirm when he was staying with us at Thebes; and there are others who say the same, although I have never understood what was meant by any of them.

Do not lose heart, replied Socrates, and the day may come when you will understand. I suppose that you wonder why, when other things which are evil may be good at certain times and to certain persons, death is to be the only exception, and why, when a man is better dead, he is not permitted to be his own benefactor, but must wait for the hand of another.

Very true, said Cebes, laughing gently and speaking in his native Boeotian.

I admit the appearance of inconsistency in what I am saying; but there may not be any real inconsistency after all. There is a doctrine whispered in secret that man is a prisoner who has no right to open the door and run away; this is a great mystery which I do not quite understand. Yet I too believe that the gods are our guardians, and that we men are a possession of theirs. Do you not agree?

Yes, I quite agree, said Cebes.

And if one of your own possessions, an ox or an ass, for example, took the liberty of putting himself out of the way when you had given no intimation of your wish that he should die, would you not be angry with him, and would you not punish him if you could?

Certainly, replied Cebes.

Then, if we look at the matter thus, there may be reason in saying that a man should wait, and not take his own life until God summons him, as he is now summoning me.

Yes, Socrates, said Cebes, there seems to be truth in what you say. And yet how can you reconcile this seemingly true belief that God is our guardian and we his possessions, with the willingness to die which you were just now attributing to the philosopher? That the wisest of men should be willing to leave a service in which they are ruled by the gods who are the best of rulers, is not reasonable; for surely no wise man thinks that when set at liberty he can take better care of himself than the gods take of him. A fool may perhaps think so—he may argue that he had better run away from his master, not considering that his duty is to remain to the end, and not to run away from the good, and that there would be no sense in his running away. The wise man will want to be ever with him who is better than himself. Now this, Socrates, is the reverse of what was just now said; for upon this view the wise man should sorrow and the fool rejoice at passing out of life.

The earnestness of Cebes seemed to please Socrates. Here, said he, turning to us, is a man who is always enquiring, and is not so easily convinced by the first thing which he hears.

And certainly, added Simmias, the objection which he is now making does appear to me to have some force. For what can be the meaning of a truly wise man wanting to fly away and lightly leave a master who is better than himself? And I rather imagine that Cebes is referring to you; he thinks that you are too ready to leave us, and too ready to leave the gods whom you acknowledge to be our good masters.

Yes, replied Socrates; there is reason in what you say. And so you think that I ought to answer your indictment as if I were in a court?

We should like you to do so, said Simmias.

Then I must try to make a more successful defence before you than I did before the judges. For I am quite ready to admit, Simmias and Cebes, that I ought to be grieved at death, if I were not persuaded in the first place that I am going to other gods who are wise and good (of which I am as certain as I can be of any such matters), and secondly (though I am not so sure of this last) to men departed, better than those whom I leave behind; and therefore I do not grieve as I might have done, for I have good hope that there is yet something remaining for the dead, and as has been said of old, some far better thing for the good than for the evil.

But do you mean to take away your thoughts with you, Socrates? said Simmias. Will you not impart them to us?—for they are a benefit in which we too are entitled to share. Moreover, if you succeed in convincing us, that will be an answer to the charge against yourself.

I will do my best, replied Socrates. But you must first let me hear what Crito wants; he has long been wishing to say something to me.

Only this, Socrates, replied Crito:—the attendant who is to give you the poison has been telling me, and he wants me to tell you, that you are not to talk much; talking, he says, increases heat, and this is apt to interfere with the action of the poison; persons who excite themselves are sometimes obliged to take a second or even a third dose.

Then, said Socrates, let him mind his business and be prepared to give the poison twice or even thrice if necessary; that is all.

I knew quite well what you would say, replied Crito; but I was obliged to satisfy him.

Never mind him, he said.

And now, O my judges, I desire to prove to you that the real philosopher has reason to be of good cheer when he is about to die, and that after death he may hope to obtain the greatest good in the other world. And how this may be, Simmias and Cebes, I will endeavour to explain. For I deem that the true votary of philosophy is likely to be misunderstood by other men; they do not perceive that he is always pursuing death and dying; and if this be so, and he has had the desire of death all his life long, why when his time comes should he repine at that which he has been always pursuing and desiring?

Simmias said laughingly: Though not in a laughing humour, you have made me laugh, Socrates; for I cannot help thinking that the many when they hear your words will say how truly you have described philosophers, and our people at home will likewise say that the life which philosophers desire is in reality death, and that they have found them out to be deserving of the death which they desire.

And they are right, Simmias, in thinking so, with the exception of the words 'they have found them out'; for they have not found out either what is the nature of that death which the true philosopher deserves, or how he deserves or desires death. But enough of them:— let us discuss the matter among ourselves. Do we believe that there is such a thing as death?

To be sure, replied Simmias.

Is it not the separation of soul and body? And to be dead is the completion of this; when the soul exists in herself, and is released from the body and the body is released from the soul, what is this but death?

Just so, he replied.

There is another question, which will probably throw light on our present enquiry if you and I can agree about it:—Ought the philosopher to care about the pleasures—if they are to be called pleasures—of eating and drinking?

Certainly not, answered Simmias.

And what about the pleasures of love—should he care for them?

By no means.

And will he think much of the other ways of indulging the body, for example, the acquisition of costly raiment, or sandals, or other adornments of the body? Instead of caring about them, does he not rather despise anything more than nature needs? What do you say?

I should say that the true philosopher would despise them.

Would you not say that he is entirely concerned with the soul and not with the body? He would like, as far as he can, to get away from the body and to turn to the soul.

Quite true.

In matters of this sort philosophers, above all other men, may be observed in every sort of way to dissever the soul from the communion of the body.

Very true.

Whereas, Simmias, the rest of the world are of opinion that to him who has no sense of pleasure and no part in bodily pleasure, life is not worth having; and that he who is indifferent about them is as good as dead.

That is also true.

What again shall we say of the actual acquirement of knowledge?—is the body, if invited to share in the enquiry, a hinderer or a helper? I mean to say, have sight and hearing any truth in them? Are they not, as the poets are always telling us, inaccurate witnesses? and yet, if even they are inaccurate and indistinct, what is to be said of the other senses?—for you will allow that they are the best of them?

Certainly, he replied.

Then when does the soul attain truth?—for in attempting to consider anything in company with the body she is obviously deceived.

True.

Then must not true existence be revealed to her in thought, if at all?

Yes.

And thought is best when the mind is gathered into herself and none of these things trouble her—neither sounds nor sights nor pain nor any pleasure,—when she takes leave of the body, and has as little as possible to do with it, when she has no bodily sense or desire, but is aspiring after true being?

Certainly.

And in this the philosopher dishonours the body; his soul runs away from his body and desires to be alone and by herself?

That is true.

Well, but there is another thing, Simmias: Is there or is there not an absolute justice?

Assuredly there is.

And an absolute beauty and absolute good?

Of course.

But did you ever behold any of them with your eyes?

Certainly not.

Or did you ever reach them with any other bodily sense?—and I speak not of these alone, but of absolute greatness, and health, and strength, and of the essence or true nature of everything. Has the reality of them ever been perceived by you through the bodily organs? or rather, is not the nearest approach to the knowledge of their several natures made by him who so orders his intellectual vision as to have the most exact conception of the essence of each thing which he considers?

Certainly.

And he attains to the purest knowledge of them who goes to each with the mind alone, not introducing or intruding in the act of thought sight or any other sense together with reason, but with the very light of the mind in her own clearness searches into the very truth of each; he who has got rid, as far as he can, of eyes and ears and, so to speak, of the whole body, these being in his opinion distracting elements which when they infect the soul hinder her from acquiring truth and knowledge —who, if not he, is likely to attain to the knowledge of true being?

What you say has a wonderful truth in it, Socrates, replied Simmias.

And when real philosophers consider all these things, will they not be led to make a reflection which they will express in words something like the following? 'Have we not found,' they will say, 'a path of thought which seems to bring us and our argument to the conclusion, that while we are in the body, and while the soul is infected with the evils of the body, our desire will not be satisfied? and our desire is of the truth. For the body is a source of endless trouble to us by reason of the mere requirement of food; and is liable also to diseases which overtake and impede us in the search after true being: it fills us full of loves, and lusts, and fears, and fancies of all kinds, and endless foolery, and in fact, as men say, takes away from us the power of thinking at all. Whence come wars, and fightings, and factions? whence but from the body and the lusts of the body? Wars are occasioned by the love of money, and money has to be acquired for the sake and in the service of the body;

and by reason of all these impediments we have no time to give to philosophy; and, last and worst of all, even if we are at leisure and betake ourselves to some speculation, the body is always breaking in upon us, causing turmoil and confusion in our enquiries, and so amazing us that we are prevented from seeing the truth. It has been proved to us by experience that if we would have pure knowledge of anything we must be quit of the body —the soul in herself must behold things in themselves: and then we shall attain the wisdom which we desire, and of which we say that we are lovers; not while we live, but after death; for if while in company with the body, the soul cannot have pure knowledge, one of two things follows—either knowledge is not to be attained at all, or, if at all, after death. For then, and not till then, the soul will be parted from the body and exist in herself alone. In this present life, I reckon that we make the nearest approach to knowledge when we have the least possible intercourse or communion with the body, and are not surfeited with the bodily nature, but keep ourselves pure until the hour when God himself is pleased to release us. And thus having got rid of the foolishness of the body we shall be pure and hold converse with the pure, and know of ourselves the clear light everywhere, which is no other than the light of truth.' For the impure are not permitted to approach the pure. These are the sort of words, Simmias, which the true lovers of knowledge cannot help saying to one another, and thinking. You would agree; would you not?

Undoubtedly, Socrates.

But, O my friend, if this be true, there is great reason to hope that, going whither I go, when I have come to the end of my journey, I shall attain that which has been the pursuit of my life. And therefore I go on my way rejoicing, and not I only, but every other man who believes that his mind has been made ready and that he is in a manner purified.

Certainly, replied Simmias.

And what is purification but the separation of the soul from the body, as I was saying before; the habit of the soul gathering and collecting herself into herself from all sides out of the body; the dwelling in her own place alone, as in another life, so also in this, as far as she can;—the release of the soul from the chains of the body?

Very true, he said.

And this separation and release of the soul from the body is termed death?

To be sure, he said.

And the true philosophers, and they only, are ever seeking to release the soul. Is not the separation and release of the soul from the body their especial study?

That is true.

And, as I was saying at first, there would be a ridiculous contradiction in men studying to live as nearly as they can in a state of death, and yet repining when it comes upon them.

Clearly.

And the true philosophers, Simmias, are always occupied in the practice of dying, wherefore also to them least of all men is death terrible. Look at the matter thus:—if they have been in every way the enemies of the body, and are wanting to be alone with the soul, when this desire of theirs is granted, how inconsistent would they be if they trembled and repined, instead of rejoicing at their departure to that place where, when they arrive, they hope to gain that which in life they desired—and this was wisdom—and at the same time to be rid of the company of their enemy. Many a man has been willing to go to the world below animated by the hope of seeing there an earthly love, or wife, or son, and conversing with them. And will he who is a true lover of wisdom, and is strongly persuaded in like manner that only in the world below he can worthily enjoy her, still repine at death? Will he not depart with joy? Surely he will, O my friend, if he be a true philosopher. For he will have a firm conviction that there, and there only, he can find wisdom in her purity. And if this be true, he would be very absurd, as I was saying, if he were afraid of death.

He would indeed, replied Simmias.

And when you see a man who is repining at the approach of death, is not his reluctance a sufficient proof that he is not a lover of wisdom, but a lover of the body, and probably at the same time a lover of either money or power, or both?

Quite so, he replied.

And is not courage, Simmias, a quality which is specially characteristic of the philosopher?

Certainly.

There is temperance again, which even by the vulgar is supposed to consist in the control and regulation of the passions, and in the sense of superiority to them— is not temperance a virtue belonging to those only who despise the body, and who pass their lives in philosophy?

Most assuredly.

For the courage and temperance of other men, if you will consider them, are really a contradiction.

How so?

Well, he said, you are aware that death is regarded by men in general as a great evil.

Very true, he said.

And do not courageous men face death because they are afraid of yet greater evils?

That is quite true.

Then all but the philosophers are courageous only from fear, and because they are afraid; and yet that a man should be courageous from fear, and because he is a coward, is surely a strange thing.

Very true.

And are not the temperate exactly in the same case? They are temperate because they are intemperate— which might seem to be a contradiction, but is nevertheless the sort of thing which happens with this foolish temperance. For there are pleasures which they are afraid of losing; and in their desire to keep them, they abstain from some pleasures, because they are overcome by others; and although to be conquered by pleasure is called by men intemperance, to them the conquest of pleasure consists in being conquered by pleasure. And that is what I mean by saying that, in a sense, they are made temperate through intemperance.

Such appears to be the case.

Yet the exchange of one fear or pleasure or pain for another fear or pleasure or pain, and of the greater for the less, as if they were coins, is not the exchange of virtue. O my blessed Simmias, is there not one true coin for which all things ought to be exchanged?—and that is wisdom; and only in exchange for this, and in company with this, is anything truly bought or sold, whether courage or temperance or justice. And is not all true virtue the companion of wisdom, no matter what fears or pleasures or other similar goods or evils may or may not attend her? But the virtue which is made up of these goods, when they are severed from wisdom and exchanged with one another, is a shadow of virtue only, nor is there any freedom or health or truth in her; but in the true exchange there is a purging away of all these things, and temperance, and justice, and courage, and wisdom herself are the purgation of them. The founders of the mysteries would appear to have had a real meaning, and were not talking nonsense when they intimated in a figure long ago that he who passes unsanctified and uninitiated into the world below will lie in a slough, but that he who arrives there after initiation and purification will dwell with the gods. For 'many,' as they say in the mysteries, 'are the thyrsus-bearers, but few are the mystics,'—meaning, as I interpret the words, 'the true philosophers.' In the number of whom, during my whole life, I have been seeking, according to my ability, to find a place;—whether I have sought in a right way or not, and whether I have succeeded or not, I shall truly know in a little while, if God will, when I myself arrive in the other world—such is my belief. And therefore I maintain that I am right, Simmias and Cebes, in not grieving or repining at parting from you and my masters in this world, for I believe that I shall equally find good masters and friends in another world. But most men do not believe this saying; if then I succeed in convincing you by my defence better than I did the Athenian judges, it will be well.

Cebes answered: I agree, Socrates, in the greater part of what you say. But in what concerns the soul, men are apt to be incredulous; they fear that when she has left the body her place may be nowhere, and that on the very day of death she may perish and come to an end— immediately on her release from the body, issuing forth dispersed like smoke or air and in her flight vanishing away into nothingness. If she could only be collected into herself after she has obtained release from the evils of which you were speaking, there would be good reason to hope, Socrates, that what you say is true. But surely it requires a great deal of argument and many proofs to show that when the man is dead his soul yet exists, and has any force or intelligence.

True, Cebes, said Socrates; and shall I suggest that we converse a little of the probabilities of these things?

I am sure, said Cebes, that I should greatly like to know your opinion about them.

I reckon, said Socrates, that no one who heard me now, not even if he were one of my old enemies, the Comic poets, would accuse me of idle talking about matters in which I have no concern:—If you please, then, we will proceed with the enquiry.

Suppose we consider the question whether the souls of men after death are or are not in the world below. There comes into my mind an ancient doctrine which affirms that they go from hence into the other world, and returning hither, are born again from the dead. Now if it be true that the living come from the dead, then our souls must exist in the other world, for if not, how could they have been born again? And this would be conclusive, if there were any real evidence that the living are only born from the dead; but if this is not so, then other arguments will have to be adduced.

Very true, replied Cebes.

Then let us consider the whole question, not in relation to man only, but in relation to animals generally, and to plants, and to everything of which there is generation, and the proof will be easier. Are not all things which have opposites generated out of their opposites? I mean such things as good and evil, just and unjust— and there are innumerable other opposites which are generated out of opposites. And I want to show that in all opposites there is of necessity a similar alternation; I mean to say, for example, that anything which becomes greater must become greater after being less.

True.

And that which becomes less must have been once greater and then have become less.

Yes.

And the weaker is generated from the stronger, and the swifter from the slower.

Very true.

And the worse is from the better, and the more just is from the more unjust.

Of course.

And is this true of all opposites? and are we convinced that all of them are generated out of opposites?

Yes.

And in this universal opposition of all things, are there not also two intermediate processes which are ever going on, from one to the other opposite, and back again; where there is a greater and a less there is also an intermediate process of increase and diminution, and that which grows is said to wax, and that which decays to wane?

Yes, he said.

And there are many other processes, such as division and composition, cooling and heating, which equally involve a passage into and out of one another. And this necessarily holds of all opposites, even though not always expressed in words—they are really generated out of one another, and there is a passing or process from one to the other of them?

Very true, he replied.

Well, and is there not an opposite of life, as sleep is the opposite of waking?

True, he said.

And what is it?

Death, he answered.

And these, if they are opposites, are generated the one

from the other, and have their two intermediate processes also?

Of course.

Now, said Socrates, I will analyze one of the two pairs of opposites which I have mentioned to you, and also its intermediate processes, and you shall analyze the other to me. One of them I term sleep, the other waking. The state of sleep is opposed to the state of waking, and out of sleeping waking is generated, and out of waking, sleeping; and the process of generation is in the one case falling asleep, and in the other waking up. Do you agree?

I entirely agree.

Then, suppose that you analyze life and death to me in the same manner. Is not death opposed to life?

Yes.

And they are generated one from the other?

Yes.

What is generated from the living?

The dead.

And what from the dead?

I can only say in answer—the living.

Then the living, whether things or persons, Cebes, are generated from the dead?

That is clear, he replied.

Then the inference is that our souls exist in the world below?

That is true.

And one of the two processes or generations is visible —for surely the act of dying is visible?

Surely, he said.

What then is to be the result? Shall we exclude the opposite process? and shall we suppose nature to walk on one leg only? Must we not rather assign to death some corresponding process of generation?

Certainly, he replied.

And what is that process?

Return to life.

And return to life, if there be such a thing, is the birth of the dead into the world of the living?

Quite true.

Then here is a new way by which we arrive at the conclusion that the living come from the dead, just as the dead come from the living; and this, if true, affords a most certain proof that the souls of the dead exist in some place out of which they come again.

Yes, Socrates, he said; the conclusion seems to flow necessarily out of our previous admissions.

And that these admissions were not unfair, Cebes, he said, may be shown, I think, as follows: If generation were in a straight line only, and there were no compensation or circle in nature, no turn or return of elements into their opposites, then you know that all things would at last have the same form and pass into the same state, and there would be no more generation of them.

What do you mean? he said.

A simple thing enough, which I will illustrate by the case of sleep, he replied. You know that if there were no alternation of sleeping and waking, the tale of the sleeping Endymion would in the end have no meaning, because all other things would be asleep too, and he would not be distinguishable from the rest. Or if there were composition only, and no division of substances, then the chaos of Anaxagoras would come again. And in like manner, my dear Cebes, if all things which partook of life were to die, and after they were dead remained in the form of death, and did not come to life again, all would at last die, and nothing would be alive —what other result could there be? For if the living spring from any other things, and they too die, must not all things at last be swallowed up in death?

There is no escape, Socrates, said Cebes; and to me your argument seems to be absolutely true.

Yes, he said, Cebes, it is and must be so, in my opinion; and we have not been deluded in making these admissions; but I am confident that there truly is such a thing as living again, and that the living spring from the dead, and that the souls of the dead are in existence, and that the good souls have a better portion than the evil.

Cebes added: Your favourite doctrine, Socrates, that knowledge is simply recollection, if true, also necessarily implies a previous time in which we have learned that which we now recollect. But this would be impossible unless our soul had been in some place before existing in the form of man; here then is another proof of the soul's immortality.

But tell me, Cebes, said Simmias, interposing, what arguments are urged in favour of this doctrine of recollection. I am not very sure at the moment that I remember them.

One excellent proof, said Cebes, is afforded by questions. If you put a question to a person in a right way, he will give a true answer of himself, but how could he do this unless there were knowledge and right reason already in him? And this is most clearly shown when he is taken to a diagram or to anything of that sort.

But if, said Socrates, you are still incredulous, Simmias, I would ask you whether you may not agree with me when you look at the matter in another way;—I mean, if you are still incredulous as to whether knowledge is recollection?

Incredulous I am not, said Simmias; but I want to

have this doctrine of recollection brought to my own recollection, and, from what Cebes has said, I am beginning to recollect and be convinced: but I should still like to hear what you were going to say.

This is what I would say, he replied:—We should agree, if I am not mistaken, that what a man recollects he must have known at some previous time.

Very true.

And what is the nature of this knowledge or recollection? I mean to ask, Whether a person who, having seen or heard or in any way perceived anything, knows not only that, but has a conception of something else which is the subject, not of the same but of some other kind of knowledge, may not be fairly said to recollect that of which he has the conception?

What do you mean?

I mean what I may illustrate by the following instance:—The knowledge of a lyre is not the same as the knowledge of a man?

True.

And yet what is the feeling of lovers when they recognize a lyre, or a garment, or anything else which the beloved has been in the habit of using? Do not they, from knowing the lyre, form in the mind's eye an image of the youth to whom the lyre belongs? And this is recollection. In like manner any one who sees Simmias may remember Cebes; and there are endless examples of the same thing.

Endless, indeed, replied Simmias.

And recollection is most commonly a process of recovering that which has been already forgotten through time and inattention.

Very true, he said.

Well; and may you not also from seeing the picture

of a horse or a lyre remember a man? and from the picture of Simmias, you may be led to remember Cebes?

True.

Or you may also be led to the recollection of Simmias himself?

Quite so.

And in all these cases, the recollection may be derived from things either like or unlike?

It may be.

And when the recollection is derived from like things, then another consideration is sure to arise, which is— whether the likeness in any degree falls short or not of that which is recollected?

Very true, he said.

And shall we proceed a step further, and affirm that there is such a thing as equality, not of one piece of wood or stone with another, but that, over and above this, there is absolute equality? Shall we say so?

Say so, yes, replied Simmias, and swear to it, with all the confidence in life.

And do we know the nature of this absolute essence?

To be sure, he said.

And whence did we obtain our knowledge? Did we not see equalities of material things, such as pieces of wood and stones, and gather from them the idea of an equality which is different from them? For you will acknowledge that there is a difference. Or look at the matter in another way:—Do not the same pieces of wood or stone appear at one time equal, and at another time unequal?

That is certain.

But are real equals ever unequal? or is the idea of equality the same as of inequality?

Impossible, Socrates.

Then these (so-called) equals are not the same with the idea of equality?

I should say, clearly not, Socrates.

And yet from these equals, although differing from the idea of equality, you conceived and attained that idea?

Very true, he said.

Which might be like, or might be unlike them?

Yes.

But that makes no difference: whenever from seeing one thing you conceived another, whether like or unlike, there must surely have been an act of recollection?

Very true.

But what would you say of equal portions of wood and stone, or other material equals? and what is the impression produced by them? Are they equals in the same sense in which absolute equality is equal? or do they fall short of this perfect equality in a measure?

Yes, he said, in a very great measure too.

And must we not allow, that when I or any one, looking at any object, observes that the thing which he sees aims at being some other thing, but falls short of, and cannot be, that other thing, but is inferior, he who makes this observation must have had a previous knowledge of that to which the other, although similar, was inferior?

Certainly.

And has not this been our own case in the matter of equals and of absolute equality?

Precisely.

Then we must have known equality previously to the time when we first saw the material equals, and reflected that all these apparent equals strive to attain absolute equality, but fall short of it?

Very true.

And we recognize also that this absolute equality has

only been known, and can only be known, through the
medium of sight or touch, or of some other of the senses,
which are all alike in this respect?

Yes, Socrates, as far as the argument is concerned,
one of them is the same as the other.

From the senses then is derived the knowledge that
all sensible things aim at an absolute equality of which
they fall short?

Yes.

Then before we began to see or hear or perceive in
any way, we must have had a knowledge of absolute
equality, or we could not have referred to that standard
the equals which are derived from the senses?—for to
that they all aspire, and of that they fall short.

No other inference can be drawn from the previous
statements.

And did we not see and hear and have the use of
our other senses as soon as we were born?

Certainly.

Then we must have acquired the knowledge of equality at some previous time?

Yes.

That is to say, before we were born, I suppose?

True.

And if we acquired this knowledge before we were
born, and were born having the use of it, then we also
knew before we were born and at the instant of birth
not only the equal or the greater or the less, but all other
ideas; for we are not speaking only of equality, but of
beauty, goodness, justice, holiness, and of all which we
stamp with the name of essence in the dialectical process, both when we ask and when we answer questions.
Of all this we may certainly affirm that we acquired the
knowledge before birth?

We may.

But if, after having acquired, we have not forgotten what in each case we acquired, then we must always have come into life having knowledge, and shall always continue to know as long as life lasts—for knowing is the acquiring and retaining knowledge and not forgetting. Is not forgetting, Simmias, just the losing of knowledge?

Quite true, Socrates.

But if the knowledge which we acquired before birth was lost by us at birth, and if afterwards by the use of the senses we recovered what we previously knew, will not the process which we call learning be a recovering of the knowledge which is natural to us, and may not this be rightly termed recollection?

Very true.

So much is clear—that when we perceive something, either by the help of sight, or hearing, or some other sense, from that perception we are able to obtain a notion of some other thing like or unlike which is associated with it but has been forgotten. Whence, as I was saying, one of two alternatives follows:—either we had this knowledge at birth, and continued to know through life; or, after birth, those who are said to learn only remember, and learning is simply recollection.

Yes, that is quite true, Socrates.

And which alternative, Simmias, do you prefer? Had we the knowledge at our birth, or did we recollect the things which we knew previously to our birth?

I cannot decide at the moment.

At any rate you can decide whether he who has knowledge will or will not be able to render an account of his knowledge? What do you say?

Certainly, he will.

But do you think that every man is able to give an

account of these very matters about which we are speaking?

Would that they could, Socrates, but I rather fear that to-morrow, at this time, there will no longer be any one alive who is able to give an account of them such as ought to be given.

Then you are not of opinion, Simmias, that all men know these things?

Certainly not.

They are in process of recollecting that which they learned before?

Certainly.

But when did our souls acquire this knowledge?—not since we were born as men?

Certainly not.

And therefore, previously?

Yes.

Then, Simmias, our souls must also have existed without bodies before they were in the form of man, and must have had intelligence.

Unless indeed you suppose, Socrates, that these notions are given us at the very moment of birth; for this is the only time which remains.

Yes, my friend, but if so, when do we lose them? for they are not in us when we are born—that is admitted. Do we lose them at the moment of receiving them, or if not at what other time?

No, Socrates, I perceive that I was unconsciously talking nonsense.

Then may we not say, Simmias, that if, as we are always repeating, there is an absolute beauty, and goodness, and an absolute essence of all things; and if to this, which is now discovered to have existed in our former state, we refer all our sensations, and with this compare them, finding these ideas to be pre-existent and our inborn possession—then our souls must have had a prior existence, but if not, there would be no force in the argument? There is the same proof that these ideas must have existed before we were born, as that our souls existed before we were born; and if not the ideas, then not the souls.

Yes, Socrates; I am convinced that there is precisely the same necessity for the one as for the other; and the argument retreats successfully to the position that the existence of the soul before birth cannot be separated from the existence of the essence of which you speak. For there is nothing which to my mind is so patent as that beauty, goodness, and the other notions of which you were just now speaking, have a most real and absolute existence; and I am satisfied with the proof.

Well, but is Cebes equally satisfied? for I must convince him too.

I think, said Simmias, that Cebes is satisfied: although he is the most incredulous of mortals, yet I believe that he is sufficiently convinced of the existence of the soul before birth. But that after death the soul will continue to exist is not yet proven even to my own satisfaction. I cannot get rid of the feeling of the many to which Cebes was referring—the feeling that when the man dies the soul will be dispersed, and that this may be the extinction of her. For admitting that she may have been born elsewhere, and framed out of other elements, and was in existence before entering the human body, why after having entered in and gone out again may she not herself be destroyed and come to an end?

Very true, Simmias, said Cebes; about half of what was required has been proven; to wit, that our souls existed before we were born:—that the soul will exist after death as well as before birth is the other half of which the proof is still wanting, and has to be supplied; when that is given the demonstration will be complete.

But that proof, Simmias and Cebes, has been already given, said Socrates, if you put the two arguments together—I mean this and the former one, in which we admitted that everything living is born of the dead. For if the soul exists before birth, and in coming to life and being born can be born only from death and dying, must she not after death continue to exist, since she has to be born again?—Surely the proof which you desire has been already furnished. Still I suspect that you and Simmias would be glad to probe the argument further. Like children, you are haunted with a fear that when the soul leaves the body, the wind may really blow her away and scatter her; especially if a man should happen to die in a great storm and not when the sky is calm.

Cebes answered with a smile: Then, Socrates, you must argue us out of our fears—and yet, strictly speaking, they are not our fears, but there is a child within us to whom death is a sort of hobgoblin: him too we must persuade not to be afraid when he is alone in the dark.

Socrates said: Let the voice of the charmer be applied daily until you have charmed away the fear.

And where shall we find a good charmer of our fears, Socrates, when you are gone?

Hellas, he replied, is a large place, Cebes, and has many good men, and there are barbarous races not a few: seek for him among them all, far and wide, sparing neither pains nor money; for there is no better way of spending your money. And you must seek among yourselves too; for you will not find others better able to make the search.

The search, replied Cebes, shall certainly be made. And now, if you please, let us return to the point of the argument at which we digressed.

By all means, replied Socrates; what else should I please?

Very good.

Must we not, said Socrates, ask ourselves what that is which, as we imagine, is liable to be scattered, and about which we fear? and what again is that about which we have no fear? And then we may proceed further to enquire whether that which suffers dispersion is or is not of the nature of soul—our hopes and fears as to our own souls will turn upon the answers to these questions.

Very true, he said.

Now the compound or composite may be supposed to be naturally capable, as of being compounded, so also of being dissolved; but that which is uncompounded, and that only, must be, if anything is, indissoluble.

Yes; I should imagine so, said Cebes.

And the uncompounded may be assumed to be the same and unchanging, whereas the compound is always changing and never the same.

I agree, he said.

Then now let us return to the previous discussion. Is that idea or essence, which in the dialectical process we define as essence or true existence—whether essence of equality, beauty, or anything else—are these essences, I say, liable at times to some degree of change? or are they each of them always what they are, having the same simple self-existent and unchanging forms, not admitting of variation at all, or in any way, or at any time?

They must be always the same, Socrates, replied Cebes.

And what would you say of the many beautiful—whether men or horses or garments or any other things which are named by the same names and may be called equal or beautiful,—are they all unchanging and the same always, or quite the reverse? May they not rather be described as almost always changing and hardly ever the same, either with themselves or with one another?

The latter, replied Cebes; they are always in a state of change.

And these you can touch and see and perceive with the senses, but the unchanging things you can only perceive with the mind—they are invisible and are not seen?

That is very true, he said.

Well then, added Socrates, let us suppose that there are two sorts of existences—one seen, the other unseen.

Let us suppose them.

The seen is the changing, and the unseen is the unchanging?

That may be also supposed.

And, further, is not one part of us body, another part soul?

To be sure.

And to which class is the body more alike and akin?

Clearly to the seen—no one can doubt that.

And is the soul seen or not seen?

Not by man, Socrates.

And what we mean by 'seen' and 'not seen' is that which is or is not visible to the eye of man?

Yes, to the eye of man.

And is the soul seen or not seen?

Not seen.

Unseen then?

Yes.

Then the soul is more like to the unseen, and the body to the seen?

That follows necessarily, Socrates.

And were we not saying long ago that the soul when using the body as an instrument of perception, that is to say, when using the sense of sight or hearing or some other sense (for the meaning of perceiving through the body is perceiving through the senses)—were we not saying that the soul too is then dragged by the body into the region of the changeable, and wanders and is confused; the world spins round her, and she is like a drunkard, when she touches change?

Very true.

But when returning into herself she reflects, then she passes into the other world, the region of purity, and eternity, and immortality, and unchangeableness, which are her kindred, and with them she ever lives, when she is by herself and is not let or hindered; then she ceases from her erring ways, and being in communion with the unchanging is unchanging. And this state of the soul is called wisdom?

That is well and truly said, Socrates, he replied.

And to which class is the soul more nearly alike and akin, as far as may be inferred from this argument, as well as from the preceding one?

I think, Socrates, that, in the opinion of every one who follows the argument, the soul will be infinitely more like the unchangeable—even the most stupid person will not deny that.

And the body is more like the changing?

Yes.

Yet once more consider the matter in another light: When the soul and the body are united, then nature orders the soul to rule and govern, and the body to obey and serve. Now which of these two functions is akin to the divine? and which to the mortal? Does not the divine appear to you to be that which naturally orders and rules, and the mortal to be that which is subject and servant?

True.

And which does the soul resemble?

The soul resembles the divine, and the body the mortal—there can be no doubt of that, Socrates.

Then reflect, Cebes: of all which has been said is not this the conclusion?—that the soul is in the very likeness of the divine, and immortal, and intellectual, and uniform, and indissoluble, and unchangeable; and that the body is in the very likeness of the human, and mortal, and unintellectual, and multiform, and dissoluble, and changeable. Can this, my dear Cebes, be denied?

It cannot.

But if it be true, then is not the body liable to speedy dissolution? and is not the soul almost or altogether indissoluble?

Certainly.

And do you further observe, that after a man is dead, the body, or visible part of him, which is lying in the visible world, and is called a corpse, and would naturally be dissolved and decomposed and dissipated, is not dissolved or decomposed at once, but may remain for some time, nay even for a long time, if the constitution be sound at the time of death, and the season of the year favourable? For the body when shrunk and embalmed, as the manner is in Egypt, may remain almost entire through infinite ages; and even in decay, there are still some portions, such as the bones and ligaments, which are practically indestructible:—Do you agree?

Yes.

And is it likely that the soul, which is invisible, in passing to the place of the true Hades, which like her is invisible, and pure, and noble, and on her way to the good and wise God, whither, if God will, my soul is also soon to go,—that soul, I repeat, if this be her nature and origin, will be blown away and destroyed immediately on quitting the body, as the many say? That can never be, my dear Simmias and Cebes. The truth rather is, that the soul which is pure at departing and draws after her no bodily taint, having never voluntarily during life had connection with the body, which she is ever avoiding, herself gathered into herself;—and making such abstraction her perpetual study—which means that she has been a true disciple of philosophy; and therefore has in fact been always engaged in the practice of dying? For is not philosophy the study of death?—

Certainly—

That soul, I say, herself invisible, departs to the invisible world—to the divine and immortal and rational: thither arriving, she is secure of bliss and is released from the error and folly of men, their fears and wild passions and all other human ills, and for ever dwells, as they say of the initiated, in company with the gods. Is not this true, Cebes?

Yes, said Cebes, beyond a doubt.

But the soul which has been polluted, and is impure at the time of her departure, and is the companion and servant of the body always, and is in love with and fascinated by the body and by the desires and pleasures of the body, until she is led to believe that the truth only exists in a bodily form, which a man may touch and see and taste, and use for the purposes of his lusts,—the soul, I mean, accustomed to hate and fear and avoid the intellectual principle, which to the bodily eye is dark and invisible, and can be attained only by philosophy;—do you suppose that such a soul will depart pure and unalloyed?

Impossible, he replied.

She is held fast by the corporeal, which the continual association and constant care of the body have wrought into her nature.

Very true.

And this corporeal element, my friend, is heavy and weighty and earthy, and is that element of sight by which a soul is depressed and dragged down again into the visible world, because she is afraid of the invisible and of the world below—prowling about tombs and sepulchres, near which, as they tell us, are seen certain ghostly apparitions of souls which have not departed pure, but are cloyed with sight and therefore visible.[1]

That is very likely, Socrates.

Yes, that is very likely, Cebes; and these must be the souls, not of the good, but of the evil, which are compelled to wander about such places in payment of the penalty of their former evil way of life; and they continue to wander until through the craving after the corporeal which never leaves them, they are imprisoned finally in another body. And they may be supposed to find their prisons in the same natures which they have had in their former lives.

What natures do you mean, Socrates?

What I mean is that men who have followed after gluttony, and wantonness, and drunkenness, and have had no thought of avoiding them, would pass into asses and animals of that sort. What do you think?

I think such an opinion to be exceedingly probable.

And those who have chosen the portion of injustice, and tyranny, and violence, will pass into wolves, or into hawks and kites;—whither else can we suppose them to go?

Yes, said Cebes; with such natures, beyond question.

---

[1] Compare Milton, *Comus*, 463 foll.

'But when lust,
By unchaste looks, loose gestures, and foul talk
But most by lewd and lavish act of sin,
Lets in defilements to the inward parts,
The soul grows clotted by contagion,
Imbodies, and imbrutes, till she quite lose,
The divine property of her first being.
Such are those thick and gloomy shadows damp
Oft seen in charnel vaults and sepulchres,
Lingering, and sitting by a new made grave,
As loath to leave the body that it lov'd,
And linked itself by carnal sensuality
To a degenerate and degraded state.'

And there is no difficulty, he said, in assigning to all of them places answering to their several natures and propensities?

There is not, he said.

Some are happier than others; and the happiest both in themselves and in the place to which they go are those who have practised the civil and social virtues which are called temperance and justice, and are acquired by habit and attention without philosophy and mind.[1]

Why are they the happiest?

Because they may be expected to pass into some gentle and social kind which is like their own, such as bees or wasps or ants, or back again into the form of man, and just and moderate men may be supposed to spring from them.

Very likely.

No one who has not studied philosophy and who is not entirely pure at the time of his departure is allowed to enter the company of the Gods, but the lover of knowledge only. And this is the reason, Simmias and Cebes, why the true votaries of philosophy abstain from all fleshly lusts, and hold out against them and refuse to give themselves up to them,—not because they fear poverty or the ruin of their families, like the lovers of money, and the world in general; nor like the lovers of power and honour, because they dread the dishonour or disgrace of evil deeds.

No, Socrates, that would not become them, said Cebes.

No indeed, he replied; and therefore they who have any care of their own souls, and do not merely live moulding and fashioning the body, say farewell to all this; they will not walk in the ways of the blind: and when philosophy offers them purification and release

[1] Cp. Rep. x. 619 C.

from evil, they feel that they ought not to resist her
influence, and whither she leads they turn and follow.

What do you mean, Socrates?

I will tell you, he said. The lovers of knowledge are
conscious that the soul was simply fastened and glued to
the body—until philosophy received her, she could only
view real existence through the bars of a prison, not in
and through herself; she was wallowing in the mire of
every sort of ignorance, and by reason of lust had become the principal accomplice in her own captivity.
This was her original state; and then, as I was saying,
and as the lovers of knowledge are well aware, philosophy, seeing how terrible was her confinement, of
which she was to herself the cause, received and gently
comforted her and sought to release her, pointing out
that the eye and the ear and the other senses are full
of deception, and persuading her to retire from them,
and abstain from all but the necessary use of them, and
be gathered up and collected into herself, bidding her
trust in herself and her own pure apprehension of pure
existence, and to mistrust whatever comes to her through
other channels and is subject to variation; for such
things are visible and tangible, but what she sees in her
own nature is intelligible and invisible. And the soul of
the true philosopher thinks that she ought not to resist
this deliverance, and therefore abstains from pleasures
and desires and pains and fears, as far as she is able;
reflecting that when a man has great joys or sorrows
or fears or desires, he suffers from them, not merely
the sort of evil which might be anticipated—as for example, the loss of his health or property which he has
sacrificed to his lusts—but an evil greater far, which is
the greatest and worst of all evils, and one of which he
never thinks.

What is it, Socrates? said Cebes.

The evil is that when the feeling of pleasure or pain is most intense, every soul of man imagines the objects of this intense feeling to be then plainest and truest: but this is not so, they are really the things of sight.

Very true.

And is not this the state in which the soul is most enthralled by the body?

How so?

Why, because each pleasure and pain is a sort of nail which nails and rivets the soul to the body, until she becomes like the body, and believes that to be true which the body affirms to be true; and from agreeing with the body and having the same delights she is obliged to have the same habits and haunts, and is not likely ever to be pure at her departure to the world below, but is always infected by the body; and so she sinks into another body and there germinates and grows, and has therefore no part in the communion of the divine and pure and simple.

Most true, Socrates, answered Cebes.

And this, Cebes, is the reason why the true lovers of knowledge are temperate and brave; and not for the reason which the world gives.

Certainly not.

Certainly not! The soul of a philosopher will reason in quite another way; she will not ask philosophy to release her in order that when released she may deliver herself up again to the thraldom of pleasures and pains, doing a work only to be undone again, weaving instead of unweaving her Penelope's web. But she will calm passion, and follow reason, and dwell in the contemplation of her, beholding the true and divine (which is not matter of opinion), and thence deriving nourishment. Thus she seeks to live while she lives, and after death she hopes to go to her own kindred and to that which is like her, and to be freed from human ills. Never fear, Simmias and Cebes, that a soul which has been thus nurtured and has had these pursuits, will at her departure from the body be scattered and blown away by the winds and be nowhere and nothing.

When Socrates had done speaking, for a considerable time there was silence; he himself appeared to be meditating, as most of us were, on what had been said; only Cebes and Simmias spoke a few words to one another. And Socrates observing them asked what they thought of the argument, and whether there was anything wanting? For, said he, there are many points still open to suspicion and attack, if any one were disposed to sift the matter thoroughly. Should you be considering some other matter I say no more, but if you are still in doubt do not hesitate to say exactly what you think, and let us have anything better which you can suggest; and if you think that I can be of any use, allow me to help you.

Simmias said: I must confess, Socrates, that doubts did arise in our minds, and each of us was urging and inciting the other to put the question which we wanted to have answered but which neither of us liked to ask, fearing that our importunity might be troublesome at such a time.

Socrates replied with a smile: O Simmias, what are you saying? I am not very likely to persuade other men that I do not regard my present situation as a misfortune, if I cannot even persuade you that I am no worse off now than at any other time in my life. Will you not allow that I have as much of the spirit of prophecy in me as the swans? For they, when they perceive that they must die, having sung all their life long, do then sing more lustily than ever, rejoicing in the thought that they are about to go away to the god whose

ministers they are. But men, because they are themselves afraid of death, slanderously affirm of the swans
that they sing a lament at the last, not considering that
no bird sings when cold, or hungry, or in pain, not even
the nightingale, nor the swallow, nor yet the hoopoe;
which are said indeed to tune a lay of sorrow, although
I do not believe this to be true of them any more than
of the swans. But because they are sacred to Apollo,
they have the gift of prophecy, and anticipate the good
things of another world; wherefore they sing and rejoice
in that day more than ever they did before. And I too,
believing myself to be the consecrated servant of the
same God, and the fellow-servant of the swans, and
thinking that I have received from my master gifts of
prophecy which are not inferior to theirs, would not go
out of life less merrily than the swans. Never mind
then, if this be your only objection, but speak and ask
anything which you like, while the eleven magistrates of
Athens allow.

Very good, Socrates, said Simmias; then I will tell
you my difficulty, and Cebes will tell you his. I feel
myself (and I daresay that you have the same feeling),
how hard or rather impossible is the attainment of any
certainty about questions such as these in the present
life. And yet I should deem him a coward who did not
prove what is said about them to the uttermost, or whose
heart failed him before he had examined them on every
side. For he should persevere until he has achieved one
of two things: either he should discover, or be taught the
truth about them; or, if this be impossible, I would have
him take the best and most irrefragable of human theories, and let this be the raft upon which he sails through
life—not without risk, as I admit, if he cannot find some
word of God which will more surely and safely carry
him. And now, as you bid me, I will venture to ques-

tion you, and then I shall not have to reproach myself
hereafter with not having said at the time what I think.
For when I consider the matter, either alone or with
Cebes, the argument does certainly appear to me, Socrates, to be not sufficient.

Socrates answered: I dare say, my friend, that you
may be right, but I should like to know in what respect
the argument is insufficient.

In this respect, replied Simmias:—Suppose a person
to use the same argument about harmony and the lyre—
might he not say that harmony is a thing invisible, incorporeal, perfect, divine, existing in the lyre which is
harmonized, but that the lyre and the strings are matter
and material, composite, earthy, and akin to mortality?
And when some one breaks the lyre, or cuts and rends
the strings, then he who takes this view would argue
as you do, and on the same analogy, that the harmony
survives and has not perished—you cannot imagine, he
would say, that the lyre without the strings, and the
broken strings themselves which are mortal remain, and
yet that the harmony, which is of heavenly and immortal nature and kindred, has perished—perished before
the mortal. The harmony must still be somewhere, and
the wood and strings will decay before anything can
happen to that. The thought, Socrates, must have occurred to your own mind that such is our conception of
the soul; and that when the body is in a manner strung
and held together by the elements of hot and cold, wet
and dry, then the soul is the harmony or due propor-
tionate admixture of them. But if so, whenever the
strings of the body are unduly loosened or overstrained
through disease or other injury, then the soul, though
most divine, like other harmonies of music or of works
of art, of course perishes at once; although the material
remains of the body may last for a considerable time,

until they are either decayed or burnt. And if any one maintans that the soul, being the harmony of the elements of the body, is first to perish in that which is called death, how shall we answer him?

Socrates looked fixedly at us as his manner was, and said with a smile: Simmias has reason on his side; and why does not some one of you who is better able than myself answer him? for there is force in his attack upon me. But perhaps, before we answer him, we had better also hear what Cebes has to say that we may gain time for reflection, and when they have both spoken, we may either assent to them, if there is truth in what they say, or if not, we will maintain our position. Please to tell me then, Cebes, he said, what was the difficulty which troubled you?

Cebes said: I will tell you. My feeling is that the argument is where it was, and open to the same objections which were urged before; for I am ready to admit that the existence of the soul before entering into the bodily form has been very ingeniously, and, if I may say so, quite sufficiently proven; but the existence of the soul after death is still, in my judgment, unproven. Now my objection is not the same as that of Simmias; for I am not disposed to deny that the soul is stronger and more lasting than the body, being of opinion that in all such respects the soul very far excels the body. Well then, says the argument to me, why do you remain unconvinced?—When you see that the weaker continues in existence after the man is dead, will you not admit that the more lasting must also survive during the same period of time? Now I will ask you to consider whether the objection, which, like Simmias, I will express in a figure, is of any weight. The analogy which I will adduce is that of an old weaver, who dies, and after his death somebody says:—He is not dead, he must be alive;

—see, there is the coat which he himself wove and wore, and which remains whole and undecayed. And then he proceeds to ask of some one who is incredulous, whether a man lasts longer, or the coat which is in use and wear; and when he is answered that a man lasts far longer, thinks that he has thus certainly demonstrated the survival of the man, who is the more lasting, because the less lasting remains. But that, Simmias, as I would beg you to remark, is a mistake; any one can see that he who talks thus is talking nonsense. For the truth is, that the weaver aforesaid, having woven and worn many such coats, outlived several of them; and was outlived by the last; but a man is not therefore proved to be slighter and weaker than a coat. Now the relation of the body to the soul may be expressed in a similar figure; and any one may very fairly say in like manner that the soul is lasting, and the body weak and shortlived in comparison. He may argue in like manner that every soul wears out many bodies, especially if a man live many years. While he is alive the body deliquesces and decays, and the soul always weaves another garment and repairs the waste. But of course, whenever the soul perishes, she must have on her last garment, and this will survive her; and then at length, when the soul is dead, the body will show its native weakness, and quickly decompose and pass away. I would therefore rather not rely on the argument from superior strength to prove the continued existence of the soul after death. For granting even more than you affirm to be possible, and acknowledging not only that the soul existed before birth, but also that the souls of some exist, and will continue to exist after death, and will be born and die again and again, and that there is a natural strength in the soul which will hold out and be born many times—nevertheless, we may be still inclined to think that she will weary in the labours of successive births, and may at last succumb in one of her deaths and utterly perish; and this death and dissolution of the body which brings destruction to the soul may be unknown to any of us, for no one of us can have had any experience of it: and if so, then I maintain that he who is confident about death has but a foolish confidence, unless he is able to prove that the soul is altogether immortal and imperishable. But if he cannot prove the soul's immortality, he who is about to die will always have reason to fear that when the body is disunited, the soul also may utterly perish.

All of us, as we afterwards remarked to one another, had an unpleasant feeling at hearing what they said. When we had been so firmly convinced before, now to have our faith shaken seemed to introduce a confusion and uncertainty, not only into the previous argument, but into any future one; either we were incapable of forming a judgment, or there were no grounds of belief.

Ech. There I feel with you—by heaven I do, Phaedo, and when you were speaking, I was beginning to ask myself the same question: What argument can I ever trust again? For what could be more convincing than the argument of Socrates, which has now fallen into discredit? That the soul is a harmony is a doctrine which has always had a wonderful attraction for me, and, when mentioned, came back to me at once, as my own original conviction. And now I must begin again and find another argument which will assure me that when the man is dead the soul survives. Tell me, I implore you, how did Socrates proceed? Did he appear to share the unpleasant feeling which you mention? or did he calmly meet the attack? And did he answer forcibly or feebly? Narrate what passed as exactly as you can.

Phaed. Often, Echecrates, I have wondered at Socrates, but never more than on that occasion. That he

should be able to answer was nothing, but what astonished me was, first, the gentle and pleasant and approving manner in which he received the words of the young
men, and then his quick sense of the wound which had
been inflicted by the argument, and the readiness with
which he healed it. He might be compared to a general
rallying his defeated and broken army, urging them to
accompany him and return to the field of argument.

Ech. What followed?

Phaed. You shall hear, for I was close to him on his
right hand, seated on a sort of stool, and he on a couch
which was a good deal higher. He stroked my head,
and pressed the hair upon my neck—he had a way of
playing with my hair; and then he said: To-morrow,
Phaedo, I suppose that these fair locks of yours will
be severed.

Yes, Socrates, I suppose that they will, I replied.

Not so, if you will take my advice.

What shall I do with them? I said.

To-day, he replied, and not to-morrow, if this argument dies and we cannot bring it to life again, you and
I will both shave our locks: and if I were you, and the
argument got away from me, and I could not hold my
ground against Simmias and Cebes, I would myself take
an oath, like the Argives, not to wear hair any more
until I had renewed the conflict and defeated them.

Yes, I said; but Heracles himself is said not to be a
match for two.

Summon me then, he said, and I will be your Iolaus
until the sun goes down.

I summon you rather, I rejoined, not as Heracles
summoned Iolaus, but as Iolaus might summon Heracles.

That will do as well, he said. But first let us take
care that we avoid a danger.

Of what nature? I said.

Lest we become misologists, he replied: no worse thing can happen to a man than this. For as there are misanthropists or haters of men, there are also misologists or haters of ideas, and both spring from the same cause, which is ignorance of the world. Misanthropy arises out of the too great confidence of inexperience;— you trust a man and think him altogether true and sound and faithful, and then in a little while he turns to be false and knavish; and then another and another, and when this has happened several times to a man, especially when it happens among those whom he deems to be his own most trusted and familiar friends, and he has often quarrelled with them, he at last hates all men, and believes that no one has any good in him at all. You must have observed this trait of character?

I have.

And is not the feeling discreditable? Is it not obvious that such an one having to deal with other men, was clearly without any experience of human nature; for experience would have taught him the true state of the case, that few are the good and few the evil, and that the great majority are in the interval between them.

What do you mean? I said.

I mean, he replied, as you might say of the very large and very small—that nothing is more uncommon than a very large or very small man; and this applies generally to all extremes, whether of great and small, or swift and slow, or fair and foul, or black and white: and whether the instances you select be men or dogs or anything else, few are the extremes, but many are in the mean between them. Did you never observe this?

Yes, I said, I have.

And do you not imagine, he said, that if there were a competition in evil, the worst would be found to be very few?

Yes, that is very likely, I said.

Yes, that is very likely, he replied; although in this respect arguments are unlike men—there I was led on by you to say more than I had intended; but the point of comparison was, that when a simple man who has no skill in dialectics believes an argument to be true which he afterwards imagines to be false, whether really false or not, and then another and another, he has no longer any faith left, and great disputers, as you know, come to think at last that they have grown to be the wisest of mankind; for they alone perceive the utter unsoundness and instability of all arguments, or indeed, of all things, which, like the currents in the Euripus, are going up and down in never-ceasing ebb and flow.

That is quite true, I said.

Yes, Phaedo, he replied, and how melancholy, if there be such a thing as truth or certainty or possibility of knowledge—that a man should have lighted upon some argument or other which at first seemed true and then turned out to be false, and instead of blaming himself and his own want of wit, because he is annoyed, should at last be too glad to transfer the blame from himself to arguments in general: and for ever afterwards should hate and revile them, and lose truth and the knowledge of realities.

Yes, indeed, I said; that is very melancholy.

Let us then, in the first place, he said, be careful of allowing or of admitting into our souls the notion that there is no health or soundness in any arguments at all. Rather say that we have not yet attained to soundness in ourselves, and that we must struggle manfully and do our best to gain health of mind—you and all other men having regard to the whole of your future life, and I myself in the prospect of death. For at this moment I am sensible that I have not the temper of a philosopher;

like the vulgar, I am only a partisan. Now the partisan, when he is engaged in a dispute, cares nothing about the rights of the question, but is anxious only to convince his hearers of his own assertions. And the difference between him and me at the present moment is merely this—that whereas he seeks to convince his hearers that what he says is true, I am rather seeking to convince myself; to convince my hearers is a secondary matter with me. And do but see how much I gain by the argument. For if what I say is true, then I do well to be persuaded of the truth; but if there be nothing after death, still, during the short time that remains, I shall not distress my friends with lamentations, and my ignorance will not last, but will die with me, and therefore no harm will be done. This is the state of mind, Simmias and Cebes, in which I approach the argument. And I would ask you to be thinking of the truth and not of Socrates: agree with me, if I seem to you to be speaking the truth; or if not, withstand me might and main, that I may not deceive you as well as myself in my enthusiasm, and like the bee, leave my sting in you before I die.

And now let us proceed, he said. And first of all let me be sure that I have in my mind what you were saying. Simmias, if I remember rightly, has fears and misgivings whether the soul, although a fairer and diviner thing than the body, being as she is in the form of harmony, may not perish first. On the other hand, Cebes appeared to grant that the soul was more lasting than the body, but he said that no one could know whether the soul, after having worn out many bodies, might not perish herself and leave her last body behind her; and that this death, which is the destruction not of the body but of the soul, for in the body the work of destruction is ever going on. Are not these, Simmias and Cebes, the points which we have to consider?

They both agreed to this statement of them.

He proceeded: And did you deny the force of the whole preceding argument, or of a part only?

Of a part only, they replied.

And what did you think, he said, of that part of the argument in which we said that knowledge was recollection, and hence inferred that the soul must have previously existed somewhere else before she was enclosed in the body?

Cebes said that he had been wonderfully impressed by that part of the argument, and that his conviction remained absolutely unshaken. Simmias agreed, and added that he himself could hardly imagine the possibility of his ever thinking differently.

But, rejoined Socrates, you will have to think differently, my Theban friend, if you still maintain that harmony is a compound, and that the soul is a harmony which is made out of strings set in the frame of the body; for you will surely never allow yourself to say that a harmony is prior to the elements which compose it.

Never, Socrates.

But do you not see that this is what you imply when you say that the soul existed before she took the form and body of man, and was made up of elements which as yet had no existence? For harmony is not like the soul, as you suppose; but first the lyre, and the strings, and the sounds exist in a state of discord, and then harmony is made last of all, and perishes first. And how can such a notion of the soul as this agree with the other?

Not at all, replied Simmias.

And yet, he said, there surely ought to be harmony in a discourse of which harmony is the theme?

There ought, replied Simmias.

But there is no harmony, he said, in the two proposition that knowledge is recollection, and that the soul is a harmony. Which of them will you retain?

I think, he replied, that I have a much stronger faith, Socrates, in the first of the two, which has been fully demonstrated to me, than in the latter, which has not been demonstrated at all, but rests only on probable and plausible grounds; and is therefore believed by the many. I know too well that these arguments from probabilities are impostors, and unless great caution is observed in the use of them, they are apt to be deceptive—in geometry, and in other things too. But the doctrine of knowledge and recollection has been proven to me on trustworthy grounds: and the proof was that the soul must have existed before she came into the body, because to her belongs the essence of which the very name implies existence. Having, as I am convinced. rightly accepted this conclusion, and on sufficient grounds, I must, as I suppose, cease to argue or allow others to argue that the soul is a harmony.

Let me put the matter, Simmias, he said, in another point of view: Do you imagine that a harmony or any other composition can be in a state other than that of the elements, out of which it is compounded?

Certainly not.

Or do or suffer anything other than they do or suffer?

He agreed.

Then a harmony does not, properly speaking, lead the parts or elements which make up the harmony, but only follows them.

He assented.

For harmony cannot possibly have any motion, or sound, or other quality which is opposed to its parts.

That would be impossible, he replied.

And does not the nature of every harmony depend upon the manner in which the elements are harmonized?

I do not understand you, he said.

I mean to say that a harmony admits of degrees, and is more of a harmony, and more completely a harmony, when more truly and fully harmonized, to any extent which is possible; and less of a harmony, and less completely a harmony, when less truly and fully harmonized.

True.

But does the soul admit of degrees? or is one soul in the very least degree more or less, or more or less completely, a soul than another?

Not in the least.

Yet surely of two souls, one is said to have intelligence and virtue, and to be good, and the other to have folly and vice, and to be an evil soul: and this is said truly?

Yes, truly.

But what will those who maintain the soul to be a harmony say of this presence of virtue and vice in the soul?—will they say that here is another harmony, and another discord, and that the virtuous soul is harmonized, and herself being a harmony has another harmony within her, and that the vicious soul is inharmonical and has no harmony within her?

I cannot tell, replied Simmias; but I suppose that something of the sort would be asserted by those who say that the soul is a harmony.

And we have already admitted that no soul is more a

soul than another; which is equivalent to admitting that harmony is not more or less harmony, or more or less completely a harmony?

Quite true.

And that which is not more or less a harmony is not more or less harmonized?

True.

And that which is not more or less harmonized cannot have more or less of harmony, but only an equal harmony?

Yes, an equal harmony.

Then one soul not being more or less absolutely a soul than another, is not more or less harmonized?

Exactly.

And therefore has neither more nor less of discord, nor yet of harmony?

She has not.

And having neither more nor less of harmony or of discord, one soul has no more vice or virtue than another, if vice be discord and virtue harmony?

Not at all more.

Or speaking more correctly, Simmias, the soul, if she is a harmony, will never have any vice; because a harmony, being absolutely a harmony, has no part in the inharmonical.

No.

And therefore a soul which is absolutely a soul has no vice?

How can she have, if the previous argument holds?

Then, if all souls are equally by their nature souls, all souls of all living creatures will be equally good?

I agree with you, Socrates, he said.

And can all this be true, think you? he said; for these are the consequences which seem to follow from the assumption that the soul is a harmony?

It cannot be true.

Once more, he said, what ruler is there of the elements of human nature other than the soul, and especially the wise soul? Do you know of any?

Indeed, I do not.

And is the soul in agreement with the affections of the body? or is she at variance with them? For example, when the body is hot and thirsty, does not the soul incline us against drinking? and when the body is hungry, against eating? And this is only one instance out of ten thousand of the opposition of the soul to the things of the body.

Very true.

But we have already acknowledged that the soul, being a harmony, can never utter a note at variance with the tensions and relaxations and vibrations and other affections of the strings out of which she is composed; she can only follow, she cannot lead them?

It must be so, he replied.

And yet do we not now discover the soul to be doing the exact opposite—leading the elements of which she is believed to be composed; almost always opposing and coercing them in all sorts of ways throughout life, sometimes more violently with the pains of medicine and gymnastic; then again more gently; now threatening, now admonishing the desires, passions, fears, as if talking to a thing which is not herself, as Homer in the Odyssee represents Odysseus doing in the words—

'He beat his breast, and thus reproached his heart:
Endure, my heart; far worse hast thou endured!'

Do you think that Homer wrote this under the idea that the soul is a harmony capable of being led by the affections of the body, and not rather of a nature which should lead and master them—herself a far diviner thing than any harmony?

Yes, Socrates, I quite think so.

Then, my friend, we can never be right in saying that the soul is a harmony, for we should contradict the divine Homer, and contradict ourselves.

True, he said.

Thus much, said Socrates, of Harmonia, your Theban goddess, who has graciously yielded to us; but what shall I say, Cebes, to her husband Cadmus, and how shall I make peace with him?

I think that you will discover a way of propitiating him, said Cebes; I am sure that you have put the argument with Harmonia in a manner that I could never have expected. For when Simmias was mentioning his difficulty, I quite imagined that no answer could be given to him, and therefore I was surprised at finding that his argument could not sustain the first onset of yours, and not impossibly the other, whom you call Cadmus, may share a similar fate.

Nay, my good friend, said Socrates, let us not boast, lest some evil eye should put to flight the word which I am about to speak. That, however, may be left in the hands of those above; while I draw near in Homeric fashion, and try the mettle of your words. Here lies the point:—You want to have it proven to you that the soul is imperishable and immortal, and the philosopher who is confident in death appears to you to have but a vain and foolish confidence, if he believes that he will fare better in the world below than one who has led another sort of life, unless he can prove this: and you say that the demonstration of the strength and divinity of the soul, and of her existence prior to our becoming men, does not necessarily imply her immortality. Admitting the soul to be longlived, and to have known and done much in a former state, still she is not on that account immortal; and her entrance into the human form may be a sort of disease which is the beginning of dissolution, and may at last, after the toils of life are over, end in that which is called death. And whether the soul enters into the body once only or many times, does not, as you say, make any difference in the fears of individuals. For any man, who is not devoid of sense, must fear, if he has no knowledge and can give no account of the soul's immortality. This, or something like this, I suspect to be your notion, Cebes; and I designedly recur to it in order that nothing may escape us, and that you may, if you wish, add or subtract anything.

But, said Cebes, as far as I see at present, I have nothing to add or subtract: I mean what you say that I mean.

Socrates paused awhile, and seemed to be absorbed in reflection. At length he said: You are raising a tremendous question, Cebes, involving the whole nature of generation and corruption, about which, if you like, I will give you my own experience; and if anything which I say is likely to avail towards the solution of your difficulty you may make use of it.

I should very much like, said Cebes, to hear what you have to say.

Then I will tell you, said Socrates. When I was young, Cebes, I had a prodigious desire to know that department of philosophy which is called the investigation of nature; to know the cause of things, and why a thing is and is created or destroyed appeared to me to be a lofty profession; and I was always agitating myself with the consideration of questions such as these:—Is the growth of animals the result of some decay which the hot and cold principle contracts, as some have said? Is the blood the element with which we think, or the air,

or the fire? or perhaps nothing of the kind—but the
brain may be the originating power of the perceptions of
hearing and sight and smell, and memory and opinion
may come from them, and science may be based on memory and opinion when they have attained fixity. And
then I went on to examine the corruption of them, and
then to the things of heaven and earth, and at last I
concluded myself to be utterly and absolutely incapable
of these enquiries, as I will satisfactorily prove to you.
For I was fascinated by them to such a degree that my
eyes grew blind to things which I had seemed to myself,
and also to others, to know quite well; I forgot what I
had before thought self-evident truths; e. g. such a fact
as that the growth of man is the result of eating and
drinking; for when by the digestion of food flesh is
added to flesh and bone to bone, and whenever there is
an aggregation of congenial elements, the lesser bulk
becomes larger and the small man great. Was not that
a reasonable notion?

Yes, said Cebes, I think so.

Well; but let me tell you something more. There was
a time when I thought that I understood the meaning of
greater and less pretty well; and when I saw a great
man standing by a little one, I fancied that one was
taller than the other by a head; or one horse would appear to be greater than another horse: and still more
clearly did I seem to perceive that ten is two more than
eight, and that two cubits are more than one, because
two is the double of one.

And what is now your notion of such matters? said
Cebes.

I should be far enough from imagining, he replied,
that I knew the cause of any of them, by heaven I
should; for I cannot satisfy myself that, when one is
added to one, the one to which the addition is made be-

comes two, or that the two units added together make two by reason of the addition. I cannot understand how, when separated from the other, each of them was one and not two, and now, when they are brought together, the mere juxtaposition or meeting of them should be the cause of their becoming two: neither can I understand how the division of one is the way to make two; for then a different cause would produce the same effect, —as in the former instance the addition and juxtaposition of one to one was the cause of two, in this the separation and subtraction of one from the other would be the cause. Nor am I any longer satisfied that I understand the reason why one or anything else is either generated or destroyed or is at all, but I have in my mind some confused notion of a new method, and can never admit the other.

Then I heard some one reading, as he said, from a book of Anaxagoras, that mind was the disposer and cause of all, and I was delighted at this notion, which appeared quite admirable, and I said to myself: If mind is the disposer, mind will dispose all for the best, and put each particular in the best place; and I argued that if any one desired to find out the cause of the generation or destruction or existence of anything, he must find out what state of being or doing or suffering was best for that thing, and therefore a man had only to consider the best for himself and others, and then he would also know the worse, since the same science comprehended both. And I rejoiced to think that I had found in Anaxagoras a teacher of the causes of existence such as I desired, and I imagined that he would tell me first whether the earth is flat or round; and whichever was true, he would proceed to explain the cause and the necessity of this being so, and then he would teach me the nature of the best and show that this was best; and if he said that the earth was in the centre, he would further explain that this position was the best, and I should be satisfied with the explanation given, and not want any other sort of cause. And I thought that I would then go on and ask him about the sun and moon and stars, and that he would explain to me their comparative swiftness, and their returnings and various states, active and passive, and how all of them were for the best. For I could not imagine that when he spoke of mind as the disposer of them, he would give any other account of their being as they are, except that this was best; and I thought that when he had explained to me in detail the cause of each and the cause of all, he would go on to explain to me what was best for each and what was good for all. These hopes I would not have sold for a large sum of money, and I seized the books and read them as fast as I could in my eagerness to know the better and the worse.

What expectations I had formed, and how grievously was I disappointed! As I proceeded, I found my philosopher altogether forsaking mind or any other principle of order, but having recourse to air, and ether, and water, and other eccentricities. I might compare him to a person who began by maintaining generally that mind is the cause of the actions of Socrates, but who, when he endeavoured to explain the causes of my several actions in detail, went on to show that I sit here because my body is made up of bones and muscles; and the bones, as he would say, are hard and have joints which divide them, and the muscles are elastic, and they cover the bones, which have also a covering or environment of flesh and skin which contains them; and as the bones are lifted at their joints by the contraction or relaxation of the muscles, I am able to bend my limbs, and this is why I am sitting here in a curved posture—that is what he would say; and he would have a similar ex-

planation of my talking to you, which he would attribute
to sound, and air, and hearing, and he would assign ten
thousand other causes of the same sort, forgetting to
mention the true cause, which is, that the Athenians have
thought fit to condemn me, and accordingly I have
thought it better and more right to remain here and undergo my sentence; for I am inclined to think that these
muscles and bones of mine would have gone off long ago
to Megara or Boeotia—by the dog they would, if they
had been moved only by their own idea of what was best,
and if I had not chosen the better and nobler part, instead of playing truant and running away, of enduring
any punishment which the state inflicts. There is surely
a strange confusion of causes and conditions in all this.
It may be said, indeed, that without bones and muscles
and the other parts of the body I cannot execute my
purposes. But to say that I do as I do because of them,
and that this is the way in which mind acts, and not
from the choice of the best, is a very careless and idle
mode of speaking. I wonder that they cannot distinguish the cause from the condition, which the many, feeling about in the dark, are always mistaking and mis-
naming. And thus one man makes a vortex all round
and steadies the earth by the heaven; another gives the
air as a support to the earth, which is a sort of broad
trough. Any power which in arranging them as they
are arranges them for the best never enters into their
minds; and instead of finding any superior strength in
it, they rather expect to discover another Atlas of the
world who is stronger and more everlasting and more
containing than the good;—of the obligatory and containing power of the good they think nothing; and yet
this is the principle which I would fain learn if any one
would teach me. But as I have failed either to discover
myself, or to learn of any one else, the nature of the

best, I will exhibit to you, if you like, what I have found
to be the second best mode of enquiring into the cause.

I should very much like to hear, he replied.

Socrates proceeded:—I thought that as I had failed
in the contemplation of true existence, I ought to be
careful that I did not lose the eye of my soul; as people
may injure their bodily eye by observing and gazing on
the sun during an eclipse, unless they take the precau-
tion of only looking at the image reflected in the water,
or in some similar medium. So in my own case, I was
afraid that my soul might be blinded altogether if I
looked at things with my eyes or tried to apprehend
them by the help of the senses. And I thought that I
had better have recourse to the world of mind and seek
there the truth of existence. I dare say that the simile
is not perfect—for I am very far from admitting that
he who contemplates existences through the medium of
thought, sees them only 'through a glass darkly,' any
more than he who considers them in action and operation. However, this was the method which I adopted:
I first assumed some principle which I judged to be the
strongest, and then I affirmed as true whatever seemed
to agree with this, whether relating to the cause or to
anything else; and that which disagreed I regarded as
untrue. But I should like to explain my meaning more
clearly, as I do not think that you as yet understand me.

No indeed, replied Cebes, not very well.

There is nothing new, he said, in what I am about to
tell you; but only what I have been always and everywhere repeating in the previous discussion and on other
occasions: I want to show you the nature of that cause
which has occupied my thoughts. I shall have to go
back to those familiar words which are in the mouth of
every one, and first of all assume that there is an absolute beauty and goodness and greatness, and the like;

grant me this, and I hope to be able to show you the nature of the cause, and to prove the immortality of the soul.

Cebes said: You may proceed at once with the proof, for I grant you this.

Well, he said, then I should like to know whether you agree with me in the next step; for I cannot help thinking, if there be anything beautiful other than absolute beauty should there be such, that it can be beautiful only in so far as it partakes of absolute beauty—and I should say the same of everything. Do you agree in this notion of the cause?

Yes, he said, I agree.

He proceeded: I know nothing and can understand nothing of any other of those wise causes which are alleged; and if a person says to me that the bloom of colour, or form, or any such thing is a source of beauty, I leave all that, which is only confusing to me, and simply and singly, and perhaps foolishly, hold and am assured in my own mind that nothing makes a thing beautiful but the presence and participation of beauty in whatever way or manner obtained; for as to the manner I am uncertain, but I stoutly contend that by beauty all beautiful things become beautiful. This appears to me to be the safest answer which I can give, either to myself or to another, and to this I cling, in the persuasion that this principle will never be overthrown, and that to myself or to any one who asks the question, I may safely reply, That by beauty beautiful things become beautiful. Do you not agree with me?

I do.

And that by greatness only great things become great and greater greater, and by smallness the less become less?

True.

Then if a person were to remark that A is taller by

a head than B, and B less by a head than A, you would
refuse to admit his statement, and would stoutly contend that what you mean is only that the greater is
greater by, and by reason of, greatness, and the less is
less only by, and by reason of, smallness; and thus you
would avoid the danger of saying that the greater is
greater and the less less by the measure of the head,
which is the same in both, and would also avoid the
monstrous absurdity of supposing that the greater man
is greater by reason of the head, which is small. You
would be afraid to draw such an inference, would you
not?

Indeed, I should, said Cebes, laughing.

In like manner you would be afraid to say that ten
exceeded eight by, and by reason of, two; but would
say by, and by reason of, number; or you would say
that two cubits exceed one cubit not by a half, but by
magnitude?—for there is the same liability to error in
all these cases.

Very true, he said.

Again, would you not be cautious of affirming that
the addition of one to one, or the division of one, is the
cause of two? And you would loudly asseverate that you
know of no way in which anything comes into existence
except by participation in its own proper essence, and
consequently, as far as you know, the only cause of two
is the participation in duality—this is the way to make
two, and the participation in one is the way to make
one. You would say: I will let alone puzzles of division and addition—wiser heads than mine may answer
them; inexperienced as I am, and ready to start, as the
proverb says, at my own shadow, I cannot afford to give
up the sure ground of a principle. And if any one
assails you there, you would not mind him, or answer
him, until you had seen whether the consequences which

follow agree with one another or not, and when you are further required to give an explanation of this principle, you would go on to assume a higher principle, and a higher, until you found a resting-place in the best of the higher; but you would not confuse the principle and the consequences in your reasoning, like the Eristics—at least if you wanted to discover real existence. Not that this confusion signifies to them, who never care or think about the matter at all, for they have the wit to be well pleased with themselves however great may be the turmoil of their ideas. But you, if you are a philosopher, will certainly do as I say.

What you say is most true, said Simmias and Cebes, both speaking at once.

Ech. Yes, Phaedo; and I do not wonder at their assenting. Any one who has the least sense will acknowledge the wonderful clearness of Socrates' reasoning.

Phaed. Certainly, Echecrates; and such was the feeling of the whole company at the time.

Ech. Yes, and equally of ourselves, who were not of the company, and are now listening to your recital. But what followed?

Phaed. After all this had been admitted, and they had agreed that ideas exist, and that other things participate in them and derive their names from them, Socrates, if I remember rightly, said:—

This is your way of speaking; and yet when you say that Simmias is greater than Socrates and less than Phaedo, do you not predicate of Simmias both greatness and smallness?

Yes, I do.

But still you allow that Simmias does not really exceed Socrates, as the words may seem to imply, because he is Simmias, but by reason of the size which he has;

just as Simmias does not exceed Socrates because he is
Simmias, any more than because Socrates is Socrates,
but because he has smallness when compared with the
greatness of Simmias?

True.

And if Phaedo exceeds him in size, this is not because
Phaedo is Phaedo, but because Phaedo has greatenss
relatively to Simmias, who is comparatively smaller?

That is true.

And therefore Simmias is said to be great, and is also
said to be small, because he is in a mean between them,
exceeding the smallness of the one by his greatness, and
allowing the greatness of the other to exceed his smallness. He added, laughing, I am speaking like a book,
but I believe that what I am saying is true.

Simmias assented.

I speak as I do because I want you to agree with me
in thinking, not only that absolute greatness will never
be great and also small, but that greatness in us or in
the concrete will never admit the small or admit of being exceeded: instead of this, one of two things will happen, either the greater will fly or retire before the opposite, which is the less, or at the approach of the less
has already ceased to exist; but will not, if allowing or
admitting of smallness, be changed by that; even as I,
having received and admitted smallness when compared
with Simmias, remain just as I was, and as the same
small person. And as the idea of greatness cannot con-
descend ever to be or become small, in like manner the
smallness in us cannot be or become great; nor can any
other opposite which remains the same ever be or become its own opposite, but either passes away or perishes in the change.

That, replied Cebes, is quite my notion.

Hereupon one of the company, though I do not exactly remember which of them, said: In heaven's name, is not this the direct contrary of what was admitted before—that out of the greater came the less and out of the less the greater, and that opposites were simply generated from opposites; but now this principle seems to be utterly denied.

Socrates inclined his head to the speaker and listened. I like your courage, he said, in reminding us of this. But you do not observe that there is a difference in the two cases. For then we were speaking of opposites in the concrete, and now of the essential opposite which, as is affirmed, neither in us nor in nature can ever be at variance with itself: then, my friend, we were speaking of things in which opposites are inherent and which are called after them, but now about the opposites which are inherent in them and which give their name to them; and these essential opposites will never, as we maintain, admit of generation into or out of one another. At the same time, turning to Cebes, he said: Are you at all disconcerted, Cebes, at our friend's objection?

No, I do not feel so, said Cebes; and yet I cannot deny that I am often disturbed by objections.

Then we are agreed after all, said Socrates, that the opposite will never in any case be opposed to itself?

To that we are quite agreed, he replied.

Yet once more let me ask you to consider the question from another point of view, and see whether you agree with me:—There is a thing which you term heat, and another thing which you term cold?

Certainly.

But are they the same as fire and snow?

Most assuredly not.

Heat is a thing different from fire, and cold is not the same with snow?

Yes.

And yet you will surely admit, that when snow, as was before said, is under the influence of heat, they will not remain snow and heat; but at the advance of the heat, the snow will either retire or perish?

Very true, he replied.

And the fire too at the advance of the cold will either retire or perish; and when the fire is under the influence of the cold, they will not remain as before, fire and cold.

That is true, he said.

And in some cases the name of the idea is not only attached to the idea in an eternal connection, but anything else which, not being the idea, exists only in the form of the idea, may also lay claim to it. I will try to make this clearer by an example:—The odd number is always called by the name of odd?

Very true.

But is this the only thing which is called odd? Are there not other things which have their own name, and yet are called odd, because, although not the same as oddness, they are never without oddness?—that is what I mean to ask—whether numbers such as the number three are not of the class of odd. And there are many other examples: would you not say, for example, that three may be called by its proper name, and also be called odd, which is not the same with three? and this may be said not only of three but also of five, and of every alternate number—each of them without being oddness is odd; and in the same way two and four, and the other series of alternate numbers, has every number even, without being evenness. Do you agree?

Of course.

Then now mark the point at which I am aiming:— not only do essential opposites exclude one another, but also concrete things, which, although not in themselves opposed, contain opposites; these, I say, likewise reject

the idea which is opposed to that which is contained in
them, and when it approaches them they either perish
or withdraw. For example: Will not the number three
endure annihilation or anything sooner than be converted into an even number, while remaining three?

Very true, said Cebes.

And yet, he said, the number two is certainly not opposed to the number three?

It is not.

Then not only do opposite ideas repel the advance of
one another, but also there are other natures which repel
the approach of opposites.

Very true, he said.

Suppose, he said, that we endeavour, if possible, to
determine what these are.

By all means.

Are they not, Cebes, such as compel the things of
which they have possession, not only to take their own
form, but also the form of some opposite?

What do you mean?

I mean, as I was just now saying, and as I am sure
that you know, that those things which are possessed by
the number three must not only be three in number, but
must also be odd.

Quite true.

And on this oddness, of which the number three has
the impress, the opposite idea will never intrude?

No.

And this impress was given by the odd principle?

Yes.

And to the odd is opposed the even?

True.

Then the idea of the even number will never arrive
at three?

No.

Then three has no part in the even?

None.

Then the triad or number three is uneven?

Very true.

To return then to my distinction of natures which are not opposed, and yet do not admit opposites—as, in the instance given, three, although not opposed to the even, does not any the more admit of the even, but always brings the opposite into play on the other side; or as two does not receive the odd, or fire the cold—from these examples (and there are many more of them) perhaps you may be able to arrive at the general conclusion, that not only opposites will not receive opposites, but also that nothing which brings the opposite will admit the opposite of that which it brings, in that to which it is brought. And here let me recapitulate— for there is no harm in repetition. The number five will not admit the nature of the even, any more than ten, which is the double of five, will admit the nature of the odd. The double has another opposite, and is not strictly opposed to the odd, but nevertheless rejects the odd altogether. Nor again will parts in the ratio 3 : 2, nor any fraction in which there is a half, nor again in which there is a third, admit the notion of the whole, although they are not opposed to the whole: You will agree?

Yes, he said, I entirely agree and go along with you in that.

And now, he said, let us begin again; and do not you answer my question in the words in which I ask it: let me have not the old safe answer of which I spoke at first, but another equally safe, of which the truth will be inferred by you from what has been just said. I mean that if any one asks you 'what that is, of which the inherence makes the body hot,' you will reply not heat (this is what I call the safe and stupid answer), but fire, a far superior answer, which we are now in a condition to give. Or if any one asks you 'why a body is diseased,' you will not say from disease, but from fever; and instead of saying that oddness is the cause of odd numbers, you will say that the monad is the cause of them: and so of things in general, as I dare say that you will understand sufficiently without my adducing any further examples.

Yes, he said, I quite understand you.

Tell me, then, what is that of which the inherence will render the body alive?

The soul, he replied.

And is this always the case?

Yes, he said, of course.

Then whatever the soul possesses, to that she comes bearing life?

Yes, certainly.

And is there any opposite to life?

There is, he said.

And what is that?

Death.

Then the soul, as has been acknowledged, will never receive the opposite of what she brings.

Impossible, replied Cebes.

And now, he said, what did we just now call that principle which repels the even?

The odd.

And that principle which repels the musical or the just?

The unmusical, he said, and the unjust.

And what do we call that principle which does not admit of death?

The immortal, he said.

And does the soul admit of death?

No.

Then the soul is immortal?

Yes, he said.

And may we say that this has been proven?

Yes, abundantly proven, Socrates, he replied.

Supposing that the odd were imperishable, must not three be imperishable?

Of course.

And if that which is cold were imperishable, when the warm principle came attacking the snow, must not the snow have retired whole and unmelted—for it could never have perished, nor could it have remained and admitted the heat?

True, he said.

Again, if the uncooling or warm principle were imperishable, the fire when assailed by cold would not have perished or have been extinguished, but would have gone away unaffected?

Certainly, he said.

And the same may be said of the immortal: if the immortal is also imperishable, the soul when attacked by death cannot perish; for the preceding argument shows that the soul will not admit of death, or ever be dead, any more than three or the odd number will admit of the even, or fire, or the heat in the fire, of the cold. Yet a person may say: 'But although the odd will not become even at the approach of the even, why may not the odd perish and the even take the place of the odd?' Now to him who makes this objection, we cannot answer that the odd principle is imperishable; for this has not been acknowledged, but if this had been acknowledged, there would have been no difficulty in contending that at the approach of the even the odd principle and the number three took their departure; and the same argument would have held good of fire and heat and any other thing.

Very true.

And the same may be said of the immortal: if the immortal is also imperishable, then the soul will be imperishable as well as immortal; but if not, some other proof of her imperishableness will have to be given.

No other proof is needed, he said; for if the immortal, being eternal, is liable to perish, then nothing is imperishable.

Yes, replied Socrates, and yet all men will agree that God, and the essential form of life, and the immortal in general, will never perish.

Yes, all men, he said—that is true; and what is more, gods, if I am not mistaken, as well as men.

Seeing then that the immortal is indestructible, must not the soul, if she is immortal, be also imperishable?

Most certainly.

Then when death attacks a man, the mortal portion of him may be supposed to die, but the immortal retires at the approach of death and is preserved safe and sound?

True.

Then, Cebes, beyond question, the soul is immortal and imperishable, and our souls will truly exist in another world!

I am convinced, Socrates, said Cebes, and have nothing more to object; but if my friend Simmias, or any one else, has any further objection to make, he had better speak out, and not keep silence, since I do not know to what other season he can defer the discussion, if there is anything which he wants to say or to have said.

But I have nothing more to say, replied Simmias; nor can I see any reason for doubt after what has been said. But I still feel and cannot help feeling uncertain in my own mind, when I think of the greatness of the subject and the feebleness of man.

Yes, Simmias, replied Socrates, that is well said: and I may add that first principles, even if they appear certain, should be carefully considered; and when they are satisfactorily ascertained, then, with a sort of hesitating confidence in human reason, you may, I think, follow the course of the argument; and if that be plain and clear, there will be no need for any further enquiry.

Very true.

But then, O my friends, he said, if the soul is really immortal, what care should be taken of her, not only in respect of the portion of time which is called life, but of eternity! And the danger of neglecting her from this point of view does indeed appear to be awful. If death had only been the end of all, the wicked would have had a good bargain in dying, for they would have been happily quit not only of their body, but of their own evil together with their souls. But now, inasmuch as the soul is manifestly immortal, there is no release or salvation from evil except the attainment of the highest virtue and wisdom. For the soul when on her progress to the world below takes nothing with her but nurture and education; and these are said greatly to benefit or greatly to injure the departed, at the very beginning of his journey thither.

For after death, as they say, the genius of each individual, to whom he belonged in life, leads him to a certain place in which the dead are gathered together, whence after judgment has been given they pass into the world below, following the guide, who is appointed to conduct them from this world to the other: and when they have there received their due and remained their time, another guide brings them back again after many revolutions of ages. Now this way to the other world is not, as Aeschylus says in the Telephus, a single and straight path—if that were so no guide would be needed, for no one could miss it; but there are many partings of the road, and windings, as I infer from the rites and sacrifices which are offered to the gods below in places where three ways meet on earth. The wise and orderly soul follows in the straight path and is conscious of her surroundings; but the soul which desires the body, and which, as I was relating before, has long been fluttering about the lifeless frame and the world of sight, is after many struggles and many sufferings hardly and with violence carried away by her attendant genius; and when she arrives at the place where the other souls are gathered, if she be impure and have done impure deeds, whether foul murders or other crimes which are the brothers of these, and the works of brothers in crime— from that soul every one flees and turns away; no one will be her companion, no one her guide, but alone she wanders in extremity of evil until certain times are fulfilled, and when they are fulfilled, she is borne irresistibly to her own fitting habitation; as every pure and just soul which has passed through life in the company and under the guidance of the gods has also her own proper home.

Now the earth has divers wonderful regions, and is indeed in nature and extent very unlike the notions of geographers, as I believe on the authority of one who shall be nameless.

What do you mean, Socrates? said Simmias. I have myself heard many descriptions of the earth, but I do not know, and I should very much like to know, in which of these you put faith.

And I, Simmias, replied Socrates, if I had the art of Glaucus would tell you; although I know not that the art of Glaucus could prove the truth of my tale, which I myself should never be able to prove, and even if I could, I fear, Simmias, that my life would come to an end before the argument was completed. I may describe to you, however, the form and regions of the earth according to my conception of them.

That, said Simmias, will be enough.

Well then, he said, my conviction is, that the earth is a round body in the centre of the heavens, and therefore has no need of air or of any similar force to be a support, but is kept there and hindered from falling or inclining any way by the equability of the surrounding heaven and by her own equipoise. For that which, being in equipoise, is in the centre of that which is equably diffused, will not incline any way in any degree, but will always remain in the same state and not deviate. And this is my first notion.

Which is surely a correct one, said Simmias.

Also I believe that the earth is very vast, and that we who dwell in the region extending from the river Phasis to the Pillars of Heracles inhabit a small portion only about the sea, like ants or frogs about a marsh, and that there are other inhabitants of many other like places; for everywhere on the face of the earth there are hollows of various forms and sizes, into which the water and the mist and the lower air collect. But the true earth is pure and situated in the pure heaven—there are the stars also; and it is the heaven which is commonly spoken of by us as the ether, and of which our own earth is the sediment gathering in the hollows beneath. But we who live in these hollows are deceived into the notion that we are dwelling above on the surface of the earth; which is just as if a creature who was at the bottom of the sea were to fancy that he was on the surface of the water, and that the sea was the heaven through which he saw the sun and the other stars, he having never come to the surface by reason of his feebleness and sluggishness, and having never lifted up his head and seen, nor ever heard from one who had seen, how much purer and fairer the world above is than his own. And such is exactly our case: for we are dwelling in a hollow of the earth, and fancy that we are on the surface; and the air we call the heaven, in which we imagine that the stars move. But the fact is, that owing to our feebleness and sluggishness we are prevented from reaching the surface of the air: for if any man could arrive at the exterior limit, or take the wings of a bird and come to the top, then like a fish who puts his head out of the water and sees this world, he would see a world beyond; and, if the nature of man could sustain the sight, he would acknowledge that this other world was the place of the true heaven and the true light and the true earth. For our earth, and the stones, and the entire region which surrounds us, are spoilt and corroded, as in the sea all things are corroded by the brine, neither is there any noble or perfect growth, but caverns only, and sand, and an endless slough of mud; and even the shore is not to be compared to the fairer sights of this world. And still less is this our world to be compared with the other. Of that upper earth which is under the heaven, I can tell you a charming tale, Simmias, which is well worth hearing.

And we, Socrates, replied Simmias, shall be charmed to listen to you.

The tale, my friend, he said, is as follows:—In the first place, the earth, when looked at from above, is in appearance streaked like one of those balls which have leather coverings in twelve pieces, and is decked with various colours, of which the colours used by painters on earth are in a manner samples. But there the whole earth is made up of them, and they are brighter far and clearer than ours; there is a purple of wonderful lustre, also the radiance of gold, and the white which is in the

earth is whiter than any chalk or snow. Of these and
other colours the earth is made up, and they are more in
number and fairer than the eye of man has ever seen;
the very hollows (of which I was speaking) filled with
air and water have a colour of their own, and are seen
like light gleaming amid the diversity of the other colours, so that the whole presents a single and continuous
appearance of variety in unity. And in this fair region
everything that grows—trees, and flowers, and fruits—
are in a like degree fairer than any here; and there are
hills, having stones in them in a like degree smoother,
and more transparent, and fairer in colour than our
highly-valued emeralds and sardonyxes and jaspers, and
other gems, which are but minute fragments of them:
for there all the stones are like our precious stones, and
fairer still. The reason is, that they are pure, and not,
like our precious stones, infected or corroded by the corrupt briny elements which coagulate among us, and
which breed foulness and disease both in earth and
stones, as well as in animals and plants. They are the
jewels of the upper earth, which also shines with gold
and silver and the like, and they are set in the light of
day and are large and abundant and in all places, making the earth a sight to gladden the beholder's eye. And
there are animals and men, some in a middle region,
others dwelling about the air as we dwell about the sea;
others in islands which the air flows round, near the
continent; and in a word, the air is used by them as
the water and the sea are by us, and the ether is to them
what the air is to us. Moreover, the temperament of
their seasons is such that they have no disease, and live
much longer than we do, and have sight and hearing
and smell, and all the other senses, in far greater perfection, in the same proportion that air is purer than

water or the ether than air. Also they have temples
and sacred places in which the gods really dwell, and
they hear their voices and receive their answers, and are
conscious of them and hold converse with them; and they
see the sun, moon, and stars as they truly are, and their
other blessedness is of a piece with this.

Such is the nature of the whole earth, and of the
things which are around the earth; and there are divers
regions in the hollows on the face of the globe everywhere, some of them deeper and more extended than
that which we inhabit, others deeper but with a nar-
rower opening than ours, and some are shallower and
also wider. All have numerous perforations, and there
are passages broad and narrow in the interior of the
earth, connecting them with one another; and there flows
out of and into them, as into basins, a vast tide of water,
and huge subterranean streams of perennial rivers, and
springs hot and cold, and a great fire, and great rivers
of fire, and streams of liquid mud, thin or thick (like
the rivers of mud in Sicily, and the lava streams which
follow them), and the regions about which they happen
to flow are filled up with them. And there is a swinging
or see-saw in the interior of the earth which moves all
this up and down, and is due to the following cause:—
There is a chasm which is the vastest of them all, and
pierces right through the whole earth; this is that chasm
which Homer describes in the words,—

'Far off, where is the inmost depth beneath the earth;'

and which he in other places, and many other poets,
have called Tartarus. And the see-saw is caused by the
streams flowing into and out of this chasm, and they
each have the nature of the soil through which they
flow. And the reason why the streams are always flow-

ing in and out, is that the watery element has no bed or bottom, but is swinging and surging up and down, and the surrounding wind and air do the same; they follow the water up and down, hither and thither, over the earth—just as in the act of respiration the air is always in process of inhalation and exhalation;—and the wind swinging with the water in and out produces fearful and irresistible blasts: when the waters retire with a rush into the lower parts of the earth, as they are called, they flow through the earth in those regions, and fill them up like water raised by a pump, and then when they leave those regions and rush back hither, they again fill the hollows here, and when these are filled, flow through subterranean channels and find their way to their several places, forming seas, and lakes, and rivers, and springs. Thence they again enter the earth, some of them making a long circuit into many lands, others going to a few places and not so distant; and again fall into Tartarus, some at a point a good deal lower than that at which they rose, and others not much lower, but all in some degree lower than the point from which they came. And some burst forth again on the opposite side, and some on the same side, and some wind round the earth with one or many folds like the coils of a serpent, and descend as far as they can, but always return and fall into the chasm. The rivers flowing in either direction can descend only to the centre and no further, for opposite to the rivers is a precipice.

Now these rivers are many, and mighty, and diverse, and there are four principal ones, of which the greatest and outermost is that called Oceanus, which flows round the earth in a circle; and in the opposite direction flows Acheron, which passes under the earth through desert places into the Acherusian lake: this is the lake to the shores of which the souls of the many go when they are dead, and after waiting an appointed time, which is to some a longer and to some a shorter time, they are sent back to be born again as animals. The third river passes out between the two, and near the place of outlet pours into a vast region of fire, and forms a lake larger than the Mediterranean Sea, boiling with water and mud; and proceeding muddy and turbid, and winding about the earth, comes, among other places, to the extremities of the Acherusian lake, but mingles not with the waters of the lake, and after making many coils about the earth plunges into Tartarus at a deeper level. This is that Pyriphlegethon, as the stream is called, which throws up jets of fire in different parts of the earth. The fourth river goes out on the opposite side, and falls first of all into a wild and savage region, which is all of a dark blue colour, like lapis lazuli; and this is that river which is called the Stygian river, and falls into and forms the Lake Styx, and after falling into the lake and receiving strange powers in the waters, passes under the earth, winding round in the opposite direction, and comes near the Acherusian lake from the opposite side to Pyriphlegethon. And the water of this river too mingles with no other, but flows round in a circle and falls into Tartarus over against Pyriphlegethon; and the name of the river, as the poets say, is Cocytus.

Such is the nature of the other world; and when the dead arrive at the place to which the genius of each severally guides them, first of all, they have sentence passed upon them, as they have lived well and piously or not. And those who appear to have lived neither well nor ill, go to the river Acheron, and embarking in any vessels which they may find, are carried in them to the lake, and there they dwell and are purified of their evil deeds, and having suffered the penalty of the wrongs which they have done to others, they are absolved, and receive the rewards of their good deeds, each of them according to his deserts. But those who appear to be incurable by reason of the greatness of their crimes —who have committed many and terrible deeds of sacrilege, murders foul and violent, or the like—such are hurled into Tartarus which is their suitable destiny, and they never come out. Those again who have committed crimes, which, although great, are not irremediable— who in a moment of anger, for example, have done some violence to a father or a mother, and have repented for the remainder of their lives, or, who have taken the life of another under the like extenuating circumstances— these are plunged into Tartarus, the pains of which they are compelled to undergo for a year, but at the end of the year the wave casts them forth—mere homicides by way of Cocytus, parricides and matricides by Pyriphlegethon—and they are borne to the Acherusian lake, and there they lift up their voices and call upon the victims whom they have slain or wronged, to have pity on them, and to be kind to them, and let them come out into the lake. And if they prevail, then they come forth and cease from their troubles; but if not, they are carried back again into Tartarus and from thence into the rivers unceasingly, until they obtain mercy from those whom they have wronged: for that is the sentence inflicted upon them by their judges. Those too who have been pre-eminent for holiness of life are released from this earthly prison, and go to their pure home which is above, and dwell in the purer earth; and of these, such as have duly purified themselves with philosophy live henceforth altogether without the body, in mansions fairer still which may not be described, and of which the time would fail me to tell.

Wherefore, Simmias, seeing all these things, what ought not we to do that we may obtain virtue and wisdom in this life? Fair is the prize, and the hope great!

A man of sense ought not to say, nor will I be very confident, that the description which I have given of the soul and her mansions is exactly true. But I do say that, inasmuch as the soul is shown to be immortal, he may venture to think, not improperly or unworthily, that something of the kind is true. The venture is a glorious one, and he ought to comfort himself with words like these, which is the reason why I lengthen out the tale. Wherefore, I say, let a man be of good cheer about his soul, who having cast away the pleasures and ornaments of the body as alien to him and working harm rather than good, has sought after the pleasures of knowledge; and has arrayed the soul, not in some foreign attire, but in her own proper jewels, temperance, and justice, and courage, and nobility, and truth—in these adorned she is ready to go on her journey to the world below, when her hour comes. You, Simmias and Cebes, and all other men, will depart at some time or other. Me already, as a tragic poet would say, the voice of fate calls. Soon I must drink the poison; and I think that I had better repair to the bath first, in order that the women may not have the trouble of washing my body after I am dead.

When he had done speaking, Crito said: And have you any commands for us, Socrates—anything to say about your children, or any other matter in which we can serve you?

Nothing particular, Crito, he replied: only, as I have always told you, take care of yourselves; that is a service which you may be ever rendering to me and mine and to all of us, whether you promise to do so or not. But if you have no thought for yourselves, and care not to walk according to the rule which I have prescribed for you, not now for the first time, however much you may profess or promise at the moment, it will be of no avail.

We will do our best, said Crito: And in what way shall we bury you?

In any way that you like; but you must get hold of me, and take care that I do not run away from you. Then he turned to us, and added with a smile:—I cannot make Crito believe that I am the same Socrates who have been talking and conducting the argument; he fancies that I am the other Socrates whom he will soon see, a dead body—and he asks, How shall he bury me? And though I have spoken many words in the endeavour to show that when I have drunk the poison I shall leave you and go to the joys of the blessed,—these words of mine, with which I was comforting you and myself, have had, as I perceive, no effect upon Crito. And therefore I want you to be surety for me to him now, as at the trial he was surety to the judges for me: but let the promise be of another sort; for he was surety for me to the judges that I would remain, and you must be my surety to him that I shall not remain, but go away and depart; and then he will suffer less at my death, and not be grieved when he sees my body being burned or buried. I would not have him sorrow at my hard lot, or say at the burial, Thus we lay out Socrates, or, Thus we follow him to the grave or bury him; for false words are not only evil in themselves, but they infect the soul with evil. Be of good cheer then, my dear Crito, and say that you are burying my body only, and do with that whatever is usual, and what you think best.

When he had spoken these words, he arose and went into a chamber to bathe; Crito followed him and told us to wait. So we remained behind, talking and thinking of the subject of discourse, and also of the greatness of our sorrow; he was like a father of whom we were being bereaved, and we were about to pass the rest of our lives as orphans. When he had taken the bath his children were brought to him—(he had two young sons and an elder one); and the women of his family also came, and he talked to them and gave them a few directions in the presence of Crito; then he dismissed them and returned to us.

Now the hour of sunset was near, for a good deal of time had passed while he was within. When he came out, he sat down with us again after his bath, but not much was said. Soon the jailer, who was the servant of the Eleven, entered and stood by him, saying:—To you, Socrates, whom I know to be the noblest and gentlest and best of all who ever came to this place, I will not impute the angry feelings of other men, who rage and swear at me, when, in obedience to the authorities, I bid them drink the poison—indeed, I am sure that you will not be angry with me; for others, as you are aware, and not I, are to blame. And so fare you well, and try to bear lightly what must needs be—you know my errand. Then bursting into tears he turned away and went out.

Socrates looked at him and said: I return your good wishes, and will do as you bid. Then turning to us, he said, How charming the man is: since I have been in prison he has always been coming to see me, and at times he would talk to me, and was as good to me as could be, and now see how generously he sorrows on my account. We must do as he says, Crito; and therefore let the cup be brought, if the poison is prepared: if not, let the attendant prepare some.

Yet, said Crito, the sun is still upon the hill-tops, and I know that many a one has taken the draught late, and after the announcement has been made to him, he has eaten and drunk, and enjoyed the society of his beloved; do not hurry—there is time enough.

Socrates said: Yes, Crito, and they of whom you speak

are right in so acting, for they think that they will be gainers by the delay; but I am right in not following their example, for I do not think that I should gain anything by drinking the poison a little later; I should only be ridiculous in my own eyes for sparing and saving a life which is already forfeit. Please then to do as I say, and not to refuse me.

Crito made a sign to the servant, who was standing by; and he went out, and having been absent for some time, returned with the jailer carrying the cup of poison. Socrates said: You, my good friend, who are experienced in these matters, shall give me directions how I am to proceed. The man answered: You have only to walk about until your legs are heavy, and then to lie down, and the poison will act. At the same time he handed the cup to Socrates, who in the easiest and gentlest manner, without the least fear or change of colour or feature, looking at the man with all his eyes, Echecrates, as his manner was, took the cup and said: What do you say about making a libation out of this cup to any god? May I, or not? The man answered: We only prepare, Socrates, just so much as we deem enough. I understand, he said: but I may and must ask the gods to prosper my journey from this to the other world—even so—and so be it according to my prayer. Then raising the cup to his lips, quite readily and cheerfully he drank off the poison. And hitherto most of us had been able to control our sorrow; but now when we saw him drinking, and saw too that he had finished the draught, we could no longer forbear, and in spite of myself my own tears were flowing fast; so that I covered my face and wept, not for him, but at the thought of my own calamity in having to part from such a friend. Nor was I the first; for Crito, when he found himself unable to restrain his tears, had got up, and I followed; and at that moment, Apollodorus, who had been weeping all the time, broke out in a loud and passionate cry which made cowards of us all. Socrates alone retained his calmness: What is this strange outcry? he said. I sent away the women mainly in order that they might not misbehave in this way, for I have been told that a man should die in peace. Be quiet then, and have patience. When we heard his words we were ashamed, and refrained our tears; and he walked about until, as he said, his legs began to fail, and then he lay on his back, according to the directions, and the man who gave him the poison now and then looked at his feet and legs; and after a while he pressed his foot hard, and asked him if he could feel; and he said, No; and then his leg, and so upwards and upwards, and showed us that he was cold and stiff. And he felt them himself, and said: When the poison reaches the heart, that will be the end. He was beginning to grow cold about the groin, when he uncovered his face, for he had covered himself up, and said—they were his last words—he said: Crito, I owe a cock to Asclepius; will you remember to pay the debt? The debt shall be paid, said Crito; is there anything else? There was no answer to this question; but in a minute or two a movement was heard, and the attendants uncovered him; his eyes were set, and Crito closed his eyes and mouth.

Such was the end, Echecrates, of our friend; concerning whom I may truly say, that of all the men of his time whom I have known, he was the wisest and justest and best.

ION

PERSONS OF THE DIALOGUE

Socrates   Ion

Socrates. Welcome, Ion. Are you from your native city of Ephesus?

Ion. No, Socrates; but from Epidaurus, where I attended the festival of Asclepius.

Soc. And do the Epidaurians have contests of rhapsodes at the festival?

Ion. O yes; and of all sorts of musical performers.

Soc. And were you one of the competitors—and did you succeed?

Ion. I obtained the first prize of all, Socrates.

Soc. Well done; and I hope that you will do the same for us at the Panathenaea.

Ion. And I will, please heaven.

Soc. I often envy the profession of a rhapsode, Ion; for you have always to wear fine clothes, and to look as beautiful as you can is a part of your art. Then, again, you are obliged to be continually in the company of many good poets; and especially of Homer, who is the best and most divine of them; and to understand him, and not merely learn his words by rote, is a thing greatly to be envied. And no man can be a rhapsode who does not understand the meaning of the poet. For the rhapsode ought to interpret the mind of the poet to his hearers, but how can he interpret him well unless he knows what he means? All this is greatly to be envied.

Ion. Very true, Socrates; interpretation has certainly been the most laborious part of my art; and I believe myself able to speak about Homer better than any man; and that neither Metrodorus of Lampsacus, nor Stesimbrotus of Thasos, nor Glaucon, nor any one else who ever was, had as good ideas about Homer as I have, or as many.

Soc. I am glad to hear you say so, Ion; I see that you will not refuse to acquaint me with them.

Ion. Certainly, Socrates; and you really ought to hear how exquisitely I render Homer. I think that the Homeridae should give me a golden crown.

Soc. I shall take an opportunity of hearing your embellishments of him at some other time. But just now I should like to ask you a question: Does your art extend to Hesiod and Archilochus, or to Homer only?

Ion. To Homer only; he is in himself quite enough.

Soc. Are there any things about which Homer and Hesiod agree?

Ion. Yes; in my opinion there are a good many.

Soc. And can you interpret better what Homer says, or what Hesiod says, about these matters in which they agree?

Ion. I can interpret them equally well, Socrates, where they agree.

Soc. But what about matters in which they do not agree?—for example, about divination, of which both Homer and Hesiod have something to say,—

Ion. Very true:

Soc. Would you or a good prophet be a better interpreter of what these two poets say about divination, not only when they agree, but when they disagree?

Ion. A prophet.

Soc. And if you were a prophet, would you not be able to interpret them only when they disagree as well as when they agree?

Ion. Clearly.

Soc. But how did you come to have this skill about Homer only, and not about Hesiod or the other poets? Does not Homer speak of the same themes which all other poets handle? Is not war his great argument? and does he not speak of human society and of intercourse of men, good and bad, skilled and unskilled, and of the gods conversing with one another and with mankind, and about what happens in heaven and in the world below, and the generations of gods and heroes? Are not these the themes of which Homer sings?

Ion. Very true, Socrates.

Soc. And do not the other poets sing of the same?

Ion. Yes, Socrates; but not in the same way as Homer.

Soc. What, in a worse way?

Ion. Yes, in a far worse.

Soc. And Homer in a better way?

Ion. He is incomparably better.

Soc. And yet surely, my dear friend Ion, in a discussion about arithmetic, where many people are speaking, and one speaks better than the rest, there is somebody who can judge which of them is the good speaker?

Ion. Yes.

Soc. And he who judges of the good will be the same as he who judges of the bad speakers?

Ion. The same.

Soc. And he will be the arithmetician?

Ion. Yes.

Soc. Well, and in discussions about the wholesomeness of food, when many persons are speaking, and one speaks better than the rest, will he who recognizes the better speaker be a different person from him who recognizes the worse, or the same?

Ion. Clearly the same.

Soc. And who is he, and what is his name?

Ion. The physician.

Soc. And speaking generally, in all discussions in which the subject is the same and many men are speaking, will not he who knows the good know the bad speaker also? For if he does not know the bad, neither will he know the good when the same topic is being discussed.

Ion. True.

Soc. Is not the same person skilful in both?

Ion. Yes.

Soc. And you say that Homer and the other poets, such as Hesiod and Archilochus, speak of the same things, although not in the same way; but the one speaks well and the other not so well?

Ion. Yes; and I am right in saying so.

Soc. And if you knew the good speaker, you would also know the inferior speakers to be inferior?

Ion. That is true.

Soc. Then, my dear friend, can I be mistaken in saying that Ion is equally skilled in Homer and in other poets, since he himself acknowledges that the same person will be a good judge of all those who speak of the same things; and that almost all poets do speak of the same things?

Ion. Why then, Socrates, do I lose attention and go to sleep and have absolutely no ideas of the least value, when any one speaks of any other poet; but when Homer is mentioned, I wake up at once and am all attention and have plenty to say?

Soc. The reason, my friend, is obvious. No one can fail to see that you speak of Homer without any art or knowledge. If you were able to speak of him by rules of art, you would have been able to speak of all other poets; for poetry is a whole.

Ion. Yes.

Soc. And when any one acquires any other art as a whole, the same may be said of them. Would you like me to explain my meaning, Ion?

Ion. Yes, indeed, Socrates; I very much wish that you would: for I love to hear you wise men talk.

Soc. O that we were wise, Ion, and that you could truly call us so; but you rhapsodes and actors, and the poets whose verses you sing, are wise; whereas I am a common man, who only speak the truth. For consider what a very commonplace and trivial thing is this which I have said—a thing which any man might say: that when a man has acquired a knowledge of a whole art, the enquiry into good and bad is one and the same. Let us consider this matter; is not the art of painting a whole?

Ion. Yes.

Soc. And there are and have been many painters good and bad?

Ion. Yes.

Soc. And did you ever know any one who was skilful in pointing out the excellences and defects of Polygnotus the son of Aplaophon, but incapable of criticizing other painters; and when the work of any other painter was produced, went to sleep and was at a loss, and had no ideas; but when he had to give his opinion about Polygnotus, or whoever the painter might be, and about him only, woke up and was attentive and had plenty to say?

Ion. No indeed, I have never known such a person.

Soc. Or did you ever know of any one in sculpture, who was skilful in expounding the merits of Daedalus the son of Metion, or of Epeis the son of Panopeus, or of Theodorus the Samian, or of any individual sculptor; but when the works of sculptors in general were produced, was at a loss and went to sleep and had nothing to say?

Ion. No indeed; no more than the other.

Soc. And if I am not mistaken, you never met with any one among flute-players or harp-players or singers to the harp or rhapsodes who was able to discourse of Olympus or Thamyras or Orpheus, or Phemius the rhapsode of Ithaca, but was at a loss when he came to speak of Ion of Ephesus, and had no notion of his merits or defects?

Ion. I cannot deny what you say, Socrates. Nevertheless I am conscious in my own self, and the world agrees with me in thinking that I do speak better and have more to say about Homer than any other man. But I do not speak equally well about others—tell me the reason of this.

Soc. I perceive, Ion; and I will proceed to explain to you what I imagine to be the reason of this. The gift which you possess of speaking excellently about Homer is not an art, but, as I was just saying, an inspiration; there is a divinity moving you, like that contained in the stone which Euripides calls a magnet, but which is commonly known as the stone of Heraclea. This stone not only attracts iron rings, but also imparts to them a similar power of attracting other things; and sometimes you may see a number of pieces of iron and rings suspended from one another so as to form quite a long chain: and all of them derive their power of suspension from the original stone. In like manner the Muse first of all inspires men herself; and from these inspired persons a chain of other persons is suspended, who take the inspiration. For all good poets, epic as well as lyric, compose their beautiful poems not by art, but because they are inspired and possessed. And as the Corybantian revellers when they dance are not in their right mind, so the lyric poets are not in their right mind when they are composing their beautiful strains; but when falling under the power of music and metre they are inspired and possessed; like Bacchic maidens who draw milk and honey from the rivers when they are under the influence of Dionysus but not when they are in their right mind. And the soul of the lyric poet does the same, as they themselves say; for they tell us that they bring songs from honeyed fountains, culling them out of the gardens and dells of the Muses; they, like the bees, winging their way from flower to flower. And this is true. For the poet is a light and winged and holy thing, and there is no invention in him until he has been inspired and is out of his senses, and the mind is no longer in him: when he has not attained to this state, he is powerless and is unable to utter his oracles. Many are the noble words in which poets speak concerning the actions of men; but like yourself when speaking about Homer, they do not speak of them by any rules of art: they are simply inspired to utter that to which the Muse impels them, and that only; and when inspired, one of them will make dithyrambs, another hymns of praise, another choral strains, another epic or iambic verses—and he who is good at one is not good at any other kind of verse: for not by art does the poet sing, but by power divine. Had he learned by rules of art, he would have known how to speak not of one theme only, but of all; and therefore God takes away the minds of poets, and uses them as his ministers, as he also uses diviners and holy prophets, in order that we who hear them may know them to be speaking not of themselves who utter these priceless words in a state of unconsciousness, but that God himself is the speaker, and that through them he is conversing with us. And Tynnichus the Chalcidian affords a striking instance of what I am saying: he wrote nothing that any one would care to remember but the famous paean which is in every one's mouth, one of the finest poems ever written, simply an invention of the Muses, as he himself says. For in this way the God would seem to indicate to us and not allow us to doubt that these beautiful poems are not human, or the work of man, but divine and the work of God; and that the poets are only the interpreters of the Gods by whom they are severally possessed. Was not this the lesson which the God intended to teach when by the mouth of the worst of poets he sang the best of songs. Am I not right, Ion?

Ion. Yes, indeed, Socrates, I feel that you are; for your words touch my soul, and I am persuaded that good poets by a divine inspiration interpret the things of the Gods to us.

Soc. And you rhapsodists are the interpreters of the poets?

Ion. There again you are right.

Soc. Then you are the interpreters of interpreters?

Ion. Precisely.

Soc. I wish you would frankly tell me, Ion, what I am going to ask of you: When you produce the greatest effect upon the audience in the recitation of some striking passage, such as the apparition of Odysseus leaping forth on the floor, recognized by the suitors and casting his arrows at his feet, or the description of Achilles rushing at Hector, or the sorrows of Andromache, Hecuba, or Priam,—are you in your right mind? Are you not carried out of yourself, and does not your soul in an ecstasy seem to be among the persons or places of which you are speaking, whether they are in Ithaca or in Troy or whatever may be the scene of the poem?

Ion. That proof strikes home to me, Socrates. For I must frankly confess that at the tale of pity my eyes are filled with tears, and when I speak of horrors, my hair stands on end and my heart throbs.

Soc. Well, Ion, and what are we to say of a man who

at a sacrifice or festival, when he is dressed in holiday attire, and has golden crowns upon his head, of which nobody has robbed him, appears weeping or panic-stricken in the presence of more than twenty thousand friendly faces, when there is no one despoiling or wrong-ing him;—is he in his right mind or is he not?

Ion. No indeed, Socrates, I must say that, strictly speaking, he is not in his right mind.

Soc. And are you aware that you produce similar effects on most of the spectators?

Ion. Only too well; for I look down upon them from the stage, and behold the various emotions of pity, won-der, sternness, stamped upon their countenances when I am speaking: and I am obliged to give my very best at-tention to them; for if I make them cry I myself shall laugh, and if I make them laugh I myself shall cry when the time of payment arrives.

Soc. Do you know that the spectator is the last of the rings which, as I am saying, receive the power of the original magnet from one another? The rhapsode like yourself and the actor are intermediate links, and the poet himself is the first of them. Through all these the God sways the souls of men in any direction which he pleases, and makes one man hang down from an-other. Thus there is a vast chain of dancers and mas-ters and under-masters of choruses, who are suspended, as if from the stone, at the side of the rings which hang down from the Muse. And every poet has some Muse from whom he is suspended, and by whom he is said to be possessed, which is nearly the same thing; for he is taken hold of. And from these first rings, which are the poets, depend others, some deriving their inspiration from Orpheus, others from Musaeus; but the greater number are possessed and held by Homer. Of whom, Ion, you are one, and are possessed by Homer; and when any one repeats the words of another poet you go to

sleep, and know not what to say; but when any one re-
cites a strain of Homer you wake up in a moment, and
your soul leaps within you, and you have plenty to say;
for not by art or knowledge about Homer do you say
what you say, but by divine inspiration and by possession; just as the Corybantian revellers too have a quick
perception of that strain only which is appropriated to
the God by whom they are possessed, and have plenty
of dances and words for that, but take no heed of any
other. And you, Ion, when the name of Homer is mentioned have plenty to say, and have nothing to say of
others. You ask, 'Why is this?' The answer is that
you praise Homer not by art but by divine inspiration.

Ion. That is good, Socrates; and yet I doubt whether
you will ever have eloquence enough to persuade me that
I praise Homer only when I am mad and possessed;
and if you could hear me speak of him I am sure you
would never think this to be the case.

Soc. I should like very much to hear you, but not
until you have answered a question which I have to ask.
On what part of Homer do you speak well?—not surely
about every part.

Ion. There is no part, Socrates, about which I do
not speak well; of that I can assure you.

Soc. Surely not about things in Homer of which you
have no knowledge?

Ion. And what is there in Homer of which I have
no knowledge?

Soc. Why, does not Homer speak in many passages
about arts? For example, about driving; if I can only
remember the lines I will repeat them.

Ion. I remember, and will repeat them.

Soc. Tell me then, what Nestor says to Antilochus,
his son, where he bids him be careful of the turn at the
horserace in honour of Patroclus.

Ion. ' "Bend gently," he says, "in the polished chariot

to the left of them, and urge the horse on the right hand
with whip and voice; and slacken the rein. And when
you are at the goal, let the left horse draw near, yet so
that the nave of the well-wrought wheel may not even
seem to touch the extremity; and avoid catching the
stone," ' [1]

Soc. Enough. Now, Ion, will the charioteer or the
physician be the better judge of the propriety of these
lines?

Ion. The charioteer, clearly.

Soc. And will the reason be that this is his art, or
will there be any other reason?

Ion. No, that will be the reason.

Soc. And every art is appointed by God to have
knowledge of a certain work; for that which we know by
the art of the pilot we do not know by the art of medicine?

Ion. Certainly not.

Soc. Nor do we know by the art of the carpenter
that which we know by the art of medicine?

Ion. Certainly not.

Soc. And this is true of all the arts;—that which
we know with one art we do not know with the other?
But let me ask a prior question: You admit that there
are differences of arts?

Ion. Yes.

Soc. You would argue, as I should, that when one
art is of one kind of knowledge and another of another,
they are different?

Ion. Yes.

Soc. Yes, surely; for if the subject of knowledge
were the same, there would be no meaning in saying
that the arts were different,—if they both gave the same

[1] *Il,* xxiii, 335.

knowledge. For example, I know that here are five fingers, and you know the same. And if I were to ask whether I and you became acquainted with this fact by the help of the same art of arithmetic, you would acknowledge that we did?

Ion. Yes.

Soc. Tell me, then, what I was intending to ask you —whether this holds universally? Must the same art have the same subject of knowledge, and different arts other subjects of knowledge?

Ion. That is my opinion, Socrates.

Soc. Then he who has no knowledge of a particular art will have no right judgment of the sayings and doings of that art?

Ion. Very true.

Soc. Then which will be a better judge of the lines which you were reciting from Homer, you or the charioteer?

Ion. The charioteer.

Soc. Why, yes, because you are a rhapsode and not a charioteer.

Ion. Yes.

Soc. And the art of the rhapsode is different from that of the charioteer?

Ion. Yes.

Soc. And if a different knowledge, then a knowledge of different matters?

Ion. True.

Soc. You know the passage in which Hecamede, the concubine of Nestor, is described as giving to the wounded Machaon a posset, as he says, 'Made with Pramnian wine; and she grated cheese of goat's milk with a grater of bronze, and at his side placed an onion which gives a relish to drink.' [1] Now would you say

[1] *Il*, xi, 630, 638.

that the art of the rhapsode or the art of medicine was better able to judge of the propriety of these lines?

Ion. The art of medicine.

Soc. And when Homer says, 'And she descended into the deep like a leaden plummet, which, set in the horn of ox that ranges in the fields, rushes along carrying death among the ravenous fishes,'— [1] will the art of the fisherman or of the rhapsode be better able to judge whether these lines are rightly expressed or not?

Ion. Clearly, Socrates, the art of the fisherman.

Soc. Come now, suppose that you were to say to me: 'Since you, Socrates, are able to assign different passages in Homer to their corresponding arts, I wish that you would tell me what are the passages of which the excellence ought to be judged by the prophet and prophetic art'; and you will see how readily and truly I shall answer you. For there are many such passages, particularly in the Odyssey; as for example, the passage in which Theoclymenus the prophet of the house of Melampus says to the suitors:— [2] 'Wretched men! what is happening to you? Your heads and your faces and your limbs underneath are shrouded in night; and the voice of lamentation bursts forth, and your cheeks are wet with tears. And the vestibule is full, and the court is full, of ghosts descending into the darkness of Erebus, and the sun has perished out of heaven, and an evil mist is spread abroad.' And there are many such passages in the Iliad also; as for example in the description of the battle near the rampart, where he says:—'As they were eager to pass the ditch, there came to them an omen: a soaring eagle, holding back the people on the left, bore a huge bloody dragon in his talons, still living and panting; nor had he yet resigned the strife, for he bent back and smote the bird which

[1] *Il,* xxiv, 80.   [2] *Od.* xxi, 351.

carried him on the breast by the neck, and he in pain
let him fall from him to the ground into the midst of
the multitude. And the eagle, with a cry, was borne
afar on the wings of the wind.' [1] These are the sort
of things which I should say that the prophet ought to
consider and determine.

Ion. And you are quite right, Socrates, in saying so.

Soc. Yes, Ion, and you are right also. And as I
have seleced from the Iliad and Odyssey for you passages which describe the office of the prophet and the
physician and the fisherman, do you, who know Homer
so much better than I do, Ion, select for me passages
which relate to the rhapsode and the rhapsode's art, and
which the rhapsode ought to examine and judge of better than other men.

Ion. All passages, I should say, Socrates.

Soc. Not all, Ion, surely. Have you already forgotten what you were saying? A rhapsode ought to
have a better memory.

Ion. Why, what am I forgetting?

Soc. Do you not remember that you declared the art
of the rhapsode to be different from the art of the
charioteer?

Ion. Yes, I remember.

Soc. And you admitted that being different they
would have different subjects of knowledge?

Ion. Yes.

Soc. Then upon your own showing the rhapsode,
and the art of the rhapsode, will not know everything?

Ion. I should exclude certain things, Socrates.

Soc. You mean to say that you would exclude pretty
much the subjects of the other arts. As he does not
know all of them, which of them will he know?

Ion. He will know what a man and what a woman

[1] *Il,* xii, 200.

ought to say, and what a freeman and what a slave ought to say, and what a ruler and what a subject.

Soc. Do you mean that a rhapsode will know better than the pilot what the ruler of a sea-tossed vessel ought to say?

Ion. No; the pilot will know best.

Soc. Or will the rhapsode know better than the physician what the ruler of a sick man ought to say?

Ion. He will not.

Soc. But he will know what a slave ought to say?

Ion. Yes.

Soc. Suppose the slave to be a cowherd; the rhapsode will know better than the cowherd what he ought to say in order to soothe the infuriated cows?

Ion. No, he will not.

Soc. But he will know what a spinning-woman ought to say about the working of wool?

Ion. No.

Soc. At any rate he will know what a general ought to say when exhorting his soldiers?

Ion. Yes, that is the sort of thing which the rhapsode will be sure to know.

Soc. Well, but is the art of the rhapsode the art of the general?

Ion. I am sure that I should know what a general ought to say.

Soc. Why, yes, Ion, because you may possibly have a knowledge of the art of the general as well as of the rhapsode; and you may also have a knowledge of horsemanship as well as of the lyre; and then you would know when horses were well or ill managed. But suppose I were to ask you: By the help of which art, Ion, do you know whether horses are well managed, by your skill as a horseman or as a performer on the lyre—what would you answer?

Ion. I should reply, by my skill as a horseman.

Soc. And if you judged of performers on the lyre, you would admit that you judged of them as a performer on the lyre, and not as a horseman?

Ion. Yes.

Soc. And in judging of the general's art, do you judge of it as a general or a rhapsode?

Ion. To me there appears to be no difference between them.

Soc. What do you mean? Do you mean to say that the art of the rhapsode and of the general is the same?

Ion. Yes, one and the same.

Soc. Then he who is a good rhapsode is also a good general?

Ion. Certainly, Socrates.

Soc. And he who is a good general is also a good rhapsode?

Ion. No; I do not say that.

Soc. But you do say that he who is a good rhapsode is also a good general.

Ion. Certainly.

Soc. And you are the best of Hellenic rhapsodes?

Ion. Far the best Socrates.

Soc. And are you the best general, Ion?

Ion. To be sure, Socrates; and Homer was my master.

Soc. But then, Ion, what in the name of goodness can be the reason why you, who are the best of generals as well as the best of rhapsodes in all Hellas, go about as a rhapsode when you might be a general? Do you think that the Hellenes want a rhapsode with his golden crown, and do not want a general?

Ion. Why, Socrates, the reason is, that my countrymen, the Ephesians, are the servants and soldiers of Athens, and do not need a general; and you and Sparta are not likely to have me, for you think that you have enough generals of your own.

Soc. My good Ion, did you never hear of Apollodorus of Cyzicus?

Ion. Who may he be?

Soc. One who, though a foreigner, has often been chosen their general by the Athenians: and there is Phanosthenes of Andros, and Heraclides of Clazomenae, whom they have also appointed to the command of their armies and to other offices, although aliens, after they had shown their merit. And will they not choose Ion the Ephesian to be their general, and honour him, if he prove himself worthy? Were not the Ephesians originally Athenians, and Ephesus is no mean city? But, indeed, Ion, if you are correct in saying that by art and knowledge you are able to praise Homer, you do not deal fairly with me, and after all your professions of knowing many glorious things about Homer, and promises that you would exhibit them, you are only a deceiver, and so far from exhibiting the art of which you are a master, will not, even after my repeated entreaties, explain to me the nature of it. You have literally as many forms as Proteus; and now you go all manner of ways, twisting and turning, and, like Proteus, become all manner of people at once, and at last slip away from me in the disguise of a general, in order that you may escape exhibiting your Homeric lore. And if you have art, then, as I was saying, in falsifying your promise that you would exhibit Homer, you are not dealing fairly with me. But if, as I believe, you have no art, but speak all these beautiful words about Homer unconsciously under his inspiring influence, then I acquit you of dishonesty, and shall only say that you are inspired. Which do you prefer to be thought, dishonest or inspired?

Ion. There is a great difference, Socrates, between the two alternatives; and inspiration is by far the nobler.

Soc. Then, Ion, I shall assume the nobler alternative; and attribute to you in your praises of Homer inspiration, and not art.

SYMPOSIUM

PERSONS OF THE DIALOGUE

APOLLODORUS, *who repeats to
his companion the dia-
logue which he had heard
from Aristodemus, and
had already once nar-
rated to Glaucon.*
PHAEDRUS

PAUSANIAS
ERYXIMACHUS
ARISTOPHANES
AGATHON
SOCRATES
ALCIBIADES
A TROOP OF REVELLERS

SCENE:—The House of Agathon

[*Apollodorus gives an account of a banquet at the
house of Agathon, at which discourses in praise of love
are delivered by Socrates and his friends. In this selection, the discourse of Socrates only is given, coming as
it does at the conclusion of the other discourses.*]

Socrates proceeded as follows:—

In the magnificent oration which you have just
uttered, I think that you were right, my dear Agathon,
in proposing to speak of the nature of Love first and
afterwards of his works—that is a way of beginning
which I very much approve. And as you have spoken
so eloquently of his nature, may I ask you further,
Whether love is the love of something or of nothing?
And here I must explain myself: I do not want you to
say that love is the love of a father or the love of a
mother—that would be ridiculous; but to answer as you
would, if I asked is a father a father of something? to
which you would find no difficulty in replying, of a son
or daughter: and the answer would be right.

Very true, said Agathon.

And you would say the same of a mother?

He assented.

Yet let me ask you one more question in order to illustrate my meaning: Is not a brother to be regarded essentially as a brother of something?

Certainly, he replied.

That is, of a brother or sister?

Yes, he said.

And now, said Socrates, I will ask about Love:—Is Love of something or of nothing?

Of something, surely, he replied.

Keep in mind what this is, and tell me what I want to know—whether Love desires that of which love is.

Yes, surely.

And does he possess, or does he not possess, that which he loves and desires?

Probably not, I should say.

Nay, replied Socrates, I would have you consider whether 'necessarily' is not rather the word. The inference that he who desires something is in want of something, and that he who desires nothing is in want of nothing, is in my judgment, Agathon, absolutely and necessarily true. What do you think?

I agree with you, said Agathon.

Very good. Would he who is great, desire to be great, or he who is strong, desire to be strong?

That would be inconsistent with our previous admissions.

True. For he who is anything cannot want to be that which he is?

Very true.

And yet, added Socrates, if a man being strong desired to be strong, or being swift desired to be swift, or being healthy desired to be healthy, in that case he might be thought to desire something which he already has or is. I give the example in order that we may avoid misconception. For the possessors of these qualities, Agathon, must be supposed to have their respective advantages at the time, whether they choose or not; and who can desire that which he has? Therefore, when a person says, I am well and wish to be well, or I am rich and wish to be rich, and I desire simply to have what I have —to him we shall reply: 'You, my friend, having wealth and health and strength, want to have the continuance of them; for at this moment, whether you choose or no, you have them. And when you say, I desire that which I have and nothing else, is not your meaning that you want to have what you now have in the future?' He must agree with us—must he not?

He must, replied Agathon.

Then, said Socrates, he desires that what he has at present may be preserved to him in the future, which is equivalent to saying that he desires something which is non-existent to him, and which as yet he has not got.

Very true, he said.

Then he and every one who desires, desires that which he has not already, and which is future and not present, and which he has not, and is not, and of which he is in want;—these are the sort of things which love and desire seek?

Very true, he said.

Then now, said Socrates, let us recapitulate the argument. First, is not love of something, and of something too which is wanting to a man?

Yes, he replied.

Remember further what you said in your speech, or if you do not remember I will remind you: you said that the love of the beautiful set in order the empire of the gods, for that of deformed things there is no love—did you not say something of that kind?

Yes, said Agathon.

Yes, my friend, and the remark was a just one. And if this is true, Love is the love of beauty and not of deformity?

He assented.

And the admission has been already made that Love is of something which a man wants and has not?

True, he said.

Then Love wants and has not beauty?

Certainly, he replied.

And would you call that beautiful which wants and does not possess beauty?

Certainly not.

Then would you still say that love is beautiful?

Agathon replied: I fear that I did not understand what I was saying.

You made a very good speech, Agathon, replied Socrates; but there is yet one small question which I would fain ask:—Is not the good also the beautiful?

Yes.

Then in wanting the beautiful, love wants also the good?

I cannot refute you, Socrates, said Agathon:—Let us assume that what you say is true.

Say rather, beloved Agathon, that you cannot refute the truth; for Socrates is easily refuted.

And now, taking my leave of you, I will rehearse a tale of love which I heard from Diotima of Mantineia, a woman wise in this and in many other kinds of knowledge, who in the days of old, when the Athenians offered sacrifice before the coming of the plague, delayed the disease ten years. She was my instructress in the art of love, and I shall repeat to you what she said to me, beginning with the admissions made by Agathon, which are nearly if not quite the same which I made to the wise woman when she questioned me: I think that this will be the easiest way, and I shall take both parts myself as well as I can. As you, Agathon, suggested, I must speak first of the being and nature of Love, and then of his works. First I said to her in nearly the same words which he used to me, that Love was a mighty god, and likewise fair; and she proved to me as I proved to him that, by my own showing, Love was neither fair nor good. 'What do you mean, Diotima,' I said, 'is love then evil and foul?' 'Hush,' she cried; 'must that be foul which is not fair?' 'Certainly,' I said. 'And is that which is not wise, ignorant? do you not see that there is a mean between wisdom and ignorance?' 'And what may that be?' I said. 'Right opinion,' she replied; 'which, as you know, being incapable of giving a reason, is not knowledge (for how can knowledge be devoid of reason? nor again, ignorance, for neither can ignorance attain the truth), but is clearly something which is a mean between ignorance and wisdom.' 'Quite true,' I replied. 'Do not then insist,' she said, 'that what is not fair is of necessity foul, or what is not good evil; or infer that because love is not fair and good he is therefore foul and evil; for he is in a mean between them.' 'Well,' I said, 'Love is surely admitted by all to be a great god.' 'By those who know or by those who do not know?' 'By all.' 'And how, Socrates,' she said with a smile, 'can Love be acknowledged to be a great god by those who say that he is not a god at all?' 'And who are they?' I said. 'You and I are two of them,' she replied. 'How can that be?' I said. 'It is quite intelligible,' she replied; 'for you yourself would acknowledge that the gods are happy and fair—of course you would—would you dare to say that any god was not?' 'Certainly not,' I replied. 'And you mean by the happy,

those who are the possessors of things good or fair?'
'Yes.' 'And you admitted that Love, because he was in
want, desires those good and fair things of which he is
in want?' 'Yes, I did.' 'But how can he be a god who
has no portion in what is either good or fair?' 'Impossible.' 'Then you see that you also deny the divinity of
Love.'

'What then is Love?' I asked; 'Is he mortal?' 'No.'
'What then?' 'As in the former instance, he is neither
mortal nor immortal, but in a mean between the two.'
'What is he, Diotima?' 'He is a great spirit (δαίμων),
and like all spirits he is intermediate between the divine
and the mortal.' 'And what,' I said, 'is his power?'
'He interprets,' she replied, 'between gods and men,
conveying and taking across to the gods the prayers and
sacrifices of men, and to men the commands and replies
of the gods; he is the mediator who spans the chasm
which divides them, and therefore in him all is bound
together, and through him the arts of the prophet and
the priest, their sacrifices and mysteries and charms, and
all prophecy and incantation, find their way. For God
mingles not with man; but through Love all the intercourse and converse of God with man, whether awake or
asleep, is carried on. The wisdom which understands
this is spiritual; all other wisdom, such as that of arts
and handicrafts, is mean and vulgar. Now these spirits
or intermediate powers are many and diverse, and one
of them is Love.' 'And who, I said, 'was his father, and
who his mother?' 'The tale,' she said, 'will take time;
nevertheless I will tell you. On the birthday of Aphrodite there was a feast of the gods, at which the god
Poros or Plenty, who is the son of Metis or Discretion,
was one of the guests. When the feast was over, Penia
or Poverty, as the manner is on such occasions, came
about the doors to beg. Now Plenty, who was the worse

Diotima explains love to Socrates

for nectar (there was no wine in those days), went into
the garden of Zeus and fell into a heavy sleep; and
Poverty considering her own straitened circumstances,
plotted to have a child by him, and accordingly she lay
down at his side and conceived Love, who partly because he is naturally a lover of the beautiful, and because Aphrodite is herself beautiful, and also because
he was born on her birthday, is her follower and attendant. And as his parentage is, so also are his for-
tunes. In the first place he is always poor, and anything but tender and fair, as the many imagine him;
and he is rough and squalid, and has no shoes, nor a
house to dwell in; on the bare earth exposed he lies under the open heaven, in the streets, or at the doors of
houses, taking his rest; and like his mother he is always
in distress. Like his father too, whom he also partly
resembles, he is always plotting against the fair and
good; he is bold, enterprising, strong, a mighty hunter,
always weaving some intrigue or other, keen in the pursuit of wisdom, fertile in resources; a philosopher at all
times, terrible as an enchanter, sorcerer, sophist. He is
by nature neither mortal nor immortal, but alive and
flourishing at one moment when he is in plenty, and dead
at another moment, and again alive by reason of his
father's nature. But that which is always flowing in is
always flowing out, and so he is never in want and never
in wealth; and, further, he is in a mean between ignorance and knowledge. The truth of the matter is this: No
god is a philosopher or seeker after wisdom, for he is
wise already; nor does any man who is wise seek after
wisdom. Neither do the ignorant seek after wisdom.
For herein is the evil of ignorance, that he who is neither
good nor wise is nevertheless satisfied with himself: he
has no desire for that of which he feels no want.' 'But
who then, Diotima,' I said, 'are the lovers of wisdom, if

they are neither the wise nor the foolish?' 'A child may answer that question,' she replied; 'they are those who are in a mean between the two; Love is one of them. For wisdom is a most beautiful thing, and Love is of the beautiful; and therefore Love is also a philosopher or lover of wisdom, and being a lover of wisdom is in a mean between the wise and the ignorant. And of this too his birth is the cause; for his father is wealthy and wise, and his mother poor and foolish. Such, my dear Socrates, is the nature of the spirit Love. The error in your conception of him was very natural, and as I imagine from what you say, has arisen out of a confusion of love and the beloved, which made you think that love was all beautiful. For the beloved is the truly beautiful, and delicate, and perfect, and blessed; but the principle of love is of another nature, and is such as I have described.'

I said: 'O thou stranger woman, thou sayest well; but, assuming Love to be such as you say, what is the use of him to men?' 'That, Socrates,' she replied, 'I will attempt to unfold: of his nature and birth I have already spoken; and you acknowledge that love is of the beautiful. But some one will say: Of the beautiful in what, Socrates and Diotima?—or rather let me put the question more clearly, and ask: When a man loves the beautiful, what does he desire?' I answered her 'That the beautiful may be his.' 'Still,' she said, 'the answer suggests a further question: What is given by the possession of beauty?' 'To what you have asked,' I replied, 'I have no answer ready.' 'Then,' she said, 'let me put the word "good" in the place of the bautiful, and repeat the question once more: If he who loves loves the good, what is it then that he loves?' 'The possession of the good,' I said. 'And what does he gain who possesses the good?' 'Happiness,' I replied; 'there is less difficulty in answering that question. 'Yes,' she said, 'the happy are made happy by the acquisition of good things. Nor is there any need to ask why a man desires happiness; the answer is already final.' 'You are right,' I said. 'And is this wish and this desire common to all? and do all men always desire their own good, or only some men?—what say you?' 'All men,' I replied; 'the desire is common to all.' 'Why, then,' she rejoined, 'are not all men, Socrates, said to love, but only some of them? whereas you say that all men are always loving the same things.' 'I myself wonder,' I said, 'why this is.' 'There is nothing to wonder at,' she replied; 'the reason is that one part of love is separated off and receives the name of the whole, but the other parts have other names.' 'Give an illustration,' I said. She answered me as follows: 'There is poetry, which, as you know, is complex and manifold. All creation or passage of non-being into being is poetry or making, and the processes of all art are creative; and the masters of arts are all poets or makers.' 'Very true.' 'Still,' she said, 'you know that they are not called poets, but have other names; only that portion of the art which is separated off from the rest, and is concerned with music and metre, is termed poetry, and they who possess poetry in this sense of the word are called poets.' 'Very true,' I said. 'And the same holds of love. For you may say generally that all desire of good and happiness is only the great and subtle power of love; but they who are drawn towards him by any other path, whether the path of money-making or gymnastics or philosophy, are not called lovers—the name of the whole is appropriated to those whose affection takes one form only—they alone are said to love, or to be lovers.' 'I dare say,' I replied, 'that you are right.' 'Yes,' she added, 'and you hear people say that lovers are seeking for their other

half; but I say that they are seeking neither for the
half of themselves, nor for the whole, unless the half or
the whole be also a good. And they will cut off their
own hands and feet and cast them away, if they are evil;
for they love not what is their own, unless perchance
there be some one who calls what belongs to him the
good, and what belongs to another the evil. For there
is nothing which men love but the good. Is there anything?' 'Certainly, I should say, that there is nothing.'
'Then,' she said, 'the simple truth is, that men love the
good.' 'Yes,' I said. 'To which must be added that they
love the possession of the good?' 'Yes, that must be
added.' 'And not only the possession, but the everlasting possession of the good?' 'That must be added too.'
'Then love,' she said, 'may be described generally as the
love of the everlasting possession of the good?' 'That is
most true.'

'Then if this be the nature of love, can you tell me
further,' she said, 'what is the manner of the pursuit?
what are they doing who show all this eagerness and
heat which is called love? and what is the object which
they have in view? Answer me.' 'Nay, Diotima,' I replied, 'if I had known, I should not have wondered at
your wisdom, neither should I have come to learn from
you about this very matter.' 'Well,' she said, 'I will
teach you:—The object which they have in view is birth
in beauty, whether of body or soul.' 'I do not understand you,' I said; 'the oracle requires an explanation.'
'I will make my meaning clearer,' she replied. 'I mean
to say, that all men are bringing to the birth in their
bodies and in their souls. There is a certain age at
which human nature is desirous of procreation—procreation which must be in beauty and not in deformity; and
this procreation is the union of man and woman, and is
a divine thing; for conception and generation are an im-

mortal principle in the mortal creature, and in the inharmonious they can never be. But the deformed is
always inharmonious with the divine, and the beautiful
harmonious. Beauty, then, is the destiny or goddess
of parturition who presides at birth, and therefore, when
approaching beauty, the conceiving power is propitious,
and diffusive, and benign, and begets and bears fruit:
at the sight of ugliness she frowns and contracts and has
a sense of pain, and turns away, and shrivels up, and
not without a pang refrains from conception. And this
is the reason why, when the hour of conception arrives,
and the teeming nature is full, there is such a flutter and
ecstasy about beauty whose approach is the alleviation
of the pain of travail. For love, Socrates, is not, as you
imagine, the love of the beautiful only.' 'What then?'
'The love of generation and of birth in beauty.' 'Yes,'
I said. 'Yes, indeed,' she replied. 'But why of generation?' [Because to the mortal creature, generation is a
sort of eternity and immortality,' she replied; 'and if,
as has been already admitted, love is of the everlasting
possession of the good, all men will necessarily desire
immortality together with good: Wherefore love is of
immortality.']

All this she taught me at various times when she spoke
of love. And I remember her once saying to me, 'What
is the cause, Socrates, of love, and the attendant desire? See you not how all animals, birds, as well as
beasts, in their desire of procreation, are in agony when
they take the infection of love, which begins with the
desire of union; whereto is added the care of offspring,
on whose behalf the weakest are ready to battle against
the strongest even to the uttermost, and to die for them,
and will let themselves be tormented with hunger or suffer anything in order to maintain their young. Man
may be supposed to act thus from reason; but why

should animals have these passionate feelings? Can you tell me why?' Again I replied that I did not know. She said to me: 'And do you expect ever to become a master in the art of love, if you do not know this?' 'But I have told you already, Diotima, that my ignorance is the reason why I come to you; for I am conscious that I want a teacher; tell me then the cause of this and of the other mysteries of love.' 'Marvel not,' she said, 'if you believe that love is of the immortal, as we have several times acknowledged; for here again, and on the same principle too, the mortal nature is seeking as far as is possible to be everlasting and immortal: and this is only to be attained by generation, because generation always leaves behind a new existence in the place of the old. Nay even in the life of the same individual there is succession and not absolute unity: a man is called the same, and yet in the short interval which elapses between youth and age, and in which every animal is said to have life and identity, he is undergoing a perpetual process of loss and reparation—hair, flesh, bones, blood, and the whole body are always changing. Which is true not only of the body, but also of the soul, whose habits, tempers, opinions, desires, pleasures, pains, fears, never remain the same in any one of us, but are always coming and going; and equally true of knowledge, and what is still more surprising to us mortals, not only do the sciences in general spring up and decay, so that in respect of them we are never the same; but each of them individually experiences a like change. For what is implied in the word "recollection," but the departure of knowledge, which is ever being forgotten, and is renewed and preserved by recollection, and appears to be the same although in reality new, according to that law of succession by which all mortal things are preserved, not absolutely the same, but by substitution, the old worn-

out mortality leaving another new and similar existence
behind—unlike the divine, which is always the same and
not another? And in this way, Socrates, the mortal
body, or mortal anything, partakes of immortality; but
the immortal in another way. Marvel not then at the
love which all men have of their offspring; for that
universal love and interest is for the sake of immortality.'

I was astonished at her words, and said: Is this really
true, O thou wise Diotima?' And she answered with all
the authority of an accomplished sophist: 'Of that, Socrates, you may be assured;—think only of the ambition
of men, and you will wonder at the senselessness of their
ways, unless you consider how they are stirred by the
love of an immortality of fame. They are ready to run
all risks greater far than they would have run for their
children, and to spend money and undergo any sort of
toil, and even to die, for the sake of leaving behind them
a name which shall be eternal. Do you imagine that
Alcestis would have died to save Admetus, or Achilles
to avenge Patroclus, or your own Codrus in order to
preserve the kingdom for his sons, if they had not imagined that the memory of their virtues, which still survives among us, would be immortal? Nay,' she said, 'I
am persuaded that all men do all things, and the better
they are the more they do them, in hope of the glorious
fame of immortal virtue; for they desire the immortal.

'Those who are pregnant in the body only, betake
themselves to women and beget children—this is the
character of their love; their offspring, as they hope, will
preserve their memory and give them the blessedness
and immortality which they desire in the future. But
souls which are pregnant—for there certainly are men
who are more creative in their souls than in their bodies
—conceive that which is proper for the soul to conceive

or contain. And what are these conceptions?—wisdom
and virtue in general. And such creators are poets and
all artists who are deserving of the name inventor. But
the greatest and fairest sort of wisdom by far is that
which is concerned with the ordering of states and families, and which is called temperance and justice. And
he who in youth has the seed of these implanted in him
and is himself inspired, when he comes to maturity desires to beget and generate. He wanders about seeking
beauty that he may beget offspring—for in deformity he
will beget nothing—and naturally embraces the beautiful rather than the deformed body; above all when he
finds a fair and noble and well-nurtured soul, he embraces the two in one person, and to such an one he is
full of speech about virtue and the nature and pursuits
of a good man; and he tries to educate him; and at the
touch of the beautiful which is ever present to his memory, even when absent, he brings forth that which he had
conceived long before, and in company with him tends
that which he brings forth; and they are married by a
far nearer tie and have a closer friendship than those
who beget mortal children, for the children who are their
common offspring are fairer and more immortal. Who,
when he thinks of Homer and Hesiod and other great
poets, would not rather have their children than ordinary human ones? Who would not emulate them in the
creation of children such as theirs, which have preserved
their memory and given them everlasting glory? Or
who would not have such children as Lycurgus left behind him to be the saviours, not only of Lacedaemon, but
of Hellas, as one may say? There is Solon, too, who is
the revered father of Athenian laws; and many others
there are in many other places, both among Hellenes
and barbarians, who have given to the world many noble
works, and have been the parents of virtue of every

kind; and many temples have been raised in their honour for the sake of children such as theirs; which were never raised in honour of any one, for the sake of his mortal children.

'These are the lesser mysteries of love, into which even you, Socrates, may enter; to the greater and more hidden ones which are the crown of these, and to which, if you pursue them in a right spirit, they will lead, I know not whether you will be able to attain. But I will do my utmost to inform you, and do you follow if you can. For he who would proceed aright in this matter should begin in youth to visit beautiful forms; and first, if he be guided by his instructor aright, to love one such form only—out of that he should create fair thoughts; and soon he will of himself perceive that the beauty of one form is akin to the beauty of another; and then if beauty of form in general is his pursuit, how foolish would he be not to recognize that the beauty in every form is one and the same! And when he perceives this he will abate his violent love of the one, which he will despise and deem a small thing, and will become a lover of all beautiful forms; in the next stage he will consider that the beauty of the mind is more honourable than the beauty of the outward form. So that if a virtuous soul have but a little comeliness, he will be content to love and tend him, and will search out and bring to the birth thoughts which may improve the young, until he is compelled to contemplate and see the beauty of institutions and laws, and to understand that the beauty of them all is of one family, and that personal beauty is a trifle; and after laws and institutions he will go on to the sciences, that he may see their beauty, being not like a servant in love with the beauty of one youth or man or institution, himself a slave mean and narrow-minded, but drawing towards and contem-

plating the vast sea of beauty, he will create many fair
and noble thoughts and notions in boundless love of
wisdom; until on that shore he grows and waxes strong,
and at last the vision is revealed to him of a single science, which is the science of beauty everywhere.   To
this I will proceed; please to give me your very best
attention:

'He who has been instructed thus far in the things of
love, and who has learned to see the beautiful in due
order and succession, when he comes toward the end
will suddenly perceive a nature of wondrous beauty
(and this, Socrates, is the final cause of all our former
toils)—a nature which in the first place is everlasting,
not growing and decaying, or waxing and waning; secondly, not fair in one point of view and foul in another,
or at one time or in one relation or at one place fair, at
another time or in another relation or at another place
foul, as if fair to some and foul to others, or in the likeness of a face or hands or any other part of the bodily
frame, or in any form of speech or knowledge, or existing in any other being, as for example, in an animal,
or in heaven, or in earth, or in any other place; but
beauty absolute, separate, simple, and everlasting, which
without diminution and without increase, or any change,
is imparted to the ever-growing and perishing beauties
of all other things.   He who from these ascending under the influence of true love, begins to perceive that
beauty, is not far from the end.   And the true order
of going, or being led by another, to the things of love,
is to begin from the beauties of earth and mount upwards for the sake of that other beauty, using these as
steps only, and from one going on to two, and from two
to all fair forms, and from fair forms to fair practices,
and from fair practices to fair notions, until from fair
notions he arrives at the notion of absolute beauty, and

at last knows what the essence of beauty is. This, my dear Socrates,' said the stranger of Mantineia, 'is that life above all others which man should live, in the contemplation of beauty absolute; a beauty which if you once beheld, you would see not to be after the measure of gold, and garments, and fair boys and youths, whose presence now entrances you; and you and many a one would be content to live seeing them only and conversing with them without meat or drink, if that were possible— you only want to look at them and to be with them. But what if man had eyes to see the true beauty—the divine beauty, I mean, pure and clear and unalloyed, not clogged with the pollutions of mortality and all the colours and vanities of human life—thither looking, and holding converse with the true beauty simple and divine? Remember how in that communion only, beholding beauty with the eye of the mind, he will be enabled to bring forth, not images of beauty, but realities (for he has hold not of an image but of a reality), and bringing forth and nourishing true virtue to become the friend of God and be immortal, if mortal man may. Would that be an ignoble life?'

Such, Phaedrus—and I speak not only to you, but to all of you—were the words of Diotima; and I am persuaded of their truth. And being persuaded of them, I try to persuade others, that in the attainment of this end human nature will not easily find a helper better than love. And therefore, also, I say that every man ought to honour him as I myself honour him, and walk in his ways, and exhort others to do the same, and praise the power and spirit of love according to the measure of my ability now and ever.

The words which I have spoken, you, Phaedrus, may call an encomium of love, or anything else which you please.

When Socrates had done speaking, the company applauded, and Aristophanes was beginning to say something in answer to the allusion which Socrates had made to his own speech, when suddenly there was a great knocking at the door of the house, as of revellers, and the sound of a flute-girl was heard. Agathon told the attendants to go and see who were the intruders. 'If they are friends of ours,' he said, 'invite them in, but if not, say that the drinking is over.' A little while afterwards they heard the voice of Alcibiades resounding in the court; he was in a great state of intoxication, and kept roaring and shouting 'Where is Agathon? Lead me to Agathon,' and at length, supported by the flute-girl and some of his attendants, he found his way to them. 'Hail, friends,' he said, appearing at the door crowned with a massive garland of ivy and violets, his head flowing with ribands. 'Will you have a very drunken man as a companion of your revels? Or shall I crown Agathon, which was my intention in coming, and go away? For I was unable to come yesterday, and therefore I am here to-day, carrying on my head these ribands, that taking them from my own head, I may crown the head of this fairest and wisest of men, as I may be allowed to call him. Will you laugh at me because I am drunk? Yet I know very well that I am speaking the truth, although you may laugh. But first tell me; if I come in shall we have the understanding of which I spoke? Will you drink with me or not?'

The company were vociferous in begging that he would take his place among them, and Agathon specially invited him. Thereupon he was led in by the people who were with him; and as he was being led, intending to crown Agathon, he took the ribands from his own head and held them in front of his eyes; he was thus prevented from seeing Socrates, who made way for him,

and Alcibiades took the vacant place between Agathon
and Socrates, and in taking the place he embraced Agathon and crowned him.   Take off his sandals, said
Agathon, and let him make a third on the same couch.

By all means; but who makes the third partner in our
revels? said Alcibiades, turning round and starting up
as he caught sight of Socrates.   By Heracles, he said,
what is this? here is Socrates always lying in wait for
me, and always, as his way is, coming out at all sorts
of unsuspected places: and now, what have you to say
for yourself, and why are you lying here, where I perceive that you have contrived to find a place, not by a
joker or lover of jokes, like Aristophanes, but by the
fairest of the company?

Socrates turned to Agathon and said: I must ask you
to protect me, Agathon; for the passion of this man has
grown quite a serious matter to me.   Since I became his
admirer I have never been allowed to speak to any
other fair one, or so much as to look at them.   If I do,
he goes wild with envy and jealousy, and not only abuses
me but can hardly keep his hands off me, and at this moment he may do me some harm.   Please to see to this,
and either reconcile me to him, or, if he attempts violence, protect me, as I am in bodily fear of his mad and
passionate attempts.

There can never be reconciliation between you and me,
said Alcibiades; but for the present I will defer your
chastisement.   And I must beg you, Agathon, to give me
back some of the ribands that I may crown the marvellous head of this universal despot—I would not have
him complain of me for crowning you, and neglecting
him, who in conversation is the conqueror of all mankind; and this not only once, as you were the day before
yesterday, but always.   Whereupon, taking some of the
ribands, he crowned Socrates, and again reclined.

Then he said: You seem, my friends, to be sober, which is a thing not to be endured; you must drink—for that was the agreement under which I was admitted—and I elect myself master of the feast until you are well drunk. Let us have a large goblet, Agathon, or rather, he said, addressing the attendant, bring me that wine-cooler. The wine-cooler which had caught his eye was a vessel holding more than two quarts—this he filled and emptied, and bade the attendant fill it again for Socrates. Observe, my friends, said Alcibiades, that this ingenious trick of mine will have no effect on Socrates, for he can drink any quantity of wine and not be at all nearer being drunk. Socrates drank the cup which the attendant filled for him.

Eryximachus said: What is this, Alcibiades? Are we to have neither conversation nor singing over our cups; but simply to drink as if we were thirsty?

Alcibiades replied: Hail, worthy son of a most wise and worthy sire!

The same to you, said Eryximachus; but what shall we do?

That I leave to you, said Alcibiades. *head of feast now.*

'The wise physician skilled our wounds to heal' [1]

shall prescribe and we will obey. What do you want?

Well, said Eryximachus, before you appeared we had passed a resolution that each one of us in turn should make a speech in praise of love, and as good a one as he could: the turn was passed round from left to right; and as all of us have spoken, and you have not spoken but have well drunken, you ought to speak, and then impose upon Socrates any task which you please, and he on his right hand neighbour, and so on.

[1] From Pope's Homer, *Il.* xi. 514.

That is good, Eryximachus, said Alcibiades; and yet the comparison of a drunken man's speech with those of sober men is hardly fair; and I should like to know, sweet friend, whether you really believe what Socrates was just now saying; for I can assure you that the very reverse is the fact, and that if I praise any one but himself in his presence, whether God or man, he will hardly keep his hands off me.

For shame, said Socrates.

Hold your tongue, said Alcibiades, for by Poseidon, there is no one else whom I will praise when you are of the company.

Well then, said Eryximachus, if you like praise Socrates.

What do you think, Eryximachus? said Alcibiades: shall I attack him and inflict the punishment before you all?

What are you about? said Socrates; are you going to raise a laugh at my expense? Is that the meaning of your praise?

I am going to speak the truth, if you will permit me.

I not only permit, but exhort you to speak the truth.

Then I will begin at once, said Alcibiades, and if I say anything which is not true, you may interrupt me if you will, and say 'that is a lie,' though my intention is to speak the truth. But you must not wonder if I speak any how as things come into my mind; for the fluent and orderly enumeration of all your singularities is not a task which is easy to a man in my condition.

And now, my boys, I shall praise Socrates in a figure which will appear to him to be a caricature, and yet I speak, not to make fun of him, but only for the truth's sake. I say, that he is exactly like the busts of Silenus,

which are set up in the statuaries' shops, holding pipes
and flutes in their mouths; and they are made to open
in the middle, and have images of gods inside them.   I
say also that he is like Marsyas the satyr.   You yourself
will not deny, Socrates, that your face is like that of a
satyr.   Aye, and there is a resemblance in other points
too.   For example, you are a bully, as I can prove by
witnesses, if you will not confess.   And are you not a
flute-player?   That you are, and a performer far more
wonderful than Marsyas.   He indeed with instruments
used to charm the souls of men by the power of his
breath, and the players of his music do so still: for the
melodies of Olympus are derived from Marsyas who
taught them, and these, whether they are played by a
great master or by a miserable flute-girl, have a power
which no others have; they alone possess the soul and
reveal the wants of those who have need of gods and
mysteries, because they are divine.   But you produce the
same effect with your words only, and do not require
the flute: that is the difference between you and him.
When we hear any other speaker, even a very good one,
he produces absolutely no effect upon us, or not much,
whereas the mere fragments of you and your words, even
at second-hand, and however imperfectly repeated,
amaze and possess the souls of every man, woman, and
child who comes within hearing of them.   And if I were
not afraid that you would think me hopelessly drunk, I
would have sworn as well as spoken to the influence
which they have always had and still have over me.
For my heart leaps within me more than that of any
Corybantian reveller, and my eyes rain tears when I
hear them.   And I observe that many others are affected
in the same manner.   I have heard Pericles and other
great orators, and I thought that they spoke well, but

I never had any similar feeling; my soul was not stirred
by them, nor was I angry at the thought of my own
slavish state. But this Marsyas has often brought me
to such a pass, that I have felt as if I could hardly endure the life which I am leading (this, Socrates, you
will admit); and I am conscious that if I did not shut
my ears against him, and fly as from the voice of the
siren, my fate would be like that of others,—he would
transfix me, and I should grow old sitting at his feet.
For he makes me confess that I ought not to live as I
do, neglecting the wants of my own soul, and busying
myself with the concerns of the Athenians; therefore I
hold my ears and tear myself away from him. And he
is the only person who ever made me ashamed, which
you might think not to be in my nature, and there is no
one else who does the same. For I know that I cannot
answer him or say that I ought not to do as he bids,
but when I leave his presence the love of popularity gets
the better of me. And therefore I run away and fly
from him, and when I see him I am ashamed of what
I have confessed to him. Many a time have I wished
that he were dead, and yet I know that I should be
much more sorry than glad, if he were to die: so that I
am at my wit's end.

And this is what I and many others have suffered
from the flute-playing of this satyr. Yet hear me once
more while I show you how exact the image is, and how
marvellous his power. For let me tell you; none of you
know him; but I will reveal him to you; having begun,
I must go on. See you how fond he is of the fair? He
is always with them and is always being smitten by
them, and then again he knows nothing and is ignorant
of all things—such is the appearance which he puts on.
Is he not like a Silenus in this? To be sure he is: his
outer mask is the carved head of the Silenus; but, O my

companions in drink, when he is opened, what temperance there is residing within! Know you that beauty and wealth and honour, at which the many wonder, are of no account with him, and are utterly despised by him: he regards not at all the persons who are gifted with them; mankind are nothing to him; all his life is spent in mocking and flouting at them. But when I opened him, and looked within at his serious purpose, I saw in him divine and golden images of such fascinating beauty that I was ready to do in a moment whatever Socrates commanded: they may have escaped the observation of others, but I saw them. Now I fancied that he was seriously enamoured of my beauty, and I thought that I should therefore have a grand opportunity of hearing him tell what he knew, for I had a wonderful opinion of the attractions of my youth. In the prosecution of this design, when I next went to him, I sent away the attendant who usually accompanied me (I will confess the whole truth, and beg you to listen; and if I speak falsely, do you, Socrates, expose the falsehood). Well, he and I were alone together, and I thought that when there was nobody with us, I should hear him speak the language which lovers use to their loves when they are by themselves, and I was delighted. Nothing of the sort; he conversed as usual, and spent the day with me and then went away. Afterwards I challenged him to the palaestra; and he wrestled and closed with me several times when there was no one present; I fancied that I might succeed in this manner. Not a bit; I made no way with him. Lastly, as I had failed hitherto, I thought that I must take stronger measures and attack him boldly, and, as I had begun, not give him up, but see how matters stood between him and me. So I invited him to sup with me, just as if he were a fair youth, and I a designing lover. He was not easily persuaded to come; he did, however, after a while accept the invitation, and when he came the first time, he wanted to go away at once as soon as supper was over, and I had not the face to detain him. The second time, still in pursuance of my design, after we had supped, I went on conversing far into the night, and when he wanted to go away, I pretended that the hour was late and that he had much better remain. So he lay down on the couch next to me, the same on which he had supped, and there was no one but ourselves sleeping in the apartment. All this may be told without shame to any one. But what follows I could hardly tell you if I were sober. Yet as the proverb says, 'In vino veritas,' whether with boys, or without them; [1] and therefore I must speak. Nor, again, should I be justified in concealing the lofty actions of Socrates when I come to praise him. Moreover I have felt the serpent's sting; and he who has suffered, as they say, is willing to tell his fellow-sufferers only, as they alone will be likely to understand him, and will not be extreme in judging of the sayings or doings which have been wrung from his agony. For I have been bitten by a more than viper's tooth; I have known in my soul, or in my heart, or in some other part, that worst of pangs, more violent in ingenuous youth than any serpent's tooth, the pang of philosophy, which will make a man say or do anything. And you whom I see around me, Phaedrus and Agathon and Eryximachus and Pausanias and Aristodemus and Aristophanes, all of you, and I need not say Socrates himself, have had experience of the same madness and passion in your longing after wisdom. Therefore listen and excuse my doings then and my sayings now. But let the attendants and other profane and unmannered persons close up the doors of their ears.

[1] In allusion to the two proverbs, οἶνος καὶ παῖδες ἀληθεῖς, and οἶνος καὶ ἀλήθεια.

When the lamp was put out and the servants had
gone away, I thought that I must be plain with him and
have no more ambiguity. So I gave him a shake, and
I said: 'Socrates, are you asleep?' 'No,' he said. 'Do
you know what I am meditating?' 'What are you meditating?' he said. 'I think,' I replied, 'that of all the
lovers whom I have ever had you are the only one who
is worthy of me, and you appear to be too modest to
speak. Now I feel that I should be a fool to refuse
you this or any other favour, and therefore I come to
lay at your feet all that I have and all that my friends
have, in the hope that you will assist me in the way of
virtue, which I desire above all things, and in which I
believe that you can help me better than any one else.
And I should certainly have more reason to be ashamed
of what wise men would say if I were to refuse a favour
to such as you, than of what the world, who are mostly
fools, would say of me if I granted it.' To these words
he replied in the ironical manner which is so characteristic of him:—'Alcibiades, my friend, you have indeed an
elevated aim if what you say is true, and if there really
is in me any power by which you may become better;
truly you must see in me some rare beauty of a kind infinitely higher than any which I see in you. And therefore, if you mean to share with me and to exchange
beauty for beauty, you will have greatly the advantage
of me; you will gain true beauty in return for appearance—like Diomede, gold in exchange for brass. But
look again, sweet friend, and see whether you are not
deceived in me. The mind begins to grow critical when
the bodily eye fails, and it will be a long time before you
get old.' Hearing this, I said: 'I have told you my purpose, which is quite serious, and do you consider what
you think best for you and me.' 'That is good,' he said;
'at some other time then we will consider and act as
seems best about this and about other matters.' Where-

upon, I fancied that he was smitten, and that the words which I had uttered like arrows had wounded him, and so without waiting to hear more I got up, and throwing my coat about him crept under his threadbare cloak, as the time of year was winter, and there I lay during the whole night having this wonderful monster in my arms. This again, Socrates, will not be denied by you. And yet, notwithstanding all, he was so superior to my solicitations, so contemptuous and derisive and disdainful of my beauty—which really, as I fancied, had some attractions—hear, O judges; for judges you shall be of the haughty virtue of Socrates—nothing more happened, but in the morning when I awoke (let all the gods and goddesses be my witnesses) I arose as from the couch of a father or an elder brother.

What do you suppose must have been my feelings, after this rejection, at the thought of my own dishonour? And yet I could not help wondering at his natural temperance and self-restraint and manliness. I never imagined that I could have met with a man such as he is in wisdom and endurance. And therefore I could not be angry with him or renounce his company, any more than I could hope to win him. For I well knew that if Ajax could not be wounded by steel, much less he by money; and my only chance of captivating him by my personal attractions had failed. So I was at my wit's end; no one was ever more hopelessly enslaved by another. All this happened before he and I went on the expedition to Potidaea; there we messed together, and I had the opportunity of observing his extraordinary power of sustaining fatigue. His endurance was simply marvellous when, being cut off from our supplies, we were compelled to go without food—on such occasions, which often happen in time of war, he was superior not only to me but to everybody; there was no one to be compared to him. Yet at a festival he was the only person who had any real powers of enjoyment; though not willing to drink, he could if compelled beat us all at that,—wonderful to relate! no human being had ever seen Socrates drunk; and his powers, if I am not mistaken, will be tested before long. His fortitude in enduring cold was also surprising. There was a severe frost, for the winter in that region is really tremendous, and everybody else either remained indoors, or if they went out had on an amazing quantity of clothes, and were well shod, and had their feet swathed in felt and fleeces: in the midst of this, Socrates with his bare foot on the ice and in his ordinary dress marched better than the other soldiers who had shoes, and they looked daggers at him because he seemed to despise them.

I have told you one tale, and now I must tell you another, which is worth hearing,

'Of the doings and sufferings of the enduring man'

while he was on the expedition. One morning he was thinking about something which he could not resolve; he would not give it up, but continued thinking from early dawn until noon—there he stood fixed in thought; and at noon attention was drawn to him, and the rumour ran through the wondering crowd that Socrates had been standing and thinking about something ever since the break of day. At last, in the evening after supper, some Ionians out of curiosity (I should explain that this was not in winter but in summer), brought out their mats and slept in the open air that they might watch him and see whether he would stand all night. There he stood until the following morning; and with the return of light he offered up a prayer to the sun, and went his way. I will also tell, if you please—and indeed I

am bound to tell—of his courage in battle; for who but
he saved my life? Now this was the engagement in
which I received the prize of valour: for I was wounded
and he would not leave me, but he rescued me and my
arms; and he ought to have received the prize of valour
which the generals wanted to confer on me partly on
account of my rank, and I told them so (this, again,
Socrates will not impeach or deny), but he was more
eager than the generals that I and not he should have
the prize. There was another occasion on which his behaviour was very remarkable—in the flight of the army
after the battle of Delium, where he served among the
heavy-armed,—I had a better opportunity of seeing him
than at Potidaea, for I was myself on horseback, and
therefore comparatively out of danger. He and Laches
were retreating, for the troops were in flight, and I met
them and told them not to be discouraged, and promised
to remain with them; and there you might see him,
Aristophanes, as you describe,[1] just as he is in the streets
of Athens, stalking like a pelican, and rolling his eyes,
calmly contemplating enemies as well as friends, and
making very intelligible to anybody, even from a distance, that whoever attacked him would be likely to
meet with a stout resistance; and in this way he and his
companion escaped—for this is the sort of man who is
never touched in war; those only are pursued who are
running away headlong. I particularly observed how
superior he was to Laches in presence of mind. Many
are the marvels which I might narrate in praise of Socrates; most of his ways might perhaps be paralleled in
another man, but his absolute unlikeness to any human
being that is or ever has been is perfectly astonishing.
You may imagine Brasidas and others to have been like
Achilles; or you may imagine Nestor and Antenor to

[1] Aristoph. *Clouds*, 362.

Tells what a superior man Socrates is.

have been like Pericles; and the same may be said of other famous men, but of this strange being you will never be able to find any likeness, however remote, either among men who now are or who ever have been—other than that which I have already suggested of Silenus and the satyrs; and they represent in a figure not only himself, but his words. For, although I forgot to mention this to you before, his words are like the images of Silenus which open; they are ridiculous when you first hear them; he clothes himself in language that is like the skin of the wanton satyr—for his talk is of packasses and smiths and cobblers and curriers, and he is always repeating the same things in the same words, so that any ignorant or inexperienced person might feel disposed to laugh at him; but he who opens the bust and sees what is within will find that they are the only words which have a meaning in them, and also the most divine, abounding in fair images of virtue, and of the widest comprehension, or rather extending to the whole duty of a good and honourable man.

This, friends, is my praise of Socrates. I have added my blame of him for his ill-treatment of me; and he has ill-treated not only me, but Charmides the son of Glaucon, and Euthydemus the son of Diocles, and many others in the same way—beginning as their lover he has ended by making them pay their addresses to him. Wherefore I say to you, Agathon, 'Be not deceived by him; learn from me and take warning, and do not be a fool and learn by experience, as the proverb says.'

When Alcibiades had finished, there was a laugh at his outspokenness; for he seemed to be still in love with Socrates. You are sober, Alcibiades, said Socrates, or you would never have gone so far about to hide the purpose of your satyr's praises, for all this long story is only an ingenious circumlocution, of which the point comes in by the way at the end; you want to get up a quarrel between me and Agathon, and your notion is that I ought to love you and nobody else, and that you and you only ought to love Agathon. But the plot of this Satyric or Silenic drama has been detected, and you must not allow him, Agathon, to set us at variance.

I believe you are right, said Agathon, and I am disposed to think that his intention in placing himself between you and me was only to divide us; but he shall gain nothing by that move; for I will go and lie on the couch next to you.

Yes, yes, replied Socrates, by all means come here and lie on the couch below me.

Alas, said Alcibiades, how I am fooled by this man; he is determined to get the better of me at every turn. I do beseech you, allow Agathon to lie between us.

Certainly not, said Socrates; as you praised me, and I in turn ought to praise my neighbor on the right, he will be out of order in praising me again when he ought rather to be praised by me, and I must entreat you to consent to this, and not be jealous, for I have a great desire to praise the youth.

Hurrah! cried Agathon, I will rise instantly, that I may be praised by Socrates.

The usual way, said Alcibiades; where Socrates is, no one else has any chance with the fair; and now how readily has he invented a specious reason for attracting Agathon to himself.

Agathon arose in order that he might take his place on the couch by Socrates, when suddenly a band of revellers entered, and spoiled the order of the banquet. Some one who was going out having left the door open, they had found their way in, and made themselves at home; great confusion ensued, and every one was compelled to drink large quantities of wine. Aristodemus said that Eryxi-

machus, Phaedrus, and others went away—he himself
fell asleep, and as the nights were long took a good
rest: he was awakened towards daybreak by a crowing
of cocks, and when he awoke, the others were either
asleep, or had gone away; there remained only Socrates,
Aristophanes, and Agathon, who were drinking out of a
large goblet which they passed round, and Socrates was
discoursing to them. Aristodemus was only half awake,
and he did not hear the beginning of the discourse; the
chief thing which he remembered was Socrates compell-
ing the other two to acknowledge that the genius of
comedy was the same with that of tragedy, and that the
true artist in tragedy was an artist in comedy also. To
this they were constrained to assent, being drowsy, and
not quite following the argument. And first of all
Aristophanes dropped off, then, when the day was already dawning, Agathon. Socrates, having laid them to
sleep, rose to depart; Aristodemus, as his manner was,
following him. At the Lyceum he took a bath, and passed
the day as usual. In the evening he retired to rest at his
own home.

PHAEDRUS

PERSONS OF THE DIALOGUE

SOCRATES   PHAEDRUS

SCENE:—Under a plane-tree, by the banks of the Ilissus

Socrates. My dear Phaedrus, whence come you, and whither are you going?

Phaedrus. I have come from Lysias the son of Cephalus, and I am going to take a walk outside the wall, for I have been sitting with him the whole morning; and our common friend Acumenus tells me that it is much more refreshing to walk in the open air than to be shut up in a cloister.

Soc. There he is right. Lysias then, I suppose, was in the town?

Phaedr. Yes, he was staying with Epicrates, here at the house of Morychus; that house which is near the temple of Olympian Zeus.

Soc. And how did he entertain you? Can I be wrong in supposing that Lysias gave you a feast of discourse?

Phaedr. You shall hear, if you can spare time to accompany me.

Soc. And should I not deem the conversation of you and Lysias 'a thing of higher import,' as I may say in the words of Pindar, 'than any business?'

Phaedr. Will you go on?

Soc. And will you go on with the narration?

Phaedr. My tale, Socrates, is one of your sort, for love was the theme which occupied us—love after a fashion: Lysias has been writing about a fair youth who

284

was being tempted, but not by a lover; and this was the point: he ingeniously proved that the non-lover should be accepted rather than the lover.

Soc. O that is noble of him! I wish that he would say the poor man rather than the rich, and the old man rather than the young one;—then he would meet the case of me and of many a man; his words would be quite refreshing, and he would be a public benefactor. For my part, I do so long to hear his speech, that if you walk all the way to Megara, and when you have reached the wall come back, as Herodicus recommends, without going in, I will keep you company.

Phaedr. What do you mean, my good Socrates? How can you imagine that my unpractised memory can do justice to an elaborate work, which the greatest rhetorician of the age spent a long time in composing. Indeed, I cannot; I would give a great deal if I could.

Soc. I believe that I know Phaedrus about as well as I know myself, and I am very sure that the speech of Lysias was repeated to him, not once only, but again and again;—he insisted on hearing it many times over and Lysias was very willing to gratify him; at last, when nothing else would do, he got hold of the book, and looked at what he most wanted to see,—this occupied him during the whole morning;—and then when he was tired with sitting, he went out to take a walk, not until, by the dog, as I believe, he had simply learned by heart the entire discourse, unless it was unusually long, and he went to a place outside the wall that he might practise his lesson. There he saw a certain lover of discourse who had a similar weakness;—he saw and rejoiced; now thought he, 'I shall have a partner in my revels.' And he invited him to come and walk with him. But when the lover of discourse begged that he would repeat the tale, he gave himself airs and said, 'No I cannot,' as if he were indisposed; although, if the hearer had refused, he would sooner or later have been compelled by him to listen whether he would or no. Therefore, Phaedrus, bid him do at once what he will soon do whether bidden or not.

Phaedr. I see that you will not let me off until I speak in some fashion or other; verily therefore my best plan is to speak as I best can.

Soc. A very true remark, that of yours.

Phaedr. I will do as I say; but believe me, Socrates, I did not learn the very words—O no; nevertheless I have a general notion of what he said, and will give you a summary of the points in which the lover differed from the non-lover. Let me begin at the beginning.

Soc. Yes, my sweet one; but you must first of all show what you have in your left hand under your cloak, for that roll, as I suspect, is the actual discourse. Now, much as I love you, I would not have you suppose that I am going to have your memory exercised at my expense, if you have Lysias himself here.

Phaedr. Enough; I see that I have no hope of practising my art upon you. But if I am to read, where would you please to sit?

Soc. Let us turn aside and go by the Ilissus; we will sit down at some quiet spot.

Phaedr. I am fortunate in not having my sandals, and as you never have any, I think that we may go along the brook and cool our feet in the water; this will be the easiest way, and at midday and in the summer is far from being unpleasant.

Soc. Lead on, and look out for a place in which we can sit down.

Phaedr. Do you see that tallest plane-tree in the distance?

Soc. Yes.

Phaedr. There are shade and gentle breezes, and grass on which we may either sit or lie down.

Soc. Move forward.

Phaedr. I should like to know, Socrates, whether the place is not somewhere here at which Boreas is said to have carried off Orithyia from the banks of the Ilissus?

Soc. Such is the tradition.

Phaedr. And is this the exact spot? The little stream is delightfully clear and bright; I can fancy that there might be maidens playing near.

Soc. I believe that the spot is not exactly here, but about a quarter of a mile lower down, where you cross to the temple of Artemis, and there is, I think, some sort of an altar of Boreas at the place.

Phaedr. I have never noticed it; but I beseech you to tell me, Socrates, do you believe this tale?

Soc. The wise are doubtful, and I should not be singular if, like them, I too doubted. I might have a rational explanation that Orithyia was playing with Pharmacia, when a northern gust carried her over the neighbouring rocks; and this being the manner of her death, she was said to have been carried away by Boreas. There is a discrepancy, however, about the locality; according to another version of the story she was taken from the Areopagus, and not from this place. Now I quite acknowledge that these allegories are very nice, but he is not to be envied who has to invent them; much labour and ingenuity will be required of him; and when he has once begun, he must go on and rehabilitate Hippocentaurs and chimeras dire. Gorgons and winged steeds flow in apace, and numberless other inconceivable and portentous natures. And if he is sceptical about them, and would fain reduce them one after another to the rules of probability, this sort of crude philosophy will take up a great deal of time. Now I have no leisure

for such enquiries; shall I tell you why? I must first
know myself, as the Delphian inscription says; to be
curious about that which is not my concern, while I am
still in ignorance of my own self, would be ridiculous.
And therefore I bid farewell to all this; the common
opinion is enough for me. For, as I was saying, I want
to know not about this, but about myself: am I a monster more complicated and swollen with passion than the
serpent Typho, or a creature of a gentler and simpler
sort, to whom Nature has given a diviner and lowlier
destiny? But let me ask you, friend: have we not reached
the plane-tree to which you were conducting us?

Phaedr. Yes, this is the tree.

Soc. By Herè, a fair resting-place, full of summer
sounds and scents. Here is this lofty and spreading
plane-tree, and the agnus castus high and clustering, in
the fullest blossom and the greatest fragrance; and the
stream which flows beneath the plane-tree is deliciously
cold to the feet. Judging from the ornaments and
images, this must be a spot sacred to Achelous and the
Nymphs. How delightful is the breeze:—so very
sweet; and there is a sound in the air shrill and sum-
merlike which makes answer to the chorus of the cicadae.
But the greatest charm of all is the grass, like a pillow
gently sloping to the head. My dear Phaedrus, you have
been an admirable guide.

Phaedr. What an incomprehensible being you are,
Socrates: when you are in the country, as you say, you
really are like some stranger who is led about by a guide.
Do you ever cross the border? I rather think that you
never venture even outside the gates.

Soc. Very true, my good friend; and I hope that you
will excuse me when you hear the reason, which is, that
I am a lover of knowledge, and the men who dwell in
the city are my teachers, and not the trees or the coun-

try. Though I do indeed believe that you have found
a spell with which to draw me out of the city into the
country, like a hungry cow before whom a bough or a
bunch of fruit is waved. For only hold up before me
in like manner a book, and you may lead me all round
Attica, and over the wide world. And now having arrived, I intend to lie down, and do you choose any posture in which you can read best.

[*They then discuss the nature of love, after which
Socrates delivers the following discourse on the nature
and life of the soul.*]

The soul through all her being is immortal, for that
which is ever in motion is immortal; but that which
moves another and is moved by another, in ceasing to
move ceases also to live. Only the self-moving, never
leaving self, never ceases to move, and is the fountain
and beginning of motion to all that moves besides. Now,
the beginning is unbegotten, for that which is begotten
has a beginning; but the beginning is begotten of nothing, for if it were begotten of something, then the begotten would not come from a beginning. But if unbegotten, it must also be indestructible; for if beginning were
destroyed, there could be no beginning out of anything,
nor anything out of a beginning; and all things must
have a beginning. And therefore the self-moving is the
beginning of motion; and this can neither be destroyed
nor begotten, else the whole heavens and all creation
would collapse and stand still, and never again have motion or birth. But if the self-moving is proved to be
immortal, he who affirms that self-motion is the very idea
and essence of the soul will not be put to confusion.
For the body which is moved from without is soulless;
but that which is moved from within has a soul, for such

is the nature of the soul. But if this be true, must not
the soul be the self-moving, and therefore of necessity
unbegotten and immortal? Enough of the soul's immortality.

Of the nature of the soul, though her true form be
ever a theme of large and more than mortal discourse,
let me speak briefly, and in a figure. And let the figure
be composite—a pair of winged horses and a charioteer.
Now the winged horses and the charioteers of the gods
are all of them noble and of noble descent, but those
of other races are mixed; the human charioteer drives
his in a pair; and one of them is noble and of noble
breed, and the other is ignoble and of ignoble breed;
and the driving of them of necessity gives a great deal
of trouble to him. I will endeavour to explain to you
in what way the mortal differs from the immortal creature. The soul in her totality has the care of inanimate
being everywhere, and traverses the whole heaven in
divers forms appearing;—when perfect and fully winged
she soars upward, and orders the whole world; whereas
the imperfect soul, losing her wings and drooping in her
flight at last settles on the solid ground—there, finding
a home, she receives an earthly frame which appears to
be self-moved, but is really moved by her power; and
this composition of soul and body is called a living and
mortal creature. For immortal no such union can be
reasonably believed to be; although fancy, not having
seen nor surely known the nature of God, may imagine
an immortal creature having both a body and also a soul
which are united throughout all time. Let that, however, be as God wills, and be spoken of acceptably to
him. And now let us ask the reason why the soul loses
her wings!

The wing is the corporeal element which is most akin
to the divine, and which by nature tends to soar aloft

and carry that which gravitates downwards into the upper region, which is the habitation of the gods. The divine is beauty, wisdom, goodness, and the like; and by these the wing of the soul is nourished, and grows apace; but when fed upon evil and foulness and the opposite of good, wastes and falls away. Zeus, the mighty lord, holding the reins of a winged chariot, leads the way in heaven, ordering all and taking care of all; and there follows him the array of gods and demi-gods, marshalled in eleven bands; Hestia alone abides at home in the house of heaven; of the rest they who are reckoned among the princely twelve march in their appointed order. They see many blessed sights in the inner heaven, and there are many ways to and fro, along which the blessed gods are passing, every one doing his own work; he may follow who will and can, for jealousy has no place in the celestial choir. But when they go to banquet and festival, then they move up the steep to the top of the vault of heaven. The chariots of the gods in even poise, obeying the rein, glide rapidly; but the others labour, for the vicious steed goes heavily, weighing down the charioteer to the earth when his steed has not been thoroughly trained:—and this is the hour of agony and extremest conflict for the soul. For the immortals, when they are at the end of their course, go forth and stand upon the outside of heaven, and the revolution of the spheres carries them round, and they behold the things beyond. But of the heaven which is above the heavens, what earthly poet ever did or ever will sing worthily? It is such as I will describe; for I must dare to speak the truth, when truth is my theme. There abides the very being with which true knowledge is concerned; the colourless, formless, intangible essence, visible only to mind, the pilot of the soul. The divine intelligence, being nurtured upon mind and pure knowl-

edge, and the intelligence of every soul which is capable
of receiving the food proper to it, rejoices at beholding
reality, and once more gazing upon truth, is replenished
and made glad, until the revolution of the worlds brings
her round again to the same place. In the revolution
she beholds justice, and temperance, and knowledge absolute, not in the form of generation or of relation,
which men call existence, but knowledge absolute in existence absolute; and beholding the other true existences
in like manner, and feasting upon them, she passes down
into the interior of the heavens and returns home; and
there the charioteer putting up his horses at the stall,
gives them ambrosia to eat and nectar to drink.

Such is the life of the gods; but of other souls, that
which follows God best and is likest to him lifts the
head of the charioteer into the outer world, and is carried round in the revolution, troubled indeed by the
steeds, and with difficulty beholding true being; while
another only rises and falls, and sees, and again fails to
see by reason of the unruliness of the steeds. The rest
of the souls are also longing after the upper world and
they all follow, but not being strong enough they are
carried round below the surface, plunging, treading on
one another, each striving to be first; and there is confusion and perspiration and the extremity of effort; and
many of them are lamed or have their wings broken
through the ill-driving of the charioteers; and all of
them after a fruitless toil, not having attained to the
mysteries of true being, go away, and feed upon opinion. The reason why the souls exhibit this exceeding
eagerness to behold the plain of truth is that pasturage
is found there, which is suited to the highest part of the
soul; and the wing on which the soul soars is nourished
with this. And there is a law of Destiny, that the soul
which attains any vision of truth in company with a god

is preserved from harm until the next period, and if attaining always is always unharmed. But when she is unable to follow, and fails to behold the truth, and through some ill-hap sinks beneath the double load of forgetfulness and vice, and her wings fall from her and she drops to the ground, then the law ordains that this soul shall at her first birth pass, not into any other animal, but only into man; and the soul which has seen most of truth shall come to the birth as a philosopher, or artist, or some musical and loving nature; that which has seen truth in the second degree shall be some righteous king or warrior chief; the soul which is of the third class shall be a politician, or economist, or trader; the fourth shall be a lover of gymnastic toils, or a physician; the fifth shall lead the life of a prophet or hierophant; to the sixth the character of a poet or some other imitative artist will be assigned; to the seventh the life of an artisan or husbandman; to the eighth that of a sophist or demagogue; to the ninth that of a tyrant;—all these are states of probation, in which he who does righteously improves, and he who does unrighteously, deteriorates his lot.

Ten thousand years must elapse before the soul of each one can return to the place from whence she came, for she cannot grow her wings in less; only the soul of a philosopher, guileless and true, or the soul of a lover, who is not devoid of philosophy, may acquire wings in the third of the recurring periods of a thousand years; he is distinguished from the ordinary good man who gains wings in three thousand years:—and they who choose this life three times in succession have wings given them, and go away at the end of three thousand years. But the others [1] receive judgment when they

---

[1] The philosopher alone is not subject to judgment (χρίσις) for he has never lost the vision of truth.

have completed their first life, and after the judgment
they go, some of them to the houses of correction which
are under the earth, and are punished; others to some
place in heaven whither they are lightly borne by justice, and there they live in a manner worthy of the life
which they led here when in the form of men. And at
the end of the first thousand years the good souls and
also the evil souls both come to draw lots and choose
their second life, and they may take any which they
please. The soul of a man may pass into the life of a
beast, or from the beast return again into the man. But
the soul which has never seen the truth will not pass
into the human form. For a man must have intelligence
of universals, and be able to proceed from the many particulars of sense to one conception of reason;—this is
the recollection of those things which our soul once saw
while following God—when regardless of that which we
now call being she raised her head up towards the true
being. And therefore the mind of the philosopher alone
has wings; and this is just, for he is always, according
to the measure of his abilities, clinging in recollection
to those things in which God abides, and in beholding
which He is what He is. And he who employs aright
these memories is ever being initiated into perfect mysteries and alone becomes truly perfect. But, as he forgets earthly interests and is rapt in the divine, the vulgar deem him mad, and rebuke him; they do not see that
he is inspired.

Thus far I have been speaking of the fourth and last
kind of madness, which is imputed to him who, when he
sees the beauty of earth, is transported with the recollection of the true beauty; he would like to fly away,
but he cannot; he is like a bird fluttering and looking upward and careless of the world below; and he is therefore thought to be mad. And I have shown this of all

inspirations to be the noblest and highest and the offspring of the highest to him who has or shares in it, and
that he who loves the beautiful is called a lover because
he partakes of it. For, as has been already said, every
soul of man has in the way of nature beheld true being; this was the condition of her passing into the form
of man. But all souls do not easily recall the things of
the other world; they may have seen them for a short
time only, or they may have been unfortunate in their
earthly lot, and, having had their hearts turned to unrighteousness through some corrupting influence, they
may have lost the memory of the holy things which once
they saw. Few only retain an adequate remembrance of
them; and they, when they behold here any image of
that other world, are rapt in amazement; but they are
ignorant of what this rapture means, because they do
not clearly perceive. For there is no light of justice or
temperance or any of the higher ideas which are precious
to souls in the earthly copies of them: they are seen
through a glass dimly; and there are few who, going to
the images, behold in them the realities, and these only
with difficulty. There was a time when with the rest of
the happy band they saw beauty shining in brightness,
—we philosophers following in the train of Zeus, others in company with other gods; and then we beheld the
beatific vision and were initiated into a mystery which
may be truly called most blessed, celebrated by us in our
state of innocence, before we had any experience of
evils to come, when we were admitted to the sight of
apparitions innocent and simple and calm and happy,
which we beheld shining in pure light, pure ourselves
and not yet enshrined in that living tomb which we carry
about, now that we are imprisoned in the body, like an
oyster in his shell. Let me linger over the memory of
scenes which have passed away.

But of beauty, I repeat again that we saw her there shining in company with the celestial forms; and coming to earth we find her here too, shining in clearness through the clearest aperture of sense. For sight is the most piercing of our bodily senses; though not by that is wisdom seen; her loveliness would have been transporting if there had been a visible image of her, and the other ideas, if they had visible counterparts, would be equally lovely. But this is the privilege of beauty, that being the loveliest she is also the most palpable to sight. Now he who is not newly initiated or who has become corrupted, does not easily rise out of this world to the sight of true beauty in the other; he looks only at her earthly namesake, and instead of being awed at the sight of her, he is given over to pleasure, and like a brutish beast he rushes on to enjoy and beget; he consorts with wantonness, and is not afraid or ashamed of pursuing pleasure in violation of nature. But he whose initiation is recent, and who has been the spectator of many glories in the other world, is amazed when he sees any one having a godlike face or form, which is the expression of divine beauty; and at first a shudder runs through him, and again the old awe steals over him; then looking upon the face of his beloved as of a god he reverences him, and if he were not afraid of being thought a downright madman, he would sacrifice to his beloved as to the image of a god; then while he gazes on him there is a sort of reaction, and the shudder passes into an unusual heat and perspiration; for, as he receives the effluence of beauty through the eyes, the wing moistens and he warms. And as he warms, the parts out of which the wing grew, and which had been hitherto closed and rigid, and had prevented the wing from shooting forth, are melted, and as nourishment streams upon him, the lower end of the wing begins to swell and grow from the root

upwards; and the growth extends under the whole soul—
for once the whole was winged. During this process the
whole soul is all in a state of ebullition and effervescence,
—which may be compared to the irritation and uneasiness in the gums at the time of cutting teeth,—bubbles
up, and has a feeling of uneasiness and tickling; but
when in like manner the soul is beginning to grow wings,
the beauty of the beloved meets her eye and she receives the sensible warm motion of particles which flow
towards her, therefore called emotion (ἵμερος), and is
refreshed and warmed by them, and then she ceases from
her pain with joy. But when she is parted from her
beloved and her moisture fails, then the orifices of the
passage out of which the wing shoots dry up and close,
and intercept the germ of the wing; which, being shut
up with the emotion, throbbing as with the pulsations of
an artery, pricks the aperture which is nearest, until
at length the entire soul is pierced and maddened and
pained, and at the recollection of beauty is again delighted. And from both of them together the soul is
oppressed at the strangeness of her condition, and is in
a great strait and excitement, and in her madness can
neither sleep by night nor abide in her place by day.
And wherever she thinks that she will behold the beautiful one, thither in her desire she runs. And when she
has seen him, and bathed herself in the waters of beauty,
her constraint is loosened, and she is refreshed, and has
no more pangs and pains; and this is the sweetest of all
pleasures at the time, and is the reason why the soul
of the lover will never forsake his beautiful one, whom
he esteems above all; he has forgotten mother and brethren and companions, and he thinks nothing of the neglect
and loss of his property; the rules and proprieties of
life, on which he formerly prided himself, he now de-
spises, and is ready to sleep like a servant, wherever he

is allowed, as near as he can to his desired one, who is the object of his worship, and the physician who can alone assuage the greatness of his pain. And this state, my dear imaginary youth to whom I am talking, is by men called love, and among the gods has a name at which you, in your simplicity, may be inclined to mock; there are two lines in the apocryphal writings of Homer in which the name occurs. One of them is rather outrageous, and not altogether metrical. They are as follows:—

'Mortals call him fluttering love,
But the immortals call him winged one,
Because the growing of wings [1] is a necessity to him.'

You may believe this, but not unless you like. At any rate the loves of lovers and their causes are such as I have described.

Now the lover who is taken to be the attendant of Zeus is better able to bear the winged god, and can endure a heavier burden; but the attendants and companions of Ares, when under the influence of love, if they fancy that they have been at all wronged, are ready to kill and put an end to themselves and their beloved. And he who follows in the train of any other god, while he is unspoiled and the impression lasts, honours and imitates him, as far as he is able; and after the manner of his God he behaves in his intercourse with his beloved and with the rest of the world during the first period of his earthly existence. Every one chooses his love from the ranks of beauty according to his character, and this he makes his god, and fashions and adorns as a sort of image which he is to fall down and worship. The followers of Zeus desire that their beloved should have a

---

[1] Or, reading πτερόφοιτον 'the movement of wings.'

soul like him; and therefore they seek out some one of a philosophical and imperial nature, and when they have found him and loved him, they do all they can to confirm such a nature in him, and if they have no experience of such a disposition hitherto, they learn of any one who can teach them, and themselves follow in the same way. And they have the less difficulty in finding the nature of their own god in themselves, because they have been compelled to gaze intensely on him; their recollection clings to him, and they become possessed of him, and receive from him their character and disposition, so far as man can participate in God. The qualities of their god they attribute to the beloved, wherefore they love him all the more, and if, like the Bacchic Nymphs, they draw inspiration from Zeus, they pour out their own fountain upon him, wanting to make him as like as possible to their own god. But those who are the followers of Herè seek a royal love, and when they have found him they do just the same with him; and in like manner the followers of Apollo, and of every other god walking in the ways of their god, seek a love who is to be made like him whom they serve, and when they have found him, they themselves imitate their god, and persuade their love to do the same, and educate him into the manner and nature of the god as far as they each can; for no feelings of envy or jealousy are entertained by them towards their beloved, but they do their utmost to create in him the greatest likeness of themselves and of the god whom they honour. Thus fair and blissful to the beloved is the desire of the inspired lover, and the initiation of which I speak into the mysteries of true love, if he be captured by the lover and their purpose is effected. Now the beloved is taken captive in the following manner:—

As I said at the beginning of this tale, I divided each

soul into three—two horses and a charioteer; and one of
the horses was good and the other bad: the division may
remain, but I have not yet explained in what the goodness or badness of either consists, and to that I will now
proceed. The right-hand horse is upright and cleanly
made; he has a lofty neck and an aquiline nose; his
colour is white, and his eyes dark; he is a lover of honour
and modesty and temperance, and the follower of true
glory; he needs no touch of the whip, but is guided by
word and admonition only. The other is a crooked lum-
bering animal, put together anyhow; he has a short thick
neck; he is flat-faced and of a dark colour, with grey
eyes and blood-red complexion; [1] the mate of insolence
and pride, shag-eared and deaf, hardly yielding to whip
and spur. Now when the charioteer beholds the vision
of love, and has his whole soul warmed through sense,
and is full of the prickings and ticklings of desire, the
obedient steed, then as always under the government of
shame, refrains from leaping on the beloved; but the
other, heedless of the pricks and of the blows of the
whip, plunges and runs away, giving all manner of
trouble to his companion and the charioteer, whom he
forces to approach the beloved and to remember the joys
of love. They at first indignantly oppose him and will
not be urged on to do terrible and unlawful deeds; but
at last, when he persists in plaguing them, they yield
and agree to do as he bids them. And now they are at
the spot and behold the flashing beauty of the beloved;
which when the charioteer sees, his memory is carried
to the true beauty, whom he beholds in company with
Modesty like an image placed upon a holy pedestal. He
sees her, but he is afraid and falls backwards in adora-
tion, and by his fall is compelled to pull back the reins
with such violence as to bring both the steeds on their

[1] Or with grey and blood-shot eyes.

haunches, the one willing and unresisting, the unruly
one very unwilling; and when they have gone back a
little, the one is overcome with shame and wonder, and
his whole soul is bathed in perspiration; the other, when
the pain is over which the bridle and the fall had given
him, having with difficulty taken breath, is full of wrath
and reproaches, which he heaps upon the charioteer and
his fellow-steed, for want of courage and manhood, declaring that they have been false to their agreement and
guilty of desertion.   Again they refuse, and again he
urges them on, and will scarce yield to their prayer that
he would wait until another time. When the appointed
hour comes, they make as if they had forgotten, and he
reminds them, fighting and neighing and dragging them
on, until at length he on the same thoughts intent, forces
them to draw near again.   And when they are near he
stoops his head and puts up his tail, and takes the bit
in his teeth and pulls shamelessly.   Then the charioteer
is worse off than ever; he falls back like a racer at the
barrier, and with a still more violent wrench drags the
bit out of the teeth of the wild steed and covers his
abusive tongue and jaws with blood, and forces his legs
and haunches to the ground and punishes him sorely.
And when this has happened several times and the villain has ceased from his wanton way, he is tamed and
humbled, and follows the will of the charioteer, and
when he sees the beautiful one he is ready to die of fear.
And from that time forward the soul of the lover follows the beloved in modesty and holy fear.

And so the beloved who, like a god, has received every
true and loyal service from his lover, not in pretence
but in reality, being also himself of a nature friendly to
his admirer,[1] if in former days he has blushed to own
his passion and turned away his lover, because his youth-

---

[1] Omitting εἰς ταὐτὸν ἄγει τὴν φιλίαν.

ful companions or others slanderously told him that he would be disgraced, now as years advance, at the appointed age and time, is led to receive him into communion. For fate which has ordained that there shall be no friendship among the evil has also ordained that there shall ever be friendship among the good. And the beloved when he has received him into communion and intimacy, is quite amazed at the good-will of the lover; he recognises that the inspired friend is worth all other friends or kinsmen; they have nothing of friendship in them worthy to be compared with his. And when this feeling continues and he is nearer to him and embraces him, in gymnastic exercises and at other times of meeting, then the fountain of that stream, which Zeus when he was in love with Ganymede named Desire, overflows upon the lover, and some enters into his soul, and some when he is filled flows out again; and as a breeze or an echo rebounds from the smooth rocks and returns whence it came, so does the stream of beauty, passing through the eyes which are the windows of the soul, come back to the beautiful one; there arriving and quickening the passages of the wings, watering them and inclining them to grow, and filling the soul of the beloved also with love. And thus he loves, but he knows not what; he does not understand and cannot explain his own state; he appears to have caught the infection of blindness from another; the lover is his mirror in whom he is beholding himself, but he is not aware of this. When he is with the lover, both cease from their pain, but when he is away then he longs as he is longed for, and has love's image, love for love (Anteros) lodging in his breast, which he calls and believes to be not love but friendship only, and his desire is as the desire of the other, but weaker; he wants to see him, touch him, kiss, embrace him, and probably not long afterwards his de-

sire is accomplished. When they meet, the wanton
steed of the lover has a word to say to the charioteer; he
would like to have a little pleasure in return for many
pains, but the wanton steed of the beloved says not a
word, for he is bursting with passion which he understands not;—he throws his arms round the lover and
embraces him as his dearest friend; and, when they are
side by side, he is not in a state in which he can refuse
the lover anything, if he ask him; although his fellow-
steed and the charioteer oppose him with the arguments
of shame and reason. After this their happiness depends upon their self-control; if the better elements of
the mind which lead to order and philosophy prevail,
then they pass their life here in happiness and harmony
—masters of themselves and orderly—enslaving the
vicious and emancipating the virtuous elements of the
soul; and when the end comes, they are light and winged
for flight, having conquered in one of the three heavenly
or truly Olympian victories; nor can human discipline
or divine inspiration confer any greater blessing on man
than this. If, on the other hand, they leave philosophy
and lead the lower life of ambition, then probably, after
wine or in some other careless hour, the two wanton animals take the two souls when off their guard and bring
them together, and they accomplish that desire of their
hearts which to the many is bliss; and this having once
enjoyed they continue to enjoy, yet rarely because they
have not the approval of the whole soul. They too are
dear, but not so dear to one another as the others, either
at the time of their love or afterwards. They consider
that they have given and taken from each other the
most sacred pledges, and they may not break them and
fall into enmity. At last they pass out of the body, un-
winged, but eager to soar, and thus obtain no mean reward of love and madness. For those who have once

begun the heavenward pilgrimage may not go down again to darkness and the journey beneath the earth, but they live in light always; happy companions in their pilgrimage, and when the time comes at which they receive their wings they have the same plumage because of their love.

Thus great are the heavenly blessings which the friendship of a lover will confer upon you, my youth. Whereas the attachment of the non-lover, which is alloyed with a worldly prudence and has worldly and niggardly ways of doling out benefits, will breed in your soul those vulgar qualities which the populace applaud, will send you bowling round the earth during a period of nine thousand years, and leave you a fool in the world below.

[The rest of the dialogue is omitted.]

THEAETETUS

PERSONS OF THE DIALOGUE

SOCRATES THEODORUS THEAETETUS

Euclid and Terpsion meet in front of Euclid's house in Megara; they enter the house, and the dialogue is read to them by a servant

[*This dialogue is an investigation into the nature of knowledge. Socrates urges Theaetetus to venture an opinion on the subject, and proceeds to compare himself to a midwife.*]

Socrates. Have you never heard, simpleton, that I am the son of a midwife, brave and burly, whose name was Phaenarete?

Theaetetus. Yes, I have.

Soc. And that I myself practise midwifery?

Theaet. No, never.

Soc. Let me tell you that I do though, my friend: but you must not reveal the secret, as the world in general have not found me out; and therefore they only say of me, that I am the strangest of mortals and drive men to their wits' end. Did you ever hear that too?

Theaet. Yes.

Soc. Shall I tell you the reason?

Theaet. By all means.

Soc. Bear in mind the whole business of the midwives, and then you will see my meaning better:—No woman, as you are probably aware, who is still able to conceive and bear, attends other women, but only those who are past bearing.

305

Theaet. Yes, I know.

Soc. The reason of this is said to be that Artemis—the goddess of childbirth—is not a mother, and she honours those who are like herself; but she could not allow the barren to be midwives, because human nature cannot know the mystery of an art without experience; and therefore she assigned this office to those who are too old to bear.

Theaet. I dare say.

Soc. And I dare say too, or rather I am absolutely certain, that the midwives know better than others who is pregnant and who is not?

Theaet. Very true.

Soc. And by the use of potions and incantations they are able to arouse the pangs and to soothe them at will; they can make those bear who have a difficulty in bearing, and if they think fit they can smother the embryo in the womb.

Theaet. They can.

Soc. Did you ever remark that they are also most cunning matchmakers, and have a thorough knowledge of what unions are likely to produce a brave brood?

Theaet. No, never.

Soc. Then let me tell you that this is their greatest pride, more than cutting the umbilical cord. And if you reflect, you will see that the same art which cultivates and gathers in the fruits of the earth, will be most likely to know in what soils the several plants or seeds should be deposited.

Theaet. Yes, the same art.

Soc. And do you suppose that with women the case is otherwise?

Theaet. I should think not.

Soc. Certainly not; but midwives are respectable women who have a character to lose, and they avoid this

department of their profession, because they are afraid
of being called procuresses, which is a name given to
those who join together man and woman in an unlawful
and unscientific way; and yet the true midwife is also
the true and only matchmaker.

Theaet. Clearly.

Soc. Such are the midwives, whose task is a very
important one, but not so important as mine; for women
do not bring into the world at one time real children,
and at another time counterfeits which are with difficulty
distinguished from them; if they did, then the discern-
ment of the true and false birth would be the crowning
achievement of the art of midwifery—you would think
so?

Theaet. Indeed I should.

Soc. Well, my art of midwifery is in most respects
like theirs; but differs, in that I attend men and not
women, and I look after their souls when they are in labour, and not after their bodies: and the triumph of my
art is in thoroughly examining whether the thought which
the mind of the young man brings forth is a false idol
or a noble and true birth. And like the midwives, I am
barren, and the reproach which is often made against
me, that I ask questions of others and have not the wit
to answer them myself, is very just—the reason is, that
the god compels me to be a midwife, but does not allow
me to bring forth. And therefore I am not myself at all
wise, nor have I anything to show which is the invention or birth of my own soul, but those who converse
with me profit. Some of them appear dull enough at
first, but afterwards, as our acquaintance ripens, if the
god is gracious to them, they all make astonishing progress; and this in the opinion of others as well as in
their own. It is quite clear that they never learned anything from me; the many fine discoveries to which they

cling are of their own making. But to me and the god
they owe their delivery. And the proof of my words is,
that many of them in their ignorance, either in their
self-conceit despising me, or falling under the influence
of others,[1] have gone away too soon; and have not only
lost the children of whom I had previously delivered
them by an ill bringing up, but have stifled whatever
else they had in them by evil communications, being
fonder of lies and shams than of the truth; and they
have at last ended by seeing themselves, as others see
them, to be great fools. Aristeides, the son of Lysi-
machus, is one of them, and there are many others. The
truants often return to me, and beg that I would consort
with them again—they are ready to go to me on their
knees—and then, if my familiar allows, which is not always the case, I receive them, and they begin to grow
again. Dire are the pangs which my art is able to
arouse and to allay in those who consort with me, just
like the pangs of women in childbirth; night and day
they are full of perplexity and travail which is even
worse than that of the women. So much for them. And
there are others, Theaetetus, who come to me apparently
having nothing in them; and as I know that they have
no need of my art, I coax them into marrying some one,
and by the grace of God I can generally tell who is
likely to do them good. Many of them I have given
away to Prodicus, and many to other inspired sages. I
tell you this long story, friend Theaetetus, because I suspect, as indeed you seem to think yourself, that you are
in labour—great with some conception. Come then to
me, who am a midwife's son and myself a midwife, and
do your best to answer the questions which I will ask
you. And if I abstract and expose your first-born, because I discover upon inspection that the conception

[1] Reading with the Bodleian MS. ἢ αὐτοὶ ὑπ' ἄλλων πεισθέντες.

which you have formed is a vain shadow, do not quarrel with me on that account, as the manner of women is when their first children are taken from them. For I have actually known some who were ready to bite me when I deprived them of a darling folly; they did not perceive that I acted from goodwill, not knowing that no god is the enemy of man—that was not within the range of their ideas; neither am I their enemy in all this, but it would be wrong for me to admit falsehood, or to stifle the truth. Once more, then, Theaetetus, I repeat my old question, 'What is knowledge?'—and do not say that you cannot tell; but quit yourself like a man, and by the help of God you will be able to tell.

Theaet. At any rate, Socrates, after such an exhortation I should be ashamed of not trying to do my best. Now he who knows perceives what he knows, and, as far as I can see at present, knowledge is perception.

Soc. Bravely said, boy; that is the way in which you should express your opinion. And now, let us examine together this conception of yours, and see whether it is a true birth or a mere wind-egg:—You say that knowledge is perception?

Theaet. Yes.

Soc. Well, you have delivered yourself of a very important doctrine about knowledge; it is indeed the opinion of Protagoras, who has another way of expressing it. Man, he says, is the measure of all things, of the existence of things that are, and of the non-existence of things that are not:—You have read him?

Theaet. O yes, again and again.

Soc. Does he not say that things are to you such as they appear to you, and to me such as they appear to me, and that you and I are men?

Theaet. Yes, he says so.

Soc. A wise man is not likely to talk nonsense. Let

us try to understand him: the same wind is blowing, and yet one of us may be cold and the other not, or one may be slightly and the other very cold?

Theaet. Quite true.

Soc. Now is the wind, regarded not in relation to us but absolutely, cold or not; or are we to say, with Protagoras, that the wind is cold to him who is cold, and not to him who is not?

Theaet. I suppose the last.

Soc. Then it must appear so to each of them?

Theaet. Yes.

Soc. And 'appears to him' means the same as 'he perceives.'

Theaet. True.

Soc. Then appearing and perceiving coincide in the case of hot and cold, and in similar instances; for things appear, or may be supposed to be, to each one such as he perceives them?

Theaet. Yes.

Soc. Then perception is always of existence, and being the same as knowledge is unerring?

Theaet. Clearly.

Soc. In the name of the Graces, what an almighty wise man Protagoras must have been! He spoke these things in a parable to the common herd, like you and me, but told the truth, 'his Truth,' [1] in secret to his own disciples.

Theaet. What do you mean, Socrates?

Soc. I am about to speak of a high argument, in which all things are said to be relative; you cannot rightly call anything by any name, such as great or small, heavy or light, for the great will be small and the heavy light—there is no single thing or quality, but out of motion and change and admixture all things are be-

---

[1] In allusion to a book of Protagoras' which bore this title.

coming relatively to one another, which 'becoming' is by us incorrectly called being, but is really becoming, for nothing ever is, but all things are becoming. Summon all philosophers—Protagoras, Heracleitus, Empedocles, and the rest of them, one after another, and with the exception of Parmenides they will agree with you in this. Summon the great masters of either kind of poetry— Epicharmus, the prince of Comedy, and Homer of Tragedy; when the latter sings of

'Ocean whence sprang the gods, and mother Tethys,'

does he not mean that all things are the offspring of flux and motion?

Theaet. I think so.

Soc. And who could take up arms against such a great army having Homer for its general, and not appear ridiculous?

Theaet. Who, indeed, Socrates?

Soc. Yes, Theaetetus; and there are plenty of other proofs which will show that motion is the source of what is called being and becoming, and inactivity of not-being and destruction; for fire and warmth, which are supposed to be the parent and guardian of all other things, are born of movement and of friction, which is a kind of motion; [1]—is not this the origin of fire?

Theaet. It is.

Soc. And the race of animals is generated in the same way?

Theaet. Certainly.

Soc. And is not the bodily habit spoiled by rest and idleness, but preserved for a long time [2] by motion and exercise?

[1] Reading τοῦτο δὲ κίνησις.
[2] Reading ἐπὶ πολύ.

Theaet. True.

Soc. And what of the mental habit? Is not the soul informed, and improved, and preserved by study and attention, which are motions; but when at rest, which in the soul only means want of attention and study, is uninformed, and speedily forgets whatever she has learned?

Theaet. True.

Soc. Then motion is a good, and rest an evil, to the soul as well as to the body?

Theaet. Clearly.

Soc. I may add, that breathless calm, stillness and the like waste and impair, while wind and storm preserve; and the palmary argument of all, which I strongly urge, is the golden chain in Homer, by which he means the sun, thereby indicating that so long as the sun and the heavens go round in their orbits, all things human and divine are and are preserved, but if they were chained up and their motions ceased, then all things would be destroyed, and, as the saying is, turned upside down.

Theaet. I believe, Socrates, that you have truly explained his meaning.

Soc. Then now apply his doctrine to perception, my good friend, and first of all to vision; that which you call white colour is not in your eyes, and is not a distinct thing which exists out of them. And you must not assign any place to it: for if it had position it would be, and be at rest, and there would be no process of becoming.

Theaet. Then what is colour?

Soc. Let us carry out the principle which has just been affirmed, that nothing is self-existent, and then we shall see that white, black, and every other colour, arises out of the eye meeting the appropriate motion, and that what we call a colour is in each case neither the active nor the passive element, but something which passes between them, and is peculiar to each percipient; are you quite certain that the several colours appear to a dog or to any animal whatever as they appear to you?

Theaet. Far from it.

Soc. Or that anything appears the same to you as to another man? Are you so profoundly convinced of this? Rather would it not be true that it never appears exactly the same to you, because you are never exactly the same?

Theaet. The latter.

Soc. And if that with which I compare myself in size,[1] or which I apprehend by touch, were great or white or hot, it could not become different by mere contact with another unless it actually changed; nor again, if the comparing or apprehending subject were great or white or hot, could this, when unchanged from within, become changed by any approximation or affection of any other thing. The fact is that in our ordinary way of speaking we allow ourselves to be driven into most ridiculous and wonderful contradictions, as Protagoras and all who take his line of argument would remark.

Theaet. How? and of what sort do you mean?

Soc. A little instance will sufficiently explain my meaning: Here are six dice, which are more by a half when compared with four, and fewer by a half than twelve—they are more and also fewer. How can you or any one maintain the contrary?

Theaet. Very true.

Soc. Well, then, suppose that Protagoras or some one asks whether anything can become greater or more if not by increasing, how would you answer him, Theaetetus?

Theaet. I should say 'No,' Socrates, if I were to

---

[1] Reading with the MSS. ᾧ παραμετρούμεθα.

speak my mind in reference to this last question, and if I were not afraid of contradicting my former answer.

Soc. Capital! excellent! spoken like an oracle, my boy! And if you reply 'Yes,' there will be a case for Euripides; for our tongue will be unconvinced, but not our mind.[1]

Theaet. Very true.

Soc. The thoroughbred Sophists, who know all that can be known about the mind, and argue only out of the superfluity of their wits, would have had a regular sparring-match over this, and would have knocked their arguments together finely. But you and I, who have no professional aims, only desire to see what is the mutual relation of these principles,—whether they are consistent with each other or not.

Theaet. Yes, that would be my desire.

Soc. And mine too. But since this is our feeling, and there is plenty of time, why should we not calmly and patiently review our own thoughts, and thoroughly examine and see what these appearances in us really are? If I am not mistaken, they will be described by us as follows:—first, that nothing can become greater or less, either in number or magnitude, while remaining equal to itself—you would agree?

Theaet. Yes.

Soc. Secondly, that without addition or subtraction there is no increase or diminution of anything, but only equality.

Theaet. Quite true.

Soc. Thirdly, that what was not before cannot be afterwards, without becoming and having become.

Theaet. Yes, truly.

Soc. These three axioms, if I am not mistaken, are

---

[1] In allusion to the well-known line of Euripides, *Hippol.* 612: ἡ γλῶσσ' ὀμώμοχ, ἡ δὲ φρὴν ἀνώμοτος.

fighting with one another in our minds in the case of the dice, or, again, in such a case as this—if I were to say that I, who am of a certain height and taller than you, may within a year, without gaining or losing in height, be not so tall—not that I should have lost, but that you would have increased. In such a case, I am afterwards what I once was not, and yet I have not become; for I could not have become without becoming, neither could I have become less without losing somewhat of my height; and I could give you ten thousand examples of similar contradictions, if we admit them at all. I believe that you follow me, Theaetetus; for I suspect that you have thought of these questions before now.

Theaet. Yes, Socrates, and I am amazed when I think of them; by the Gods I am! and I want to know what on earth they mean; and there are times when my head quite swims with the contemplation of them.

Soc. I see, my dear Theaetetus, that Theodorus had a true insight into your nature when he said that you were a philosopher, for wonder is the feeling of a philosopher, and philosophy begins in wonder. He was not a bad genealogist who said that Iris (the messenger of heaven) is the child of Thaumas (wonder). But do you begin to see what is the explanation of this perplexity on the hypothesis which we attribute to Protagoras?

Theaet. Not as yet.

Soc. Then you will be obliged to me if I help you to unearth the hidden 'truth' of a famous man or school.

Theaet. To be sure, I shall be very much obliged.

Soc. Take a look round, then, and see that none of the uninitiated are listening. Now by the uninitiated I mean the people who believe in nothing but what they can grasp in their hands, and who will not allow that action or generation or anything invisible can have real existence.

same things appear dif to people

Theaet. Yes, indeed, Socrates, they are very hard and impenetrable mortals.

Soc. Yes, my boy, outer barbarians. Far more ingenious are the brethren whose mysteries I am about to reveal to you. Their first principle is, that all is motion, and upon this all the affections of which we were just now speaking are supposed to depend: there is nothing but motion, which has two forms, one active and the other passive, both in endless number; and out of the union and friction of them there is generated a progeny endless in number, having two forms, sense and the object of sense, which are ever breaking forth and coming to the birth at the same moment. The senses are variously named hearing, seeing, smelling; there is the sense of heat, cold, pleasure, pain, desire, fear, and many more which have names, as well as innumerable others which are without them; each has its kindred object,—each variety of colour has a corresponding variety of sight, and so with sound and hearing, and with the rest of the senses and the objects akin to them. Do you see, Theaetetus, the bearings of this tale on the preceding argument?

Theaet. Indeed I do not.

Soc. Then attend, and I will try to finish the story. The purport is that all these things are in motion, as I was saying, and that this motion is of two kinds, a slower and a quicker; and the slower elements have their motions in the same place and with reference to things near them, and so they beget; but what is begotten is swifter, for it is carried to and fro, and moves from place to place. Apply this to sense:—When the eye and the appropriate object meet together and give birth to whiteness and the sensation connatural with it, which could not have been given by either of them going elsewhere, then, while the sight is flowing from the eye,

whiteness proceeds from the object which combines in
producing the colour; and so the eye is fulfilled with
sight, and really sees, and becomes, not sight, but a seeing eye; and the object which combined to form the
colour is fulfilled with whiteness, and becomes not whiteness but a white thing, whether wood or stone or whatever the object may be which happens to be coloured
white.[1] And this is true of all sensible objects, hard.
warm, and the like, which are similarly to be regarded,
as I was saying before, not as having any absolute existence, but as being all of them of whatever kind generated by motion in their intercourse with one another;
for of the agent and patient, as existing in separation,
no trustworthy conception, as they say, can be formed,
for the agent has no existence until united with the patient, and the patient has no existence until united with
the agent; and that which by uniting with something becomes an agent, by meeting with some other thing is
converted into a patient. And from all these considerations, as I said at first, there arises a general reflection, that there is no one self-existent thing, but everything is becoming and in relation; and being must be
altogether abolished, although from habit and ignorance
we are compelled even in this discussion to retain the
use of the term. But great philosophers tell us that we
are not to allow either the word 'something,' or 'belonging to something,' or 'to me,' or 'this' or 'that,' or any
other detaining name to be used; in the language of nature all things are being created and destroyed, coming
into being and passing into new forms; nor can any
name fix or detain them; he who attempts to fix them
is easily refuted. And this should be the way of speaking, not only of particulars but of aggregates; such
aggregates as are expressed in the word 'man,' or 'stone,'

[1] Reading ὁτιοῦν or ὑτῳοῦν and omitting χρῶμα

or any name of an animal or of a class. O Theaetetus,
are not these speculations sweet as honey? And do you
not like the taste of them in the mouth?

Theaet. I do not know what to say, Socrates; for,
indeed, I cannot make out whether you are giving your
own opinion or only wanting to draw me out.

Soc. You forget, my friend, that I neither know, nor
profess to know, anything of these matters; you are the
person who is in labour, I am the barren midwife; and
this is why I soothe you, and offer you one good thing
after another, that you may taste them. And I hope
that I may at last help to bring your own opinion into
the light of day: when this has been accomplished, then
we will determine whether what you have brought forth
is only a wind-egg or a real and genuine birth. Therefore, keep up your spirits, and answer like a man what
you think.

Theaet. Ask me.

Soc. Then once more: Is it your opinion that nothing is but what becomes?—the good and the noble, as
well as all the other things which we were just now
mentioning?

Theaet. When I hear you discoursing in this style,
I think that there is a great deal in what you say, and
I am very ready to assent.

Soc. Let us not leave the argument unfinished, then;
for there still remains to be considered an objection
which may be raised about dreams and diseases, in particular about madness, and the various illusions of hearing and sight, or of other senses. For you know that in
all these cases the *esse-percipi* theory appears to be un-
mistakably refuted, since in dreams and illusions we
certainly have false perceptions; and far from saying
that everything is which appears, we should rather say
that nothing is which appears.

Theaet. Very true, Socrates.

Soc. But then, my boy, how can any one contend that knowledge is perception, or that to every man what appears is?

Theaet. I am afraid to say, Socrates, that I have nothing to answer, because you rebuked me just now for making this excuse; but I certainly cannot undertake to argue that madmen or dreamers think truly, when they imagine, some of them that they are gods, and others that they can fly, and are flying in their sleep.

Soc. Do you see another question which can be raised about these phenomena, notably about dreaming and waking?

Theaet. What question?

Soc. A question which I think that you must often have heard persons ask:—How can you determine whether at this moment we are sleeping, and all our thoughts are a dream; or whether we are awake, and talking to one another in the waking state?

Theaet. Indeed, Socrates, I do not know how to prove the one any more than the other, for in both cases the facts precisely correspond; and there is no difficulty in supposing that during all this discussion we have been talking to one another in a dream; and when in a dream [1] we seem to be narrating dreams, the resemblance of the two states is quite astonishing.

Soc. You see, then, that a doubt about the reality of sense is easily raised, since there may even be a doubt whether we are awake or in a dream. And as our time is equally divided between sleeping and waking, in either sphere of existence the soul contends that the thoughts which are present to our minds at the time are true; and during one half of our lives we affirm the truth of the one, and, during the other half, of the other; and are equally confident of both.

Theaet. Most true.

[1] Or perhaps, reading ὕπαρ, 'in our waking state.'

Soc. And may not the same be said of madness and other disorders? the difference is only that the times are not equal.

Theaet. Certainly.

Soc. And is truth or falsehood to be determined by duration of time?

Theaet. That would be in many ways ridiculous.

Soc. But can you certainly determine by any other means which of these opinions is true?

Theaet. I do not think that I can.

Soc. Listen, then, to a statement of the other side of the argument, which is made by the champions of appearance. They would say, as I imagine—Can that which is wholly other than something, have the same quality as that from which it differs? and observe, Theaetetus, that the word 'other' means not 'partially,' but 'wholly other.'

Theaet. Certainly, putting the question as you do, that which is wholly other cannot either potentially or in any other way be the same.

Soc. And must therefore be admitted to be unlike?

Theaet. True.

Soc. If, then, anything happens to become like or unlike itself or another, when it becomes like we call it the same—when unlike, other?

Theaet. Certainly.

Soc. Were we not saying that there are agents many and infinite, and patients many and infinite?

Theaet. Yes.

Soc. And also that different combinations will produce results which are not the same, but different?

Theaet. Certainly.

Soc. Let us take you and me, or anything as an example:—There is Socrates in health, and Socrates sick —Are they like or unlike?

Theaet. You mean to compare Socrates in health as a whole, and Socrates in sickness as a whole?

Soc. Exactly; that is my meaning.

Theaet. I answer, they are unlike.

Soc. And if unlike, they are other?

Theaet. Certainly.

Soc. And would you not say the same of Socrates sleeping and waking, or in any of the states which we were mentioning?

Theaet. I should.

Soc. All agents have a different patient in Socrates, accordingly as he is well or ill.

Theaet. Of course.

Soc. And I who am the patient, and that which is the agent, will produce something different in each of the two cases?

Theaet. Certainly.

Soc. The wine which I drink when I am in health, appears sweet and pleasant to me?

Theaet. True.

Soc. For, as has been already acknowledged, the patient and agent meet together and produce sweetness and a perception of sweetness, which are in simultaneous motion, and the perception which comes from the patient makes the tongue percipient, and the quality of sweetness which arises out of and is moving about the wine, makes the wine both to be and to appear sweet to the healthy tongue.

Theaet. Certainly; that has been already acknowledged.

Soc. But when I am sick, the wine really acts upon another and a different person?

Theaet. Yes.

Soc. The combination of the draught of wine, and the Socrates who is sick, produces quite another result;

which is the sensation of bitterness in the tongue, and the motion and creation of bitterness in and about the wine, which becomes not bitterness but something bitter; as I myself become not perception but percipient?

Theaet. True.

Soc. There is no other object of which I shall ever have the same perception, for another object would give another perception, and would make the percipient other and different; nor can that object which affects me, meeting another subject, produce the same, or become similar, for that too will produce another result from another subject, and become different.

Theaet. True.

Soc. Neither can I by myself, have this sensation, nor the object by itself, this quality.

Theaet. Certainly not.

Soc. When I perceive I must become percipient of something—there can be no such thing as perceiving and perceiving nothing; the object, whether it become sweet, bitter, or of any other quality, must have relation to a percipient; nothing can become sweet which is sweet to no one.

Theaet. Certainly not.

Soc. Then the inference is, that we [the agent and patient] are or become in relation to one another; there is a law which binds us one to the other, but not to any other existence, nor each of us to himself; and therefore we can only be bound to one another; so that whether a person says that a thing is or becomes, he must say that it is or becomes to or of or in relation to something else; but he must not say or allow any one else to say that anything is or becomes absolutely:— such is our conclusion.

Theaet. Very true, Socrates.

Soc. Then, if that which acts upon me has relation

to me and to no other, I and no other am the percipient
of it?

Theaet. Of course.

Soc. Then my perception is true to me, being in-
separable from my own being; and, as Protagoras says,
to myself I am judge of what is and what is not to me.

Theaet. I suppose so.

Soc. How then, if I never err, and if my mind never
trips in the conception of being or becoming, can I fail
of knowing that which I perceive?

Theat. You cannot.

Soc. Then you were quite right in affirming that
knowledge is only perception; and the meaning turns
out to be the same, whether with Homer and Heracleitus, and all that company, you say that all is motion
and flux, or with the great sage Protagoras, that man
is the measure of all things; or with Theaetetus, that,
given these premises, perception is knowledge. Am I
not right, Theaetetus, and is not this your new-born
child, of which I have delivered you? What say you?

Theaet. I cannot but agree, Socrates.

Soc. Then this is the child, however he may turn
out, which you and I have with difficulty brought into
the world. And now that he is born, we must run
round the hearth with him, and see whether he is worth
rearing, or is only a wind-egg and a sham. Is he to be
reared in any case, and not exposed? or will you bear
to see him rejected, and not get into a passion if I take
away your first-born?

Theod. Theaetetus will not be angry, for he is very
good-natured. But tell me, Socrates, in heaven's name,
is this, after all, not the truth?

Soc. You, Theodorus, are a lover of theories, and
now you innocently fancy that I am a bag full of them,
and can easily pull one out which will overthrow its

predecessor. But you do not see that in reality none of these theories come from me; they all come from him who talks with me. I only know just enough to extract them from the wisdom of another, and to receive them in a spirit of fairness. And now I shall say nothing myself, but shall endeavour to elicit something from our young friend.

Theod. Do as you say, Socrates; you are quite right.

Soc. Shall I tell you, Theodorus, what amazes me in your acquaintance Protagoras.

Theod. What is it?

Soc. I am charmed with his doctrine, that what appears is to each one, but I wonder that he did not begin his book on Truth with a declaration that a pig or a dog-faced baboon, or some other yet stranger monster which has sensation, is the measure of all things; then he might have shown a magnificent contempt for our opinion of him by informing us at the outset that while we were reverencing him like a God for his wisdom he was no better than a tadpole, not to speak of his fellow-men— would not this have produced an overpowering effect? For if truth is only sensation, and no man can discern another's feelings better than he, or has any superior right to determine whether his opinion is true or false, but each, as we have several times repeated, is to himself the sole judge, and everything that he judges is true and right, why, my friend, should Protagoras be preferred to the place of wisdom and instruction, and deserve to be well paid, and we poor ignoramuses have to go to him, if each one is the measure of his own wisdom? Must he not be talking 'ad captandum' in all this? I say nothing of the ridiculous predicament in which my own midwifery and the whole art of dialectic is placed; for the attempt to supervise or refute the notions or opinions of others would be a tedious and enormous piece of folly, if to each man his own are right; and this must be the case if Protagoras' Truth is the real truth, and the philosopher is not merely amusing himself by giving oracles out of the shrine of his book.

Theod. He was a friend of mine, Socrates, as you were saying, and therefore I cannot have him refuted by my lips, nor can I oppose you when I agree with you; please, then, to take Theaetetus again; he seemed to answer very nicely.

Soc. If you were to go into a Lacedaemonian palestra, Theodorus, would you have a right to look on at the naked wrestlers, some of them making a poor figure, if you did not strip and give them an opportunity of judging of your own person?

Theod. Why not, Socrates, if they would allow me, as I think you will, in consideration of my age and stiffness; let some more supple youth try a fall with you, and do not drag me into the gymnasium.

Soc. Your will is my will, Theodorus, as the proverbial philosophers say, and therefore I will return to the sage Theaetetus: Tell me, Theaetetus, in reference to what I was saying, are you not lost in wonder, like myself, when you find that all of a sudden you are raised to the level of the wisest of men, or indeed of the gods? —for you would assume the measure of Protagoras to apply to the gods as well as men?

Theaet. Certainly I should, and I confess to you that I am lost in wonder. At first hearing, I was quite satisfied with the doctrine, that whatever appears is to each one, but now the face of things has changed.

Soc. Why, my dear boy, you are young, and therefore your ear is quickly caught and your mind influenced by popular arguments. Protagoras, or some one speaking on his behalf, will doubtless say in reply,—Good people, young and old, you meet and harangue, and bring in the gods, whose existence or non-existence I banish from writing and speech, or you talk about the reason of man being degraded to the level of the brutes, which is a telling argument with the multitude, but not one word of proof or demonstration do you offer. All is probability with you, and yet surely you and Theodorus had better reflect whether you are disposed to admit of probability and figures of speech in matters of such importance. He or any other mathematician who argued from probabilities and likelihoods in geometry, would not be worth an ace.

Theaet. But neither you nor we, Socrates, would be satisfied with such arguments.

Soc. Then you and Theodorus mean to say that we must look at the matter in some other way?

Theaet. Yes, in quite another way.

Soc. And the way will be to ask whether perception is or is not the same as knowledge; for this was the real point of our argument, and with a view to this we raised (did we not?) those many strange questions.

Theat. Certainly.

Soc. Shall we say that we know every thing which we see and hear? for example, shall we say that not having learned, we do not hear the language of foreigners when they speak to us? or shall we say that we not only hear, but know what they are saying? Or again, if we see letters which we do not understand, shall we say that we do not see them? or shall we aver that, seeing them, we must know them?

Theat. We shall say, Socrates, that we know what we actually see and hear of them—that is to say, we see and know the figure and colour of the letters, and we hear and know the elevation or depression of the sound of them; but we do not perceive by sight and hearing, or know, that which grammarians and interpreters teach about them.

Soc. Capital, Theaetetus; and about this there shall be no dispute, because I want you to grow; but there is another difficulty coming, which you will also have to repulse.

Theaet. What is it?

Soc. Some one will say, Can a man who has ever known anything, and still has and preserves a memory of that which he knows, not know that which he remembers at the time when he remembers? I have, I fear, a tedious way of putting a simple question, which is only, whether a man who has learned, and remembers, can fail to know?

Theaet. Impossible, Socrates; the supposition is monstrous.

Soc. Am I talking nonsense, then? Think: is not seeing perceiving, and is not sight perception?

Theaet. True.

Soc. And if our recent definition holds, every man knows that which he has seen?

Theaet. Yes.

Soc. And you would admit that there is such a thing as memory?

Theaet. Yes.

Soc. And is memory of something or of nothing?

Theaet. Of something, surely.

Soc. Of things learned and perceived, that is?

Theaet. Certainly.

Soc. Often a man remembers that which he has seen?

Theaet. True.

Soc. And if he closed his eyes, would he forget?

Theaet. Who, Socrates, would dare to say so?

Soc. But we must say so, if the previous argument is to be maintained.

Theaet. What do you mean? I am not quite sure

that I understand you, though I have a strong suspicion that you are right.

Soc. As thus: he who sees knows, as we say, that which he sees; for perception and sight and knowledge are admitted to be the same.

Theaet. Certainly.

Soc. But he who saw, and has knowledge of that which he saw, remembers, when he closes his eyes, that which he no longer sees.

Theaet. True.

Soc. And seeing is knowing, and therefore not-seeing is not-knowing.

Theaet. Very true.

Soc. Then the inference is, that a man may have attained the knowledge of something, which he may remember and yet not know, because he does not see; and this has been affirmed by us to be a monstrous supposition.

Theaet. Most true.

Soc. Thus, then, the assertion that knowledge and perception are one, involves a manifest impossibility?

Theaet. Yes.

Soc. Then they must be distinguished?

Theaet. I suppose that they must.

Soc. Once more we shall have to begin, and ask, 'What is knowledge?' and yet, Theaetetus, what are we going to do?

Theaet. About what?

Soc. Like a good-for-nothing cock, without having won the victory, we walk away from the argument and crow.

Theaet. How do you mean?

Soc. After the manner of disputers, we were satisfied with mere verbal consistency, and were well pleased if in this way we could gain an advantage. Although professing not to be mere Eristics, but philosophers, I suspect that we have unconsciously fallen into the error of that ingenious class of persons.

Theaet. I do not as yet understand you.

Soc. Then I will try to explain myself: just now we asked the question, whether a man who had learned and remembered could fail to know, and we showed that a person who had seen might remember when he had his eyes shut and could not see, and then he would at the same time remember and not know. But this was an impossibility. And so the Protagorean fable came to nought, and yours also, who maintained that knowledge is the same as perception.

Theaet. True.

Soc. And yet, my friend, I rather suspect that the result would have been different if Protagoras, who was the father of the first of the two brats, had been alive; he would have had a great deal to say on their behalf. But he is dead, and we insult over his orphan child; and even the guardians whom he left, and of whom our friend Theodorus is one, are unwilling to give any help, and therefore I suppose that I must take up his cause myself, and see justice done?

Theod. Not I, Socrates, but rather Callias, the son of Hipponicus, is guardian of his orphans. I was too soon diverted from the abstractions of dialectic to geometry. Nevertheless, I shall be grateful to you if you assist him.

Soc. Very good, Theodorus; you shall see how I will come to the rescue. If a person does not attend to the meaning of terms as they are commonly used in argument, he may be involved even in greater paradoxes than these. Shall I explain this matter to you or to Theaetetus?

Theod. To both of us, and let the younger answer; he will incur less disgrace if he is discomfited.

Soc. Then now let me ask the awful question, which is this:—Can a man know and also not know that w he knows?

Theod. How shall we answer, Theaetetus?

Theaet. He cannot, I should say.

Soc. He can, if you maintain that seeing is knowing. When you are imprisoned in a well, as the saying is, and the self-assured adversary closes one of your eyes with his hand, and asks whether you can see his cloak with the eye which he has closed, how will you answer the inevitable man?

Theaet. I should answer, 'Not with that eye but with the other.'

Soc. Then you see and do not see the same thing at the same time.

Theaet. Yes, in a certain sense.

Soc. None of that, he will reply; I do not ask or bid you answer in what sense you know, but only whether you know that which you do not know. You have been proved to see that which you do not see; and you have already admitted that seeing is knowing, and that not-seeing is not-knowing: I leave you to draw the inference.

Theaet. Yes; the inference is the contradictory of my assertion.

Soc. Yes, my marvel, and there might have been yet worse things in store for you, if an opponent had gone on to ask whether you can have a sharp and also a dull knowledge, and whether you can know near, but not at a distance, or know the same thing with more or less intensity, and so on without end. Such questions might have been put to you by a light-armed mercenary, who argued for pay. He would have lain in wait for you, and when you took up the position, that sense is knowledge, he would have made an assault upon hearing, smelling, and the other senses;—he would have shown you no mercy; and while you were lost in envy and admiration of his wisdom, he would have got you into his net, out of which you would not have escaped until you had come to an understanding about the sum to be paid for your release. Well, you ask, and how will Protagoras reinforce his position? Shall I answer for him?

Theaet. By all means.

Soc. He will repeat all those things which we have been urging on his behalf, and then he will close with us in disdain, and say:—The worthy Socrates asked a little boy, whether the same man could remember and not know the same thing, and the boy said No, because he was frightened, and could not see what was coming, and then Socrates made fun of poor me. The truth is, O slatternly Socrates, that when you ask questions about any assertion of mine, and the person asked is found tripping, if he has answered as I should have answered, then I am refuted, but if he answers something else, then he is refuted and not I. For do you really suppose that any one would admit the memory which a man has of an impression which has passed away to be the same with that which he experienced at the time? Assuredly not. Or would he hesitate to acknowledge that the same man may know and not know the same thing? Or, if he is afraid of making this admission, would he ever grant that one who has become unlike is the same as before he became unlike? Or would he admit that a man is one at all, and not rather many and infinite as the changes which take place in him? I speak by the card in order to avoid entanglements of words. But, O my good sir, he will say, come to the argument in a more

generous spirit; and either show, if you can, that our
sensations are not relative and individual, or, if you admit them to be so, prove that this does not involve the
consequence that the appearance becomes, or, if you will
have the word, is, to the individual only. As to your
talk about pigs and baboons, you are yourself behaving
like a pig, and you teach your hearers to make sport of
my writings in the same ignorant manner; but this is not
to your credit. For I declare that the truth is as I have
written, and that each of us is a measure of existence
and of non-existence. Yet one man may be a thousand
times better than another in proportion as different
things are and appear to him. And I am far from saying that wisdom and the wise man have no existence;
but I say that the wise man is he who makes the evils
which appear and are to a man, into goods which are
and appear to him. And I would beg you not to press
my words in the letter, but to take the meaning of them
as I will explain them. Remember what has been already said,—that to the sick man his food appears to
be and is bitter, and to the man in health the opposite
of bitter. Now I cannot conceive that one of these men
can be or ought to be made wiser than the other: nor can
you assert that the sick man because he has one impression is foolish, and the healthy man because he has another is wise; but the one state requires to be changed
into the other, the worse into the better. As in education, a change of state has to be effected, and the sophist
accomplishes by words the change which the physician
works by the aid of drugs. Not that any one ever made
another think truly, who previously thought falsely.
For no one can think what is not, or, think anything
different from that which he feels; and this is always
true. But as the inferior habit of mind has thoughts of
a kindred nature, so I conceive that a good mind causes

mcn to have good thoughts; and these which the inexperienced call true, I maintain to be only better, and not
truer than others. And, O my dear Socrates, I do not
call wise men tadpoles: far from it; I say that they are
the physicians of the human body, and the husbandmen
of plants—for the husbandmen also take away the evil
and disordered sensations of plants, and infuse into them
good and healthy sensations—aye and true ones; and
the wise and good rhetoricians make the good instead of
the evil to seem just to states; for whatever appears to a
state to be just and fair, so long as it is regarded as
such, is just and fair to it; but the teacher of wisdom
causes the good to take the place of the evil, both in
appearance and in reality. And in like manner the
Sophist who is able to train his pupils in this spirit is a
wise man, and deserves to be well paid by them. And
so one man is wiser than another; and no one thinks
falsely, and you, whether you will or not, must endure
to be a measure. On these foundations the argument
stands firm, which you, Socrates, may, if you please,
overthrow by an opposite argument, or if you like you
may put questions to me—a method to which no intelligent person will object, quite the reverse. But I must
beg you to put fair questions: for there is great inconsistency in saying that you have a zeal for virtue, and
then always behaving unfairly in argument. The un-
fairness of which I complain is that you do not distinguish between mere disputation and dialectic: the dis-
puter may trip up his opponent as often as he likes, and
make fun; but the dialectician will be in earnest, and
only correct his adversary when necessary, telling him
the errors into which he has fallen through his own fault,
or that of the company which he has previously kept.
If you do so, your adversary will lay the blame of his
own confusion and perplexity on himself, and not on

you. He will follow and love you, and will hate himself, and escape from himself into philosophy, in order that he may become different from what he was. But the other mode of arguing, which is practised by the many, will have just the opposite effect upon him; and as he grows older, instead of turning philosopher, he will come to hate philosophy. I would recommend you, therefore, as I said before, not to encourage yourself in this polemical and controversial temper, but to find out, in a friendly and congenial spirit, what we really mean when we say that all things are in motion, and that to every individual and state what appears, is. In this manner you will consider whether knowledge and sensation are the same or different, but you will not argue, as you were just now doing, from the customary use of names and words, which the vulgar pervert in all sorts of ways, causing infinite perplexity to one another. Such, Theodorus, is the very slight help which I am able to offer to your old friend; [1] had he been living, he would have helped himself in a far more glorious style.

Theod. You are jesting, Socrates; indeed, your defence of him has been most valorous.

Soc. Thank you, friend; and I hope that you observed Protagoras bidding us be serious, as the text, 'Man is the measure of all things,' was a solemn one; and he reproached us with making a boy the medium of discourse, and said that the boy's timidity was made to tell against his argument; he also declared that we made a joke of him.

Theod. How could I fail to observe all that, Socrates?

Soc. Well, and shall we do as he says?

Theod. By all means.

Soc. But if his wishes are to be regarded, you and I

[1] Reading προσήρχεσα

must take up the argument, and in all seriousness,[1] and
ask and answer one another, for you see that the rest
of us are nothing but boys. In no other way can we escape the imputation, that in our fresh analysis of his
thesis we are making fun with boys.

Theod. Well, but is not Theaetetus better able to follow a philosophical enquiry than a great many men who
have long beards?

Soc. Yes, Theodorus, but not better than you; and
therefore please not to imagine that I am to defend by
every means in my power your departed friend; and that
you are to defend nothing and nobody. At any rate, my
good man, do not sheer off until we know whether you
are a true measure of diagrams, or whether all men are
equally measures and sufficient for themselves in astronomy and geometry, and the other branches of knowledge
in which you are supposed to excel them.

Theod. He who is sitting by you, Socrates, will not
easily avoid being drawn into an argument; and when I
said just now that you would excuse me, and not, like
the Lacedaemonians, compel me to strip and fight, I
was talking nonsense—I should rather compare you to
Scirrhon, who threw travellers from the rocks; for the
Lacedemonian rule is 'strip or depart,' but you seem to
go about your work more after the fashion of Antaeus:
you will not allow any one who approaches you to depart
until you have stripped him, and he has been compelled
to try a fall with you in argument.

Soc. There, Theodorus, you have hit off precisely
the nature of my complaint; but I am even more pug-
nacious than the giants of old, for I have met with no
end of heroes; many a Heracles, many a Theseus, mighty
in words, has broken my head; nevertheless I am always at this rough exercise, which inspires me like a

---

[1] Reading αὐτοῦ τῶν λόγων

passion. Please, then, to try a fall with me, whereby you will do yourself good as well as me.

Theod. I consent; lead me whither you will, for I know that you are like destiny; no man can escape from any argument which you may weave for him. But I am not disposed to go further than you suggest.

Soc. Once will be enough; and now take particular care that we do not again unwittingly expose ourselves to the reproach of talking childishly.

Theod. I will do my best to avoid that error.

Soc. In the first place, let us return to our old objection, and see whether we were right in blaming and taking offence at Protagoras on the ground that he assumed all to be equal and sufficient in wisdom; although he admitted that there was a better and worse, and that in respect of this, some who as he said were the wise excelled others.

Theod. Very true.

Soc. Had Protagoras been living and answered for himself, instead of our answering for him, there would have been no need of our reviewing or reinforcing the argument. But as he is not here, and some one may accuse us of speaking without authority on his behalf, had we not better come to a clearer agreement about his meaning, for a great deal may be at stake?

Theod. True.

Soc. Then let us obtain, not through any third person, but from his own statement and in the fewest words possible, the basis of agreement.

Theod. In what way?

Soc. In this way:—His words are, 'What seems to a man, is to him.'

Theod. Yes, so he says.

Soc. And are not we, Protagoras, uttering the opinion of man, or rather of all mankind, when we say that every one thinks himself wiser than other men in some things, and their inferior in others? In the hour of danger, when they are in perils of war, or of the sea, or of sickness, do they not look up to their commanders as if they were gods, and expect salvation from them, only because they excel them in knowledge? Is not the world full of men in their several employments, who are looking for teachers and rulers of themselves and of the animals? and there are plenty who think that they are able to teach and able to rule. Now, in all this is implied that ignorance and wisdom exist among them, at least in their own opinion.

Theod. Certainly.

Soc. And wisdom is assumed by them to be true thought, and ignorance to be false opinion.

Theod. Exactly.

Soc. How then, Protagoras, would you have us treat the argument? Shall we say that the opinions of men are always true, or sometimes true and sometimes false? In either case, the result is the same, and their opinions are not always true, but sometimes true and sometimes false. For tell me, Theodorus, do you suppose that you yourself, or any other follower of Protagoras, would contend that no one deems another ignorant or mistaken in his opinion?

Theod. The thing is incredible, Socrates.

Soc. And yet that absurdity is necessarily involved in the thesis which declares man to be the measure of all things.

Theod. How so?

Soc. Why, suppose that you determine in your own mind something to be true, and declare your opinion to me; let us assume, as he argues, that this is true to you. Now, if so, you must either say that the rest of us are not the judges of this opinion or judgment of yours, or

that we judge you always to have a true opinion? But
are there not thousands upon thousands who, whenever
you form a judgment, take up arms against you and are
of an opposite judgment and opinion, deeming that you
judge falsely?

Theod. Yes, indeed, Socrates, thousands and tens of
thousands, as Homer says, who give me a world of
trouble.

Soc. Well, but are we to assert that what you think
is true to you and false to the ten thousand others?

Theod. No other inference seems to be possible.

Soc. And how about Protagoras himself? If neither
he nor the multitude thought, as indeed they do not
think, that man is the measure of all things, must it
not follow that the truth of which Protagoras wrote
would be true to no one? But if you suppose that he
himself thought this, and that the multitude does not
agree with him, you must begin by allowing that in whatever proportion the many are more than one, in that
proportion his truth is more untrue than true.

Theod. That would follow if the truth is supposed
to vary with individual opinion.

Soc. And the best of the joke is, that he acknowledges the truth of their opinion who believe his own
opinion to be false; for he admits that the opinions of
all men are true.

Theod. Certainly.

Soc. And does he not allow that his own opinion is
false, if he admits that the opinion of those who think
him false is true?

Theod. Of course.

Soc. Whereas the other side do not admit that they
speak falsely?

Theod. They do not.

Soc. And he, as may be inferred from his writings, agrees that this opinion is also true.

Theod. Clearly.

Soc. Then all mankind, beginning with Protagoras, will contend, or rather, I should say that he will allow, when he concedes that his adversary has a true opinion —Protagoras, I say, will himself allow that neither a dog nor any ordinary man is the measure of anything which he has not learned—am I not right?

Theod. Yes.

Soc. And the truth of Protagoras being doubted by all, will be true neither to himself nor to any one else?

Theod. I think, Socrates, that we are running my old friend too hard.

Soc. But I do not know that we are going beyond the truth. Doubtless, as he is older, he may be expected to be wiser than we are. And if he could only just get his head out of the world below, he would have overthrown both of us again and again, me for talking nonsense and you for assenting to me, and have been off and underground in a trice. But as he is not within call, we must make the best use of our own faculties, such as they are, and speak out what appears to us to be true. And one thing which no one will deny is, that there are great differences in the understandings of men.

Theod. In that opinion I quite agree.

Soc. And is there not most likely to be firm ground in the distinction which we were indicating on behalf of Protagoras, viz. that most things, and all immediate sensations, such as hot, dry, sweet, are only such as they appear; if however difference of opinion is to be allowed at all, surely we must allow it in respect of health or disease? for every woman, child, or living creature has not such a knowledge of what conduces to health as to enable them to cure themselves.

Theod. I quite agree.

Soc. Or again, in politics, while affirming that just and unjust, honourable and disgraceful, holy and unholy, are in reality to each state such as the state thinks and makes lawful, and that in determining these matters no individual or state is wiser than another, still the followers of Protagoras will not deny that in determining what is or is not expedient for the community one state is wiser and one counsellor better than another—they will scarcely venture to maintain, that what a city enacts in the belief that it is expedient will always be really expedient. But in the other case, I mean when they speak of justice and injustice, piety and impiety, they are confident that in nature these have no existence or essence of their own—the truth is that which is agreed on at the time of the agreement, and as long as the agreement lasts; and this is the philosophy of many who do not altogether go along with Protagoras. Here arises a new question, Theodorus, which threatens to be more serious than the last.

Theod. Well, Socrates, we have plenty of leisure.

Soc. That is true, and your remark recalls to my mind an observation which I have often made, that those who have passed their days in the pursuit of philosophy are ridiculously at fault when they have to appear and speak in court. How natural is this!

Theod. What do you mean?

Soc. I mean to say, that those who have been trained in philosophy and liberal pursuits are as unlike those who from their youth upwards have been knocking about in the courts and such places, as a freeman is in breeding unlike a slave.

Theod. In what is the difference seen?

Soc. In the leisure spoken of by you, which a freeman can always command: he has his talk out in peace,

and, like ourselves, he wanders at will from one subject
to another, and from a second to a third,—if the fancy
takes him, he begins again, as we are doing now, caring
not whether his words are many or few; his only aim
is to attain the truth. But the lawyer is always in a
hurry; there is the water of the clepsydra driving him
on, and not allowing him to expatiate at will: and there
is his adversary standing over him, enforcing his rights;
the indictment, which in their phraseology is termed the
affidavit, is recited at the time: and from this he must not
deviate. He is a servant, and is continually disputing
about a fellow-servant before his master, who is seated,
and has the cause in his hands; the trial is never about
some indifferent matter, but always concerns himself;
and often the race is for his life. The consequence has
been, that he has become keen and shrewd; he has
learned how to flatter his master in word and indulge
him in deed; but his soul is small and unrighteous. His
condition, which has been that of a slave from his youth
upwards, has deprived him of growth and uprightness
and independence; dangers and fears, which were too
much for his truth and honesty, came upon him in early
years, when the tenderness of youth was unequal to them,
and he has been driven into crooked ways; from the first
he has practised deception and retaliation, and has become stunted and warped. And so he has passed out of
youth into manhood, having no soundness in him; and
is now, as he thinks, a master in wisdom. Such is the
lawyer, Theodorus. Will you have the companion picture of the philosopher, who is of our brotherhood; or
shall we return to the argument? Do not let us abuse
the freedom of digression which we claim.

Theod. Nay, Socrates, not until we have finished
what we are about; for you truly said that we belong to
a brotherhood which is free, and are not the servants

of the argument; but the argument is our servant, and must wait our leisure. Who is our judge? Or where is the spectator having any right to censure or control us, as he might the poets?

Soc. Then, as this is your wish, I will describe the leaders; for there is no use in talking about the inferior sort. In the first place, the lords of philosophy have never, from their youth upwards, known their way to the Agora, or the dicastery, or the council, or any other political assembly; they neither see nor hear the laws or decrees, as they are called, of the state written or recited; the eagerness of political societies in the attainment of offices—clubs, and banquets, and revels, and singing-maidens,—do not enter even into their dreams. Whether any event has turned out well or ill in the city, what disgrace may have descended to any one from his ancestors, male or female, are matters of which the philosopher no more knows than he can tell, as they say, how many pints are contained in the ocean. Neither is he conscious of his ignorance. For he does not hold aloof in order that he may gain a reputation; but the truth is, that the outer form of him only is in the city: his mind, disdaining the littlenesses and nothingnesses of human things, is 'flying all abroad' as Pindar says, measuring earth and heaven and the things which are under and on the earth and above the heaven, interrogating the whole nature of each and all in their entirety, but not condescending to anything which is within reach.

Theod. What do you mean, Socrates?

Soc. I will illustrate my meaning, Theodorus, by the jest which the clever witty Thracian handmaid is said to have made about Thales, when he fell into a well as he was looking up at the stars. She said, that he was so eager to know what was going on in heaven, that he could not see what was before his feet. This is a jest which is equally applicable to all philosophers. For the philosopher is wholly unacquainted with his next-door neighbour; he is ignorant, not only of what he is doing, but he hardly knows whether he is a man or an animal; he is searching into the essence of man, and busy in enquiring what belongs to such a nature to do or suffer different from any other;—I think that you understand me, Theodorus?

Theod. I do, and what you say is true.

Soc. And thus, my friend, on every occasion, private as well as public, as I said at first, when he appears in a law-court, or in any place in which he has to speak of things which are at his feet and before his eyes, he is the jest, not only of Thracian handmaids but of the general herd, tumbling into wells and every sort of disaster through his inexperience. His awkwardness is fearful, and gives the impression of imbecility. When he is reviled, he has nothing personal to say in answer to the civilities of his adversaries, for he knows no scandals of any one, and they do not interest him; and therefore he is laughed at for his sheepishness; and when others are being praised and glorified, in the simplicity of his heart he cannot help going into fits of laughter, so that he seems to be a downright idiot. When he hears a tyrant or king eulogized, he fancies that he is listening to the praises of some keeper of cattle—a swineherd, or shepherd, or perhaps a cowherd, who is congratulated on the quantity of milk which he squeezes from them; and he remarks that the creature whom they tend, and out of whom they squeeze the wealth, is of a less tractable and more insidious nature. Then, again, he observes that the great man is of necessity as ill-mannered and un-educated as any shepherd—for he has no leisure, and he is surrounded by a wall, which is his mountain-pen. Hearing of enormous landed proprietors of ten thousand acres and more, our philosopher deems this to be a trifle, because he has been accustomed to think of the whole earth; and when they sing the praises of family, and say that some one is a gentleman because he can show seven generations of wealthy ancestors, he thinks that their sentiments only betray a dull and narrow vision in those who utter them, and who are not educated enough to look at the whole, nor to consider that every man has had thousands and ten thousands of progenitors, and among them have been rich and poor, kings and slaves, Hellenes and barbarians, innumerable. And when people pride themselves on having a pedigree of twenty-five ancestors, which goes back to Heracles, the son of Amphitryon, he cannot understand their poverty of ideas. Why are they unable to calculate that Amphitryon had a twenty-fifth ancestor, who might have been anybody, as was such as fortune made him, and he had a fiftieth, and so on? He amuses himself with the notion that they cannot count, and thinks that a little arithmetic would have got rid of their senseless vanity. Now, in all these cases our philosopher is derided by the vulgar, partly because he is thought to despise them, and also because he is ignorant of what is before him, and always at a loss.

Theod. That is very true, Socrates.

Soc. But, O my friend, when he draws the other into upper air, and gets him out of his pleas and rejoinders into the contemplation of justice and injustice in their own nature and in their difference from one another and from all other things; or from the commonplaces about the happiness of a king or of a rich man to the consideration of government, and of human happiness and misery in general—what they are, and how a man is to attain the one and avoid the other—when that narrow, keen, little legal mind is called to account about all this, he gives the philosopher his revenge; for dizzied by the height at which he is hanging, whence he looks down into space, which is a strange experience to him, he being dismayed, and lost, and stammering broken words, is laughed at, not by Thracian handmaidens or any other uneducated persons, for they have no eye for the situation, but by every man who has not been brought up a slave. Such are the two characters, Theodorus: the one of the freeman, who has been trained in liberty and leisure, whom you call the philosopher,—him we cannot blame because he appears simple and of no account when he has to perform some menial task, such as packing up bed-clothes, or flavouring a sauce or fawning speech; the other character is that of the man who is able to do all this kind of service smartly and neatly, but knows not how to wear his cloak like a gentleman; still less with the music of discourse can he hymn the true life aright which is lived by immortals or men blessed of heaven.

Theod. If you could only persuade everybody, Socrates, as you do me, of the truth of your words, there would be more peace and fewer evils among men.

Soc. Evils, Theodorus, can never pass away; for there must always remain something which is antagonistic to good. Having no place among the gods in heaven, of necessity they hover around the mortal nature, and this earthly sphere. Wherefore we ought to fly away from earth to heaven as quickly as we can; and to fly away is to become like God, as far as this is possible; and to become like him, is to become holy, just, and wise. But, O my friend, you cannot easily convince mankind that they should pursue virtue or avoid vice, not merely in order that a man may seem to be good, which is the reason given by the world, and in my judgment is only a repetition of an old wives' fable.

Whereas, the truth is that God is never in any way un-righteous—he is perfect righteousness; and he of us who is the most righteous is most like him. Herein is seen the true cleverness of a man, and also his nothing-ness and want of manhood. For to know this is true wisdom and virtue, and ignorance of this is manifest folly and vice. All other kinds of wisdom or cleverness, which seem only, such as the wisdom of politicians, or the wisdom of the arts, are coarse and vulgar. The un-righteous man, or the sayer and doer of unholy things, had far better not be encouraged in the illusion that his roguery is clever; for men glory in their shame—they fancy that they hear others saying of them, 'These are not mere good-for-nothing persons, mere burdens of the earth, but such as men should be who mean to dwell safely in a state.' Let us tell them that they are all the more truly what they do not think they are because they do not know it; for they do not know the penalty of in-justice, which above all things they ought to know—not stripes and death, as they suppose, which evil-doers often escape, but a penalty which cannot be escaped.

Theod. What is that?

Soc. There are two patterns eternally set before them; the one blessed and divine, the other godless and wretched: but they do not see them, or perceive that in their utter folly and infatuation they are growing like the one and unlike the other, by reason of their evil deeds; and the penalty is, that they lead a life answer-ing to the pattern which they are growing like. And if we tell them, that unless they depart from their cun-ning, the place of innocence will not receive them after death; and that here on earth, they will live ever in the likeness of their own evil selves, and with evil friends—when they hear this they in their superior cunning will seem to be listening to the talk of idiots.

Theod. Very true, Socrates.

Soc. Too true, my friend, as I well know; there is, however, one peculiarity in their case: when they begin to reason in private about their dislike of philosophy, if they have the courage to hear the argument out, and do not run away, they grow at last strangely discontented with themselves; their rhetoric fades away, and they become helpless as children. These however are digressions from which we must now desist, or they will overflow, and drown the original argument; to which, if you please, we will now return.

Theod. For my part, Socrates, I would rather have the digressions, for at my age I find them easier to follow; but if you wish, let us go back to the argument.

Soc. Had we not reached the point at which the partisans of the perpetual flux, who say that things are as they seem to each one, were confidently maintaining that the ordinances which the state commanded and thought just, were just to the state which imposed them, while they were in force; this was especially asserted of justice; but as to the good, no one had any longer the hardihood to contend of any ordinances which the state thought and enacted to be good that these, while they were in force, were really good;—he who said so would be playing with the name 'good,' and would not touch the real question—it would be a mockery, would it not?

Theod. Certainly it would.

Soc. He ought not to speak of the name, but of the thing which is contemplated under the name.

Theod. Right.

Soc. Whatever be the term used, the good or expedient is the aim of legislation, and as far as she has an opinion, the state imposes all laws with a view to the greatest expediency; can legislation have any other aim?

Theod. Certainly not.

Soc. But is the aim attained always? do not mistakes often happen?

Theod. Yes, I think that there are mistakes.

Soc. The possibility of error will be more distinctly recognised, if we put the question in reference to the whole class under which the good or expedient falls. That whole class has to do with the future, and laws are passed under the idea that they will be useful in after-time; which, in other words, is the future.

Theod. Very true.

Soc. Suppose now, that we ask Protagoras, or one of his disciples, a question:—O, Protagoras, we will say to him, Man is, as you declare, the measure of all things —white, heavy, light: of all such things he is the judge; for he has the criterion of them in himself, and when he thinks that things are such as he experiences them to be, he thinks what is and is true to himself. Is it not so?

Theod. Yes.

Soc. And do you extend your doctrine, Protagoras (as we shall further say), to the future as well as to the present; and has he the criterion not only of what in his opinion is but of what will be, and do things always happen to him as he expected? For example, take the case of heat:—When an ordinary man thinks that he is going to have a fever, and that this kind of heat is coming on, and another person, who is a physician, thinks the contrary, whose opinion is likely to prove right? Or are they both right?—he will have a heat and fever in his own judgment, and not have a fever in the phy·sician's judgment?

Theod. How ludicrous!

Soc. And the vinegrower, if I am not mistaken, is a better judge of the sweetness or dryness of the vintage which is not yet gathered than the harp-player?

Theod. Certainly.

Soc. And in musical composition the musician will know better than the training master what the training master himself will hereafter think harmonious or the reverse?

Theod. Of course.

Soc. And the cook will be a better judge than the guest, who is not a cook, of the pleasure to be derived from the dinner which is in preparation; for of present or past pleasure we are not as yet arguing; but can we say that every one will be to himself the best judge of the pleasure which will seem to be and will be to him in the future?—nay, would not you, Protagoras, better guess which arguments in a court would convince any one of us than the ordinary man?

Theod. Certainly, Socrates, he used to profess in the strongest manner that he was the superior of all men in this respect.

Soc. To be sure, friend: who would have paid a large sum for the privilege of talking to him, if he had really [1] persuaded his visitors that neither a prophet nor any other man was better able to judge what will be and seem to be in the future than every one could for himself?

Theod. Who indeed?

Soc. And legislation and expediency are all concerned with the future; and every one will admit that states, in passing laws, must often fail of their highest interests?

Theod. Quite true.

Soc. Then we may fairly argue against your master, that he must admit one man to be wiser than another, and that the wiser is a measure: but I, who know nothing, am not at all obliged to accept the honour

[1] Reading δή.

which the advocate of Protagoras was just now forcing upon me, whether I would or not, of being a measure of anything.

Theod. That is the best refutation of him, Socrates; although he is also caught when he ascribes truth to the opinions of others, who give the lie direct to his own opinion.

Soc. There are many ways, Theodorus, in which the doctrine that every opinion of every man is true may be refuted; but there is more difficulty in proving that states of feeling, which are present to a man, and out of which arise sensations and opinions in accordance with them, are also untrue. And very likely I have been talking nonsense about them; for they may be unassailable, and those who say that there is clear evidence of them, and that they are matters of knowledge, may probably be right; in which case our friend Theaetetus was not far from the mark when he identified perception and knowledge. And therefore let us draw nearer, as the advocate of Protagoras desires, and give the truth of the universal flux a ring: is the theory sound or not? at any rate, no small war is raging about it, and there are combatants not a few.

Theod. No small war, indeed, for in Ionia the sect makes rapid strides; the disciples of Heracleitus are most energetic upholders of the doctrine.

Soc. Then we are the more bound, my dear Theodorus, to examine the question from the foundation as it is set forth by themselves.

Theod. Certainly we are. About these speculations of Heracleitus, which, as you say, are as old as Homer, or even older still, the Ephesians themselves, who profess to know them, are downright mad, and you cannot talk with them on the subject. For, in accordance with their text-books, they are always in motion; but as for dwelling upon an argument or a question, and quietly asking and answering in turn, they can no more do so than they can fly; or rather, the determination of these fellows not to have a particle of rest in them is more than the utmost powers of negation can express. If you ask any of them a question, he will produce, as from a quiver, sayings brief and dark, and shoot them at you; and if you enquire the reason of what he has said, you will be hit by some other new-fangled word, and will make no way with any of them, nor they with one another; their great care is, not to allow of any settled principle either in their arguments or in their minds, conceiving, as I imagine, that any such principle would be stationary; for they are at war with the stationary, and do what they can to drive it out everywhere.

Soc. I suppose, Theodorus, that you have only seen them when they were fighting, and have never stayed with them in time of peace, for they are no friends of yours; and their peace doctrines are only communicated by them at leisure, as I imagine, to those disciples of theirs whom they want to make like themselves.

Theod. Disciples! my good sir, they have none; men of their sort are not one another's disciples, but they grow up at their own sweet will, and get their inspiration anywhere, each of them saying of his neighbour that he knows nothing. From these men, then, as I was going to remark, you will never get a reason, whether with their will or without their will; we must take the question out of their hands, and make the analysis ourselves, as if we were doing a geometrical problem.

Soc. Quite right too; but as touching the aforesaid problem, have we not heard from the ancients, who concealed their wisdom from the many in poetical figures, that Oceanus and Tethys, the origin of all things, are streams, and that nothing is at rest? And now the moderns, in their superior wisdom, have declared the same openly, that the cobbler too may hear and learn of them, and no longer foolishly imagine that some things are at rest and others in motion—having learned that all is motion, he will duly honour his teachers. I had almost forgotten the opposite doctrine, Theodorus,

'Alone Being remains unmoved, which is the name for the all.'

This is the language of Parmenides, Melissus, and their followers, who stoutly maintain that all being is one and self-contained, and has no place in which to move. What shall we do, friend, with all these people; for, advancing step by step, we have imperceptibly got between the combatants, and, unless we can protect our retreat, we shall pay the penalty of our rashness—like the players in the palaestra who are caught upon the line, and are dragged different ways by the two parties. Therefore I think that we had better begin by considering those whom we first accosted, 'the river-gods,' and, if we find any truth in them, we will help them to pull us over, and try to get away from the others. But if the partisans of 'the whole' appear to speak more truly, we will fly off from the party which would move the immovable, to them. And if we find that neither of them have anything reasonable to say, we shall be in a ridiculous position, having so great a conceit of our own poor opinion and rejecting that of ancient and famous men. O Theodorus, do you think that there is any use in proceeding when the danger is so great?

Theod. Nay, Socrates, not to examine thoroughly what the two parties have to say would be quite intolerable.

Soc. Then examine we must, since you, who were so

reluctant to begin, are so eager to proceed. The nature of motion appears to be the question with which we begin. What do they mean when they say that all things are in motion? Is there only one kind of motion, or, as I rather incline to think, two? I should like to have your opinion upon this point in addition to my own, that I may err, if I must err, in your company; tell me, then, when a thing changes from one place to another, or goes round in the same place, is not that what is called motion?

Theod. Yes.

Soc. Here then we have one kind of motion. But when a thing, remaining on the same spot, grows old, or becomes black from being white, or hard from being soft, or undergoes any other change, may not this be properly called motion of another kind?

Theod. I think so.

Soc. Say rather that it must be so. Of motion then there are these two kinds, 'change,' and 'motion in place.' [1]

Theod. You are right.

Soc. And now, having made this distinction, let us address ourselves to those who say that all is motion, and ask them whether all things according to them have the two kinds of motion, and are changed as well as move in place, or is one thing moved in both ways, and another in one only?

Theod. Indeed, I do not know what to answer; but I think they would say that all things are moved in both ways.

Soc. Yes, comrade; for, if not, they would have to say that the same things are in motion and at rest, and there would be no more truth in saying that all things are in motion, than that all things are at rest.

[1] Reading φοράν

Theod. To be sure.

Soc. And if they are to be in motion, and nothing is to be devoid of motion, all things must always have every sort of motion?

Theod. Most true.

Soc. Consider a further point: did we not understand them to explain the generation of heat, whiteness, or anything else, in some such manner as the following: —were they not saying that each of them is moving between the agent and the patient, together with a perception, and that the patient ceases to be a perceiving power and becomes a percipient, and the agent a quale instead of a quality? I suspect that quality may appear a strange and uncouth term to you, and that you do not understand the abstract expression. Then I will take concrete instances: I mean to say that the producing power or agent becomes neither heat nor whiteness, but hot and white, and the like of other things. For I must repeat what I said before, that neither the agent nor patient have any absolute existence, but when they come together and generate sensations and their objects, the one becomes a thing of a certain quality, and the other a percipient. You remember?

Theod. Of course.

Soc. We may leave the details of their theory unexamined, but we must not forget to ask them the only question with which we are concerned: Are all things in motion and flux?

Theod. Yes, they will reply.

Soc. And they are moved in both those ways which we distinguished; that is to say, they move in place and are also changed?

Theod. Of course, if the motion is to be perfect.

Soc. If they only moved in place and were not

changed, we should be able to say what is the nature of the things which are in motion and flux?

Theod. Exactly.

Soc. But now, since not even white continues to flow white, and whiteness itself is a flux or change which is passing into another colour, and is never to be caught standing still, can the name of any colour be rightly used at all?

Theod. How is that possible, Socrates, either in the case of this or of any other quality—if while we are using the word the object is escaping in the flux?

Soc. And what would you say of perceptions, such as sight and hearing, or any other kind of perception? Is there any stopping in the act of seeing and hearing?

Theod. Certainly not, if all things are in motion.

Soc. Then we must not speak of seeing any more than of not-seeing, nor of any other perception more than of any non-perception, if all things partake of every kind of motion?

Theod. Certainly not.

Soc. Yet perception is knowledge: so at least Theaetetus and I were saying.

Theod. Very true.

Soc. Then when we were asked what is knowledge, we no more answered what is knowledge than what is not knowledge?

Theod. I suppose not.

Soc. Here, then, is a fine result: we corrected our first answer in our eagerness to prove that nothing is at rest. But if nothing is at rest, every answer upon whatever subject is equally right: you may say that a thing is or is not thus; or, if you prefer, 'becomes' thus; and if we say 'becomes,' we shall not then hamper them with words expressive of rest.

Theod. Quite true.

Soc. Yes, Theodorus, except in saying 'thus' and 'not thus.' But you ought not to use the word 'thus,' for there is no motion in 'thus' or in 'not thus.' The maintainers of the doctrine have as yet no words in which to express themselves, and must get a new language. I know of no word that will suit them, except perhaps 'no how,' which is perfectly indefinite.

Theod. Yes, that is a manner of speaking in which they will be quite at home.

Soc. And so, Theodorus, we have got rid of your friend without assenting to his doctrine, that every man is the measure of all things—a wise man only is a measure; neither can we allow that knowledge is perception, certainly not on the hypothesis of a perpetual flux, unless perchance our friend Theaetetus is able to convince us that it is.

PARMENIDES

PERSONS OF THE DIALOGUE

CEPHALUS
ADEIMANTUS
GLAUCON
ANTIPHON.
PYTHODORUS

SOCRATES
ZENO
PARMENIDES
ARISTOTELES

[*Cephalus rehearses a dialogue which is supposed to have been narrated in his presence by Antiphon, the half-brother of Adeimantus and Glaucon, to certain Clazomenians.*]

WE had come from our home at Clazomenae to Athens, and met Adeimantus and Glaucon in the Agora. Welcome, Cephalus, said Adeimantus, taking me by the hand; is there anything which we can do for you in Athens?

Yes; that is why I am here; I wish to ask a favour of you.

What may that be? he said.

I want you to tell me the name of your half-brother, which I have forgotten; he was a mere child when I last came hither from Clazomenae, but that was a long time ago; his father's name, if I remember rightly, was Pyrilampes?

Yes, he said, and the name of our brother, Antiphon; but why do you ask?

Let me introduce some countrymen of mine, I said; they are lovers of philosophy, and have heard that Antiphon was intimate with a certain Pythodorus, a friend of Zeno, and remembers a conversation which took place between Socrates, Zeno, and Parmenides many years ago, Pythodorus having often recited it to him.

357

Quite true.

And could we hear it? I asked.

Nothing easier, he replied; when he was a youth he made a careful study of the piece; at present his thoughts run in another direction; like his grandfather Antiphon he is devoted to horses. But, if that is what you want, let us go and look for him; he dwells at Melita, which is quite near, and he has only just left us to go home.

Accordingly we went to look for him; he was at home, and in the act of giving a bridle to a smith to be fitted. When he had done with the smith, his brothers told him the purpose of our visit; and he saluted me as an acquaintance whom he remembered from my former visit, and we asked him to repeat the dialogue. At first he was not very willing, and complained of the trouble, but at length he consented. He told us that Pythodorus had described to him the appearance of Parmenides and Zeno; they came to Athens, as he said, at the great Panathenaea; the former was, at the time of his visit, about 65 years old, very white with age, but well favoured. Zeno was nearly 40 years of age, tall and fair to look upon; in the days of his youth he was reported to have been beloved by Parmenides. He said that they lodged with Pythodorus in the Ceramicus, outside the wall, whither Socrates, then a very young man, came to see them, and many others with him; they wanted to hear the writings of Zeno, which had been brought to Athens for the first time on the occasion of their visit. These Zeno himself read to them in the absence of Parmenides, and had very nearly finished when Pythodorus entered, and with him Parmenides and Aristoteles who was afterwards one of the Thirty, and heard the little that remained of the dialogue. Pythodorus had heard Zeno repeat them before.

When the recitation was completed, Socrates requested that the first thesis of the first argument might be read over again, and this having been done, he said: What is your meaning, Zeno? Do you maintain that if being is many, it must be both like and unlike, and that this is impossible, for neither can the like be unlike, nor the unlike like—is that your position?

Just so, said Zeno.

And if the unlike cannot be like, or the like unlike, then according to you, being could not be many; for this would involve an impossibility. In all that you say have you any other purpose except to disprove the being of the many? and is not each division of your treatise intended to furnish a separate proof of this, there being in all as many proofs of the not-being of the many as you have composed arguments? Is that your meaning, or have I misunderstood you?

No, said Zeno; you have correctly understood my general purpose.

I see, Parmenides, said Socrates, that Zeno would like to be not only one with you in friendship but your second self in his writings too; he puts what you say in another way, and would fain make believe that he is telling us something which is new. For you, in your poems, say The All is one, and of this you adduce excellent proofs; and he on the other hands says There is no many; and on behalf of this he offers overwhelming evidence. You affirm unity, he denies plurality. And so you deceive the world into believing that you are saying different things when really you are saying much the same. This is a strain of art beyond the reach of most of us.

Yes, Socrates, said Zeno. But although you are as keen as a Spartan hound in pursuing the track, you do not fully apprehend the true motive of the composition, which is not really such an artificial work as you imagine; for what you speak of was an accident; there was no pretence of a great purpose; nor any serious intention of deceiving the world. The truth is, that these writings of mine were meant to protect the arguments of Parmenides against those who make fun of him and seek to show the many ridiculous and contradictory results which they suppose to follow from the affirmation of the one. My answer is addressed to the partisans of the many, whose attack I return with interest by retorting upon them that their hypothesis of the being of many, if carried out, appears to be still more ridiculous than the hypothesis of the being of one. Zeal for my master led me to write the book in the days of my youth, but some one stole the copy; and therefore I had no choice whether it should be published or not; the motive, however, of writing, was not the ambition of an elder man, but the pugnacity of a young one. This you do not seem to see, Socrates; though in other respects, as I was saying, your notion is a very just one.

I understand, said Socrates, and quite accept your account. But tell me, Zeno, do you not further think that there is an idea of likeness in itself, and another idea of unlikeness, which is the opposite of likeness, and that in these two, you and I and all other things to which we apply the term many, participate—things which participate in likeness become in that degree and manner like; and so far as they participate in unlikeness become in that degree unlike, or both like and unlike in the degree in which they participate in both? And may not all things partake of both opposites, and be both like and unlike, by reason of this participation?—Where is the wonder? Now if a person could prove the absolute like to become unlike, or the absolute unlike to become like, that, in my opinion, would indeed be a won-

der; but there is nothing extraordinary, Zeno, in showing
that the things which only partake of likeness and unlikeness experience both. Nor, again, if a person were
to show that all is one by partaking of one, and at the
same time many by partaking of many, would that be
very astonishing. But if he were to show me that the
absolute one was many, or the absolute many one, I
should be truly amazed. And so of all the rest: I
should be surprised to hear that the natures or ideas
themselves had these opposite qualities; but not if a person wanted to prove of me that I was many and also
one. When he wanted to show that I was many he
would say that I have a right and a left side, and a front
and a back, and an upper and a lower half, for I cannot
deny that I partake of multitude; when, on the other
hand, he wants to prove that I am one, he will say, that
we who are here assembled are seven, and that I am one
and partake of the one. In both instances he proves his
case. So again, if a person shows that such things as
wood, stones, and the like, being many are also one, we
admit that he shows the coexistence of the one and many,
but he does not show that the many are one or the one
many; he is uttering not a paradox but a truism. If
however, as I just now suggested, some one were to abstract simple notions of like, unlike, one, many, rest,
motion, and similar ideas, and then to show that these
admit of admixture and separation in themselves, I
should be very much astonished. This part of the argument appears to be treated by you, Zeno, in a very spir-
ited manner; but, as I was saying, I should be far more
amazed if any one found in the ideas themselves which
are apprehended by reason, the same puzzle and entan-
glement which you have shown to exist in visible objects.

While Socrates was speaking, Pythodorus thought
that Parmenides and Zeno were not altogether pleased

at the successive steps of the argument; but still they gave the closest attention, and often looked at one another, and smiled as if in admiration of him. When he had finished, Parmenides expressed their feelings in the following words:—

Socrates, he said, I admire the bent of your mind towards philosophy; tell me now, was this your own distinction between ideas in themselves and the things which partake of them? and do you think that there is an idea of likeness apart from the likeness which we possess, and of the one and many, and of the other things which Zeno mentioned?

I think that there are such ideas, said Socrates.

Parmenides proceeded: And would you also make absolute ideas of the just and the beautiful and the good, and of all that class?

Yes, he said, I should.

And would you make an idea of man apart from us and from all other human creatures, or of fire and water?

I am often undecided, Parmenides, as to whether I ought to include them or not.

And would you feel equally undecided, Socrates, about things of which the mention may provoke a smile? —I mean such things as hair, mud, dirt, or anything else which is vile and paltry; would you suppose that each of these has an idea distinct from the actual objects with which we come into contact, or not?

Certainly not, said Socrates; visible things like these are such as they appear to us, and I am afraid that there would be an absurdity in assuming any idea of them, although I sometimes get disturbed, and begin to think that there is nothing without an idea; but then again, when I have taken up this position, I run away, because I am afraid that I may fall into a bottomless pit of nonsense, and perish; and so I return to the ideas of which I was just now speaking, and occupy myself with them.

Yes, Socrates, said Parmenides; that is because you are still young; the time will come, if I am not mistaken, when philosophy will have a firmer grasp of you, and then you will not despise even the meanest things; at your age, you are too much disposed to regard the opinions of men. But I should like to know whether you mean that there are certain ideas of which all other things partake, and from which they derive their names; that similars, for example, become similar, because they partake of similarity; and great things become great, because they partake of greatness; and that just and beautiful things become just and beautiful, because they partake of justice and beauty?

Yes, certainly, said Socrates, that is my meaning.

Then each individual partakes either of the whole of the idea or else of a part of the idea? Can there be any other mode of participation?

There cannot be, he said.

Then do you think that the whole idea is one, and yet, being one, is in each one of the many?

Why not, Parmenides? said Socrates.

Because one and the same thing will exist as a whole at the same time in many separate individuals, and will therefore be in a state of separation from itself.

Nay, but the idea may be like the day which is one and the same in many places at once, and yet continuous with itself; in this way each idea may be one and the same in all at the same time.

I like your way, Socrates, of making one in many places at once. You mean to say, that if I were to spread out a sail and cover a number of men, there would be one whole including many—is not that your meaning?

I think so.

And would you say that the whole sail includes each man, or a part of it only, and different parts different men?

The latter.

Then, Socrates, the ideas themselves will be divisible, and things which participate in them will have a part of them only and not the whole idea existing in each of them?

That seems to follow.

Then would you like to say, Socrates, that the one idea is really divisible and yet remains one?

Certainly not, he said.

Suppose that you divide absolute greatness, and that of the many great things, each one is great in virtue of a portion of greatness less than absolute greatness—is that conceivable?

No.

Or will each equal thing, if possessing some small portion of equality less than absolute equality, be equal to some other thing by virtue of that portion only?

Impossible.

Or suppose one of us to have a portion of smallness; this is but a part of the small, and therefore the absolutely small is greater; if the absolutely small be greater, that to which the part of the small is added will be smaller and not greater than before.

How absurd!

Then in what way, Socrates, will all things participate in the ideas, if they are unable to participate in them either as parts or wholes?

Indeed, he said, you have asked a question which is not easily answered.

Well, said Parmenides, and what do you say of another question?

What question?

I imagine that the way in which you are led to assume one idea of each kind is as follows:—You see a number of great objects, and when you look at them there seems to you to be one and the same idea (or nature) in them all; hence you conceive of greatness as one.

Very true, said Socrates.

And if you go on and allow your mind in like manner to embrace in one view the idea of greatness and of great things which are not the idea, and to compare them, will not another greatness arise, which will appear to be the source of all these?

It would seem so.

Then another idea of greatness now comes into view over and above absolute greatness, and the individuals which partake of it; and then another, over and above all these, by virtue of which they will all be great, and so each idea instead of being one will be infinitely multiplied.

But may not the ideas, asked Socrates, be thoughts only, and have no proper existence except in our minds, Parmenides? For in that case each idea may still be one, and not experience this infinite multiplication.

And can there be individual thoughts which are thoughts of nothing?

Impossible, he said.

The thought must be of something?

Yes.

Of something which is or which is not?

Of something which is.

Must it not be of a single something, which the thought recognizes as attaching to all, being a single form or nature?

Yes.

And will not the something which is apprehended as one and the same in all, be an idea?

From that, again, there is no escape.

Then, said Parmenides, if you say that everything else participates in the ideas, must you not say either that everything is made up of thoughts, and that all things think; or that they are thoughts but have no thought?

The latter view, Parmenides, is no more rational than the previous one. In my opinion, the ideas are, as it were, patterns fixed in nature, and other things are like them, and resemblances of them—what is meant by the participation of other things in the ideas, is really assimilation to them.

But if, said he, the individual is like the idea, must not the idea also be like the individual, in so far as the individual is a resemblance of the idea? That which is like, cannot be conceived of as other than the like of like.

Impossible.

And when two things are alike, must they not partake of the same idea?

They must.

And will not that of which the two partake, and which makes them alike, be the idea itself?

Certainly.

Then the idea cannot be like the individual, or the individual like the idea; for if they are alike, some further idea of likeness will always be coming to light, and if that be like anything else, another; and new ideas will be always arising, if the idea resembles that which partakes of it?

Quite true.

The theory, then, that other things participate in the ideas by resemblance, has to be given up, and some other mode of participation devised?

It would seem so.

Do you see then, Socrates, how great is the difficulty of affirming the ideas to be absolute?

Yes, indeed.

And, further, let me say that as yet you only understand a small part of the difficulty which is involved if you make of each thing a single idea, parting it off from other things.

What difficulty? he said.

There are many, but the greatest of all is this:—If an opponent argues that these ideas, being such as we say they ought to be, must remain unknown, no one can prove to him that he is wrong, unless he who denies their existence be a man of great ability and knowledge, and is willing to follow a long and laborious demonstration; he will remain unconvinced, and still insist that they cannot be known.

What do you mean, Parmenides? said Socrates.

In the first place, I think, Socrates, that you, or any one who maintains the existence of absolute essences, will admit that they cannot exist in us.

No, said Socrates; for then they would be no longer absolute.

True, he said; and therefore when ideas are what they are in relation to one another, their essence is determined by a relation among themselves, and has nothing to do with the resemblances, or whatever they are to be termed, which are in our sphere, and from which we receive this or that name when we partake of them. And the things which are within our sphere and have the same names with them, are likewise only relative to one another, and not to the ideas which have the same names with them, but belong to themselves and not to them.

What do you mean? said Socrates.

I may illustrate my meaning in this way, said Parmenides:—A master has a slave; now there is nothing absolute in the relation between them, which is simply a relation of one man to another. But there is also an idea of mastership in the abstract, which is relative to the idea of slavery in the abstract. These natures have nothing to do with us, nor we with them; they are concerned with themselves only, and we with ourselves. Do you see my meaning?

Yes, said Socrates, I quite see your meaning.

And will not knowledge—I mean absolute knowledge —answer to absolute truth?

Certainly.

And each kind of absolute knowledge will answer to each kind of absolute being?

Yes.

But the knowledge which we have, will answer to the truth which we have; and again, each kind of knowledge which we have, will be a knowledge of each kind of being which we have?

Certainly.

But the ideas themselves, as you admit, we have not, and cannot have?

No, we cannot.

And the absolute natures or kinds are known severally by the absolute idea of knowledge?

Yes.

And we have not got the idea of knowledge?

No.

Then none of the ideas are known to us, because we have no share in absolute knowledge?

I suppose not.

Then the nature of the beautiful in itself, and of the good in itself, and all other ideas which we suppose to exist absolutely, are unknown to us?

It would seem so.

I think that there is a stranger consequence still.

What is it?

Would you, or would you not say, that absolute knowledge, if there is such a thing, must be far more exact knowledge than our knowledge; and the same of beauty and of the rest?

Yes.

And if there be such a thing as participation in absolute knowledge, no one is more likely than God to have this most exact knowledge?

Certainly.

But then, will God, having absolute knowledge, have a knowledge of human things?

Why not?

Because, Socrates, said Parmenides, we have admitted that the ideas are not valid in relation to human things; nor human things in relation to them; the relations of either are limited to their respective spheres.

Yes, that has been admitted.

And if God has this perfect authority, and perfect knowledge, his authority cannot rule us, nor his knowledge know us, or any human thing; just as our authority does not extend to the gods, nor our knowledge know anything which is divine, so by parity of reason they, being gods, are not our masters, neither do they know the things of men.

Yet, surely, said Socrates, to deprive God of knowledge is monstrous.

These, Socrates, said Parmenides, are a few, and only a few of the difficulties in which we are involved if ideas really are and we determine each one of them to be an absolute unity. He who hears what may be said against them will deny the very existence of them—and even if they do exist, he will say that they must of necessity be unknown to man; and he will seem to have reason on his side, and as we were remarking just now, will be very difficult to convince; a man must be gifted with very considerable ability before he can learn that everything has a class and an absolute essence; and still more remarkable will he be who discovers all these things for himself, and having thoroughly investigated them is able to teach them to others.

I agree with you, Parmenides, said Socrates; and what you say is very much to my mind.

And yet, Socrates, said Parmenides, if a man, fixing his attention on these and the like difficulties, does away with ideas of things and will not admit that every individual thing has its own determinate idea which is always one and the same, he will have nothing on which his mind can rest; and so he will utterly destroy the power of reasoning, as you seem to me to have particularly noted.

Very true, he said.

But, then, what is to become of philosophy? Whither shall we turn, if the ideas are unknown?

I certainly do not see my way at present.

Yes, said Parmenides; and I think that this arises, Socrates, out of your attempting to define the beautiful, the just, the good, and the ideas generally, without sufficient previous training.

[The rest of the dialogue is omitted.]

PHILEBUS

PERSONS OF THE DIALOGUE

SOCRATES   PROTARCHUS   PHILEBUS

[*This dialogue is a discussion of the nature of the good, and of the relative importance of wisdom and pleasure in the good. The selection here given consists of the concluding portion of the dialogue, which is in the nature of a summing up of the whole discussion.*]

Socrates. Philebus says that pleasure is the true end of all living beings, at which all ought to aim, and moreover that it is the chief good of all, and that the two names 'good' and 'pleasant' are correctly given to one thing and one nature; Socrates, on the other hand, begins by denying this, and further says, that in nature as in name they are two, and that wisdom partakes more than pleasure of the good. Is not and was not this what we were saying, Protarchus?

Protarchus. Certainly.

Soc. And is there not and was there not a further point which was conceded between us?

Pro. What was it?

Soc. That the good differs from all other things.

Pro. In what respect?

Soc. In that the being who possesses good always everywhere and in all things has the most perfect sufficiency, and is never in need of anything else.

Pro. Exactly.

Soc. And did we not endeavour to make an imagi-

371

nary separation of wisdom and pleasure, assigning to each a distinct life, so that pleasure was wholly excluded from wisdom, and wisdom in like manner had no part whatever in pleasure?

Pro. We did.

Soc. And did we think that either of them alone would be sufficient?

Pro. Certainly not.

Soc. And if we erred in any point, then let any one who will, take up the enquiry again and set us right; and assuming memory and wisdom and knowledge and true opinion to belong to the same class, let him consider whether he would desire to possess or acquire,—I will not say pleasure, however abundant or intense, if he has no real perception that he is pleased, nor any consciousness of what he feels, nor any recollection, however momentary, of the feeling,—but would he desire to have anything at all, if these faculties were wanting to him? And about wisdom I ask the same question; can you conceive that any one would choose to have all wisdom absolutely devoid of pleasure, rather than with a certain degree of pleasure, or all pleasure devoid of wisdom rather than with a certain degree of wisdom?

Pro. Certainly not, Socrates; but why repeat such questions any more?

Soc. Then the perfect and universally eligible and entirely good cannot possibly be either of them?

Pro. Impossible.

Soc. Then now we must ascertain the nature of the good more or less accurately, in order, as we were saying, that the second place may be duly assigned?

Pro. Right.

Soc. Have we not found a road which leads towards the good?

Pro. What road?

Soc. Supposing that a man had to be found, and you could discover in what house he lived, would not that be a great step towards the discovery of the man himself?

Pro. Certainly.

Soc. And now reason intimates to us, as at our first beginning, that we should seek the good, not in the unmixed life but in the mixed.

Pro. True.

Soc. There is greater hope of finding that which we are seeking in the life which is well mixed than in that which is not?

Pro. Far greater.

Soc. Then now let us mingle, Protarchus, at the same time offering up a prayer to Dionysus or Hephaestus, or whoever is the god who presides over the ceremony of mingling.

Pro. By all means.

Soc. Are not we the cup-bearers? and here are two fountains which are flowing at our side: one, which is pleasure, may be likened to a fountain of honey; the other, wisdom, a sober draught in which no wine mingles, is of water unpleasant but healthful; out of these we must seek to make the fairest of all possible mixtures.

Pro. Certainly.

Soc. Tell me first;—should we be most likely to succeed if we mingled every sort of pleasure with every sort of wisdom?

Pro. Perhaps we might.

Soc. But I should be afraid of the risk, and I think that I can show a safer plan.

Pro. What is it?

Soc. One pleasure was supposed by us to be truer than another, and one art to be more exact than another.

Pro. Certainly.

Soc. There was also supposed to be a difference in sciences; some of them regarding only the transient and perishing, and others the permanent and imperishable and everlasting and immutable; and when judged by the standard of truth, the latter, as we thought, were truer than the former.

Pro. Very good and right.

Soc. If, then, we were to begin by mingling the sections of each class which have the most of truth, will not the union suffice to give us the loveliest of lives, or shall we still want some elements of another kind?

Pro. I think that we ought to do what you suggest.

Soc. Let us suppose a man who understands justice, and has reason as well as understanding about the true nature of this and of all other things.

Pro. We will suppose such a man.

Soc. Will he have enough of knowledge if he is acquainted only with the divine circle and sphere, and knows nothing of our human spheres and circles, but uses only divine circles and measures in the building of a house?

Pro. The knowledge which is only superhuman, Socrates, is ridiculous in man.

Soc. What do you mean? Do you mean that you are to throw into the cup and mingle the impure and uncertain art which uses the false measure and the false circle?

Pro. Yes, we must, if any of us is ever to find his way home.

Soc. And am I to include music, which, as I was saying just now, is full of guesswork and imitation, and is wanting in purity?

Pro. Yes, I think that you must, if human life is to be a life at all.

Soc. Well, then, suppose that I give way, and, like a

doorkeeper who is pushed and overborne by the mob, I open the door wide, and let knowledge of every sort stream in, and the pure mingle with the impure?

Pro. I do not know, Socrates, that any great harm would come of having them all, if only you have the first sort.

Soc. Well, then, shall I let them all flow into what Homer poetically terms 'a meeting of the waters'?

Pro. By all means.

Soc. There—I have let them in, and now I must return to the fountain of pleasure. For we were not permitted to begin by mingling in a single stream the true portions of both according to our original intention; but the love of all knowledge constrained us to let all the sciences flow in together before the pleasures.

Pro. Quite true.

Soc. And now the time has come for us to consider about the pleasures also, whether we shall in like manner let them go all at once, or at first only the true ones.

Pro. It will be by far the safer course to let flow the true ones first.

Soc. Let them flow, then; and now, if there are any necessary pleasures, as there were arts and sciences necessary, must we not mingle them?

Pro. Yes; the necessary pleasures should certainly be allowed to mingle.

Soc. The knowledge of the arts has been admitted to be innocent and useful always; and if we say of pleasures in like manner that all of them are good and innocent for all of us at all times, we must let them all mingle?

Pro. What shall we say about them, and what course shall we take?

Soc. Do not ask me, Protarchus; but ask the daughters of pleasure and wisdom to answer for themselves.

Pro. How?

Soc. Tell us, O beloved—shall we call you pleasures or by some other name?—would you rather live with or without wisdom? I am of opinion that they would certainly answer as follows:

Pro. How?

Soc. They would answer, as we said before, that for any single class to be left by itself pure and isolated is not good, nor altogether possible; and that if we are to make comparisons of one class with another and choose, there is no better companion than knowledge of things in general, and likewise the perfect knowledge, if that may be, of ourselves in every respect.[1]

Pro. And our answer will be:—In that ye have spoken well.

Soc. Very true. And now let us go back and interrogate wisdom and mind: Would you like to have any pleasures in the mixture? And they will reply:—'What pleasures do you mean?'

Pro. Likely enough.

Soc. And we shall take up our parable and say: Do you wish to have the greatest and most vehement pleasures for your companions in addition to the true ones? 'Why, Socrates,' they will say, 'how can we? seeing that they are the source of ten thousand hindrances to us; they trouble the souls of men, which are our habitation, with their madness; they prevent us from coming to the birth, and are commonly the ruin of the children which are born to us, causing them to be forgotten and unheeded; but the true and pure pleasures, of which you spoke, know to be of our family, and also those pleasures which accompany health and temperance, and which every Virtue, like a goddess, has in her train to

[1] Reading αὐτῶν ἡμῶν.

follow her about wherever she goes,—mingle these and not the others; there would be great want of sense in any one who desires to see a fair and perfect mixture, and to find in it what is the highest good in man and in the universe, and to divine what is the true form of good—there would be great want of sense in his allowing the pleasures, which are always in the company of folly and vice, to mingle with mind in the cup.'—Is not this a very rational and suitable reply, which mind has made, both on her own behalf, as well as on the behalf of memory and true opinion?

Pro. Most certainly.

Soc. And still there must be something more added, which is a necessary ingredient in every mixture.

Pro. What is that?

Soc. Unless truth enter into the composition, nothing can truly be created or subsist.

Pro. Impossible.

Soc. Quite impossible; and now you and Philebus must tell me whether anything is still wanting in the mixture, for to my way of thinking the argument is now completed, and may be compared to an incorporeal law, which is going to hold fair rule over a living body.

Pro. I agree with you, Socrates.

Soc. And may we not say with reason that we are now at the vestibule of the habitation of the good?

Pro. I think that we are.

Soc. What, then, is there in the mixture which is most precious, and which is the principal cause why such a state is universally beloved by all? When we have discovered it, we will proceed to ask whether this omnipresent nature is more akin to pleasure or to mind.

Pro. Quite right; in that way we shall be better able to judge.

Soc. And there is no difficulty in seeing the cause

which renders any mixture either of the highest value or
of none at all.

Pro. What do you mean?

Soc. Every man knows it.

Pro. What?

Soc. He knows that any want of measure and symmetry in any mixture whatever must always of necessity be fatal, both to the elements and to the mixture,
which is then not a mixture, but only a confused medley
which brings confusion on the possessor of it.

Pro. Most true.

Soc. And now the power of the good has retired into
the region of the beautiful; for measure and symmetry
are beauty and virtue all the world over.

Pro. True.

Soc. Also we said that truth was to form an element
in the mixture.

Pro. Certainly.

Soc. Then, if we are not able to hunt the good with
one idea only, with three we may catch our prey;
Beauty, Symmetry, Truth are the three, and these taken
together we may regard as the single cause of the mixture, and the mixture as being good by reason of the
infusion of them.

Pro. Quite right.

Soc. And now, Protarchus, any man could decide
well enough whether pleasure or wisdom is more akin to
the highest good, and more honourable among gods and
men.

Pro. Clearly, and yet perhaps the argument had better be pursued to the end.

Soc. We must take each of them separately in their
relation to pleasure and mind, and pronounce upon them;
for we ought to see to which of the two they are severally most akin.

Pro. You are speaking of beauty, truth, and measure?

Soc. Yes, Protarchus, take truth first, and, after passing in review mind, truth, pleasure, pause awhile and make answer to yourself,—as to whether pleasure or mind is more akin to truth.

Pro. There is no need to pause, for the difference between them is palpable; pleasure is the veriest impostor in the world, and it is said that in the pleasures of love, which appear to be the greatest, perjury is excused by the gods; for pleasures, like children, have not the least particle of reason in them; whereas mind is either the same as truth, or the most like truth, and the truest.

Soc. Shall we next consider measure, in like manner, and ask whether pleasure has more of this than wisdom, or wisdom than pleasure?

Pro. Here is another question which may be easily answered; for I imagine that nothing can ever be more immoderate than the transports of pleasure, or more in conformity with measure than mind and knowledge.

Soc. Very good; but there still remains the third test: Has mind a greater share of beauty than pleasure, and is mind or pleasure the fairer of the two?

Pro. No one, Socrates, either awake or dreaming, ever saw or imagined mind or wisdom to be in aught unseemly, at any time, past, present, or future.

Soc. Right.

Pro. But when we see some one indulging in pleasures, perhaps in the greatest of pleasures, the ridiculous or disgraceful nature of the action makes us ashamed; and so we put them out of sight, and consign them to darkness, under the idea that they ought not to meet the eye of day.

Soc. Then, Protarchus, you will proclaim everywhere, by word of mouth to this company, and by messengers bearing the tidings far and wide, that pleasure is not the first of possessions, nor yet the second, but that in measure, and the mean, and the suitable, and the like, the eternal nature has been found.

Pro. Yes, that seems to be the result of what has been now said.

Soc. In the second class is contained the symmetrical and beautiful and perfect or sufficient, and all which are of that family.

Pro. True.

Soc. And if you reckon in the third class mind and wisdom, you will not be far wrong, if I divine aright.

Pro. I dare say.

Soc. And would you not put in the fourth class the goods which we were affirming to appertain specially to the soul—sciences and arts and true opinions as we called them? These come after the third class, and form the fourth, as they are certainly more akin to good than pleasure is.

Pro. Surely.

Soc. The fifth class are the pleasures which were defined by us as painless, being the pure pleasures of the soul herself, as we termed them, which accompany, some the sciences, and some the senses.[1]

Pro. Perhaps.

Soc. And now, as Orpheus says,

'With the sixth generation cease the glory of my song.'

Here, at the sixth award, let us make an end; all that remains is to set the crown on our discourse.

Pro. True.

Soc. Then let us sum up and reassert what has been

[1] Reading ἐπιστήμαις, τὰς δὲ κ.τ.λ.

said, thus offering the third libation to the saviour Zeus.

Pro. How?

Soc. Philebus affirmed that pleasure was always and absolutely the good.

Pro. I understand; this third libation, Socrates, of which you spoke, meant a recapitulation.

Soc. Yes, but listen to the sequel; convinced of what I have just been saying, and feeling indignant at the doctrine, which is maintained, not by Philebus only, but by thousands of others, I affirmed that mind was far better and far more excellent, as an element of human life, than pleasure.

Pro. True.

Soc. But, suspecting that there were other things which were also better, I went on to say that if there was anything better than either, then I would claim the second place for mind over pleasure, and pleasure would lose the second place as well as the first.

Pro. You did.

Soc. Nothing could be more satisfactorily shown than the unsatisfactory nature of both of them.

Pro. Very true.

Soc. The claims both of pleasure and mind to be the absolute good have been entirely disproven in this argument, because they are both wanting in self-sufficiency and also in adequacy and perfection.

Pro. Most true.

Soc. But, though they must both resign in favour of another, mind is ten thousand times nearer and more akin to the nature of the conqueror than pleasure.

Pro. Certainly.

Soc. And, according to the judgment which has now been given, pleasure will rank fifth.

Pro. True.

Soc. But not first; no, not even if all the oxen and

horses and animals in the world by their pursuit of enjoyment proclaim her to be so;—although the many trusting in them, as diviners trust in birds, determine that pleasures make up the good of life, and deem the lusts of animals to be better witnesses than the inspirations of divine philosophy.

Pro. And now, Socrates, we tell you that the truth of what you have been saying is approved by the judgment of all of us.

Soc. And will you let me go?

Pro. There is a little which yet remains, and I will remind you of it, for I am sure that you will not be the first to go away from an argument.

TIMAEUS

PERSONS OF THE DIALOGUE

SOCRATES
TIMAEUS

CRITIAS
HERMOCRATES

[*The dialogue opens with a few remarks on the state, which are omitted in this selection.*]

Critias. I will tell an old-world story which I heard from an aged man; for Critias, at the time of telling it, was, as he said, nearly ninety years of age, and I was about ten. Now the day was that day of the Apaturia which is called the Registration of Youth, at which, according to custom, our parents gave prizes for recitations, and the poems of several poets were recited by us boys, and many of us sang the poems of Solon, which at that time had not gone out of fashion. One of our tribe, either because he thought so or to please Critias, said that in his judgment Solon was not only the wisest of men, but also the noblest of poets. The old man, as I very well remember, brightened up at hearing this and said, smiling: Yes, Amynander, if Solon had only, like other poets, made poetry the business of his life, and had completed the tale which he brought with him from Egypt, and had not been compelled, by reason of the factions and troubles which he found stirring in his own country when he came home, to attend to other matters, in my opinion he would have been as famous as Homer or Hesiod, or any poet.

And what was the tale about, Critias? said Amynander.

About the greatest action which the Athenians ever

383

did, and which ought to have been the most famous, but, through the lapse of time and the destruction of the actors, it has not come down to us.

Tell us, said the other, the whole story, and how and from whom Solon heard this veritable tradition.

He replied:—In the Egyptian Delta, at the head of which the river Nile divides, there is a certain district' which is called the district of Sais, and the great city of the district is also called Sais, and is the city from which King Amasis came. The citizens have a deity for their foundress; she is called in the Egyptian tongue Neith, and is asserted by them to be the same whom the Hellenes call Athene; they are great lovers of the Athenians, and say that they are in some way related to them. To this city came Solon, and was received there with great honour; he asked the priests who were most skilful in such matters, about antiquity, and made the discovery that neither he nor any other Hellene knew anything worth mentioning about the times of old. On one occasion, wishing to draw them on to speak of antiquity, he began to tell about the most ancient things in our part of the world—about Phoroneus, who is called 'the first man,' and about Niobe; and after the Deluge, of the surivial of Deucalion and Pyrrha; and he traced the genealogy of their descendants, and reckoning up the dates, tried to compute how many years ago the events of which he was speaking happened. Thereupon one of the priests, who was of a very great age, said: O Solon, Solon, you Hellenes are never anything but children, and there is not an old man among you. Solon in return asked him what he meant. I mean to say, he replied, that in mind you are all young; there is no old opinion handed down among you by ancient tradition, nor any science which is hoary with age. And I will tell you why. There have been, and will be again, many

destructions of mankind arising out of many causes;
the greatest have been brought about by the agencies of
fire and water, and other lesser ones by innumerable
other causes. There is a story, which even you have preserved, that once upon a time Phaëthon, the son of
Helios, having yoked the steeds in his father's chariot,
because he was not able to drive them in the path of his
father, burnt up all that was upon the earth, and was
himself destroyed by a thunderbolt. Now this has the
form of a myth, but really signifies a declination of the
bodies moving in the heavens around the earth, and a
great conflagration of things upon the earth, which re-
curs after long intervals; at such times those who live
upon the mountains and in dry and lofty places are more
liable to destruction than those who dwell by rivers or
on the seashore. And from this calamity the Nile, who
is our never-failing saviour, delivers and preserves us.
When, on the other hand, the gods purge the earth with
a deluge of water, the survivors in your country are
herdsmen and shepherds who dwell on the mountains,
but those who, like you, live in cities are carried by the
rivers into the sea. Whereas in this land, neither then
nor at any other time, does the water come down from
above on the fields, having always a tendency to come
up from below; for which reason the traditions preserved here are the most ancient. The fact is, that wherever the extremity of winter frost or of summer sun does
not prevent, mankind exist, sometimes in greater, sometimes in lesser numbers. And whatever happened either
in your country or in ours, or in any other region of
which we are informed—if there were any actions noble
or great or in any other way remarkable, they have all
been written down by us of old, and are preserved in our
temples. Whereas just when you and other nations are
beginning to be provided with letters and the other

requisites of civilized life, after the usual interval, the stream from heaven, like a pestilence, comes pouring down, and leaves only those of you who are destitute of letters and education; and so you have to begin all over again like children, and know nothing of what happened in ancient times, either among us or among yourselves. As for those genealogies of yours which you just now recounted to us, Solon, they are no better than the tales of children. In the first place you remember a single deluge only, but there were many previous ones; in the next place, you do not know that there formerly dwelt in your land the fairest and noblest race of men which ever lived, and that you and your whole city are descended from a small seed or remnant of them which survived. And this was unknown to you, because, for many generations, the survivors of that destruction died, leaving no written word. For there was a time, Solon, before the great deluge of all, when the city which now is Athens was first in war and in every way the best governed of all cities, and is said to have performed the noblest deeds and to have had the fairest constitution of any of which tradition tells, under the face of heaven. Solon marvelled at his words, and earnestly requested the priests to inform him exactly and in order about these former citizens. You are welcome to hear about them, Solon, said the priest, both for your own sake and for that of your city, and above all, for the sake of the goddess who is the common patron and parent and educator of both our cities. She founded your city a thousand years before ours,[1] receiving from the Earth and Hephaestus the seed of your race, and afterwards she founded ours, of which the constitution is recorded in our sacred registers to be 8000 years old. As touching

[1] Observe that Plato gives the same date (9000 years ago) for the foundation of Athens and for the repulse of the invasion from Atlantis.

your citizens of 9000 years ago, I will briefly inform you of their laws and of their most famous action; the exact particulars of the whole we will hereafter go through at our leisure in the sacred registers themselves. If you compare these very laws with ours you will find that many of ours are the counterpart of yours as they were in the olden time. In the first place, there is the caste of priests, which is separated from all the others; next, there are the artificers, who ply their several crafts by themselves and do not intermix; and also there is the class of shepherds and of hunters,[1] as well as that of husbandmen; and you will observe, too, that the warriors in Egypt are distinct from all the other classes, and are commanded by the law to devote themselves solely to military pursuits; moreover, the weapons which they carry are shields and spears, a style of equipment which the goddess taught of Asiatics first to us, as in your part of the world first to you. Then as to wisdom, do you observe how our law from the very first made a study of the whole order of things, extending even to prophecy and medicine which gives health; out of these divine elements deriving what was needful for human life, and adding every sort of knowledge which was akin to them. All this order and arrangement the goddess first imparted to you when establishing your city; and she chose the spot of earth in which you were born, because she saw that the happy temperament of the seasons in that land would produce the wisest of men. Wherefore the goddess, who was a lover both of war and of wisdom, selected and first of all settled that spot which was the most likely to produce men likest herself. And there you dwelt, having such laws as these and still better ones, and excelled all mankind in all virtue, as became the children and disciples of the gods.

---

[1] Reading τὸ τῶν θηρευτῶν.

Many great and wonderful deeds are recorded of your state in our histories. But one of them exceeds all the rest in greatness and valour. For these histories tell of a mighty power which unprovoked made an expedition against the whole of Europe and Asia, and to which your city put an end. This power came forth out of the Atlantic Ocean, for in those days the Atlantic was navigable; and there was an island situated in front of the straits which are by you called the pillars of Heracles; the island was larger than Libya and Asia put together, and was the way to other islands, and from these you might pass to the whole of the opposite continent which surrounded the true ocean; for this sea which is within the Straits of Heracles is only a harbour, having a narrow entrance, but that other is a real sea, and the surrounding land may be most truly called a boundless continent. Now in this island of Atlantis there was a great and wonderful empire which had rule over the whole island and several others, and over parts of the continent, and, furthermore, the men of Atlantis had subjected the parts of Libya within the columns of Heracles as far as Egypt, and of Europe as far as Tyrrhenia. This vast power, gathered into one, endeavoured to subdue at a blow our country and yours and the whole of the region within the straits; and then, Solon, your country shone forth, in the excellence of her virtue and strength, among all mankind. She was pre-eminent in courage and military skill, and was the leader of the Hellenes. And when the rest fell off from her, being compelled to stand alone, after having undergone the very extremity of danger, she defeated and triumphed over the invaders, and preserved from slavery those who were not yet subjugated, and generously liberated all the rest of us who dwell within the pillars. But afterwards there occurred violent earthquakes and floods; and in a

single day and night of misfortune all your warlike men
in a body sank into the earth, and the island of Atlantis
in like manner disappeared in the depths of the sea.
For which reason the sea in those parts is impassable
and impenetrable, because there is a shoal of mud in the
way; and this was caused by the subsidence of the
island.

I have told you briefly, Socrates, what the aged Critias heard from Solon and related to us. And when you
were speaking yesterday about your city and citizens,
the tale which I have just been repeating to you came
into my mind, and I remarked with astonishment how,
by some mysterious coincidence, you agreed in almost
every particular with the narrative of Solon; but I did
not like to speak at the moment. For a long time had
elapsed, and I had forgotten too much; I thought that
I must first of all run over the narrative in my own mind,
and then I would speak. And so I readily assented to
your request yesterday, considering that in all such cases
the chief difficulty is to find a tale suitable to our purpose, and that with such a tale we should be fairly well
provided.

And therefore, as Hermocrates has told you, on my
way home yesterday I at once communicated the tale
to my companions as I remembered it; and after I left
them, during the night by thinking, I recovered nearly
the whole of it. Truly, as is often said, the lessons of
our childhood make a wonderful impression on our memories; for I am not sure that I could remember all the
discourse of yesterday, but I should be much surprised
if I forgot any of these things which I have heard very
long ago. I listened at the time with childlike interest
to the old man's narrative; he was very ready to teach
me, and I asked him again and again to repeat his words,
so that like an indelible picture they were branded into

my mind. As soon as the day broke, I rehearsed them as he spoke them to my companions, that they, as well as myself, might have something to say. And now, Socrates, to make an end of my preface, I am ready to tell you the whole tale. I will give you not only the general heads, but the particulars, as they were told to me. The city and citizens, which you yesterday described to us in fiction, we will now transfer to the world of reality. It shall be the ancient city of Athens, and we will suppose that the citizens whom you imagined, were our veritable ancestors, of whom the priest spoke; they will perfectly harmonize, and there will be no inconsistency in saying that the citizens of your republic are these ancient Athenians. Let us divide the subject among us, and all endeavour according to our ability gracefully to execute the task which you have imposed upon us. Consider then, Socrates, if this narrative is suited to the purpose, or whether we should seek for some other instead.

Soc. And what other, Critias, can we find that will be better than this, which is natural and suitable to the festival of the goddess, and has the very great advantage of being a fact and not a fiction? How or where shall we find another if we abandon this? We cannot, and therefore you must tell the tale, and good luck to you; and I in return for my yesterday's discourse will now rest and be a listener.

Crit. Let me proceed to explain to you, Socrates, the order in which we have arranged our entertainment. Our intention is, that Timaeus, who is the most of an astronomer amongst us, and has made the nature of the universe his special study, should speak first, beginning with the generation of the world and going down to the creation of man; next, I am to receive the men whom he has created, and of whom some will have profited by the excellent education which you have given them; and then, in accordance with the tale of Solon, and equally with his law, we will bring them into court and make them citizens, as if they were those very Athenians whom the sacred Egyptian record has recovered from oblivion, and thenceforward we will speak of them as Athenians and fellow-citizens.

Soc. I see that I shall receive in my turn a perfect and splendid feast of reason. And now, Timaeus, you, I suppose, should speak next, after duly calling upon the Gods.

Tim. All men, Socrates, who have any degree of right feeling, at the beginning of every enterprise, whether small or great, always call upon God. And we, too, who are going to discourse of the nature of the universe, how created or how existing without creation, if we be not altogether out of our wits, must invoke the aid of Gods and Goddesses and pray that our words may be acceptable to them and consistent with themselves. Let this, then, be our invocation of the Gods, to which I add an exhortation of myself to speak in such manner as will be most intelligible to you, and will most accord with my own intent.

First, then, in my judgment, we must make a distinction and ask, What is that which always is and has no becoming; and what is that which is always becoming and never is? That which is apprehended by intelligence and reason is always in the same state; but that which is conceived by opinion with the help of sensation and without reason, is always in a process of becoming and perishing and never really is. Now everything that becomes or is created must of necessity be created by some cause, for without a cause nothing can be created. The work of the creator, whenever he looks to the unchangeable and fashions the form and nature of his work after an unchangeable pattern, must necessarily be made fair and perfect; but when he looks to the created only, and uses a created pattern, it is not fair or perfect. Was the heaven then or the world, whether called by this or by any other more appropriate name—assuming the name, I am asking a question which has to be asked at the beginning of an enquiry about anything—was the world, I say, always in existence and without beginning? or created, and had it a beginning? Created, I reply, being visible and tangible and having a body, and therefore sensible; and all sensible things are apprehended by opinion and sense and are in a process of creation and created. Now that which is created must, as we affirm, of necessity be created by a cause. But the father and maker of all this universe is past finding out; and even if we found him, to tell of him to all men would be impossible. And there is still a question to be asked about him: Which of the patterns had the artificer in view when he made the world,—the pattern of the unchangeable, or of that which is created? If the world be indeed fair and the artificer good, it is manifest that he must have looked to that which is eternal; but if what cannot be said without blasphemy is true, then to the created pattern. Every one will see that he must have looked to the eternal; for the world is the fairest of creations and he is the best of causes. And having been created in this way, the world has been framed in the likeness of that which is apprehended by reason and mind and is unchangeable, and must therefore of necessity, if this is admitted, be a copy of something. Now it is all-important that the beginning of everything should be according to nature. And in speaking of the copy and the original we may assume that words are akin to the matter which they describe; when they relate to the lasting and permanent and intelligible, they ought to be lasting and unalterable, and, as far as their nature allows, irrefutable and immovable—nothing less. But when they express only the copy or likeness and not the eternal things themselves, they need only be likely and analogous to the real words. As being is to becoming, so is truth to belief. If then, Socrates, amid the many opinions about the gods and the generation of the universe, we are not able to give notions which are altogether and in every respect exact and consistent with one another, do not be surprised. Enough, if we adduce probabilities as likely as any others; for we must remembr that I who am the speaker, and you who are the judges, are only mortal men, and we ought to accept the tale which is probable and enquire no further.

Soc. Excellent, Timaeus; and we will do precisely as you bid us. The prelude is charming, and is already accepted by us—may we beg of you to proceed to the strain?

Tim. Let me tell you then why the creator made this world of generation. He was good, and the good can never have any jealousy of anything. And being free from jealousy, he desired that all things should be as like himself as they could be. This is in the truest sense the origin of creation and of the world, as we shall do well in believing on the testimony of wise men: God desired that all things should be good and nothing bad, so far as this was attainable. Wherefore also finding the whole visible sphere not at rest, but moving in an irregular and disorderly fashion, out of disorder he brought order, considering that this was in every way better than the other. Now the deeds of the best could never be or have been other than the fairest; and the creator, reflecting on the things which are by nature visible, found that no unintelligent creature taken as a whole was fairer than the intelligent taken as a whole; and that intelligence could not be present in anything which was devoid of soul. For which reason, when he was framing the universe, he put intelligence in soul, and soul in body, that he might be the creator of a work which was by nature fairest and best. Wherefore, using the language of probability, we may say that the world became a living creature truly endowed with soul and intelligence by the providence of God.

This being supposed, let us proceed to the next stage: In the likeness of what animal did the Creator make the world? It would be an unworthy thing to liken it to any nature which exists as a part only; for nothing can be beautiful which is like any imperfect thing; but let us suppose the world to be the very image of that whole of which all other animals both individually and in their tribes are portions. For the original of the universe contains in itself all intelligible beings, just as this world comprehends us and all other visible creatures. For the Deity, intending to make this world like the fairest and most perfect of intelligible beings, framed one visible animal comprehending within itself all other animals of a kindred nature. Are we right in saying that there is one world, or that they are many and infinite? There must be one only, if the created copy is to accord with the original. For that which includes all other intelligible creatures cannot have a second or companion; in that case there would be need of another living being which would include both, and of which they would be parts, and the likeness would be more truly said to resemble not them, but that other which included them. In order then that the world might be solitary, like the perfect animal, the creator made not two worlds or an infinite number of them; but there is and ever will be one only-begotten and created heaven.

Now that which is created is of necessity corporeal, and also visible and tangible. And nothing is visible where there is no fire, or tangible which has no solidity, and nothing is solid without earth. Wherefore also God in the beginning of creation made the body of the universe to consist of fire and earth. But two things cannot be rightly put together without a third; there must be some bond of union between them. And the fairest bond is that which makes the most complete fusion of itself and the things which it combines; and proportion is best adapted to effect such a union. For whenever in any three numbers, whether cube or square, there is a mean, which is to the last term what the first term is to it; and again, when the mean is to the first term as the last term is to the mean,—then the mean becoming first and last, and the first and last both becoming means, they will all of them of necessity come to be the same, and having become the same with one another will be all one. If the universal frame had been created a surface only and having no depth, a single mean would have sufficed to bind together itself and the other terms; but now, as the world must be solid, and solid bodies are always compacted not by one mean but by two, God placed water and air in the mean between fire and earth, and made them to have the same proportion so far as was possible (as fire is to air so is air to water, and as air is to water so is water to earth); and thus he bound and put together a visible and tangible heaven. And for these reasons, and out of such elements which are in number four, the body of the world was created, and it was harmonized by proportion, and therefore has the spirit of friendship; and having been reconciled to itself, it was indissoluble by the hand of any other than the framer.

Now the creation took up the whole of each of the

four elements; for the Creator compounded the world out of all the fire and all the water and all the air and all the earth, leaving no part of any of them nor any power of them outside. His intention was, in the first place, that the animal should be as far as possible a perfect whole and of perfect parts: secondly, that it should be one, leaving no remnants out of which another such world might be created: and also that it should be free from old age and unaffected by disease. Considering that if heat and cold and other powerful forces which unite bodies surround and attack them from without when they are unprepared, they decompose them, and by bringing diseases and old age upon them, make them waste away—for this cause and on these grounds he made the world one whole, having every part entire, and being therefore perfect and not liable to old age and disease. And he gave to the world the figure which was suitable and also natural. Now to the animal which was to comprehend all animals, that figure was suitable which comprehends within itself all other figures. Wherefore he made the world in the form of a globe, round as from a lathe, having its extremes in every direction equidistant from the centre, the most perfect and the most like itself of all figures; for he considered that the like is infinitely fairer than the unlike. This he finished off, making the surface smooth all round for many reasons; in the first place, because the living being had no need of eyes when there was nothing remaining outside him to be seen; nor of ears when there was nothing to be heard; and there was no surrounding atmosphere to be breathed; nor would there have been any use of organs by the help of which he might receive his food or get rid of what he had already digested, since there was nothing which went from him or came into him: for there was nothing beside him. Of design he was created thus, his own waste providing his own food, and all that he did or suffered taking place in and by himself. For the Creator conceived that a being which was self-sufficient would be far more excellent than one which lacked anything; and, as he had no need to take anything or defend himself against any one, the Creator did not think it necessary to bestow upon him hands: nor had he any need of feet, nor of the whole apparatus of walking; but the movement suited to his spherical form was assigned to him, being of all the seven that which is most appropriate to mind and intelligence; and he was made to move in the same manner and on the same spot, within his own limits revolving in a circle. All the other six motions were taken away from him, and he was made not to partake of their deviations. And as this circular movement required no feet, the universe was created without legs and without feet.

Such was the whole plan of the eternal God about the god that was to be, to whom for this reason he gave a body, smooth and even, having a surface in every direction equidistant from the centre, a body entire and perfect, and formed out of perfect bodies. And in the centre he put the soul, which he diffused throughout the body, making it also to be the exterior environment of it; and he made the universe a circle moving in a circle, one and solitary, yet by reason of its excellence able to converse with itself, and needing no other friendship or acquaintance. Having these purposes in view he created the world a blessed god.

Now God did not make the soul after the body, although we are speaking of them in this order; for having brought them together he would never have allowed that the elder should be ruled by the younger; but this is a random manner of speaking which we have, because somehow we ourselves too are very much under the do-

minion of chance. Whereas he made the soul in origin
and excellence prior to and older than the body, to be
the ruler and mistress, of whom the body was to be the
subject. And he made her out of the following elements
and on this wise: Out of the indivisible and unchangeable, and also out of that which is divisible and has to
do with material bodies, he compounded a third and intermediate kind of essence, partaking of the nature of
the same [1] and of the other, and this compound he placed
accordingly in a mean between the indivisible, and the
divisible and material. He took the three elements of
the same, the other, and the essence, and mingled them
into one form, compressing by force the reluctant and
unsociable nature of the other into the same. When he
had mingled them with the essence and out of three
made one, he again divided this whole into as many portions as was fitting, each portion being a compound of
the same, the other, and the essence. And he proceeded
to divide after this manner:—First of all, he took away
one part of the whole [1], and then he separated a second part which was double the first [2], and then he
took away a third part which was half as much again
as the second and three times as much as the first [3],
and then he took a fourth part which was twice as much
as the second [4], and a fifth part which was three times
the third [9], and a sixth part which was eight times
the first [8], and a seventh part which was twenty-
seven times the first [27]. After this he filled up the
double intervals [i. e. between 1, 2, 4, 8] and the triple
[i. e. between 1, 3, 9, 27], cutting off yet other portions
from the mixture and placing them in the intervals, so
that in each interval there were two kinds of means, the
one exceeding and exceeded by equal parts of its ex-
tremes [as for example 1, $\frac{4}{3}$, 2, in which the mean $\frac{4}{3}$

[1] Omitting αὖ πέρι.

is one-third of 1 more than one, and one-third of 2 less than 2], the other being that kind of mean which exceeds and is exceeded by an equal number.[1] Where there were intervals of $\frac{3}{2}$ and of $\frac{4}{3}$ and of $\frac{9}{8}$, made by the connecting terms in the former intervals, he filled up all the intervals of $\frac{4}{3}$ with the interval of $\frac{9}{8}$, leaving a fraction over; and the interval which this fraction expressed was in the ratio of 256 to 243.[2] And thus the whole mixture out of which he cut these portions was all exhausted by him. This entire compound he divided lengthways into two parts, which he joined to one another at the centre like the letter X, and bent them into a circular form, connecting them with themselves and each other at the point opposite to their original meeting-point; and, comprehending them in a uniform revolution upon the same axis, he made the one the outer and the other the inner circle. Now the motion of the outer circle he called the motion of the same, and the motion of the inner circle the motion of the other or diverse. The motion of the same he carried round by the side [3] to the right, and the motion of the diverse diagonally [4] to the left. And he gave dominion to the motion of the same and like, for that he left single and undivided; but the inner motion he divided in six places and made seven unequal circles having their intervals in ratios of two and three, three of each, and bade the orbits proceed in a direction opposite to one another; and three [Sun, Mercury, Venus] he made to move with equal swiftness, and the remaining four [Moon, Saturn,

---

[1] e.g. $\overline{1}$, $\frac{4}{3}$, $\frac{3}{2}$, $\overline{2}$, $\frac{8}{3}$, 3, $\overline{4}$, $\frac{16}{3}$, 6, $\overline{8}$; and
$\overline{1}$, $\frac{3}{2}$, 2, $\overline{3}$, $\frac{9}{2}$, 6, $\overline{9}$, $\frac{27}{2}$, 18, $\overline{27}$.

[2] e.g. $243 : 256 :: \frac{81}{64} : \frac{4}{3} :: \frac{243}{128} : 2 :: \frac{81}{32} : \frac{8}{3} :: \frac{243}{64} : 4 :: \frac{81}{16} : \frac{16}{3} :: \frac{243}{32} : 8.$ (MARTIN).

[3] i. e. of the rectangular figure supposed to be inscribed in the circle of the same.

[4] i. e. across the rectangular figure from corner to corner.

Mars, Jupiter] to move with unequal swiftness to the three and to one another, but in due proportion.

Now when the Creator had framed the soul according to his will, he formed within her the corporeal universe, and brought the two together, and united them centre to centre. The soul, interfused everywhere from the centre to the circumference of heaven, of which also she is the external envelopment, herself turning in herself, began a divine beginning of never-ceasing and rational life enduring throughout all time. The body of heaven is visible, but the soul is invisible, and partakes of reason and harmony, and being made by the best of intellectual and everlasting natures, is the best of things created. And because she is composed of the same and of the other and of the essence, these three, and is divided and united in due proportion, and in her revolutions returns upon herself, the soul, when touching anything which has essence, whether dispersed in parts or undivided, is stirred through all her powers, to declare the sameness or difference of that thing and some other; and to what individuals are related, and by what affected, and in what way and how and when, both in the world of generation and in the world of immutable being. And when reason, which works with equal truth, whether she be in the circle of the diverse or of the same—in voiceless silence holding her onward course in the sphere of the self-moved—when reason, I say, is hovering around the sensible world and when the circle of the diverse also moving truly imparts the intimations of sense to the whole soul, then arise opinions and beliefs sure and certain. But when reason is concerned with the rational, and the circle of the same moving smoothly declares it, then intelligence and knowledge are necessarily perfected. And if any one affirms that in which these two are found to be other than the soul, he will say the very opposite of the truth.

When the father and creator saw the creature which
he had made moving and living, the created image of the
eternal gods, he rejoiced, and in his joy determined to
make the copy still more like the original; and as this
was eternal, he sought to make the universe eternal, so
far as might be. Now the nature of the ideal being was
everlasting, but to bestow this attribute in its fulness
upon a creature was impossible. Wherefore he resolved
to have a moving image of eternity, and when he set in
order the heaven, he made this image eternal but moving according to number, while eternity itself rests in
unity; and this image we call time. For there were no
days and nights and months and years before the heaven
was created, but when he constructed the heaven he created them also. They are all parts of time, and the past
and future are created species of time, which we unconsciously but wrongly transfer to the eternal essence; for
we say that he 'was,' he 'is,' he 'will be,' but the truth
is that 'is' alone is properly attributed to him, and that
'was' and 'will be' are only to be spoken of becoming in
time, for they are motions, but that which is immovably
the same cannot become older or younger by time, nor
ever did or has become, or hereafter will be, older or
younger, nor is subject at all to any of those states
which affect moving and sensible things and of which
generation is the cause. These are the forms of time,
which imitates eternity and revolves according to a law
of number. Moreover, when we say that what has become *is* become and what becomes *is* becoming, and that
what will become *is* about to become and that the non-
existent *is* non-existent,—all these are inaccurate modes
of expression. But perhaps this whole subject will be
more suitably discussed on some other occasion.

Time, then, and the heaven came into being at the
same instant in order that, having been created together,

if ever there was to be a dissolution of them, they might
be dissolved together. It was framed after the pattern
of the eternal nature, that it might resemble this as far
as was possible; for the pattern exists from eternity,
and the created heaven has been, and is, and will be, in
all time. Such was the mind and thought of God in the
creation of time. The sun and moon and five other
stars, which are called the planets, were created by him
in order to distinguish and preserve the numbers of
time; and when he had made their several bodies, he
placed them in the orbits in which the circle of the other
was revolving (cp. 36 D),—in seven orbits seven stars.
First, there was the moon in the orbit nearest the earth,
and next the sun, in the second orbit above the earth;
then came the morning star and the star sacred to
Hermes, moving in orbits which have an equal swiftness
with the sun, but in an opposite direction; and this is
the reason why the sun and Hermes and Lucifer overtake and are overtaken by each other. To enumerate
the places which he assigned to the other stars, and to
give all the reasons why he assigned them, although a
secondary matter, would give more trouble than the primary. These things at some future time, when we are at
leisure, may have the consideration which they deserve,
but not at present.

Now, when all the stars which were necessary to the
creation of time had attained a motion suitable to them,
and had become living creatures having bodies fastened
by vital chains, and learnt their appointed task, moving
in the motion of the diverse, which is diagonal, and
passes through and is governed by the motion of the
same, they revolved, some in a larger and some in a
lesser orbit,—those which had the lesser orbit revolving
faster, and those which had the larger more slowly.
Now by reason of the motion of the same, those which

revolved fastest appeared to be overtaken by those which moved slower although they really overtook them; for the motion of the same made them all turn in a spiral, and, because some went one way and some another, that which receded most slowly from the sphere of the same, which was the swiftest, appeared to follow it most nearly. That there might be some visible measure of their relative swiftness and slowness as they proceeded in their eight courses, God lighted a fire, which we now call the sun, in the second from the earth of these orbits, that it might give light to the whole of heaven, and that the animals, as many as nature intended, might participate in number, learning arithmetic from the revolution of the same and the like. Thus, then, and for this reason the night and the day were created, being the period of the one most intelligent revolution. And the month is accomplished when the moon has completed her orbit and overtaken the sun, and the year when the sun has completed his own orbit. Mankind, with hardly an exception, have not remarked the periods of the other stars, and they have no name for them, and do not measure them against one another by the help of number, and hence they can scarcely be said to know that their wanderings, being infinite in number and admirable for their variety, make up time. And yet there is no difficulty in seeing that the perfect number of time fulfils the perfect year when all the eight revolutions, having their relative degrees of swiftness, are accomplished together and attain their completion at the same time, measured by the rotation of the same and equally moving. After this manner, and for these reasons, came into being such of the stars as in their heavenly progress received reversals of motion, to the end that the created heaven might imitate the eternal nature, and be as like as possible to the perfect and intelligible animal.

Thus far and until the birth of time the created universe was made in the likeness of the original, but inasmuch as all animals were not yet comprehended therein, it was still unlike. What remained, the creator then proceeded to fashion after the nature of the pattern. Now as in the ideal animal the mind perceives ideas or species of a certain nature and number, he thought that this created animal ought to have species of a like nature and number. There are four such; one of them is the heavenly race of the gods; another, the race of birds whose way is in the air; the third, the watery species; and the fourth, the pedestrian and land creatures. Of the heavenly and divine, he created the greater part out of fire, that they might be the brightest of all things and fairest to behold, and he fashioned them after the likeness of the universe in the figure of a circle, and made them follow the intelligent motion of the supreme, distributing them over the whole circumference of heaven, which was to be a true cosmos or glorious world spangled with them all over. And he gave to each of them two movements: the first, a movement on the same spot after the same manner, whereby they ever continue to think consistently the same thoughts about the same things; the second, a forward movement, in which they are controlled by the revolution of the same and the like; but by the other five motions they were unaffected (cp. 43 B), in order that each of them might attain the highest perfection. And for this reason the fixed stars were created, to be divine and eternal animals, everabiding and revolving after the same manner and on the same spot; and the other stars which reverse their motion and are subject to deviations of this kind, were created in the manner already described. The earth, which is our nurse, clinging [1] around the pole which is

---

[1] Or 'circling.'

extended through the universe, he framed to be the guardian and artificer of night and day, first and eldest of gods that are in the interior of heaven. Vain would be the attempt to tell all the figures of them circling as in dance, and their juxtapositions, and the return of them in their revolutions upon themselves, and their approximations, and to say which of these deities in their conjunctions meet, and which of them are in opposition, and in what order they get behind and before one another, and when they are severally eclipsed to our sight and again reappear, sending terrors and intimations of the future to those who cannot calculate their movements —to attempt to tell of all this without a visible representation of the heavenly system [1] would be labour in vain. Enough on this head; and now let what we have said about the nature of the created and visible gods have an end.

To know or tell the origin of the other divinities is beyond us, and we must accept the traditions of the men of old time who affirm themselves to be the offspring of the gods—that is what they say—and they must surely have known their own ancestors. How can we doubt the word of the children of the gods? Although they give no probable or certain proofs, still, as they declare that they are speaking of what took place in their own family, we must conform to custom and believe them. In this manner, then, according to them, the genealogy of these gods is to be received and set forth.

Oceanus and Tethys were the children of Earth and Heaven, and from these sprang Phorcys and Cronos and Rhea, and all that generation; and from Cronos and Rhea sprang Zeus and Herè, and all those who are said to be their brethren, and others who were the children of these.

[1] Reading τοῖς οὐ δυν. and τούτων αὐτῶν.

Now, when all of them, both those who visibly appear in their revolutions as well as those other gods who are of a more retiring nature, had come into being, the creator of the universe addressed them in these words: 'Gods, children of gods, who are my works, and of whom I am the artificer and father, my creations are indissoluble, if so I will. All that is bound may be undone, but only an evil being would wish to undo that which is harmonious and happy. Wherefore, since ye are but creatures, ye are not altogether immortal and indissoluble, but ye shall certainly not be dissolved, nor be liable to the fate of death, having in my will a greater and mightier bond than those with which ye were bound at the time of your birth. And now listen to my instructions:—Three tribes of mortal beings remain to be created—without them the universe will be incomplete, for it will not contain every kind of animal which it ought to contain, if it is to be perfect. On the other hand, if they were created by me and received life at my hands, they would be on an equality with the gods. In order then that they may be mortal, and that this universe may be truly universal, do ye, according to your natures, betake yourselves to the formation of animals, imitating the power which was shown by me in creating you. The part of them worthy of the name immortal, which is called divine and is the guiding principle of those who are willing to follow justice and you —of that divine part I will myself sow the seed, and having made a beginning, I will hand the work over to you. And do ye then interweave the mortal with the immortal, and make and beget living creatures, and give them food, and make them to grow, and receive them again in death.'

Thus he spake, and once more into the cup in which he had previously mingled the soul of the universe he

poured the remains of the elements, and mingled them
in much the same manner; they were not, however, pure
as before, but diluted to the second and third degree.
And having made it he divided the whole mixture into
souls equal in number to the stars, and assigned each
soul to a star; and having there placed them as in a
chariot, he showed them the nature of the universe, and
declared to them the laws of destiny, according to which
their first birth would be one and the same for all,—no
one should suffer a disadvantage at his hands; they were
to be sown in the instruments of time severally adapted
to them, and to come forth the most religious of animals; and as human nature was of two kinds, the superior race would hereafter be called man. Now, when
they should be implanted in bodies by necessity, and be
always gaining or losing some part of their bodily substance, then in the first place it would be necessary that
they should all have in them one and the same faculty
of sensation, arising out of irresistible impressions; in
the second place, they must have love, in which pleasure
and pain mingle; also fear and anger, and the feelings
which are akin or opposite to them; if they conquered
these they would live righteously, and if they were conquered by them, unrighteously. He who lived well during his appointed time was to return and dwell in his
native star, and there he would have a blessed and congenial existence. But if he failed in attaining this, at
the second birth he would pass into a woman, and if,
when in that state of being, he did not desist from evil,
he would continually be changed into some brute who
resembled him in the evil nature which he had acquired,
and would not cease from his toils and transformations
until he followed the revolution of the same and the like
within him, and overcame by the help of reason the
turbulent and irrational mob of later accretions, made

up of fire and air and water and earth, and returned to the form of his first and better state. Having given all these laws to his creatures, that he might be guiltless of future evil in any of them, the creator sowed some of them in the earth, and some in the moon, and some in the other instruments of time; and when he had sown them he committed to the younger gods the fashioning of their mortal bodies, and desired them to furnish what was still lacking to the human soul, and having made all the suitable additions, to rule over them, and to pilot the mortal animal in the best and wisest manner which they could, and avert from him all but self-inflicted evils.

[Then follows a passage, principally on the constitution of the human body, which is omitted here.]

Thus far in what we have been saying, with small exceptions, the works of intelligence have been set forth; and now we must place by the side of them in our discourse the things which come into being through necessity—for the creation is mixed, being made up of necessity and mind. Mind, the ruling power, persuaded necessity to bring the greater part of created things to perfection, and thus and after this manner in the beginning, when the influence of reason got the better of necessity, the universe was created. But if a person will truly tell of the way in which the work was accomplished, he must include the other influence of the variable cause as well. Wherefore, we must return again and find another suitable beginning, as about the former matters, so also about these. To which end we must consider the nature of fire, and water, and air, and earth, such as they were prior to the creation of the heaven, and what was happening to them in this previous state; for no one has as yet explained the manner of their gen-

eration, but we speak of fire and the rest of them, whatever they mean, as though men knew their natures, and
we maintain them to be the first principles and letters or
elements of the whole, when they cannot reasonably be
compared by a man of any sense even to syllables or
first compounds. And let me say thus much: I will not
now speak of the first principle or principles of all
things, or by whatever name they are to be called, for
this reason,—because it is difficult to set forth my opinion according to the method of discussion which we are
at present employing. Do not imagine, any more than
I can bring myself to imagine, that I should be right in
undertaking so great and difficult a task. Remember-
ing what I said at first about probability, I will do my
best to give as probable an explanation as any other,—
or rather, more probable; and I will first go back to the
beginning, and try to speak of each thing and of all.[1]
Once more, then, at the commencement of my discourse,
I call upon God, and beg him to be our saviour out of
a strange and unwonted enquiry, and to bring us to the
haven of probability. So now let us begin again.

This new beginning of our discussion of the universe
requires a fuller division than the former; for then we
made two classes, now a third must be revealed. The
two sufficed for the former discussion: one, which we
assumed, was a pattern intelligible and always the same;
and the second was only the imitation of the pattern,
generated and visible. There is also a third kind which
we did not distinguish at the time, conceiving that the
two would be enough. But now the argument seems to
require that we should set forth in words another kind,

---

[1] Putting the comma after μᾶλλον δὲ; or, following Stallbaum
and omitting the comma, 'or rather, before entering on this
probable discussion, we will begin again, and try to speak of
each thing and of all.'

which is difficult of explanation and dimly seen. What nature are we to attribute to this new kind of being? We reply, that it is the receptacle, and in a manner the nurse, of all generation. I have spoken the truth; but I must express myself in clearer language, and this will be an arduous task for many reasons, and in particular because I must first raise questions concerning fire and the other elements, and determine what each of them is; for to say, with any probability or certitude, which of them should be called water rather than fire, and which should be called any of them rather than all or someone of them, is a difficult matter. How, then, shall we settle this point, and what questions about the elements may be fairly raised?

In the first place, we see that what we just now called water, by condensation, I suppose, becomes stone and earth; and this same element, when melted and dispersed, passes into vapour and air. Air, again, when inflamed, becomes fire; and again fire, when condensed and extinguished, passes once more into the form of air; and once more, air, when collected and condensed, produces cloud and mist; and from these, when still more compressed, comes flowing water, and from water comes earth and stones once more; and thus generation appears to be transmitted from one to the other in a circle. Thus, then, as the several elements never present themselves in the same form, how can any one have the assurance to assert positively that any of them, whatever it may be, is one thing rather than another? No one can. But much the safest plan is to speak of them as follows:—Anything which we see to be continually changing, as, for example, fire, we must not call 'this' or 'that,' but rather say that it is 'of such a nature;' nor let us speak of water as 'this,' but always as 'such;' nor must we imply that there is any stability in any of

those things which we indicate by the use of the words
'this' and 'that,' supposing ourselves to signify something thereby; for they are too volatile to be detained
in any such expressions as 'this,' or 'that,' or 'relative
to this,' or any other mode of speaking which represents
them as permanent. We ought not to apply 'this' to any
of them, but rather the word 'such;' which expresses the
similar principle circulating in each and all of them; for
example, that should be called 'fire' which is of such a
nature always, and so of everything that has generation. That in which the elements severally grow up, and
appear, and decay, is alone to be called by the name
'this' or 'that;' but that which is of a certain nature, hot
or white, or anything which admits of opposite qualities, and all things that are compounded of them, ought
not to be so denominated. Let me make another attempt
to explain my meaning more clearly. Suppose a person to make all kinds of figures of gold and to be always
transmuting one form into all the rest;—somebody
points to one of them and asks what it is. By far the
safest and truest answer is, That is gold; and not to call
the triangle or any other figures which are formed in
the gold 'these,' as though they had existence, since they
are in process of change while he is making the assertion; but if the questioner be willing to take the safe and
indefinite expression, 'such,' we should be satisfied. And
the same argument applies to the universal nature which
receives all bodies—that must be always called the same;
for, while receiving all things, she never departs at all
from her own nature, and never in any way, or at any
time, assumes a form like that of any of the things which
enter into her; she is the natural recipient of all impressions, and is stirred and informed by them, and appears
different from time to time by reason of them. But the
forms which enter into and go out of her are the like-

nesses of real existences modelled after their patterns in a wonderful and inexplicable manner, which we will hereafter investigate. For the present we have only to conceive of three natures: first, that which is in process of generation; secondly, that in which the generation takes place; and thirdly, that of which the thing generated is a resemblance. And we may liken the receiving principle to a mother, and the source or spring to a father, and the intermediate nature to a child; and may remark further, that if the model is to take every variety of form, then the matter in which the model is fashioned will not be duly prepared, unless it is formless, and free from the impress of any of those shapes which it is hereafter to receive from without. For if the matter were like any of the supervening forms, then whenever any opposite or entirely different nature was stamped upon its surface, it would take the impression badly, because it would intrude its own shape. Wherefore, that which is to receive all forms should have no form; as in making perfumes they first contrive that the liquid substance which is to receive the scent shall be as inodorous as possible; or as those who wish to impress figures on soft substances do not allow any previous impression to remain, but begin by making the surface as even and smooth as possible. In the same way that which is to receive perpetually and through its whole extent the resemblances of all eternal beings ought to be devoid of any particular form. Wherefore, the mother and receptacle of all created and visible and in any way sensible things, is not to be termed earth, or air, or fire, or water, or any of their compounds, or any of the elements from which these are derived, but is an invisible and formless being which receives all things and in some mysterious way partakes of the intelligible, and is most incomprehensible. In saying this we shall

not be far wrong; as far, however, as we can attain to
a knowledge of her from the previous considerations, we
may truly say that fire is that part of her nature which
from time to time is inflamed, and water that which is
moistened, and that the mother substance becomes earth
and air, in so far as she receives the impressions of them.

Let us consider this question more precisely. Is there
any self-existent fire? and do all those things which we
call self-existent exist? or are only those things which
we see, or in some way perceive through the bodily organs, truly existent, and nothing whatever besides them?
And is all that which we call an intelligible essence
nothing at all, and only a name? Here is a question
which we must not leave unexamined or undetermined,
nor must we affirm too confidently that there can be no
decision; neither must we interpolate in our present long
discourse a digression equally long, but if it is possible
to set forth a great principle in a few words, that is just
what we want.

Thus I state my view:—If mind and true opinion are
two distinct classes, then I say that there certainly are
these self-existent ideas unperceived by sense, and apprehended only by the mind; if, however, as some say,
true opinion differs in no respect from mind, then everything that we perceive through the body is to be regarded as most real and certain. But we must affirm
them to be distinct, for they have a distinct origin and
are of a different nature; the one is implanted in us by
instruction, the other by persuasion; the one is always
accompanied by true reason, the other is without reason; the one cannot be overcome by persuasion, but the
other can: and lastly, every man may be said to share in
true opinion, but mind is the attribute of the gods and of
very few men. Wherefore also we must acknowledge
that there is one kind of being which is always the same,

uncreated and indestructible, never receiving anything into itself from without, nor itself going out to any other, but invisible and imperceptible by any sense, and of which the contemplation is granted to intelligence only. And there is another nature of the same name with it, and like to it, perceived by sense, created, always in motion, becoming in place and again vanishing out of place, which is apprehended by opinion and sense. And there is a third nature, which is space, and is eternal, and admits not of destruction and provides a home for all created things, and is apprehended without the help of sense, by a kind of spurious reason, and is hardly real; which we beholding as in a dream, say of all existence that it must of necessity be in some place and occupy a space, but that what is neither in heaven nor in earth has no existence. Of these and other things of the same kind, relating to the true and waking reality of nature, we have only this dreamlike sense, and we are unable to cast off sleep and determine the truth about them. For an image, since the reality, after which it is modelled, does not belong to it,[1] and it exists ever as the fleeting shadow of some other, must be inferred to be in another [i. e. in space], grasping existence in some way or other, or it could not be at all. But true and exact reason, vindicating the nature of true being, maintains that while two things [i. e. the image and space] are different they cannot exist one of them in the other and so be one and also two at the same time.

Thus have I concisely given the result of my thoughts; and my verdict is that being and space and generation, these three, existed in their three ways before the heaven; and that the nurse of generation, moistened by water and inflamed by fire, and receiving the forms of

---

[1] Or, 'since in its very intention it is not self-existent'—which, though obscure, avoids any inaccuracy of construction.

earth and air, and experiencing all the affections which accompany these, presented a strange variety of appearances; and being full of powers which were neither similar nor equally balanced, was never in any part in a state of equipoise, but swaying unevenly hither and thither, was shaken by them, and by its motion again shook them; and the elements when moved were separated and carried continually, some one way, some another; as, when grain is shaken and winnowed by fans and other instruments used in the threshing of corn, the close and heavy particles are borne away and settle in one direction, and the loose and light particles in another. In this manner, the four kinds or elements were then shaken by the receiving vessel, which, moving like a winnowing machine, scattered far away from one another the elements most unlike, and forced the most similar elements into close contact. Wherefore also the various elements had different places before they were arranged so as to form the universe. At first, they were all without reason and measure. But when the world began to get into order, fire and water and earth and air had only certain faint traces of themselves, and were altogether such as everything might be expected to be in the absence of God; this, I say, was their nature at that time, and God fashioned them by form and number. Let it be consistently maintained by us in all that we say that God made them as far as possible the fairest and best, out of things which were not fair and good.

[The rest of the dialogue is omitted.]

LAWS

PERSONS OF THE DIALOGUE

An Athenian Stranger   Cleinias, *a Cretan*
Megillus, *a Lacedœmonian*

Book X

[*What follows is practically the whole of Book X of
the Laws. A few sentences at the very beginning and
at the end of the Book have been omitted.*]

Athenian. No one who in obedience to the laws believed that there were Gods, ever intentionally did any
unholy act, or uttered any unlawful word; but he who
did must have supposed one of three things,—either that
they did not exist,—which is the first possibility, or secondly, that, if they did, they took no care of man, or
thirdly, that they were easily appeased and turned aside
from their purpose by sacrifices and prayers.

Cleinias. What shall we say or do to these persons?

Ath. My good friend, let us first hear the jests
which I suspect that they in their superiority will utter
against us.

Cle. What jests?

Ath. They will make some irreverent speech of this
sort:—'O inhabitants of Athens, and Sparta, and Cno-
sus,' they will reply, 'in that you speak truly; for some
of us deny the very existence of the Gods, while others,
as you say, are of opinion that they do not care about
us; and others that they are turned from their course by

gifts. Now we have a right to claim, as you yourself allowed, in the matter of laws, that before you are hard upon us and threaten us, you should argue with us and convince us—you should first attempt to teach and persuade us that there are Gods by reasonable evidences, and also that they are too good to be unrighteous, or to be propitiated, or turned from their course by gifts. For when we hear such things said of them by those who are esteemed to be the best of poets, and orators, and prophets, and priests, and by innumerable others, the thoughts of most of us are not set upon abstaining from unrighteous acts, but upon doing them and atoning for them. When lawgivers profess that they are gentle and not stern, we think that they should first of all use persuasion to us, and show us the existence of Gods, if not in a better manner than other men, at any rate in a truer; and who knows but that we shall hearken to you? If then our request is a fair one, please to accept our challenge.'

Cle. But is there any difficulty in proving the existence of the Gods?

Ath. How would you prove it?

Cle. How? In the first place, the earth and the sun, and the stars and the universe, and the fair order of the seasons, and the division of them into years and months, furnish proofs of their existence; and also there is the fact that all Hellenes and barbarians believe in them.

Ath. I fear, my sweet friend, though I will not say that I much regard, the contempt with which the profane will be likely to assail us. For you do not understand the nature of their complaint, and you fancy that they rush into impiety only from a love of sensual pleasure.

Cle. Why, Stranger, what other reason is there?

Ath. One which you who live in a different atmosphere would never guess.

Cle. What is it?

Ath. A very grievous sort of ignorance which is imagined to be the greatest wisdom.

Cle. What do you mean?

Ath. At Athens there are tales preserved in writing which the virtue of your state, as I am informed, refuses to admit. They speak of the Gods in prose as well as verse, and the oldest of them tell of the origin of the heavens and of the world, and not far from the beginning of their story they proceed to narrate the birth of the Gods, and how after they were born they behaved to one another. Whether these stories have in other ways a good or a bad influence, I should not like to be severe upon them, because they are ancient; but, looking at them with reference to the duties of children to their parents, I cannot praise them, or think that they are useful, or at all true. Of the words of the ancients I have nothing more to say; and I should wish to say of them only what is pleasing to the Gods. But as to our younger generation and their wisdom, I cannot let them off when they do mischief. For do but mark the effect of their words: when you and I argue for the existence of the Gods, and produce the sun, moon, stars, and earth, claiming for them a divine being, if we would listen to the aforesaid philosophers we should say [1] that they are earth and stones only, which can have no care at all of human affairs, and that all religion is a cooking up of words and a make-believe.

Cle. One such teacher, O Stranger, would be bad enough, and you imply that there are many of them, which is worse.

Ath. Well, then; what shall we say or do?—Shall we assume that some one is accusing us among unholy

---

[1] Reading λέγοιμεν.

men, who are trying to escape from the effect of our legislation; and that they say of us—How dreadful that you should legislate on the supposition that there are Gods! Shall we make a defence of ourselves? or shall we leave them and return to our laws, lest the prelude should become longer than the law? For the discourse will certainly extend to great length, if we are to treat the impiously disposed as they desire, partly demonstrating to them at some length the things of which they demand an explanation, partly making them afraid or dissatisfied, and then proceed to the requisite enactments.

Cle. Yes, Stranger; but then how often have we repeated already that on the present occasion there is no reason why brevity should be preferred to length; for who is 'at our heels?'—as the saying goes, and it would be paltry and ridiculous to prefer the shorter to the better. It is a matter of no small consequence, in some way or other to prove that there are Gods, and that they are good, and regard justice more than men do. The demonstration of this would be the best and noblest prelude of all our laws. And therefore, without impatience, and without hurry, let us unreservedly consider the whole matter, summoning up all the power of persuasion which we possess.

Ath. Seeing you thus in earnest, I would fain offer up a prayer that I may succeed:—but I must proceed at once. Who can be calm when he is called upon to prove the existence of the Gods? Who can avoid hating and abhorring the men who are and have been the cause of this argument; I speak of those who will not believe the tales which they have heard as babes and sucklings from their mothers and nurses, repeated by them both in jest and earnest, like charms, who have also heard them in the sacrificial prayers, and seen sights accompanying them,—sights and sounds delightful to children,—and their parents during the sacrifices showing an intense earnestness on behalf of their children and of themselves, and with eager interest talking to the Gods, and beseeching them, as though they were firmly convinced of their existence; who likewise see and hear the prostrations and invocations which are made by Hellenes and barbarians at the rising and setting of the sun and moon, in all the vicissitudes of life, not as if they thought that there were no Gods, but as if there could be no doubt of their existence, and no suspicion of their non-existence; when men, knowing all these things, despise them on no real grounds, as would be admitted by all who have any particle of intelligence, and when they force us to say what we are now saying, how can any one in gentle terms remonstrate with the like of them, when he has to begin by proving to them the very existence of the Gods? Yet the attempt must be made; for it would be unseemly that one half of mankind should go mad in their lust of pleasure, and the other half in their indignation at such persons. Our address to these lost and perverted natures should not be spoken in passion; let us suppose ourselves to select some one of them, and gently reason with him, smothering our anger:—O my son, we will say to him, you are young, and the advance of time will make you reverse many of the opinions which you now hold. Wait awhile, and do not attempt to judge at present of the highest things; and that is the highest of which you now think nothing—to know the Gods rightly and to live accordingly. And in the first place let me indicate to you one point which is of great importance, and about which I cannot be deceived:—You and your friends are not the first who have held this opinion about the Gods.

LAWS

421

There have always been persons more or less numerous
who have had the same disorder. I have known many
of them, and can tell you, that no one who had taken up
in youth this opinion, that the Gods do not exist, ever
continued in the same until he was old; the two other
notions certainly do continue in some cases, but not in
many; the notion, I mean, that the Gods exist, but take
no heed of human things, and the other notion that they
do take heed of them, but are easily propitiated with
sacrifices and prayers. As to the opinion about the
Gods which may some day become clear to you, I advise you to wait and consider if it be true or not; ask
of others, and above all of the legislator. In the mean-
time take care that you do not offend against the Gods.
For the duty of the legislator is and always will be to
teach you the truth of these matters.

Cle. Our address, Stranger, thus far, is excellent.

Ath. Quite true, Megillus and Cleinias, but I am
afraid that we have unconsciously lighted on a strange
doctrine.

Cle. What doctrine do you mean?

Ath. The wisest of all doctrines, in the opinion of
many.

Cle. I wish that you would speak plainer.

Ath. The doctrine that all things do become, have
become, and will become, some by nature, some by art,
and some by chance.

Cle. Is not that true?

Ath. Well, philosophers are probably right; at any
rate we may as well follow in their track, and examine
what is the meaning of them and their disciples.

Cle. By all means.

Ath. They say that the greatest and fairest things
are the work of nature and of chance, the lesser of art,

which, receiving from nature the greater and primeval
creations, moulds and fashions all those lesser works
which are generally termed artificial.

Cle. How is that?

Ath. I will explain my meaning still more clearly.
They say that fire and water, and earth and air, all
exist by nature and chance, and none of them by art,
and that as to the bodies which come next in order,—
earth, and sun, and moon, and stars,—they have been
created by means of these absolutely inanimate existences. The elements are severally moved by chance
and some inherent force according to certain affinities
among them—of hot with cold, or of dry with moist, or
of soft with hard, and according to all the other acci-
dental admixtures of opposites which have been formed
by necessity. After this fashion and in this manner the
whole heaven has been created, and all that is in the
heaven, as well as animals and all plants, and all the
seasons come from these elements, not by the action of
mind, as they say, or of any God, or from art, but as
I was saying, by nature and chance only. Art sprang up
afterwards and out of these, mortal and of mortal birth,
and produced in play certain images and very partial
imitations of the truth, having an affinity to one another,
such as music and painting create and their companion
arts. And there are other arts which have a serious
purpose, and these co-operate with nature, such, for
example, as medicine, and husbandry, and gymnastics.
And they say that politics co-operate with nature, but in
a less degree, and have more of art; also that legislation is entirely a work of art, and is based on assumptions which are not true.

Cle. How do you mean?

Ath. In the first place, my dear friend, these people would say that the Gods exist not by nature, but

by art, and by the laws of states, which are different in different places, according to the agreement of those who make them; and that the honourable is one thing by nature and another thing by law, and that the principles of justice have no existence at all in nature, but that mankind are always disputing about them and altering them; and that the alterations which are made by art and by law have no basis in nature, but are of authority for the moment and at the time at which they are made.—These, my friends, are the sayings of wise men, poets and prose writers, which find a way into the minds of youth. They are told by them that the highest right is might, and in this way the young fall into impieties, under the idea that the Gods are not such as the law bids them imagine; and hence arise factions, these philosophers inviting them to lead a true life according to nature, that is, to live in real dominion over others, and not in legal subjection to them.

Cle. What a dreadful picture, Stranger, have you given, and how great is the injury which is thus inflicted on young men to the ruin both of states and families!

Ath. True, Cleinias; but then what should the lawgiver do when this evil is of long standing? should he only rise up in the state and threaten all mankind, proclaiming that if they will not say and think that the Gods are such as the law ordains (and this may be extended generally to the honourable, the just, and to all the highest things, and to all that relates to virtue and vice), and if they will not make their actions conform to the copy which the law gives them, then he who refuses to obey the law shall die, or suffer stripes and bonds, or privation of citizenship, or in some cases be punished by loss of property and exile? Should he not rather, when he is making laws for men, at the same

time infuse the spirit of persuasion into his words, and
mitigate the severity of them as far as he can?

Cle. Why, Stranger, if such persuasion be at all possible, then a legislator who has anything in him ought
never to weary of persuading men; he ought to leave
nothing unsaid in support of the ancient opinion that
there are Gods, and of all those other truths which you
were just now mentioning; he ought to suport the law
and also art, and acknowledge that both alike exist by
nature, and no less than nature, if they are the creations
of mind in accordance with right reason, as you appear
to me to maintain, and I am disposed to agree with you
in thinking.

Ath. Yes, my enthusiastic Cleinias; but are not these
things when spoken to a multitude hard to be understood, not to mention that they take up a dismal length
of time?

Cle. Why, Stranger, shall we, whose patience failed
not when drinking or music were the themes of discourse, weary now of discoursing about the Gods, and
about divine things? And the greatest help to rational
legislation is that the laws when once written down are
always at rest; they can be put to the test at any future
time, and therefore, if on first hearing they seem difficult, there is no reason for apprehension about them, because any man however dull can go over them and consider them again and again; nor if they are tedious but
useful, is there any reason or religion, as it seems to me,
in any man refusing to maintain the principles of them
to the utmost of his power.

Megillus. Stranger, I like what Cleinias is saying.

Ath. Yes, Megillus, and we should do as he proposes; for if impious discourses were not scattered, as
I may say, throughout the world, there would have been
no need for any vindication of the existence of the Gods

but seeing that they are spread far and wide, such arguments are needed; and who should come to the rescue of the greatest laws, when they are being undermined by bad men, but the legislator himself?

Meg. There is no more proper champion of them.

Ath. Well, then, tell me, Cleinias,—for I must ask you to be my partner,—does not he who talks in this way conceive fire and water and earth and air to be the first elements of all things? these he calls nature, and out of these he supposes the soul to be formed afterwards; and this is not a mere conjecture of ours about his meaning, but is what he really means.

Cle. Very true.

Ath. Then, by Heaven, we have discovered the source of this vain opinion of all those physical investigators; and I would have you examine their arguments with the utmost care, for their impiety is a very serious matter; they not only make a bad and mistaken use of argument, but they lead away the minds of others: that is my opinion of them.

Cle. You are right; but I should like to know how this happens.

Ath. I fear that the argument may seem singular.

Cle. Do not hesitate, Stranger; I see that you are afraid of such a discussion carrying you beyond the limits of legislation. But if there be no other way of showing our agreement in the belief that there are Gods, of whom the law is said now to approve, let us take this way, my good sir.

Ath. Then I suppose that I must repeat the singular argument of those who manufacture the soul according to their own impious notions; they affirm that which is the first cause of the generation and destruction of all things, to be not first, but last, and that which is last to be first, and hence they have fallen into error about the true nature of the Gods.

Cle. Still I do not understand you.

Ath. Nearly all of them, my friends, seem to be ignorant of the nature and power of the soul, especially in what relates to her origin: they do not know that she is among the first of things, and before all bodies, and is the chief author of their changes and transpositions. And if this is true, and if the soul is older than the body, must not the things which are of the soul's kindred be of necessity prior to those which appertain to the body?

Cle. Certainly.

Ath. Then thought and attention and mind and art and law will be prior to that which is hard and soft and heavy and light; and the great and primitive works and actions will be works of art; they will be the first, and after them will come nature and works of nature, which however is a wrong term for men to apply to them; these will follow, and will be under the government of art and mind.

Cle. But why is the word 'nature' wrong?

Ath. Because those who use the term mean to say that nature is the first creative power; but if the soul turn out to be the primeval element, and not fire or air, then in the truest sense and beyond other things the soul may be said to exist by nature; and this would be true if you proved that the soul is older than the body, but not otherwise.

Cle. You are quite right.

Ath. Shall we, then, take this as the next point to which our attention should be directed?

Cle. By all means.

Ath. Let us be on our guard lest this most deceptive argument with its youthful looks, beguiling us old men, give us the slip and make a laughing-stock of us. Who knows but we may be aiming at the greater, and fail of attaining the lesser? Suppose that we three have to pass a rapid river, and I, being the youngest of the three and experienced in rivers, take upon me the duty of making the attempt first by myself; leaving you in safety on the bank, I am to examine whether the river is passable by older men like yourselves, and if such appears to be the case then I shall invite you to follow, and my experience will help to convey you across; but if the river is impassable by you, then there will have been no danger to anybody but myself,—would not that seem to be a very fair proposal? I mean to say that the argument in prospect is likely to be too much for you, out of your depth and beyond your strength, and I should be afraid that the stream of my questions might create in you who are not in the habit of answering, giddiness and confusion of mind, and hence a feeling of unpleasantness and unsuitableness might arise. I think therefore that I had better first ask the questions and then answer them myself while you listen in safety; in that way I can carry on the argument until I have completed the proof that the soul is prior to the body.

Cle. Excellent, Stranger, and I hope that you will do as you propose.

Ath. Come, then, and if ever we are to call upon the Gods, let us call upon them now in all seriousness to come to the demonstration of their own existence. And so holding fast to the rope we will venture upon the depths of the argument. When questions of this sort are asked of me, my safest answer would appear to be as follows:—Some one says to me, 'O Stranger, are all things at rest and nothing in motion, or is the exact opposite of this true, or are some things in motion and others at rest?'—To this I shall reply that some things are in motion and others at rest. 'And do not things which move move in a place, and are not the things which are at rest at rest in a place?' Certainly. 'And some move or rest in one place and some in more places than one?' You mean to say, we shall rejoin, that those things which rest at the centre move in one place, just as the circumference goes round of globes which are said to be at rest? 'Yes.' And we observe that, in the revolution, the motion which carries round the larger and the lesser circle at the same time is proportionally distributed to greater and smaller, and is greater and smaller in a certain proportion. Here is a wonder which might be thought an impossibility, that the same motion should impart swiftness and slowness in due proportion to larger and lesser circles. 'Very true.' And when you speak of bodies moving in many places, you seem to me to mean those which move from one place to another, and sometimes have one centre of motion and sometimes more than one because they turn upon their axis; and whenever they meet anything, if it be stationary, they are divided by it; but if they get in the midst between bodies which are approaching and moving towards the same spot from opposite directions, they unite with them. 'I admit the truth of what you are saying.' Also when they unite they grow, and when they are divided they waste away,—that is, supposing the constitution of each to remain, or if that fails, then there is a second reason of their dissolution. 'And when are all things created and how?' Clearly, they are created when the first principle receives increase and attains to the second dimension, and from this arrives at the one which is neighbour to this, and after reaching the third becomes perceptible to sense. Everything which is thus changing and moving is in process of generation; only when at rest has it real existence, but when passing into another state it is destroyed utterly. Have we not mentioned all motions that there are, and comprehended them under their kinds and numbered them with the exception, my friends, of two?

Cle. Which are they?

Ath. Just the two, with which our present enquiry is concerned.

Cle. Speak plainer.

Ath. I suppose that our enquiry has reference to the soul?

Cle. Very true.

Ath. Let us assume that there is a motion able to move other things, but not to move itself;—that is one kind; and there is another kind which can move itself as well as other things, working in composition and decomposition, by increase and diminution and generation and destruction,—that is also one of the many kinds of motion.

Cle. Granted.

Ath. And we will assume that which moves other, and is changed by other, to be the ninth, and that which changes itself and others, and is co-incident with every action and every passion, and is the true principle of change and motion in all that is,—that we shall be inclined to call the tenth.

Cle. Certainly.

Ath. And which of these ten motions ought we to prefer as being the mightiest and most efficient?

Cle. I must say that the motion which is able to move itself is ten thousand times superior to all the others.

Ath. Very good; but may I make one or two corrections in what I have been saying?

Cle. What are they?

Ath. When I spoke of the tenth sort of motion, that was not quite correct.

Cle. What was the error?

Ath. According to the true order, the tenth was really the first in generation and power; then follows the second, which was strangely enough termed the ninth by us.

Cle. What do you mean?

Ath. I mean this: when one thing changes another, and that another, of such will there be any primary changing element? How can a thing which is moved by another ever be the beginning of change? Impossible. But when the self-moved changes other, and that again other, and thus thousands upon tens of thousands of bodies are set in motion, must not the beginning of all this motion be the change of the self-moving principle?

Cle. Very true, and I quite agree.

Ath. Or, to put the question in another way, making answer to ourselves:—If, as most of these philosophers have the audacity to affirm, all things were at rest in one mass, which of the above-mentioned principles of motion would first spring up among them?

Cle. Clearly the self-moving; for there could be no change in them arising out of any external cause; the change must first take place in themselves.

Ath. Then we must say that self-motion being the origin of all motions, and the first which arises among things at rest as well as among things in motion, is the eldest and mightiest principle of change, and that which is changed by another and yet moves other is second.

Cle. Quite true.

Ath. At this stage of the argument let us put a question.

Cle. What question?

Ath. If we were to see this power existing in any earthy, watery, or fiery substance, simple or compound—how should we describe it?

Cle. You mean to ask whether we should call such a self-moving power life?

Ath. I do.

Cle. Certainly we should.

Ath. And when we see soul in anything, must we not do the same—must we not admit that this is life?

Cle. We must.

Ath. And now, I beseech you, reflect;—you would admit that we have a threefold knowledge of things?

Cle. What do you mean?

Ath. I mean that we know the essence, and that we know the definition of the essence, and the name,—these are the three; and there are two questions which may be raised about anything.

Cle. How two?

Ath. Sometimes a person may give the name and ask the definition; or he may give the definition and ask the name. I may illustrate what I mean in this way.

Cle. How?

Ath. Number like some other things is capable of being divided into equal parts; when thus divided, number is named 'even,' and the definition of the name 'even' is 'number divisible into two equal parts?'

Cle. True.

Ath. I mean, that when we are asked about the definition and give the name, or when we are asked about the name and give the definition—in either case, whether we give name or definition, we speak of the same thing, calling 'even' the number which is divided into two equal parts.

Cle. Quite true.

Ath. And what is the definition of that which is

named 'soul'? Can we conceive of any other than that which has been already given—the motion which can move itself?

Cle. You mean to say that the essence which is defined as the self-moved is the same with that which has the name soul?

Ath. Yes; and if this is true, do we still maintain that there is anything wanting in the proof that the soul is the first origin and moving power of all that is, or has become, or will be, and their contraries, when she has been clearly shown to be the source of change and motion in all things?

Cle. Certainly not; the soul as being the source of motion, has been most satisfactorily shown to be the oldest of all things.

Ath. And is not that motion which is produced in another, by reason of another, but never has any self-moving power at all, being in truth the change of an inanimate body, to be reckoned second, or by any lower number which you may prefer?

Cle. Exactly.

Ath. Then we are right, and speak the most perfect and absolute truth, when we say that the soul is prior to the body, and that the body is second and comes afterwards, and is born to obey the soul, which is the ruler?

Cle. Nothing can be more true.

Ath. Do you remember our old admission, that if the soul was prior to the body the things of the soul were also prior to those of the body?

Cle. Certainly.

Ath. Then characters and manners, and wishes and reasonings, and true opinions, and reflections, and recollections are prior to length and breadth and depth and strength of bodies, if the soul is prior to the body.

Cle. To be sure.

Ath. In the next place, must we not of necessity admit that the soul is the cause of good and evil, base and honourable, just and unjust, and of all other opposites, if we suppose her to be the cause of all things?

Cle. We must.

Ath. And as the soul orders and inhabits all things that move, however moving, must we not say that she orders also the heavens?

Cle. Of course.

Ath. One soul or more? More than one—I will answer for you;—at any rate, we must not suppose that there are less than two—one the author of good, and the other of evil.

Cle. Very true.

Ath. Yes, very true; the soul then directs all things in heaven, and earth, and sea by her movements, and these are described by the terms—will, consideration, attention, deliberation, opinion true and false, joy and sorrow, confidence, fear, hatred, love, and other primary motions akin to these; which again receive the secondary motions of corporeal substances, and guide all things to growth and decay, to composition and decomposition, and to the qualities which accompany them, such as heat and cold, heaviness and lightness, hardness and softness, blackness and whiteness, bitterness and sweetness, and all those other qualities which the soul uses, herself a goddess, when truly receiving the divine mind she disciplines all things rightly to tneir happiness; but when she is the companion of folly, she does the very contrary of all this. Shall we assume so much, or do we still entertain doubts?

Cle. There is no room at all for doubt.

Ath. Shall we say then that it is the soul which controls heaven and earth, and the whole world?—that it is a principle of wisdom and virtue, or a principle which has neither wisdom nor virtue? Suppose that we make answer as follows:—

Cle. How would you answer?

Ath. If, my friend, we say that the whole path and movement of heaven, and of all that is therein, is by nature akin to the movement and revolution and calculation of mind, and proceeds by kindred laws, then, as is plain, we must say that the best soul takes care of the world and guides it along the good path.

Cle. True.

Ath. But if the world moves wildly and irregularly, then the evil soul guides it.

Cle. True again.

Ath. Of what nature is the movement of mind?—To this question it is not easy to give an intelligent answer; and therefore I ought to assist you in framing one.

Cle. Very good.

Ath. Then let us not answer as if we would look straight at the sun, making ourselves darkness at midday—I mean as if we were under the impression that we could see with mortal eyes, or know adequately the nature of mind;—it will be safer to look at the image only.

Cle. What do you mean?

Ath. Let us select of the ten motions the one which mind chiefly resembles; this I will bring to your recollection, and will then make the answer on behalf of us all.

Cle. That will be excellent.

Ath. You will surely remember our saying that all things were either at rest or in motion?

Cle. I do.

Ath. And that of things in motion some were moving in one place, and others in more than one?

Cle. Yes.

Ath. Of these two kinds of motion, that which moves in one place must move about a centre like globes made in a lathe, and is most entirely akin and similar to the circular movement of mind.

Cle. What do you mean?

Ath. In saying that both mind and the motion which is in one place move in the same and like manner, in and about the same, and in relation to the same, and according to one proportion and order, and are like the motion of a globe, we invented a fair image, which does no discredit to our ingenuity.

Cle. It does us great credit.

Ath. And the motion of the other sort which is not after the same manner, nor in the same, nor about the same, nor in relation to the same, nor in one place, nor in order, nor according to any rule or proportion, may be said to be akin to senselessness and folly?

Cle. That is most true.

Ath. Then, after what has been said, there is no difficulty in distinctly stating, that since soul carries all things round, either the best soul or the contrary must of necessity carry round and order and arrange the revolution of the heaven.

Cle. And judging from what has been said, Stranger, there would be impiety in asserting that any but the most perfect soul or souls carries round the heavens.

Ath. You have understood my meaning right well, Cleinias, and now let me ask you another question.

Cle. What are you going to ask?

Ath. If the soul carries round the sun and moon, and the other stars, does she not carry round each individual of them?

Cle. Certainly.

Ath. Then of one of them let us speak, and the same argument will apply to all.

Cle. Which will you take?

Ath. Every one sees the body of the sun, but no one sees his soul, nor the soul of any other body living or dead; and yet there is great reason to believe that this nature, unperceived by any of our senses, is circumfused around them all, but is perceived by mind; and therefore by mind and reflection only let us apprehend the following point.

Cle. What is that?

Ath. If the soul carries round the sun, we shall not be far wrong in supposing one of three alternatives.

Cle. What are they?

Ath. Either the soul which moves the sun this way and that, resides within the circular and visible body, like the soul which carries us about every way; or the soul provides herself with an external body of fire or air, as some affirm, and violently propels body by body; or thirdly, she is without such a body, but guides the sun by some extraordinary and wonderful power.

Cle. Yes, certainly; the soul can only order all things in one of these three ways.

Ath. And this soul of the sun, which is therefore better than the sun, whether taking the sun about in a chariot to give light to men, or acting from without, or in whatever way, ought by every man to be deemed a God.

Cle. Yes, by every man who has the least particle of sense.

Ath. And of the stars too, and of the moon, and of the years and months and seasons, must we not say in like manner, that since a soul or souls having every sort

of excellence are the causes of all of them, those souls
are Gods, whether they are living beings and reside in
bodies, and in this way order the whole heaven, or whatever be the place and mode of their existence;—and will
any one who admits all this venture to deny that all
things are full of Gods?

Cle. No one, Stranger, would be such a madman.

Ath. And now, Megillus and Cleinias, let us offer
terms to him who has hitherto denied the existence of
the Gods, and leave him.

Cle. What terms?

Ath. Either he shall teach us that we were wrong in
saying that the soul is the original of all things, and
arguing accordingly; or, if he be not able to say anything better, then he must yield to us and live for the
remainder of his life in the belief that there are Gods.
—Let us see, then, whether we have said enough or not
enough to those who deny that there are Gods.

Cle. Certainly,—quite enough, Stranger.

Ath. Then to them we will say no more. And now
we are to address him who, believing that there are
Gods, believes also that they take no heed of human
affairs: To him we say,—O thou best of men, in believing that there are Gods you are led by some affinity to
them, which attracts you towards your kindred and
makes you honour and believe in them. But the for-
tunes of evil and unrighteous men in private as well as
public life, which, though not really happy, are wrongly
counted happy in the judgment of men, and are celebrated both by poets and prose writers—these draw
you aside from your natural piety. Perhaps you have
seen impious men growing old and leaving their children's children in high offices, and their prosperity
shakes your faith—you have known or heard or been

yourself an eyewitness of many monstrous impieties, and
have beheld men by such criminal means from small beginnings attaining to sovereignty and the pinnacle of
greatness; and considering all these things you do not
like to accuse the Gods of them, because they are your
relatives; and so from some want of reasoning power,
and also from an unwillingness to find fault with them,
you have come to believe that they exist indeed, but
have no thought or care of human things. Now, that
your present evil opinion may not grow to still greater
impiety, and that we may if possible use arguments
which may conjure away the evil before it arrives, we
will add another argument to that originally addressed
to him who utterly denied the existence of the Gods.
And do you, Megillus and Cleinias, answer for the
young man as you did before; and if any impediment
comes in our way, I will take the word out of your
mouths, and carry you over the river as I did just now.

Cle. Very good; do as you say, and we will help
you as well as we can.

Ath. There will probably be no difficulty in proving
to him that the Gods care about the small as well as
about the great. For he was present and heard what
was said, that they are perfectly good, and that the care
of all things is most entirely natural to them.

Cle. No doubt he heard that.

Ath. Let us consider together in the next place what
we mean by this virtue which we ascribe to them. Surely
we should say that to be temperate and to possess mind
belongs to virtue, and the contrary to vice?

Cle. Certainly.

Ath. Yes; and courage is a part of virtue, and cowardice of vice?

Cle. True.

Ath. And the one is honourable, and the other dishonourable?

Cle. To be sure.

Ath. And the one, like other meaner things, is a human quality, but the Gods have no part in anything of the sort?

Cle. That again is what everybody will admit.

Ath. But do we imagine carelessness and idleness and luxury to be virtues? What do you think?

Cle. Decidedly not.

Ath. They rank under the opposite class?

Cle. Yes.

Ath. And their opposites, therefore, would fall under the opposite class?

Cle. Yes.

Ath. But are we to suppose that one who possesses all these good qualities will be luxurious and heedless and idle, like those whom the poet compares to stingless drones? [1]

Cle. And the comparison is a most just one.

Ath. Surely God must not be supposed to have a nature which He Himself hates?—he who dares to say this sort of thing must not be tolerated for a moment.

Cle. Of course not. How could He have?

Ath. Should we not on any principle be entirely mistaken in praising any one who has some special business entrusted to him, if he have a mind which takes care of great matters and no care of small ones? Reflect; he who acts in this way, whether he be God or man, must act from one of two principles.

Cle. What are they?

Ath. Either he must think that the neglect of the small matters is of no consequence to the whole, or if

[1] Hesiod, *Works and Days*, 307.

he knows that they are of consequence, and he neglects them, his neglect must be attributed to carelessness and indolence. Is there any other way in which his neglect can be explained? For surely, when it is impossible for him to take care of all, he is not negligent if he fails to attend to these things great or small, which a God or some inferior being might be wanting in strength or capacity to manage?

Cle. Certainly not.

Ath. Now, then, let us examine the offenders, who both alike confess that there are Gods, but with a difference,—the one saying that they may be appeased, and the other that they have no care of small matters: there are three of us and two of them, and we will say to them,—In the first place, you both acknowledge that the Gods hear and see and know all things, and that nothing can escape them which is matter of sense and knowledge:—do you admit this?

Cle. Yes.

Ath. And do you admit also that they have all power which mortals and immortals can have?

Cle. They will, of course, admit this also.

Ath. And surely we three and they two—five in all —have acknowledged that they are good and perfect.

Cle. Assuredly.

Ath. But, if they are such as we conceive them to be, can we possibly suppose that they ever act in the spirit of carelessness and indolence? For in us inactivity is the child of cowardice, and carelessness of inactivity and indolence.

Cle. Most true.

Ath. Then not from inactivity and carelessness is any God ever negligent; for there is no cowardice in them.

Cle. That is very true.

Ath. Then the alternative which remains is, that if the Gods neglect the lighter and lesser concerns of the universe, they neglect them because they know that they ought not to care about such matters—what other alternative is there but the opposites of their knowing?

Cle. There is none.

Ath. And, O most excellent and best of men, do I understand you to mean that they are careless because they are ignorant, and do not know that they ought to take care, or that they know, and yet like the meanest sort of men, knowing the better, choose the worse because they are overcome by pleasures and pains?

Cle. Impossible.

Ath. Do not all human things partake of the nature of soul? And is not man the most religious of all animals?

Cle. That is not to be denied.

Ath. And we acknowledge that all mortal creatures are the property of the Gods, to whom also the whole of heaven belongs?

Cle. Certainly.

Ath. And, therefore, whether a person says that these things are to the Gods great or small—in either case it would not be natural for the Gods who own us, and who are the most careful and the best of owners, to neglect us.—There is also a further consideration.

Cle. What is it?

Ath. Sensation and power are in an inverse ratio to each other in respect to their ease and difficulty.

Cle. What do you mean?

Ath. I mean that there is greater difficulty in seeing and hearing the small than the great, but more facility in moving and controlling and taking care of small and unimportant things than of their opposites.

Cle. Far more.

Ath. Suppose the case of a physician who is willing and able to cure some living thing as a whole,—how will the whole fare at his hands if he takes care only of the greater and neglects the parts which are lesser?

Cle. Decidedly not well.

Ath. No better would be the result with pilots or generals, or householders or statesmen, or any other such class, if they neglected the small and regarded only the great;—as the builders say, the larger stones do not lie well without the lesser.

Cle. Of course not.

Ath. Let us not, then, deem God inferior to human workmen, who, in proportion to their skill, finish and perfect their works, small as well as great, by one and the same art; or that God, the wisest of beings, who is both willing and able to take care, is like a lazy good-for-nothing, or a coward, who turns his back upon labour and gives no thought to smaller and easier matters, but to the greater only.

Cle. Never, Stranger, let us admit a supposition about the Gods which is both impious and false.

Ath. I think that we have now argued enough with him who delights to accuse the Gods of neglect.

Cle. Yes.

Ath. He has been forced to acknowledge that he is in error, but he still seems to me to need some words of consolation.

Cle. What consolation will you offer him?

Ath. Let us say to the youth:—The ruler of the universe has ordered all things with a view to the excellence and preservation of the whole, and each part, as far as may be, has an action and passion appropriate to it. Over these, down to the least fraction of them, ministers have been appointed to preside, who have wrought out their perfection with infinitesimal exactness. And one of these portions of the universe is thine own, unhappy man, which, however little, contributes to the whole; and you do not seem to be aware that this and every other creation is for the sake of the whole, and in order that the life of the whole may be blessed; and that you are created for the sake of the whole, and not the whole for the sake of you. For every physician and every skilled artist does all things for the sake of the whole, directing his effort towards the common good, executing the part for the sake of the whole, and not the whole for the sake of the part. And you are annoyed because you are ignorant how what is best for you happens to you and to the universe, as far as the laws of the common creation admit. Now, as the soul combining first with one body and then with another undergoes all sorts of changes, either of herself, or through the influence of another soul, all that remains to the player of the game is that he should shift the pieces; sending the better nature to the better place, and the worse to the worse, and so assigning to them their proper portion.

Cle. In what way do you mean?

Ath. In a way which may be supposed to make the care of all things easy to the Gods. If any one were to form or fashion all things without any regard to the whole,[1]—if, for example, he formed a living element of water out of fire, instead of forming many things out of one or one out of many in regular order attaining to a first or second or third birth, the transmutation would have been infinite; but now the ruler of the world has a wonderfully easy task.

Cle. How so?

Ath. I will explain:—When the king saw that our actions had life, and that there was much virtue in them

[1] Reading μὴ πρὸς τὸ ὅλον.

and much vice, and that the soul and body, although
not, like the Gods of popular opinion, eternal, yet having once come into existence, were indestructible (for
if either of them had been destroyed, there would have
been no generation of living beings); and when he observed that the good of the soul was ever by nature
designed to profit men, and the evil to harm them—he,
seeing all this, contrived so to place each of the parts
that their position might in the easiest and best manner
procure the victory of good and the defeat of evil in the
whole. And he contrived a general plan by which a
thing of a certain nature found a certain seat and room.
But the formation of qualities [1] he left to the wills of
individuals. For every one of us is made pretty much
what he is by the bent of his desires and the nature of
his soul.

Cle. Yes, that is probably true.

Ath. Then all things which have a soul change, and
possess in themselves a principle of change, and in
changing move according to law and to the order of
destiny: natures which have undergone a lesser change
move less and on the earth's surface, but those
which have suffered more change and have become more
criminal sink into the abyss, that is to say, into Hades
and other places in the world below, of which the very
names terrify men, and which they picture to themselves as in a dream, both while alive and when released
from the body. And whenever the soul receives more
of good or evil from her own energy and the strong influence of others—when she has communion with divine
virtue and becomes divine, she is carried into another
and better place, which is perfect in holiness; but when
she has communion with evil, then she also changes the
place of her life.

---

[1] Reading τοῦ ποίου.

'This is the justice of the Gods who inhabit Olympus.' [1]

O youth or young man, who fancy that you are neglected
by the Gods, know that if you become worse you shall
go to the worse souls, or if better to the better, and in
every succession of life and death you will do and suffer
what like may fitly suffer at the hands of like. This is
the justice of heaven, which neither you nor any other
unfortunate will ever glory in escaping, and which the
ordaining powers have specially ordained; take good
heed thereof, for it will be sure to take heed of you.
If you say:—I am small and will creep into the depths
of the earth, or I am high and will fly up to heaven,
you are not so small or so high but that you shall pay
the fitting penalty, either here or in the world below or
in some still more savage place whither you shall be con-
veyed. This is also the explanation of the fate of those
whom you saw, who had done unholy and evil deeds, and
from small beginnings had grown great, and you fancied that from being miserable they had become happy;
and in their actions, as in a mirror, you seemed to see
the universal neglect of the Gods, not knowing how they
make all things work together and contribute to the
great whole. And thinkest thou, bold man, that thou
needest not to know this?—he who knows it not can
never form any true idea of the happiness or unhappi-
ness of life or hold any rational discourse respecting
either. If Cleinias and this our reverend company succeed in proving to you that you know not what you say
of the Gods, then will God help you; but should you
desire to hear more, listen to what we say to the third
opponent, if you have any understanding whatsoever.
For I think that we have sufficiently proved the existence
of the Gods, and that they care for men:—The other

[1] Hom. *Odyss*. xix. 43.

notion that they are appeased by the wicked, and take
gifts, is what we must not concede to any one, and what
every man should disprove to the utmost of his power.

Cle. Very good; let us do as you say.

Ath. Well, then, by the Gods themselves I conjure
you to tell me,—if they are to be propitiated, how are
they to be propitiated? Who are they, and what is their
nature? Must they not be at least rulers who have to
order unceasingly the whole heaven?

Cle. True.

Ath. And to what earthly rulers can they be compared, or who to them? How in the less can we find an
image of the greater? Are they charioteers of contending pairs of steeds, or pilots of vessels? Perhaps they
might be compared to the generals of armies, or they
might be likened to physicians providing against the
diseases which make war upon the body, or to husbandmen observing anxiously the effects of the seasons on the
growth of plants; or perhaps to shepherds of flocks.
For as we acknowledge the world to be full of many
goods and also of evils, and of more evils than goods,
there is, as we affirm, an immortal conflict going on
among us, which requires marvellous watchfulness; and
in that conflict the Gods and demigods are our allies,
and we are their property. Injustice and insolence and
folly are the destruction of us, and justice and temperance and wisdom are our salvation; and the place of
these latter is in the life of the Gods, although some
vestige of them may occasionally be discerned among
mankind. But upon this earth we know that there dwell
souls possessing an unjust spirit,[1] who may be compared to brute animals, which fawn upon their keepers,
whether dogs or shepherds, or the best and most perfect masters; for they in like manner, as the voices of

------

[1] Reading λῆμα.

the wicked declare, prevail by flattery and prayers and incantations, and are allowed to make their gains with impunity. And this sin, which is termed dishonesty, is an evil of the same kind as what is termed disease in living bodies or pestilence in years or seasons of the year, and in cities and governments has another name, which is injustice.

Cle. Quite true.

Ath. What else can he say who declares that the Gods are always lenient to the doers of unjust acts, if they divide the spoil with them? As if wolves were to toss a portion of their prey to the dogs, and they, mollified by the gift, suffered them to tear the flocks. Must not he who maintains that the Gods can be propitiated argue thus?

Cle. Precisely so.

Ath. And to which of the above-mentioned classes of guardians would any man compare the Gods without absurdity? Will he say that they are like pilots, who are themselves turned away from their duty by 'libations of wine and the savour of fat,' and at last overturn both ship and sailors?

Cle. Assuredly not.

Ath. And surely they are not like charioteers who are bribed to give up the victory to other chariots?

Cle. That would be a fearful image of the Gods.

Ath. Nor are they like generals, or physicians, or husbandmen, or shepherds; and no one would compare them to dogs who have been silenced by wolves.

Cle. A thing not to be spoken of.

Ath. And are not all the Gods the chiefest of all guardians, and do they not guard our highest interests?

Cle. Yes; the chiefest.

Ath. And shall we say that those who guard our noblest interests, and are the best of guardians, are inferior in virtue to dogs, and to men even of moderate excellence, who would never betray justice for the sake of gifts which unjust men impiously offer them?

Cle. Certainly not; nor is such a notion to be endured, and he who holds this opinion may be fairly singled out and characterized as of all impious men the wickedest and most impious.

Ath. Then are the three assertions—that the Gods exist, and that they take care of men, and that they can never be persuaded to do injustice, now sufficiently demonstrated? May we say that they are?

Cle. You have our entire assent to your words.